Designing Websites with Publii and GitHub Pages

Create, Maintain and Host Beautiful Websites for Free

Brad Moore

Apress®

Designing Websites with Publii and GitHub Pages: Create, Maintain and Host Beautiful Websites for Free

Brad Moore
Hawesville, KY, USA

ISBN-13 (pbk): 979-8-8688-1194-4 ISBN-13 (electronic): 979-8-8688-1195-1
https://doi.org/10.1007/979-8-8688-1195-1

Managing Director, Apress Media LLC: Welmoed Spahr
Acquisitions Editor: James Robinson-Prior
Development Editor: James Markham
Coordinating Editor: Gryffin Winkler

Cover image by Moondance from Pixabay

Distributed to the book trade worldwide by Springer Science+Business Media New York, 1 New York Plaza, New York, NY 10004. Phone 1-800-SPRINGER, fax (201) 348-4505, e-mail orders-ny@springer-sbm.com, or visit www.springeronline.com. Apress Media, LLC is a Delaware LLC and the sole member (owner) is Springer Science + Business Media Finance Inc (SSBM Finance Inc). SSBM Finance Inc is a **Delaware** corporation.

For information on translations, please e-mail booktranslations@springernature.com; for reprint, paperback, or audio rights, please e-mail bookpermissions@springernature.com.

Apress titles may be purchased in bulk for academic, corporate, or promotional use. eBook versions and licenses are also available for most titles. For more information, reference our Print and eBook Bulk Sales web page at http://www.apress.com/bulk-sales.

Any source code or other supplementary material referenced by the author in this book can be found here: https://www.apress.com/gp/services/source-code.

If disposing of this product, please recycle the paper

This book is dedicated to my daughter, Jennalee, a creative soul who always dreamed of building stunning websites. May this guide make web development accessible and enjoyable, just as you would have loved.

Table of Contents

About the Author

Brad Moore is a technical writer and blogger based in Kentucky, USA, who has been involved in web development for 20 years. He has helped clients host sites with WordPress, Grav, and Publii since 2023. Brad enjoys programming, electronics, microprocessors, and model trains. Brad is married and has three children.

About the Technical Reviewer

Bob Mitro is a seasoned front-end developer and graphic designer, who is passionate about creating intuitive and visually engaging web experiences. With several years of experience in the technology industry, he specializes in front-end technologies such as HTML, CSS, and JavaScript, along with user experience and interface design. As a co-founder and one of the visionaries behind Publii, he contributes significantly to its creation by working closely with the team, ensuring that Publii fulfills its promise of simplicity and power. His role centers around enhancing the platform's user experience, ensuring it empowers anyone to build a modern, fast, and aesthetically pleasing website.

His deep understanding of successful application design and streamlined user flows is a key element of his contributions. He meticulously analyzes each element of the user journey, from initial interaction with the application to long-term engagement. Outside of his active involvement with Publii, he remains engaged with new design concepts, explores the latest front-end frameworks, and keeps a close eye on industry trends. This dedication ensures that Publii stays at the cutting edge of web development. He is deeply passionate about technology's potential to make the Web more accessible, functional, and beautiful for everyone.

Acknowledgments

I would like to thank Tom Dziuda and Bob Mitro who have passionately developed and nurtured Publii CMS since at least 2018. Their vision and along with their continued consideration of community needs have resulted in a truly phenomenal software product for creating and maintaining websites.

I would like to thank my wife and family for their patience and support during the development of this project. Without them this book would never have come into existence.

I would like to thank Bob Mitro who graciously provided the technical review for the book despite his heavy workload and personal commitments.

I would like to thank James Robinson-Prior, not just for the opportunity to write this book for Apress, but also for his encouragement and enthusiasm for this project.

The editors and staff at Apress, in particular: Gryffin Winkler, Krishnan Sathyamurthy and Dulcy Nirmala Chellappa – you all have been fantastic. You all deserve so much thanks as well. A book is a team effort.

PART I

Building the Foundation

This book is about building and publishing a website – that anyone on the Internet can access and read – easily and for free. The tools you will learn to use are Publii CMS and GitHub Pages. The material presented is easy to follow and will allow you to publish your thoughts and ideas and even publicize your business or organization.

Part 1 of this book will lay the foundations needed to be successful as well as expose you to both Publii and GitHub Pages. In the chapters ahead, you will build a simple blog, configure GitHub Pages, and upload the blog to the Internet.

My wish for you as you move forward through this book is that you enjoy yourself, don't worry too much about getting it right the first time, reread what you don't get, and be successful.

CHAPTER 1

A Small Step or a Giant Leap?

When I was a boy, NASA, the United States Space Agency, rose to the challenge that President John Kennedy made to the people in the early 1960s. They landed a human onto the surface of the moon where he subsequently walked.

I can still remember the words of Neil Armstrong on that fateful day as he descended the lander stairs to the surface of the moon the first time:

That's one small step for man, one giant leap for mankind.

—Neil Armstrong

Twenty-two years later mankind took another giant leap as the first website was published by Tim Berners-Lee. We were connected globally, and democratization had come to publishing. For me, this was a dramatic new frontier that had been opened, and this time I could be a part of the journey.

I created my first website in 1994, joining the tens of thousands of people eager to get a piece of the "web" real estate. I have been creating websites and publishing online since. At one time getting an online presence up and running meant knowing how to code, work with servers, and owning expensive software or buying services from someone else. Not so today. Today that giant leap is just a short step away.

© Brad Moore 2025
B. Moore, *Designing Websites with Publii and GitHub Pages*,
https://doi.org/10.1007/979-8-8688-1195-1_1

Introduction

You might be thumbing through this book, have just picked it up, or you might be here because you have decided you need a website but don't know where to start. A shift from traditional social media[1] underway today means that it is increasingly important to have a traditional website. Whether you're running a small business, a church, a charity, or just want to share your thoughts and stories, being online is where it's at.

You might be thinking, "I can't afford to hire someone to build a website," or "I don't know where to start." Trust me, you're not alone. But here's the good news: you don't need a big budget or a tech degree to get online. With tools like Publii CMS and GitHub Pages, anyone can create a website or blog and be online for free.[2]

Maybe you want to start a blog but found platforms like WordPress and Squarespace too complicated or expensive. Or maybe you've been relying on social media and are looking for a more personal space to share your content. This book is for you.

You might even wonder, "Why should I bother with a website or blog when I can just use social media?" Great question! Sure, social media is convenient, but we must recognize it comes with limitations and distractions. Having your own website or blog gives you full control over your content, design, and audience. No more competing with endless ads and algorithms. Plus, it makes you look more professional and credible.

Imagine reaching your audience without the clutter, sharing your story your way, and having a digital space that truly represents you. It's easier than you think, and I'll be with you every step of the way.

So, let's dive in and get you online!

---

[1] https://www.rappler.com/technology/social-media/gartner-research-2023-social-media-use-limit-prediction/

[2] A free website assumes you will use the host site root URL. Purchasing a custom domain name can add a small yearly expense.

What's in It for Me?

In this book, we will be focusing on creating a static website that can support blogging. You probably have a few questions, like: What is in it for me? What is the advantage of having a website anyway? What is blogging and who the heck is in the tomb of the unknown soldier?

I can't help you with all of these, but we will most certainly focus on the website and blogging questions.

Having a website offers many benefits over other forms of media – whether you are a small business, a church, an organization, or an individual. The primary advantages you will experience are visibility and content control. With a website, you can be accessible 24/7, allowing potential customers, members, or general audience to learn about your offerings, ideas, and information at their convenience. Having complete control over your content allows you to tailor your message or story to your audience's needs, regularly update your site with new information, and ensure that your branding remains consistent and compelling.

Having a website also boosts your professionalism and credibility. A site with good, consistent design provides a sense of legitimacy and professionalism, which is crucial for building trust with your audience. For you, a website can serve as a central hub where visitors can find information about your services, read testimonials, and contact you directly, all of which contribute to a stronger, more credible image.

Customer and community engagement is another key benefit. A website offers various tools to engage with your audience, such as blogs, newsletters, and contact forms. These features enable you to maintain an ongoing conversation with your visitors, fostering a sense of community and loyalty.

A blog is like an online journal or diary where you can share your thoughts, stories, or information with others. You can think of it as a personal space on the Internet where you can write about anything you're interested in. Sometimes these are topics to enhance your customer

5

engagement with your business; sometimes these are simply stories about your cat or family or whatever interests you. Each new post you create is like writing a new entry in a journal, and people can visit your blog to read what you've written, leave comments, and share your posts with others.

Many bloggers publish on a schedule, but it is perfectly fine publishing as the material becomes available. This allows timely and targeted delivery of information which can help you develop a community of followers and, if you are a business or organization, increase customer engagement.

The toolset we will be using is designed to create static websites. These are websites that are built on the most basic web technologies of HTML, CSS, and JavaScript. Knowing how to use these is not necessary to be successful; Publii CMS – our publishing client – will handle all that behind the scenes. Once published, the content remains static. Imagine a static website like a printed book. Once the book is printed, the words and pictures stay the same. Every time you open the book, you see the same pages with the same information. If we want to change the information, we will need to publish a new book. This is how a static website works.

Many of today's websites are dynamic. Think of a dynamic website as being like a television. The content can change every time you turn it on. Just like how different shows can appear on your TV depending on the time and channel, a dynamic website can show different information depending on what you click or what you search. Behind the scenes a server is assembling the content and serving it in response to your interactions with the website.

Note   This is not to say that a static website like those generated by Publii CMS cannot interact with the end user. With the incorporation of JavaScript, there are a lot of dynamic-like interactions possible when using a static website.

It is not necessary to have a dynamic website to have an informative and effective presence on the Internet. Static sites have huge advantages for the publisher including lightning-fast load times, greater security, and being much easier to manage.

What Lies Ahead

We will be building three websites as you and I progress through this book. The websites will all be created with Publii CMS and hosted on GitHub Pages. These are the underlying technology platforms that will allow us to get online for free.

The theme of the sites we will be building will all relate to humankind's journey to the moon:

- A blog for a moon adventure company as they prepare for their first trip to the moon.

- A landing page for a lunar vacation travel agency (this will be based on a single-page website).

- We will expand the landing page to support several additional features including

  - A blog index and blog posts

  - A photo gallery

  - An FAQ with collapsible questions and answers

Note   A single-page website, or landing page, is like a poster or flyer. Instead of having multiple sections or pages, all the important information is presented on one long page. It's designed to be simple and direct, often used to promote a specific product, service, or event.

As we work through these projects, we will explore the various features of Publii CMS and some of its add-ons. The focus of this project is getting online for free. I will be presenting an optional step in the process that will greatly enhance your online presence. It is the only non-free component of these projects requiring a small yearly fee. Several steps require this component; however, they are completely optional as noted in the outline below.

Here is the basic process you and I will be working through as we develop the first of the three websites:

1. Create a new email address just for the project.

2. Create a GitHub account.

3. Download and install Publii CMS.

4. Create and configure your new site.

5. Add your initial content.

6. Create a GitHub Pages page on the web client.

7. Configure Publii CMS to upload (Sync) to GitHub Pages.

8. Upload (Sync) your site.

9. Register a domain name (Optional).

10. Create a DNS entry that points to your GitHub Pages page (Requires a domain name – Optional).

11. Update your Publii CMS–based site on your PC as new content is needed and sync it with your GitHub Pages page (Requires a domain name – Optional).

As subsequent sites are developed, you will leverage these configurations and accounts you previously set up. It will not be necessary to go through steps 1 through 7 more than once.

As mentioned, you will be using a publishing tool called Publii CMS. Publii CMS is a free, open source desktop application that is used to create, maintain, and compile your static website for publishing. Compiling a website for publishing with Publii CMS does not get it out onto the Internet. To do that, the compiled website must be uploaded to a server that can be accessed by all the people of the world. We will use GitHub Pages as that server.

Every new website that you publish will need to have its own unique web address. That address – like `www.google.com` – is where the website lives in the larger Internet. We call that web address a Uniform Resource Locator – or URL for short.

There are a couple of optional steps (9 and 10). If you choose not to do these steps, you can still have your website on the Internet hosted by GitHub Pages. The URL will look less professional, as it will end in "github. com" instead of something like "mymoonadventure.com". The part of the URL that reads "mymoonadventure.com" or "google.com" is called a domain name. We will go over this in more depth later in the book, but for now, be aware of a couple things up front – these are optional, these must be unique (each site must have its own), and these are not free.

What Sort of Tools Will I Need?

You might be wondering what tools, equipment, or software will be needed to create and publish your own website.

The goal of this book is to get you all in at no cost; however, there are a few requirements you will need to have to be successful. The first and most obvious one is a computer. The computer you use does not need to be very powerful but should run an operating system you are familiar with. Most people this book is aimed at own or use a Microsoft Windows or Apple Macintosh. The software we will be using will work in Linux as well.

The projects shown are all completed on a Windows 11 operating system. Any 64-bit version of Windows would work as well.

The main software that you will be using is called Publii CMS. It is a free website and blogging tool that runs on your local computer. Installing Publii CMS will be addressed in Chapter 3.

A good image editor would be useful as well. I like IrfanView which you can get here: `https://www.irfanview.com/`, or here as a Windows store app: `https://apps.microsoft.com/detail/9pjz3btl5pv6?hl=en-us&gl=US`. IrfanView only runs on Windows OS; if you are looking for an alternative for MacOS, look at Nomacs: `https://nomacs.org/`. Both software products allow browsing of libraries of images as well as simple editing. They are also both free to download, install, and use.

Regardless of the operating system you are using, you will find your PC or Mac will have a good native web browser. I like to install my own browser since I am used to it. I will be using the Chrome web browser. It runs on all major operating systems and can be downloaded for free here: `https://www.google.com/chrome/`.

The last thing that I consider indispensable is paper and a pen.

Write Everything Down!

This cannot be stressed enough. You will be creating some accounts early in this process. It is easy to get carried away and set things up promising yourself that you will remember the information only to find that later you do not. Trust me – I have done this more times than I care to admit.

The lesson: Always write it down.

Now is a great time to go get a pen or pencil and a small notebook or notepad.

As you progress through the process creating unique usernames, passwords, and website addresses, be sure to record them on your notepad or in your notebook. I promise that your future self will thank your past self!

Overview of the Workflow

There is a bit of set-up work ahead to get your free website and the website editor (Publii CMS) up and running. It is not complicated, and I will be explaining each step in the process. The good news – you only need to do this work once. This book is all about getting that setup done and getting you going on your blogging journey. But what is the process of blogging once it is all set up? How will you use the toolset and update your website or blog?

That is what I want to talk about now. In this first half of the book, I will be covering how to set up, create, and manage a blog. Still not sure what a blog is? Jump ahead to Chapter 5, section: 'What is a Blog' and read more about it (don't forget to come right back here). If you are interested in just creating a simple single-page website or landing page that does not require regular updates, check out Chapter 11. You should still read Chapters 2–10 as there is valuable information you will need to know when you reach Chapter 11.

Regardless of whether you are maintaining a single-page website or a regularly updated blog, the general workflow of publishing the site remains the same. It is a simple process, which is one of the reasons I hope you are here:

1) Open Publii CMS on your local computer. Make your changes, add a blog entry, or modify the site in the desired way.

2) Save the changes, compile the site, and upload the site to your remote host (in your case, GitHub Pages); this is where your website files are publicly available on the Internet.

3) Access the updated website from a browser using its URL.

As you can see, the process described above is represented in Figure 1-1. On the left, at number 1, the user updates the website on their local computer using Publii CMS. Publii CMS is used to compile and package the source for the website and then transfer it to a cloud-based storage location. The transfer process is handled by Publii CMS using the built-in synchronization features.

At number 2, in the center, is GitHub Pages – a cloud-based storage location. It is the remote server from which your site can be accessed through the public Internet. The final step on the right, at number 3, depicts the website content being served to the end user in a browser as a web page.

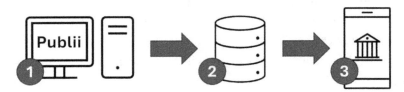

Figure 1-1. *Publii CMS publishing workflow*

It is an exciting thing to watch something you have created come alive in a web browser for the first time. This will be a fun journey as we light our rocket engines and head into space. Cyberspace in this case.

Summary

A lot of material was covered in this chapter. Here are some key takeaways:

> A blog is like an online journal where you can share your thoughts, stories, and other information.

> A static website is like a book – once published, the content remains fixed. Changing the content requires publishing once again.

> A dynamic website is more like a TV show or video game. The content that you are presented is rendered in real time in response to how you interact with the website.

> Having a website can benefit you as a business, organization, charity, or even an individual by increasing your

> > Visibility

> > Content control

> > Professionalism and credibility

> > Engagement with customers

> Every website needs to have its own address – which is called a URL.

> For someone to see your website, it must be on a remote host that is publicly accessible from the Internet.

CHAPTER 2

Getting Started

In this chapter, you will learn about setting up a GitHub account. This will be required to set up your remote storage space that will host the files that make up your website.

An email account will be required when setting up an account on GitHub. Most folks who use the Internet have at least one email account. One consideration I will discuss is whether to use an existing email address for your website or create a new address.

I recognize that everyone coming to this project has varying degrees of exposure and expertise in using online tools, executing creative endeavors, and visualizing technical processes. If for you these things come easy – you might want to build your own website on the fly as you follow along with us in this book. Others will likely benefit from reproducing the steps outlined here as they build sites like those demonstrated throughout this book.

I know that new technologies often seem intimidating to me when I first approach them. I find that following along, doing what the author of a book or tutorial teaches me allows me to get my feet wet, increasing my understanding without the fear of drowning.

If you are like me, let me suggest that you plan on working through the material in this book twice. On the first pass, create a make-believe entity like the one I will be demonstrating. Build a blog for that entity following what I do for my make-believe companies and people.

© Brad Moore 2025
B. Moore, *Designing Websites with Publii and GitHub Pages,*
https://doi.org/10.1007/979-8-8688-1195-1_2

The first project we will be working on will be called "Space B" which will feature the development of Bob's reusable "Brant"[1] rocket. This will be a blog which will feature news regarding the development process. It is of course completely fictitious. During this first project, we will cover all the required steps to get your blog or website online.

On the second pass through the book, use what you have learned and create the website or blog that you have always wanted for your real-life company, organization, church, or individual project.

As you and I progress through this book, I am going to assume you are reading and working through the examples as suggested. Enjoy the journey.

Getting an Email Address

You will need an email address so that you can later set up a GitHub account. I am going to assume you do not want to use an existing email address. Additionally, I will assume you do not sign up for a new email address every day. I will be helping you to get set up.

In the real world, when setting up your actual website or blog, you may find that you want to use an email address that has been created specifically for that use. Having a unique email address separate from existing addresses can benefit a website operator in several ways.

The primary benefit is enhanced security and privacy. A separate email address specifically for website operations limits the exposure of your personal information and reduces the risk of spam, hacking attempts, and phishing scams directed against your other accounts.

This separation can also foster a more professional image. It will show a clear delineation between your personal and professional

---

[1] The Brant is a kind of small goose, certainly not a falcon (`https://www.allaboutbirds.org/guide/Brant/id`).

communications, which is essential in building trust with clients and users. Additionally, having a dedicated email for your website helps in staying organized, making it easier to manage emails, prioritize tasks, and keep track of website-related inquiries.

If you plan to use an existing email address you already have, which you most certainly can do, please proceed to Chapter 2, section: 'Getting Started with GitHub' and set up a GitHub account.

I recommend an Outlook.com address for your website operations both when you follow examples in the book and when you are creating your actual real website. This offers several benefits. Being a service provided by Microsoft, Outlook.com enjoys a strong reputation for security and reliability. This type of email address can lend credibility to your website's communications. Many organizations look at Outlook.com addresses with greater respect, as these are often associated with businesses and other organizations.

Getting a new @outlook.com address is straightforward. You will start by visiting the Outlook.com sign-up page and fill out the registration form with the required details, including your name, desired email address, and password. You will need to verify your account, which may involve phone or email verification after submitting the registration information. This is all done on the Internet through your favorite web browser.

A word about web browsers. They tend to remember the sites you frequent and even supply user accounts and passwords to simplify the connection process. Some websites even cache your last session and allow you to pick up right where you left off – often already logged on. This will be a problem if you already have an Outlook.com or Microsoft account. Therefore, we will be using our favorite browser in Incognito mode.

Note   Incognito mode (called Private Browsing in Firefox) is a special browser mode that doesn't use or save any information from your previous browsing sessions. It also won't cache or store any session data, ensuring that nothing from the current session is remembered.

In the examples that follow, I will be using Google's Chrome as my web browser. You can perform the account setup steps with your favorite browser on your favorite operating system (Windows or Mac).

Open your web browser and open an incognito tab. Do this by clicking the Chrome options menu button (three stacked dots) in the upper right corner of the application window as shown in Figure 2-1. Click the menu item "New Incognito window".

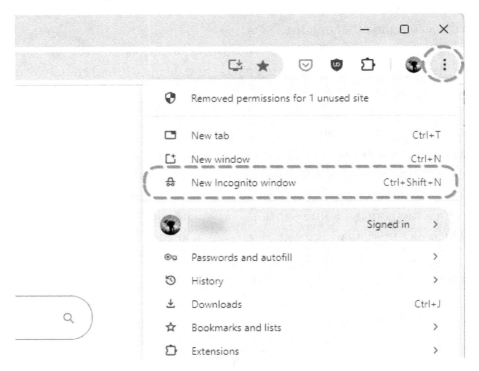

Figure 2-1. *Opening a New Incognito window*

Type the Internet address "`https://outlook.com`" into the address bar/search bar in your browser. At the time of this writing, this address took you to a website that looks like the one shown in Figure 2-2. Click the "Create free account" button in the middle of the page.

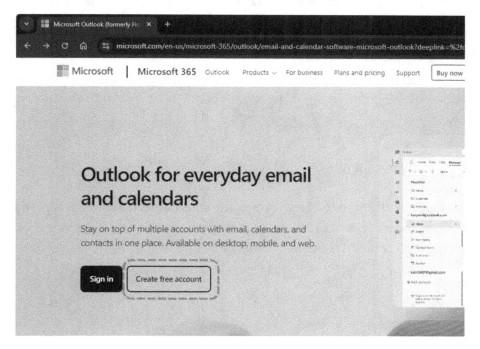

Figure 2-2. *Create free account button*

If you clicked the Create free account button, then you can skip the alternate steps to getting to the Create Account dialog window described below. Proceed to the next section Choosing an Email Address.

If the Create free account button is no longer offered or you cannot locate it when visiting this website, you can follow these alternate steps to get to the Create Account dialog window. In the first step shown in Figure 2-3, you will click the Sign in link in the upper right corner of the web page.

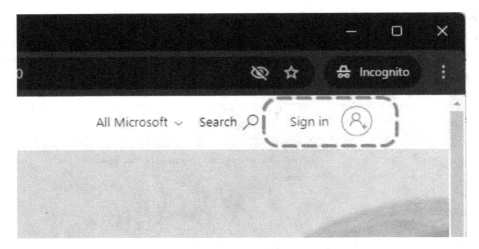

Figure 2-3. *Sign in link*

Clicking the Sign in link will open the standardized Microsoft sign in dialog window shown in Figure 2-4. Since you will be creating a new email account, click the "Create one!" link following the question "No account?".

Figure 2-4. *Create a new email account*

Microsoft assumes you will want to link an existing email account from a different service or organization to this account. This is not what you came here to do. Click the "Get a new email address" link as shown in Figure 2-5.

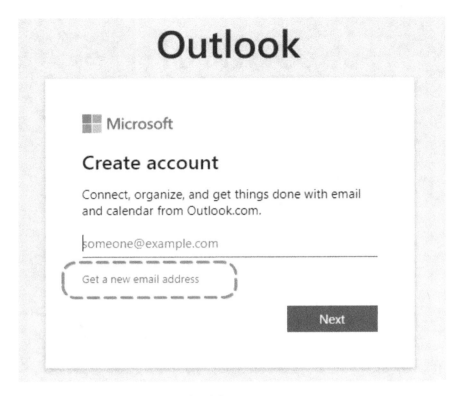

Figure 2-5. *Get a new email address*

Choosing an Email Address

There are a lot of opinions on how to choose a name for use in your email address. One of the most obvious rules is that it must be unique. You will not be able to use an email address that is already in use. I suggest keeping the name simple, not using slang or strange spellings of common words. If this is the email you use for your final website, consider keeping the name professional. Stick with something easy to remember. Perhaps incorporate your name or business name into the email name.

If you have been following along, you will be at a point where you must choose an email address name. It will also be your account name with Microsoft. In Figure 2-6, I have decided to go with the email name "example-user" which I have typed into the space provided.

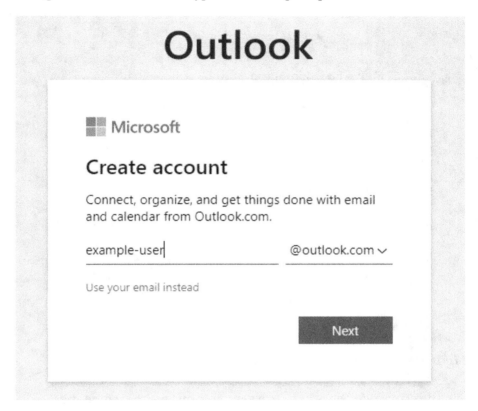

Figure 2-6. *Choosing an email address name*

Once you have typed in your choice for email name, click the **Next** button.

If you have selected a name that is already registered with Microsoft, then you will see the error message that I got in Figure 2-7.

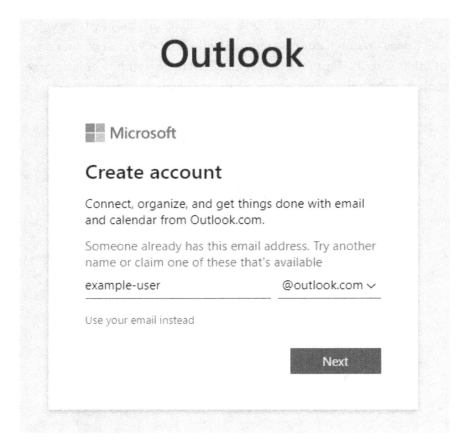

Figure 2-7. *Duplicate email address error*

The error message is in red text and informs me that someone is already using this email address name that I tried to claim. I have two choices now. I could click the browser's back button and start over trying a different email address name, or I could click the link in blue which reads "claim one of these that's available".

Clicking the link is an easy way to go, as Microsoft ensures that the various choices presented are available for use. In Figure 2-8, I have clicked the "claim one of these that's available" link, and I now have a choice of three similar options that are available.

Figure 2-8. *Available email address names*

One of these looks just right to me. If I click on it, I will be right back where I started out, but I will have a known available email address name. In Figure 2-9, I have clicked on the email address "example-user2024@ outlook.com" which was offered to me. I am now ready to proceed.

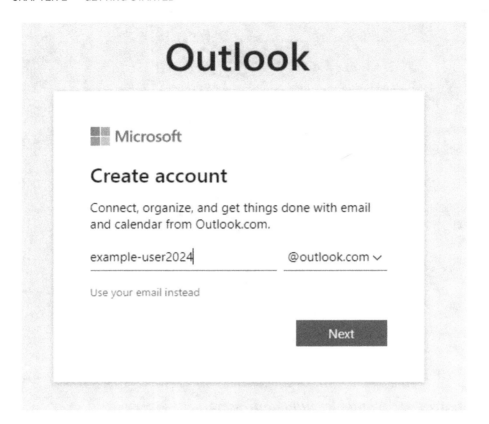

Figure 2-9. *A known good email address*

If I click the Next button, I will be granted this account name provisionally until I complete the sign-up process and claim the account permanently. The next step in the process is selecting a password for this account.

Hey – are you writing this stuff down? Remember – write everything down so that you can access your accounts later when you need to.

Choosing a Password

I don't want to use "example-user2024@outlook.com" as my email account for this project. Since I will be building a blog site for the founder and chief technologist for the little known (and completely imaginary) space company Space-B, I have decided to go with "space-b-systems@ outlook.com".

As you can see in Figure 2-10, I have typed that into the account name portion of the email address in the Microsoft Outlook Create account dialog window.

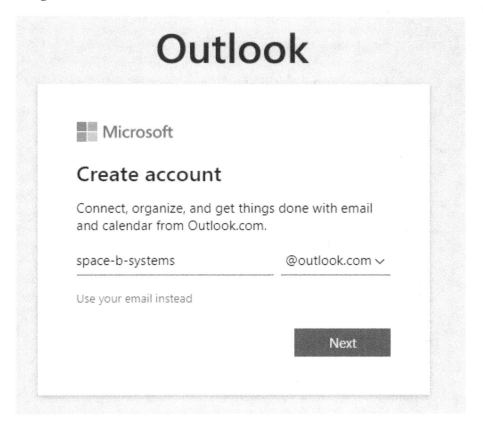

Figure 2-10. *Email account name*

I am ready to commit to this email account name. I click the Next button to move on.

After clicking the Next button, I see a new dialog window where I must select a password as shown in Figure 2-11.

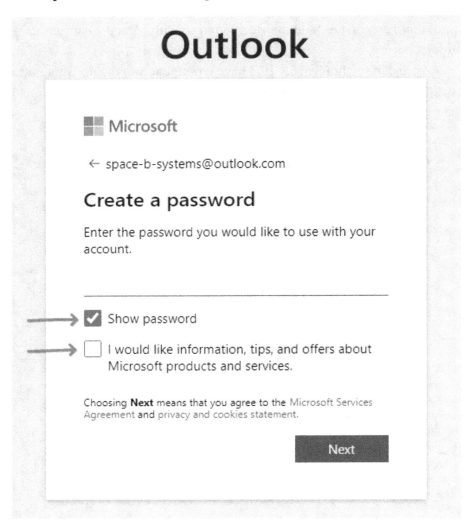

Figure 2-11. *Selecting a password*

There are some good rules for selecting a good password. I bet you have heard some, but the odds are good that the ones you have heard are wrong. This is because in the early days of security, complexity was the watch word when creating a password. Complex passwords tended to be very short. With today's technology, a short complex password can be brute force cracked in days if not hours. Better passwords today are made up of four or five short, easy-to-remember words.

Here in Figure 2-12 is Randall Munroe, author of XKCD web comics, with an informative comic illustrating the problem.

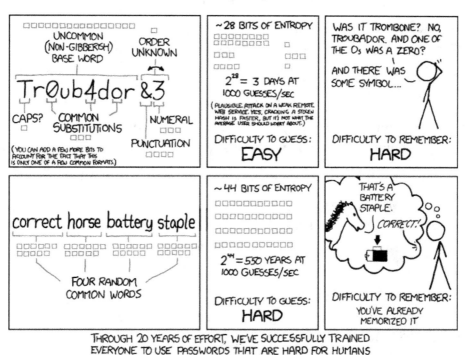

Figure 2-12. Password Strength (`https://xkcd.com/936/`) – by Randall Munroe. Used with permission

Picking a good password is less an art but more of a science. Here are some guidelines to which a good password should conform:

- Don't use your own name or other names or identifying information of significant others, dogs, cats, etc.

- Use four or five short words instead of a string of gibberish.

- Don't use "correcthorsebatterystaple" either.

- Capitalize one or more of the words.

- If you use numbers, do not use dates that are significant such as wedding anniversaries, birth dates, etc.

- No spaces.

- You can use a special character and/or number somewhere in your password, but it is not necessary unless the system you are using forces you to do that.

- Do NOT reuse a password from one system to another.

- Write down your passwords, keep them secure, or better yet track them in a program called a password safe. A good password safe can be found here: `https:// keepass.info/`.

As I filled out the Outlook Create a password dialog window, as you might notice looking at Figure 2-11, I chose to disable the offer for information, tips, and offers on other Microsoft products. That is extra noise I really don't need. I also chose to enable the show password option. This ensures that I have positive visual confirmation that what you think you typed for a password is indeed what you really typed.

Tip   Remember to write your email account and password down.

Notice the small print. You are confirming that you agree to the Microsoft Services Agreement as well as the privacy and cookies statement by clicking Next.

After typing my desired password into the form in the Create a password dialog window, I clicked Next. You should too.

There are a couple more dialog windows that you will need to work through before you are the official new owner of your new Microsoft Outlook.com account. The first of these wants your first and last name. I am sure the terms of service encourage truthfulness. Sometimes that just does not fit the need. Provide a name as you are lead. I chose a pseudonym for this project.

The next dialog window will ask you for your region as well as your birth date. The default region seemed fine for me when I was filling this out. Once again – choose a date that fits your needs.

The final set of dialog boxes are designed to prove you are human. Someone at Microsoft has a sense of humor as the caption on the first of these says "Let's beat the robots." I was given a puzzle to solve. Depending on how well you do, you may be asked to solve more than one puzzle.

Once you have completed this step, a completely new web application will open in the current tab. It is the web version of the Microsoft Outlook email client. It will look something like Figure 2-13. Of course, it will have your email account and information, not mine.

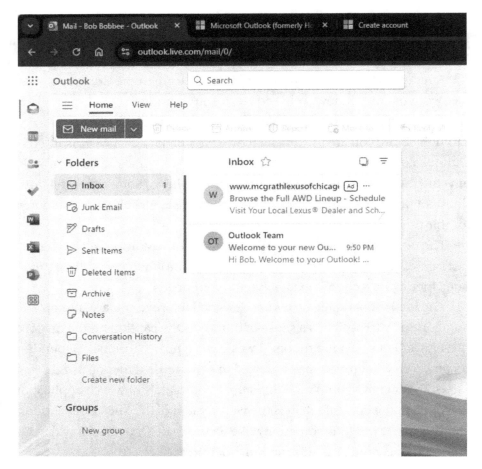

Figure 2-13. *Microsoft Outlook web email client*

Keep the email client open in one of your browser tabs. We will be using it very soon.

Getting Started with GitHub

In this section, I will be introducing GitHub and a little bit about how it works as well as setting up an account so that you can use GitHub to host your website soon.

But What Exactly Is GitHub?

GitHub is an online platform that is widely used for storing, managing, and sharing code, but it's not just for programmers and developers. Imagine it as a vast library where, instead of books, there are projects, pieces of code, and data that people from all over the world have written and shared. It's like a social network for code and data, where users can collaborate, suggest changes, and improve each other's work.

One of the great features of GitHub is GitHub Pages, a service that allows you to turn your code repository into a live website. This is particularly useful for those looking to create a portfolio, blog, or project web page without delving deep into web hosting complexities.

Getting started with GitHub is straightforward. You will need to create a GitHub account. Once your account is set up, you can create your first repository. A repository, or "repo," is like a project folder where your code and project files live. Think of it as a special storage space for everything related to your project. It can contain all sorts of things like text files, images, and data sheets – anything your project needs. In our case, it will contain all the files that make a static website function. When you create a new repository, GitHub guides you through a few simple steps, letting you name your repo and add a brief description of what your project is about.

A repository is required before you can start using GitHub Pages. It's the foundation of your project on GitHub, acting as the central hub where all your files are stored and managed. This makes it easy to keep everything organized and accessible, whether you're working alone or collaborating with others.

Once your repository is created, you can configure it for GitHub Pages. This feature takes the files in your repository and turns them into a live website. You don't need to understand web hosting or domain names; GitHub handles it all. You simply upload your content (like your portfolio pieces or blog posts) and publish it. This user-friendly approach makes GitHub an invaluable tool not only for coders but for anyone looking to showcase their work online in a professional and accessible manner.

Creating a New GitHub Account

The process of creating a new GitHub account will be like that of creating a new email account. We will once again work in your browser's incognito or private browsing mode.

As before I will be using Google's Chrome as my web browser. You can perform the account setup steps with your favorite browser on your favorite operating system (Windows or Mac).

Open your web browser and open an incognito tab. Do this by clicking the Chrome options menu button (three stacked dots) in the upper right corner of the application window as shown in Figure 2-1. Click the menu item "New Incognito window".

Type the internet address "https://github.com" into the address bar/search bar in the browser. At the time of this writing, this address took you to a website that looks like the one shown in Figure 2-14.

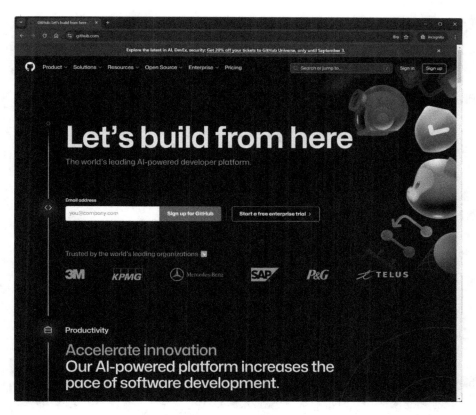

Figure 2-14. *GitHub.com welcome page*

In the upper right corner of the website, you will see options to "Sign in" and "Sign up". To create my account, I clicked the "Sign up" button as shown in Figure 2-15. You should too.

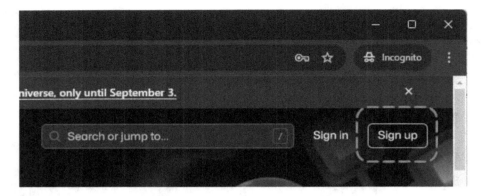

Figure 2-15. *GitHub Sign up button*

GitHub has a smooth sign-up process. It begins with a simple dialog window asking what email address you want to use to sign up as shown in Figure 2-16. I used the email address created earlier in this chapter. In my case, I used "space-b-systems@outlook.com". You should use the email address you created as you followed along.

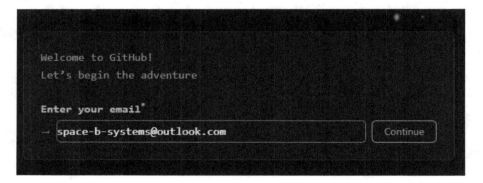

Figure 2-16. *Enter your email*

Clicking the Continue button will expand the dialog window adding a field for you to create a password as shown in Figure 2-17. Remember the password discussion for when you created a password for your email account. Do not use the same password here that you created for your email account. I know it is tempting.

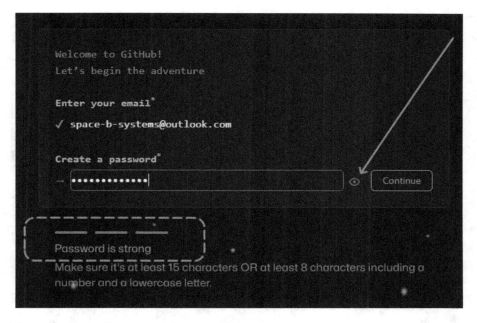

Figure 2-17. *Create a password*

Notice a couple things about the password creation process. As you type your password, GitHub will provide feedback below the dialog window as to just how strong your password is. Your goal is to have a strong password.

Another thing to notice is the little eye that the arrow is pointing to. Clicking this eye will allow you to see your password that you typed in plain text. I think this is a good idea as it will let you verify that the password you think you typed is really the password that you did type.

Remember – write it down.

Once you have created your password and you are sure it meets the guidelines for a good password, click the "Continue" button. The dialog window will be expanded a little more, this time giving you a chance to create a username as shown in Figure 2-18.

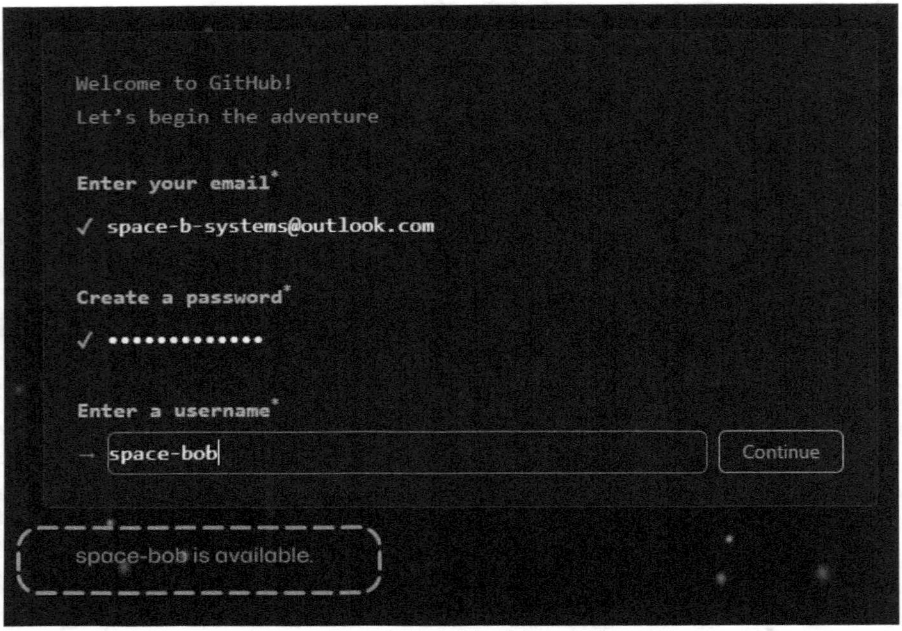

Figure 2-18. *Enter a username*

GitHub usernames are unique across the platform, just like email accounts were unique in Outlook.com. As you type your username, GitHub will provide feedback as to whether it meets this criteria.

You will see in my case as I created a username, the name I supplied is available as specified in the area below the dialog window.

There are no screenshots of the next few steps as they are quite simple. After supplying a username that is available and clicking "Continue", you will be offered the opportunity to receive product information from GitHub. The option is unchecked, so just click "Continue" and move to the next step.

Verifying your account is the next step. Like when your email account was created, you will be presented with a puzzle (perhaps several) to solve so that you may prove you are a real human and not a robot.

One last step needs to be taken. This is essentially verifying that you really own the email account that you used to register this GitHub account. GitHub will send to your email account a "launch code" which you will need to enter in the next dialog window that opens as shown in Figure 2-19.

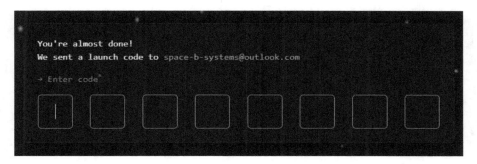

Figure 2-19. *The launch code*

As you can see from the screenshot, my launch code was sent to my email address "space-b-systems@outlook.com".

Remember that I left the Microsoft Outlook web application open in a tab in my browser. Checking my email account in that tab, I found that I already had mail from GitHub.com. As you can see in Figure 2-20, I had received a launch code from GitHub.

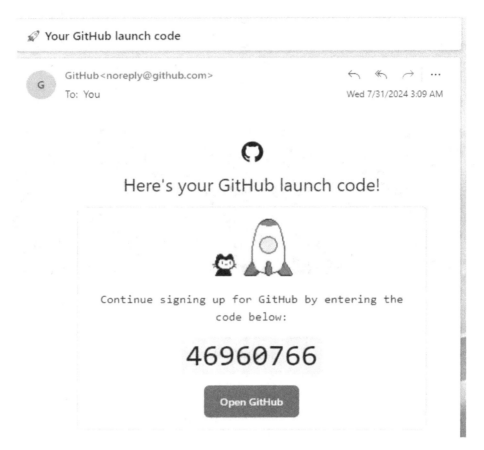

Figure 2-20. GitHub launch code

I entered that launch code into the space labeled Enter code with eight empty boxes on the GitHub site as shown in Figure 2-19.

After entering the code, GitHub opened a large web page welcoming me to GitHub. This page also began the process of personalizing my account. This is part of the GitHub on-boarding process, and it helps the system to adapt to my needs. In my case, I do not require any personalization. You won't either.

In the lower middle of the web page, there is a small link that says, "skip personalization". You can safely click this and skip these last steps. I did.

That ended the account creation and on-boarding process. I now have a GitHub account. If you followed along, you too should have one also.

Signing In to GitHub

The account creation process flows smoothly from the personalization process to the sign-in page which is shown in Figure 2-21. This is the standard GitHub logon screen which you will use to sign in to GitHub whenever you need to use the system.

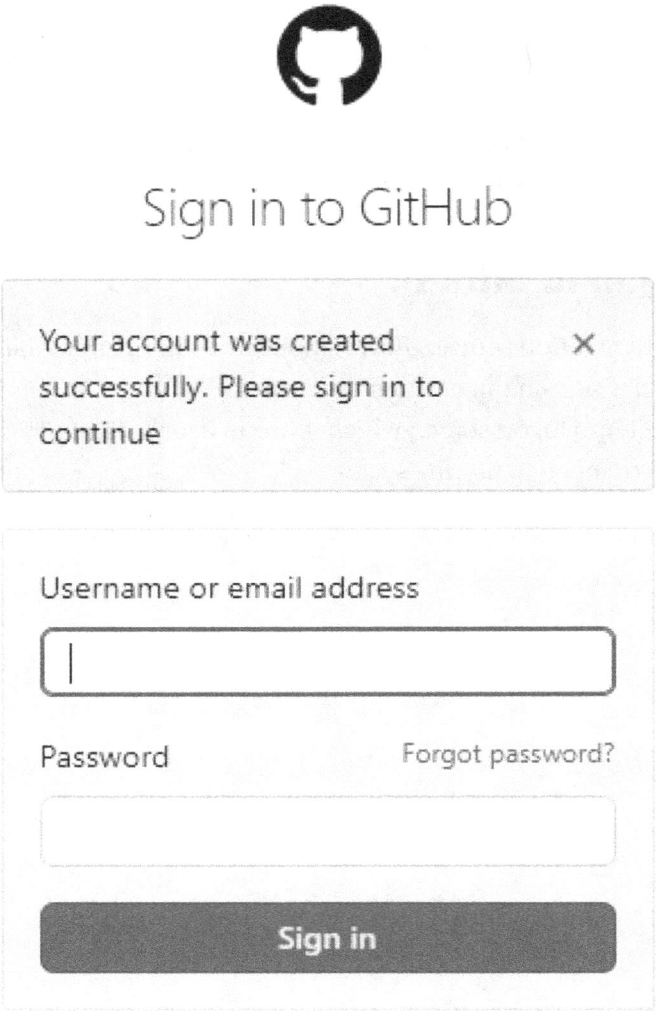

Sign in to GitHub

Your account was created   ✕
successfully. Please sign in to
continue

Username or email address

|

Password   Forgot password?

Sign in

Figure 2-21. *Sign in to GitHub*

Go ahead and enter your username and password and click the "Sign in" button. What you see next is your first brief glimpse of the GitHub user interface as shown in Figure 2-22.

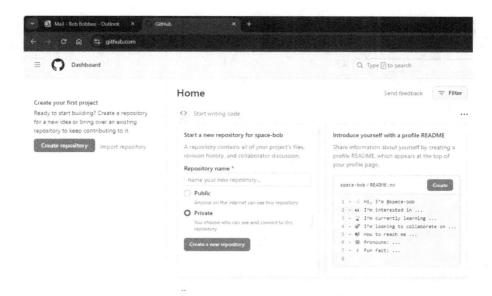

Figure 2-22. *The GitHub website and user interface*

GitHub is a very powerful tool that can do many things. It is often used as a version control tool by developers to make sure everyone is working on the latest versions of programming source code. As you begin to use Publii and GitHub together, you will barely scratch the surface of the capabilities of GitHub. In fact, other than setting a few things up, you will not ever need to visit GitHub again. Don't burn your username and password just yet. You will be back soon.

In the meantime, if you want to learn more about GitHub, feel free to check out some videos on YouTube or read up on the system at the site's documentation hub: `https://docs.github.com/en/get-started`.

Summary

I covered a lot of ground in this chapter. Luckily much of it was stuff you have probably done before in one form or another. Let's look at some of the key points:

Email accounts must be unique.

A dedicated email account for your website has several benefits:

- Security and privacy

- Greater professionalism

- Better organization

Private Browsing (or Incognito mode) in web browsers creates an isolated browsing environment which will not save information from your browsing sessions such as history, cookies, form information, or session information.

Short complex passwords are no longer desirable today as they are insecure.

Longer passwords made up of four or five short, easy-to-remember words will provide far better security over the short complex password of yesteryear.

Here are some guidelines to which a good password should conform:

- Don't use your own name or other names or identifying information of significant others, dogs, cats, etc.

- Use four or five short words instead of a string of gibberish.

- Capitalize one or more of the words.

- If you use numbers, do not use dates that are significant such as wedding anniversaries, birth dates, etc.

- No spaces.

- You can use a special character and/or numbers in your password, but it is not necessary unless the system you are using forces you to do that.

- Do NOT reuse a password from one system to another.

Always write down the account names and passwords that you create. Even better you should use a software-based password safe.

GitHub allows you to share files and manage file versions and encourages collaboration.

Files are stored in GitHub in a repository which is like a project folder that can store electronic information.

CHAPTER 3

Getting Publii CMS Running

In this chapter, you will install Publii CMS on your Windows PC or macOS system and perform some basic configuration.

Introduction to Publii CMS

Publii CMS is a simple, lightweight Content Management System (CMS) designed specifically for bloggers, personal portfolios, galleries, and documentation sites. It's beginner-friendly and provides all the tools you need to create a fully functional website quickly and easily, yet it packs a punch allowing the seasoned publisher to get online and be heard. Publii CMS is used by agencies as well as the platform of choice building out sites for customers.

The latest Publii CMS release allows us to create pages and provides the option to display a different homepage and a blog in a subfolder with its own index post page. This makes it ideal for small business websites as well. We will be exploring this functionality in Part 2 of this book.

Websites created with Publii CMS are considered static in nature, meaning they consist of fixed HTML files. Static sites load quickly and are highly secure. Unlike traditional CMS tools that generate pages dynamically, Publii's static sites don't rely on databases or content

© Brad Moore 2025
B. Moore, *Designing Websites with Publii and GitHub Pages*,
https://doi.org/10.1007/979-8-8688-1195-1_3

generation on a server (called server-side processing) to render a page. This makes them faster, more reliable, and less vulnerable to security risks.

Creating a website with Publii CMS is straightforward. First, download and install the Publii CMS application on your computer. This process will be covered in this chapter. The user-friendly interface allows you to manage your site with ease, choose from various templates, and customize them to fit your style. Adding content is as simple as typing in a text editor – you can include images and links and format your text without writing any code.

One of Publii CMS's best features is its offline functionality. You can create and edit your website without an Internet connection. When you're ready, Publii CMS uploads the static files to your web host with just a few clicks. This is different from online platforms like Wix and Squarespace, where you build and manage your site entirely online. With Publii CMS, there's no need to worry about databases or complex setups. It's a great choice for individuals, small businesses, and organizations of all kinds who want a secure, fast, and easy-to-maintain website without needing deep technical skills.

> *"Publii CMS generates static websites that are really fast; they avoid all the unnecessary bells and whistles that slow down modern sites and negatively impact their rating in searches."*
>
> –Publii.com

WHAT IS GDPR AND CCPA?

The General Data Protection Regulation (GDPR) is a set of rules created by the European Union to protect people's personal data. It requires websites to get permission before collecting or using your information, like your name or email address. Websites must also keep your data safe and let you know what they do with it. The California Consumer Privacy Act (CCPA) is similar but applies to people in California. It gives you the right to know what personal data websites collect about you and to ask them to delete it or not sell it to others. Both GDPR and CCPA help ensure your privacy is protected online. In later chapters, you will learn more about achieving the best compliance possible with Publii.

Publii CMS's focus on privacy and data protection means compliance with various laws comes built in. Publii CMS–based websites do not collect personal information, ensuring a GDPR-compliant, privacy-focused experience (see the side panel "What is GDPR and CCPA?"). If you want to use third-party tools for tracking or analytics, Publii CMS provides easy-to-use privacy tools to make your site GDPR and CCPA compliant without dealing with complex code. This ensures that your website respects user privacy while still allowing you to gather valuable insights.

A key advantage of Publii CMS is its optimization for search engines (learn more about SEO in the section "Search Engine Optimization" later in this chapter). Static websites generated by Publii CMS load quickly because they avoid unnecessary features that slow down modern sites. With no databases to check or external data requests, the essential files are sent directly from the server to the browser, ensuring smooth and rapid loading. Search engines prioritize fast-loading websites, so using Publii CMS can help improve your search ranking. This means more visitors are likely to find and stay on your site, increasing your audience and engagement.

Publii CMS is available for Windows, macOS (both Intel and Apple architectures), and several Linux versions. In this chapter, we will focus on installing Publii CMS in both the Windows and macOS environments.

Downloading Publii CMS

In this section, you will be downloading Publii CMS for the Windows operating system. If you are using macOS, proceed to the section titled "macOS Installation" for downloading and installation instructions.

Visit the Publii CMS website using your favorite web browser at `https://getpublii.com/`. The version of Publii CMS at the time of this writing is 0.46.2, released on November 1, 2024, as shown in Figure 3-1.

Create SEO & privacy-focused super fast website.

Creating a website doesn't have to be complicated or expensive. With the Publii app, the most intuitive CMS for static sites, you can create a beautiful, safe, and privacy-friendly website quickly and easily; perfect for anyone who wants a fast, secure website in a flash.

Win 64-bit 10+ | macOS 11+ | Linux 64-bit
Updated on November 1, 2024

Figure 3-1. *The Publii homepage*

To begin downloading Publii, click the "Download Publii 0.46.2" button in the middle of the page, or the download button in the upper right corner of the page. Both will take you to the download page as shown in Figure 3-2.

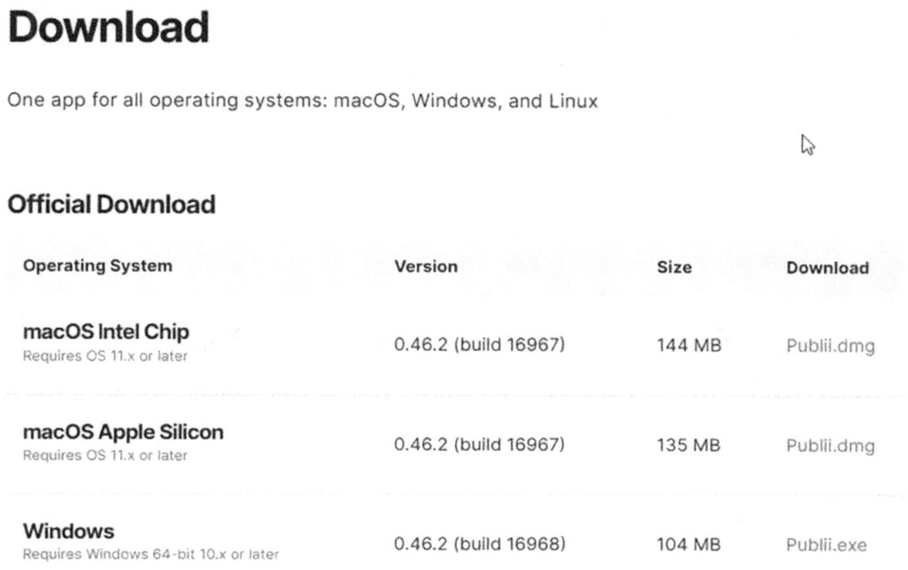

Download

One app for all operating systems: macOS, Windows, and Linux

Official Download

Operating System	Version	Size	Download
macOS Intel Chip Requires OS 11.x or later	0.46.2 (build 16967)	144 MB	Publii.dmg
macOS Apple Silicon Requires OS 11.x or later	0.46.2 (build 16967)	135 MB	Publii.dmg
Windows Requires Windows 64-bit 10.x or later	0.46.2 (build 16968)	104 MB	Publii.exe

Figure 3-2. *Publii CMS download page*

You will notice that Publii CMS is offered on several platforms including Windows, macOS, and Linux. This section specifically focuses on downloading and installing the Windows version of the application. If you are a Mac user, you should proceed to the section titled "macOS Installation" later in this chapter.

This book does not cover installation on the Linux platform. It is assumed that most Linux users are well versed in installing applications on their specific version of Linux. If you are a Linux user and need help installing Publii CMS, please visit the Publii CMS User Forums for assistance: https://github.com/GetPublii/Publii/discussions.

Click the blue Publii.exe link to begin the download of the Windows version. You can find that in the fourth column of the third row labeled "Windows" in the downloads table as seen in Figure 3-2.

The folks at Publii CMS are interested in staying in touch and offer you an option to sign up to receive occasional emails and product updates from the team as seen in Figure 3-3. If you will be using Publii CMS regularly, this is not a bad thing to do. It is completely optional.

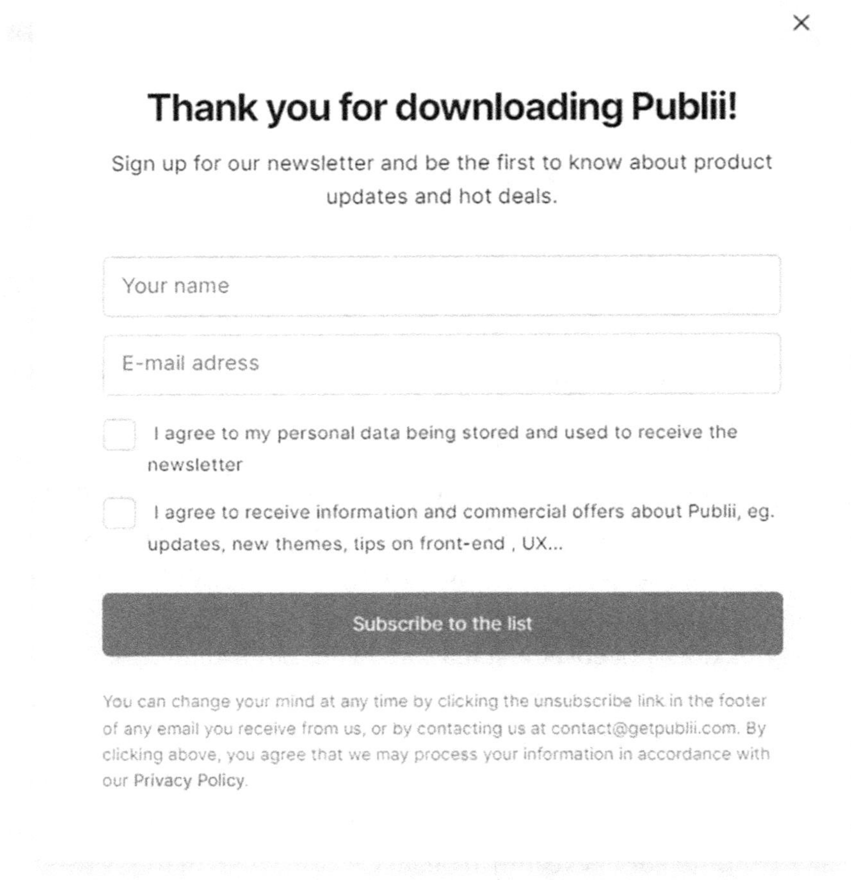

Figure 3-3. *Sign up to the newsletter*

Note   Publii CMS is headquartered in the European Union and complies with all EU data protection laws. They consider it a privilege to host your data when you sign up for a newsletter and will treat it with the highest care and in complete compliance with GDPR regulations.

Click the "X" in the upper right corner of the dialog to close it should you opt not to sign up.

Installing Publii CMS

Installing Publii CMS is an easy and painless process whether you are a Windows or macOS user. You will find below the information you need to install Publii CMS on either operating system.

Windows Installation

This section explains how to install the Windows version of Publii CMS on your Windows 10 or 11 operating system – you should be able to install the application on any 64-bit Windows OS.

At this point, you should have clicked the download link for the Windows version of Publii CMS. The file is about 104 MB in size. The time required to download the executable will depend greatly on your Internet connection speed.

Once the download is completed, open the folder where it was saved. Chrome lets you do that by clicking the download manager icon in the upper right of the browser as seen in Figure 3-4.

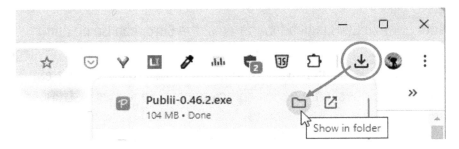

Figure 3-4. *Chrome's Show in folder feature*

Go ahead and click the Show in folder icon in the small window that pops up to open Windows File Explorer to the location where this file was downloaded.

Note   You can skip this step and simply launch the installer – since this is a Windows executable file – by clicking the file name ("Publii-0.46.2.exe") in the small window that popped open.

Figure 3-5 shows the file that was downloaded from the Publii CMS website in my Windows file explorer. Yours will look similar.

Figure 3-5. *Publii CMS installation file*

Double-click the file in the Windows File Explorer to begin the installation. (You might be here already if you launched the installation from Chrome.) Windows will warn you about the security risks installing a file that was downloaded from the Internet as shown in Figure 3-6.

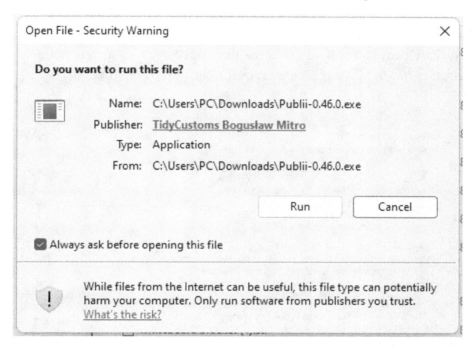

Figure 3-6. *File Security Warning*

This warning will always pop up when executing files downloaded from the Internet. This is because some software can be dangerous for your computer if you do not know where it came from or what it does. As the dialog window suggests – only run software from publishers you trust.

The developers of Publii CMS take security seriously which is why the Publii app is signed by an EV Code Signing certificate, ensuring the highest level of identity verification. This certificate is recognized and trusted by Microsoft. Additionally, Publii CMS is also signed with an Apple Developer

Certificate, which ensures compatibility with macOS and enhances security. For this reason, you can safely install the downloaded program.

Click the "Run" button to launch the installer.

Once the installation begins running, you will be presented with the application license agreement as shown in Figure 3-7. Publii CMS is open source software licensed under the GNU General Public License version 3. You can learn more about the licensing of open source software here: https://www.gnu.org/licenses/quick-guide-gplv3.html.

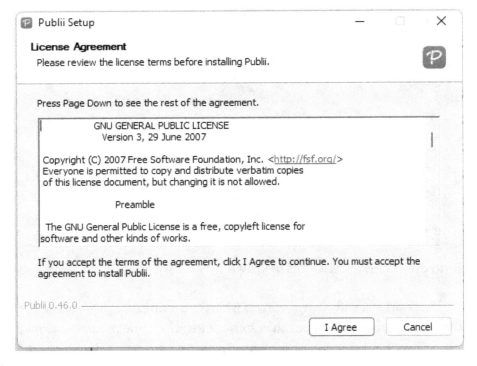

Figure 3-7. Publii CMS Licensing dialog

Click the "I Agree" button once you have read the license (if you are the kind of person to read software licensing agreements). Of course, you must agree to the license before you can install the software.

That's it. The installation is on its way. Figure 3-8 shows the file copy process of the installation as it runs.

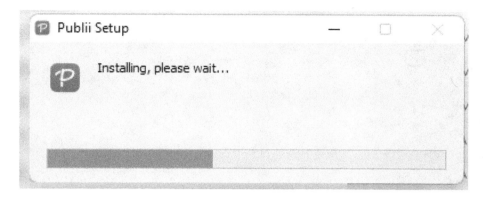

Figure 3-8. *Publii CMS being installed*

Once Publii CMS has been installed, the application will begin running automatically. The first thing it wants to do is create a website as shown in Figure 3-9. We will do this in the section below titled "Create Your First Website."

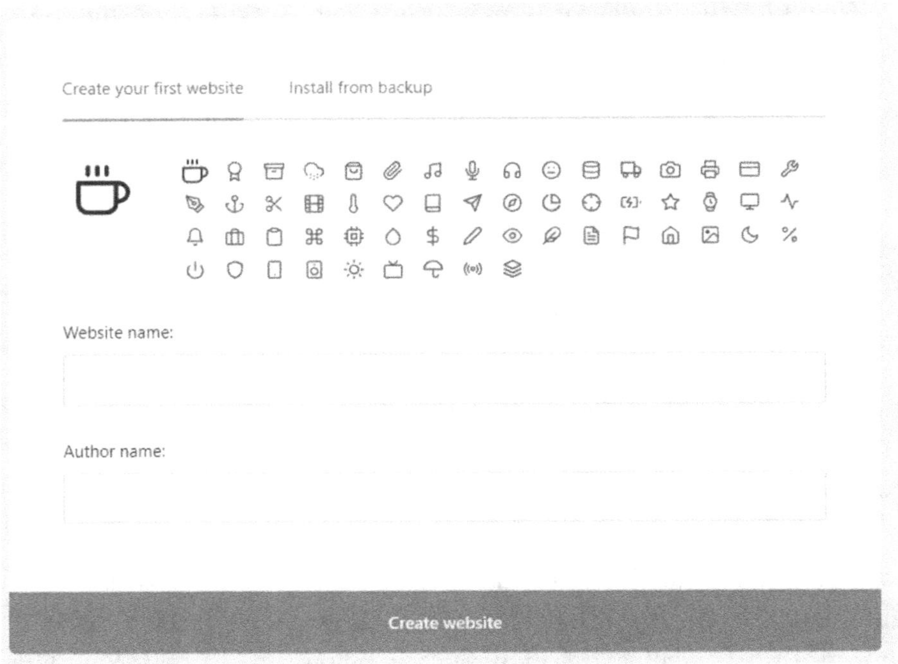

Figure 3-9. *Create your first website*

macOS Installation

In this section, you will download and install the macOS version of Publii CMS. If you have already installed the Windows version and want to continue with setting up your first website, then please skip ahead to the next Create Your First Website.

The Publii download page is shown in Figure 3-10. You can get here by opening your favorite browser to https://getpublii.com/ and then clicking one of the blue download buttons on the Publii homepage. See Figure 3-1 for an example of this web page.

Download

One app for all operating systems: macOS, Windows, and Linux

Official Download

Operating System	Version	Size	Download
macOS Intel Chip Requires OS 11.x or later	0.46.2 (build 16967)	144 MB	Publii.dmg
macOS Apple Silicon Requires OS 11.x or later	0.46.2 (build 16967)	135 MB	Publii.dmg

Figure 3-10. *Publii CMS download page*

On the Publii CMS download page, you will see several platforms that Publii CMS supports. As a macOS user, you will notice that there are two platforms listed. Most Mac users will know a little bit about the history of the Mac architecture. Since 2005, Apple manufactured Mac computers using an Intel-based CPU at the heart of the machine. In 2020, Apple began transitioning from the Intel processor to a CPU of their own design – which is refered to as Apple Silicon. Depending on the age and model of your Mac, you may have an Intel or an Apple Silicon processor inside. See the following website for more information on the transition: https://support.apple.com/en-us/116943.

It is important that you download the correct version of the application as the most current macOS will not support Intel-designed applications on Apple Silicon. If you are not sure what you have, then find your computer's model number and google it for more information.

I have a fairly new Mac Mini running Apple Silicon, so I chose to download that version of the application by clicking the blue link in the fourth column of the table labeled "Publii.dmg". Download the "dmg" file that matches the architecture of your Mac.

I am using Chrome as my preferred browser on my Mac. You may use Safari or any other browser you like.

The "dmg" file has been downloaded as can be seen from Figure 3-11. The Mac typically downloads all files to the Downloads folder. Once the download is completed, open the folder where the file was saved. Chrome lets you do that by clicking the download manager icon in the upper right of the browser and clicking the folder icon.

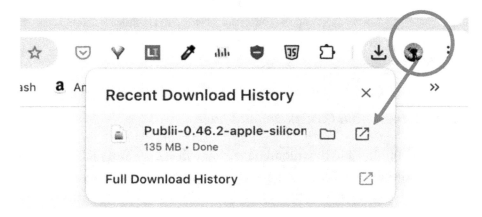

Figure 3-11. *Publii CMS Installation file as seen in the Download Manager*

Locate the downloaded file in your downloaded files list in the Mac Finder window as shown in Figure 3-12.

Name

📄 Publii-0.46.2-apple-silicon.dmg

Figure 3-12. *Mac Finder showing the file in the Downloads folder*

Note   You can skip this step and simply launch the installer from Chrome – since this is an executable file – by clicking the file name ("Publii-0.46.2-apple-silicon.dmg") in the small window that popped open.

Double-click the file that you downloaded to launch the installer. In my case, I downloaded "Publii-0.46.2-apple-silicon.dmg".

Once the installation begins running, you will be presented with the application license agreement as shown in Figure 3-13. Publii CMS is open source software licensed under the GNU General Public License version 3. You can learn more about the licensing of open source software here: https://www.gnu.org/licenses/quick-guide-gplv3.html.

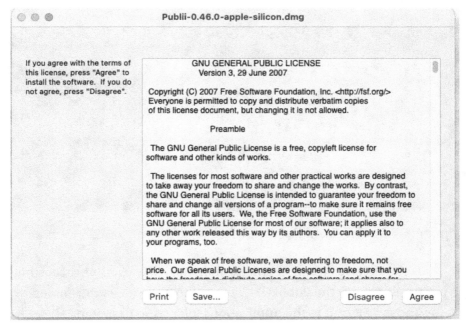

Figure 3-13. Publii CMS License dialog

Click the "Agree" button once you have read the license (if you are the kind of person to read software licensing agreements – you should be). Of course, you must agree to the license before you can install the software.

The operating system will quickly unpack the "dmg" file and validate it. It is still not installed. You must drag the Publii CMS application icon into the Applications folder on your Mac. To simplify this process, the installer opens a Finder window with the application icon and a shortcut to the Applications folder as shown in Figure 3-14.

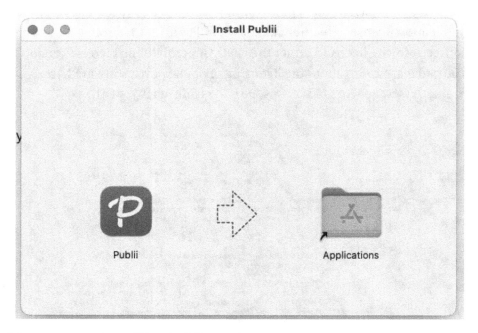

Figure 3-14. *Installing Publii CMS*

This should be a common process that most Mac users are accustomed to performing. Click the Publii CMS icon on the left side of the Finder dialog and drag it over to the Applications folder and drop it in.

This will install the application onto your Mac. Most Macs are so fast, and this application is so small you will probably not see it being copied. You can open a new Finder window and locate the file as shown in Figure 3-15.

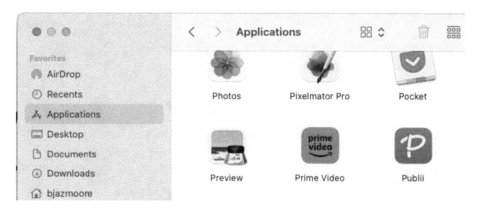

Figure 3-15. *Applications folder in Finder*

Tip   Open a new Finder window by first clicking on Finder in your Mac dock at the bottom of the screen. Next, in the upper left corner of the screen, click File, then New Finder Window.

Click the Applications shortcut in the left pane of the Finder window to view the programs that are installed into the Applications folder.

Double-click the Publii CMS icon to launch the program. The macOS will warn you that this file was downloaded from the Internet as shown in Figure 3-16.

Figure 3-16. *Application Security Warning*

Notice that the file was checked by Apple for the presence of malicious software. Apple calls this type of validation done by the publisher as application notarization. Since this has been notarized by a trusted publisher, you can safely click the "Open" button to launch the application.

Apple explains notarization and software security as it regards running software downloaded from the Internet here: `https://support.apple. com/en-us/102445`.

In addition to being notarized, Publii CMS is also signed with an Apple Developer Certificate, which ensures compatibility with macOS and enhances security. For this reason, you can safely install the downloaded program.

When first opened, Publii CMS will begin the process of creating your first website as shown in Figure 3-17 of the next section titled "Create Your First Website." Proceed there to continue setting up Publii CMS.

Create Your First Website

In this section, you will create your first website. You should have come here from installing Publii CMS either on a Mac or a Windows PC.

The remainder of the book will use examples from the Windows operating system. In all cases, the Publii CMS application operates the same apart from file system management. When necessary, I will mention major differences to be aware of if you are a Mac user.

Whether you installed the Windows version of Publii CMS or the macOS version, you should now be looking at the dialog window as shown in Figure 3-17.

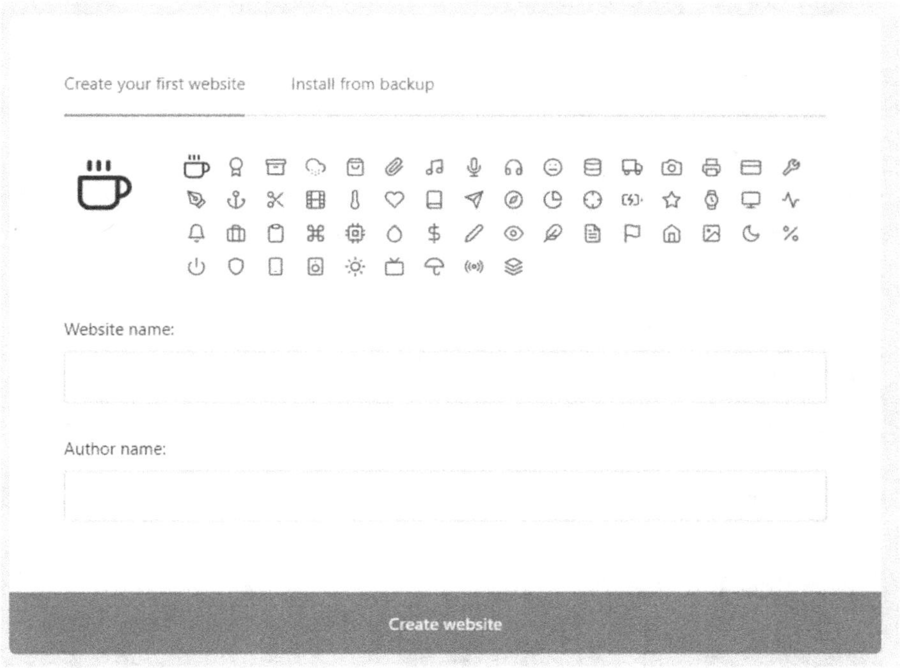

Figure 3-17. *Create your first website*

You probably noticed that there are two options available in this dialog form for creating a website. The form has a tabbed interface. The default operation is to create a new website from scratch. If you click the words

"Install from backup", the dialog window will change to reflect the input needed to restore a website from a backup that was previously created. We will review this functionality in Chapter 9, Backups and Sites.

To create your first website in Publii CMS, you need only to provide a name for the website and your name as the author. As I develop this first example for you to follow, I will be creating a blog site detailing an imaginary rocket company developing equipment and preparing to go to the moon. I will be writing under the pseudonym Bob Bobbee. You may follow along mirroring my project or you can branch out and do your own thing. Maybe a coffee shop or a community gardening patch. Whatever strikes your fancy.

As you can see, I have given my website a name and provided the name of the author in Figure 3-18. Do the same for your project.

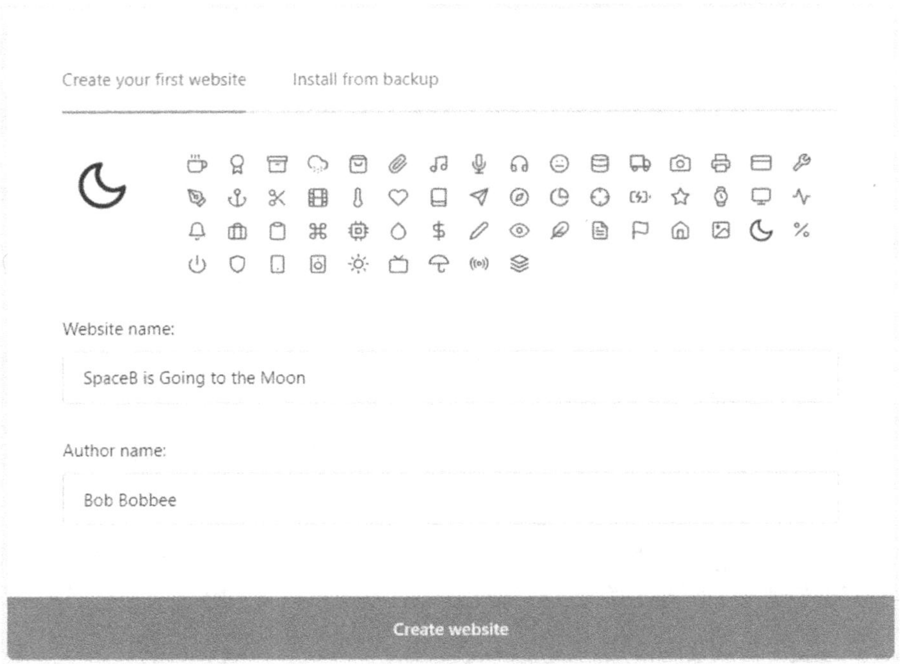

Figure 3-18. *Creating your first website*

Also notice that I have changed the icon for the site to a moon. This icon is only for site management and will not be presented to the end user when they visit your finished website. You can leave it as a coffee cup or select any other icon you like.

Make sure you are on the tab "Create your first website" and have supplied a website name and an author name. Click the large blue button on the bottom labeled "Create website".

If Publii CMS looks like Figure 3-19, which it should, you have successfully created your first website.

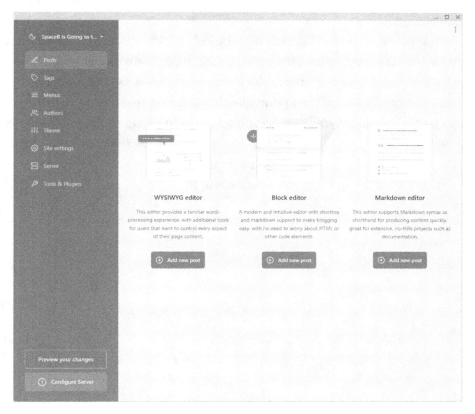

Figure 3-19. *Publii CMS with a fresh website just created*

We will learn a lot more about using Publii CMS to create posts and pages and publish our site in the chapters to come. The rest of this chapter will focus on making a few settings changes required to get the most out of Publii CMS.

Modifying Publii CMS Site Settings

In this section, we will focus on making a few settings modifications from the default settings so that we can have the best Publii CMS publishing experience.

You probably noticed already that the Publii CMS interface is divided into two panes. The narrow blue left pane has the application main menu. This will allow you to move around in the application as you use the program.

On the right side of the application is a large pane (I often refer to it as a panel) used to display the various parts of the program as you use different functions. Sometimes this section will be divided further into different sections to facilitate maintaining application settings.

Looking at the main menu as shown in Figure 3-20, click on the menu item "Site settings".

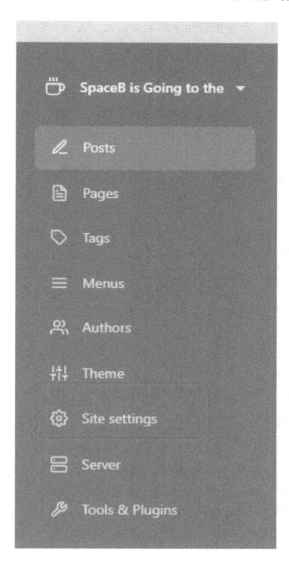

Figure 3-20. *Application main menu*

Observe that the right pane has changed context and now reflects the site settings options and menus as shown in Figure 3-21.

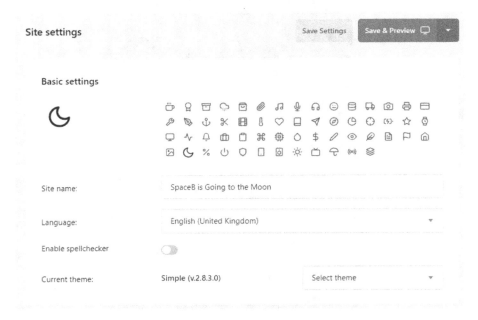

Figure 3-21. *Publii CMS Site Settings*

One of the first things I change when installing Publii CMS is the site language. I live, write, and publish in the United States, so I choose the USA version of English. If you do not live in an area that uses the United Kingdom version of English spelling, then select the drop-down arrow on the right of the Language picker field as shown in Figure 3-22 and choose your native language.

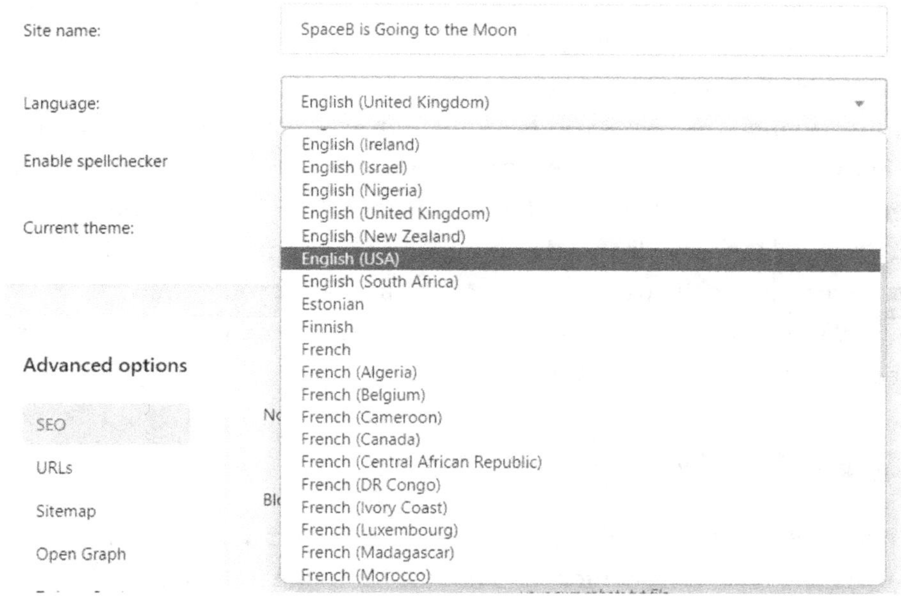

Figure 3-22. *Language picker*

Another very useful option I recommend enabling is the spellchecker as shown in Figure 3-23. When I was in second grade, my teacher told my parents that my spelling was atrocious. You know what – it has not improved much since. Thank you Publii CMS (and its creators) for the spellchecker feature!

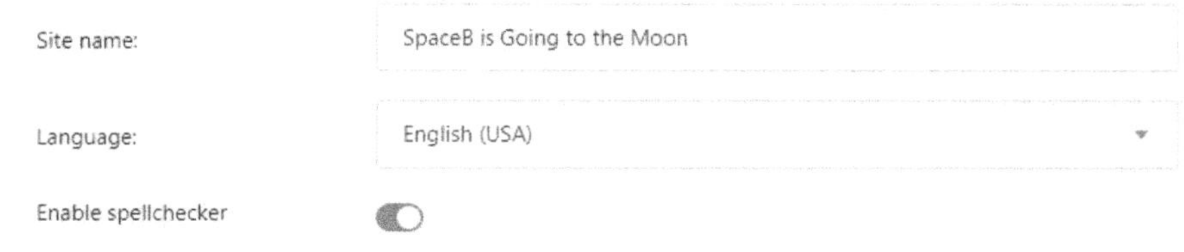

Figure 3-23. *Enable spellchecker*

Enable the spellchecker by sliding the toggle switch to the right. The toggle option will turn blue indicating it is active.

When you make changes, be sure to click the light blue "Save Settings" button in the upper right corner of the right application panel as seen in Figure 3-21. Notice that there are two save options there. The light-colored button will simply save the changes you made. Clicking the darker "Save & Preview" button will save the settings and then launch your default web browser loading the website you are working on for you to view.

We will intentionally preview the website at the end of this chapter, but feel free to peek ahead of time.

Advanced Options

In this section, I will be discussing the other options that you can modify to get ready for creating content and publishing to the Internet.

There is another section of the settings interface below the Basic settings in the right pane labelled Advance Options. This part of the interface has a submenu on the right side of the panel and settings for each submenu on the left side as shown in Figure 3-24.

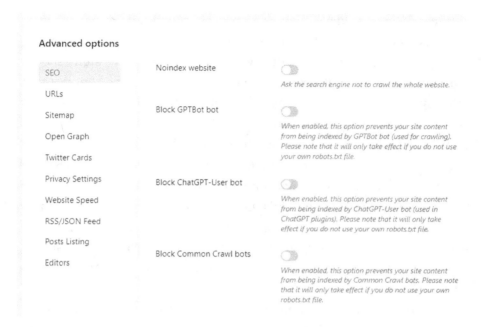

Advanced options

SEO	Noindex website
URLs	*Ask the search engine not to crawl the whole website.*
Sitemap	Block GPTBot bot
Open Graph	*When enabled, this option prevents your site content from being indexed by GPTBot bot (used for crawling). Please note that it will only take effect if you do not use your own robots.txt file.*
Twitter Cards	
Privacy Settings	Block ChatGPT-User bot
Website Speed	*When enabled, this option prevents your site content from being indexed by ChatGPT-User bot (used in ChatGPT plugins). Please note that it will only take effect if you do not use your own robots.txt file.*
RSS/JSON Feed	
Posts Listing	Block Common Crawl bots
Editors	*When enabled, this option prevents your site content from being indexed by Common Crawl bots. Please note that it will only take effect if you do not use your own robots.txt file.*

Figure 3-24. *SEO options*

You will notice in the figure below that the SEO section is selected.

Search Engine Optimization

In this section, you will learn about SEO and how to use it to make your website more accessible.

SEO is an abbreviation that stands for "Search Engine Optimization." These are strategies you use to help your website to get noticed or make it easier to find on the Internet. Think of it as if your website were a book and you are trying to get it noticed in a giant library filled with millions of books. When someone searches for something online – like "best local restaurants" – search engines like Google scan through all the websites they have cataloged and show the ones that seem most relevant and trustworthy at the top of the results. Our goal with SEO is to make sure our website is one of those that gets noticed.

Search engines like Google use a process called **indexing** to create a catalog of websites and determine where they should appear in search results. This begins with **crawling**, where automated bots (often called "spiders") systematically explore the Internet, visiting page after page by following links. As the bots crawl your website, they analyze its content, structure, and links and then store this information in a massive database known as the **index**. The index acts like a digital library or catalog, organizing web pages by content, relevance, and quality. When someone searches for a term – on Google, for instance – the search engine retrieves the most relevant pages from this index. Where these pages appear in the search results is called ranking. Pages are ranked on various factors like keywords, page speed, and backlink authority. Ensuring your site is properly indexed is crucial for appearing in search results and improving your visibility online.

SEO is important to remember as you develop your website. Imagine having a beautifully designed website full of valuable content, but no one ever visits because it doesn't show up in search results. Without good SEO, your website is like a hidden gem that no one ever discovers. By considering SEO as you develop your site, you ensure that your site is visible to people who are searching for the kind of content you offer. This can lead to more visitors, more people reading your information, and, ultimately, more success for whatever goals you have – whether it's sharing your ideas, growing your business, or building a community.

Winning at SEO involves a few key strategies. First, you need to use the right words – called keywords – that people are likely to type into a search engine when looking for content like yours. These keywords should appear naturally in your website's text, titles, and descriptions. But SEO is more than just using the right words; it's also about creating high-quality content that provides real value to our visitors. I will discuss content later as we develop the demonstration website and blog.

The thing to remember is that search engines – like Google and Bing – prefer to show content that is informative, well written, and useful, so focusing on the quality of what you write is crucial.

Another important aspect of SEO is making sure our website is easy to navigate and loads quickly. Search engines like Google pay attention to how user-friendly your site is. If your pages take too long to load or if visitors can't easily find what they're looking for, search engines might penalize your site by listing it lower in the results they return. This means you should aim for a clean, organized layout and ensure your site performs well on both computers and mobile devices. Publii CMS makes this easy as it is designed to be search engine friendly. Also, static websites such as those Publii CMS generates are extremely lean and tend to load very quickly.

Finally, we win at SEO by building credibility. This involves getting other reputable websites to link to our site, which acts like a vote of confidence. The more high-quality links you have pointing to your content, the more likely search engines are to trust your site and list it with higher search results. This is a strategic endeavor that requires effort. I will not be covering this specific technique in this book. You can learn a lot more about SEO and backlinking on the Internet. Specifically look at this article discussing backlinking: `https://ahrefs.com/blog/what-are-backlinks/`.

Engaging with your audience, sharing your content on social media, and building relationships with other website owners can all help increase the results of your SEO efforts. I will be pointing out ways to improve your SEO performance as I progress through the content development stage of this project. SEO is not a one-and-done feature of getting your information onto the Internet – the better you want your site to perform, the more effort you will need to invest into the process.

In Figure 3-24, there were four different page indexing options we can enable or disable. These will affect how various website crawlers access your website and collect information.

When I publish with Publii CMS, I leave this set at the default settings given to them when Publii CMS was installed. Depending on your specific needs, you may find you want to change these. It is not uncommon for publishers to choose to block AI crawlers which scrape data from websites and use it to train AI models. The practice of scraping websites is controversial currently, as it likely violates copyright law in many countries.

Setting the GPTBot and ChatGPT-User bots to prevent scraping is done by sliding the toggle button to the right for the second and third options as seen in Figure 3-24. The switch will become blue.

Be careful enabling the "Noindex website" option as this will prevent your website from being indexed by most crawlers including Google's. It will also cause some of the Publii CMS features to stop working, such as the sitemap not being generated.

This is the equivalent of becoming invisible on the Internet. The same is true for the fourth option – blocking common Crawl bots.

The safest path forward here if you are unsure is to not make any changes. However, you should understand what is being asked in case you want to make changes in the future.

If you made changes, be sure to click the light blue "Save settings" button in the upper right corner of the right application panel as seen in Figure 3-21.

Homepage SEO Settings

In this section, I will discuss setting up a meta description for your website homepage.

Scroll the right panel down a little so that you can see the SEO settings for the homepage as shown in Figure 3-25.

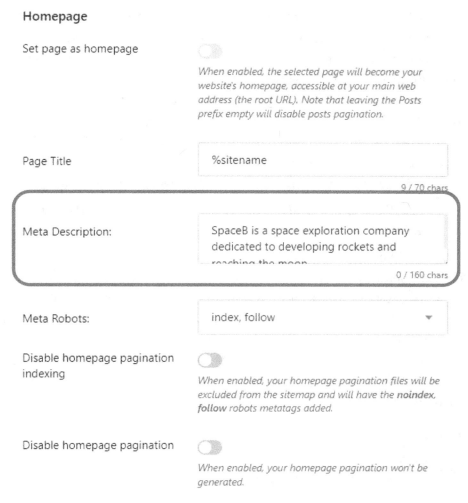

Homepage

Set page as homepage

When enabled, the selected page will become your website's homepage, accessible at your main web address (the root URL). Note that leaving the Posts prefix empty will disable posts pagination.

Page Title

%sitename

9 / 70 chars

Meta Description:

SpaceB is a space exploration company dedicated to developing rockets and reaching the moon

0 / 160 chars

Meta Robots:

index, follow

Disable homepage pagination indexing

When enabled, your homepage pagination files will be excluded from the sitemap and will have the **noindex, follow** robots metatags added.

Disable homepage pagination

When enabled, your homepage pagination won't be generated.

Figure 3-25. *Homepage settings for SEO*

Generally, I leave these settings on this panel at the default settings they had when Publii CMS was installed – with one exception. I always provide a meta description for the homepage.

There is a lot of debate regarding whether a meta description for the site homepage is an asset for SEO. In 2024, there was a leak of the Google page ranking algorithm which seemed to suggest that it still plays a factor in the process despite denials from Google.

The meta description is highly useful in helping Google and other search engines decide how to summarize your website when listing it in the results from a search. For this reason alone, you need to provide a meta description for your front page.

In the meta description (highlighted in Figure 3-25), write a short, keyword-intensive description of your site, products, and services. Keep your keywords on point so that they describe what you are offering. The field will permit up to 160 characters.

For the site I am building, I have chosen to write the following:

SpaceB is a space exploration company dedicated to developing rockets and reaching the moon.

You will not need to make any other changes to the SEO settings. Meta descriptions for posts and pages are assigned to each specific post or page. Other page types (tags, author, etc.) should not be indexed – as defined by their Meta Robot's default setting of "noindex, follow" – therefore, they will not require a meta description. Leave these as set to their default values.

Don't forget to save your changes; be sure to click the light blue "Save Settings" button in the upper right corner of the right application panel as seen in Figure 3-21.

Pretty URLs

In this section, you will enable pretty URLs for your Publii CMS–generated website.

Pretty URLs are another great option to enable. It does not come enabled so you will need to make that change. URLs that have been made pretty are easier for humans to deal with and enhance the SEO performance of your website.

Enabling this option will be important for us later (in Part 2) when we set a specific page as the new homepage and choose to have the post index in a subfolder, like /blog/. This option is also critical to the function of page nesting, which will not work without it.

In the Advanced Options menu in the right panel, click on the item labeled URLs as shown in Figure 3-26.

Advanced options

SEO	Use pretty URLs	◯
URLs		When enabled, your post URLs won't contain the .html suffix e.g. it will change URLs from https://example.com/post.html to https://example.com/post/.
Sitemap		
Open Graph	Always add index.html in URLs	◯
Twitter Cards		Enable this option if you cannot enable loading index.html files by default when a folder on your server
Privacy Settings		is opened.
Website Speed		
	Tag prefix:	tags
RSS/JSON Feed		
		Prefixes entered here will be added before the tag slug in the URL e.g. https://example.com/TAG_PREFIX/tag-slug.
Posts Listing		
		This prefix is also used to generate the tags list page (if
Editors		supported in your theme) e.g.

Figure 3-26. *URL settings*

In this section, I recommend only this one change. Enable the "Use pretty URLs" feature by sliding the toggle switch to the right for that option. The toggle switch will turn blue to indicate it is enabled.

Since you have changed the option for "Use pretty URLs", you should save your settings. Click the light blue "Save Settings" button in the upper right corner of the right application panel as seen in Figure 3-21 to save the changes made.

There are many other options available in the "Advanced Options" menu, as you can see from Figure 3-26. We may choose to modify some of these in the future. Generally, you are safe leaving this set to default settings as they are best for the general use of Publii CMS for website creation and publishing.

Some of these settings are purely optional and designed to enhance your website's visibility on various social media platforms such as Facebook (Open Graph) and Twitter (Twitter Cards). I will not cover these, but some searching on Google can help you utilize these for greater site visibility should you choose. Don't forget you can also ask questions in the Publii forum should you need help. It is located here: `https://github.com/GetPublii/Publii/discussions`.

Previewing the Site

In this section, you will learn the two different ways to preview changes you have made to your Publii CMS website.

As you work on your website, you will probably want to see how things will look when the site is published. I know I often do. This is done by previewing the site. There are two different ways to generate a preview of the site. In both cases, the preview is generated and saved to your Publii working directory. Your default browser is then used to display the local copy of the website as it was generated.

Preview should not be confused with uploading your site to the Internet. A site when previewed is stored locally on your computer and cannot be accessed by outside users. Uploading your site to the Internet, what I call publishing, is a different process which we will cover in Chapter 8: Configure Publii CMS for Sync.

The first way to preview your site is to click the dark blue "Save & Preview" button on the top or bottom of the right panel of the application as shown in Figure 3-27. These buttons do the same functions, which are to save any changes made in the user interface and then generate the site displaying it in your default web browser.

Figure 3-27. *Save & Preview button*

Typically, this process of previewing is done in conjunction with making changes to a post, page, or Publii CMS setting.

Sometimes you might just want to generate a preview and see your site even though you have not made changes to the site or site settings. This is where the second method comes in handy.

There is a button on the bottom of the blue main menu that is nearly always available (except when editing a post or page) labeled "Preview your changes" as shown in Figure 3-28. Clicking this button will also generate a preview of your Publii CMS website as it exists. (If you are making changes to settings – be sure to save them first or they will be discarded.)

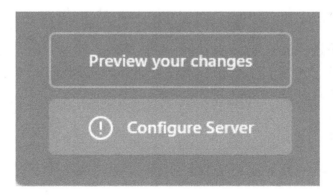

Figure 3-28. *Preview your changes button*

Both buttons will generate a preview of your site, and you can use either one interchangeably. When clicking the preview buttons, Publii CMS will generate your site from the post, page, themes, images, and other content settings, compiling it into a complete website. That website is saved on your local PC or Mac.

I clicked the "Preview your changes" button to generate the website in its current form which can be seen in Figure 3-29.

Figure 3-29. *Preview of my blog after initial configuration*

I admit the site is not very exciting. There is a huge black section and a few words. There are no other links or content. Of course I have not developed any of that yet.

Summary

Here are some of the key points covered in this chapter.

You were introduced to Publii CMS as a website generator.

- It is used to create static websites.

- The sites it creates are fast and secure by virtue of the technology used.

- They are also search engine optimized.

- Publii CMS is available for multiple platforms including Windows, macOS, and Linux.

You were also introduced to the concepts of privacy and compliance as it relates to GDPR and CCPA.

The preceding chapter covered how to download and install Publii CMS on both Windows and macOS.

Also covered was the process of creating your first website.

You were introduced to the concept of Search Engine Optimization (SEO):

- The process of indexing was discussed.

- Bots and crawlers used for discovering web pages was explored.

- The importance of good SEO was stressed (as it will be going forward).

Meta descriptions are important both for the home page and for pages and posts. These will be covered once again when we begin creating pages and posts.

We concluded the chapter by previewing our website. Preview often as you develop your site to make sure it looks the way you think it should.

CHAPTER 4

Getting Ready for Content

In this chapter, I will be discussing some basic theme settings, completing configuration of the author information, creating a main menu, and setting up tags for the website project. All these activities get Publii CMS ready for adding content.

Theme Settings

Publii CMS ships with a theme called Simple. The version of the theme available with Publii CMS 0.46.2 is Simple 3.0.0.0. Publii CMS offers many official themes – I will cover installing additional themes in Chapter 10: Themes.

Themes in Publii CMS have multiple customization features that allow you to adjust the look and feel of your website. In the sections that follow, I will discuss some simple changes you can make to give your site some visual polish.

Theme settings are under the main menu item labeled "Theme" as shown in Figure 4-1.

© Brad Moore 2025
B. Moore, *Designing Websites with Publii and GitHub Pages*,
https://doi.org/10.1007/979-8-8688-1195-1_4

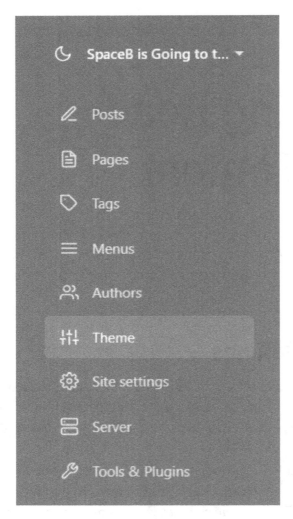

Figure 4-1. *Publii CMS main menu*

Clicking "Theme" in the main menu changes the context of the right panel to display theme options. Basic settings are displayed initially as shown in Figure 4-2.

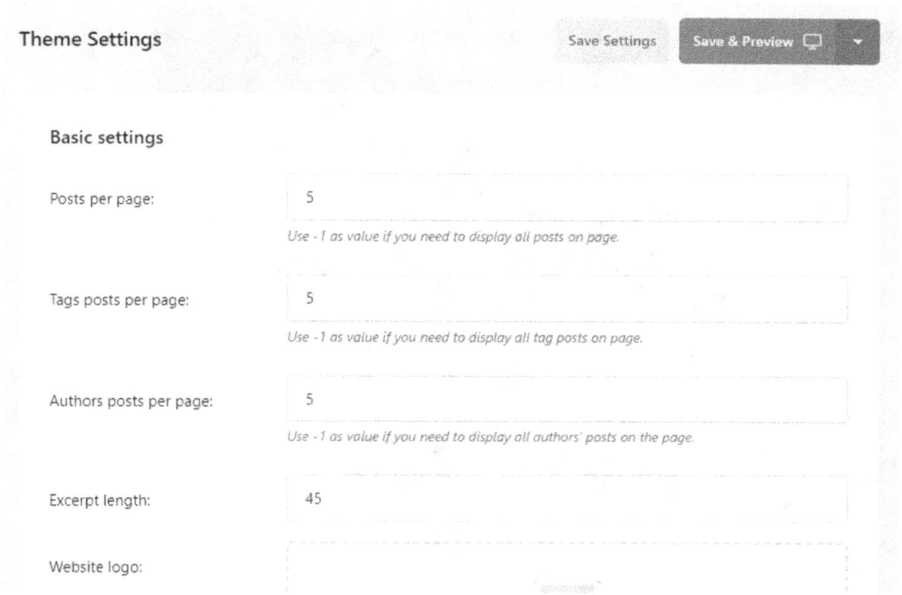

Figure 4-2. *Theme Settings*

You can achieve many different looks for a given theme by making changes to the various settings. In the case of this project, I will be making very few changes. I encourage you to experiment and see what various settings changes make to the website.

In the Basic settings section, I want to apply a custom image as my website logo. I will be using a black and white rocket image that I downloaded from OpenClipArt.org as shown in Figure 4-3. Clipart on this website is licensed under Creative Commons "CC0," making them public domain. Learn more about Creative Commons "CC0" licensing here: `https://creativecommons.org/publicdomain/zero/1.0/legalcode`.

Figure 4-3. *Rocket-15 from OpenClipArt.org*

This image can be downloaded from this URL: `https://openclipart.org/detail/260817/rocket15`. You can also find this image in this book's GitHub repository at `https://github.com/Apress/Designing-Websites-with-Publii-and-GitHub-Pages`.

If you are following along, then download the image. Locate the image in your computer's file system – usually in the Downloads folder. Drag the image file from the Downloads folder to the large rectangular field for the website which instructs us to "Drop to upload your photo" as shown in Figure 4-4.

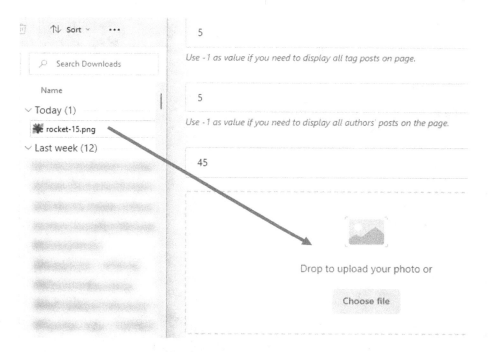

Figure 4-4. *Drag and drop the image into the photo picker field*

The field we dropped the image into is called a "photo picker." It supports browsing your file system for images by clicking "Choose file" or dragging and dropping images into the field as I have done here.

Picker fields exist for other file types as well. When encountered later in the book, I will simply suggest dragging and dropping a file into the picker field. Once the file is dropped into the field, Publii CMS will display a thumbnail of the image as seen in Figure 4-5.

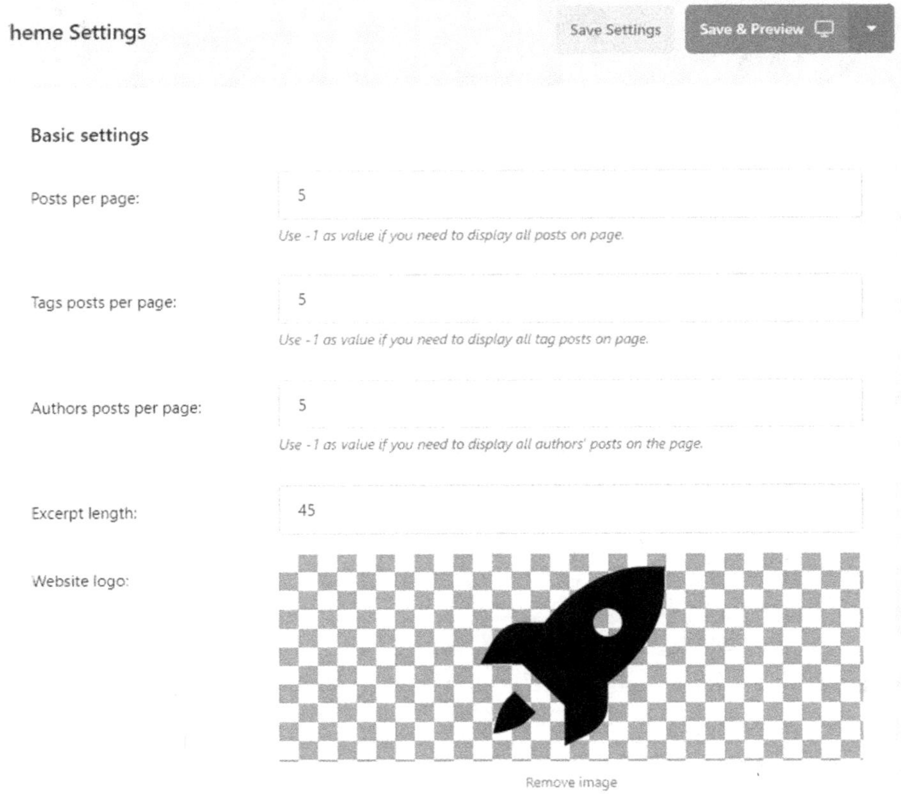

heme Settings   Save Settings   Save & Preview ⌐ ▾

Basic settings

Posts per page: 5

Use -1 as value if you need to display all posts on page.

Tags posts per page: 5

Use -1 as value if you need to display all tag posts on page.

Authors posts per page: 5

Use -1 as value if you need to display all authors' posts on the page.

Excerpt length: 45

Website logo:

Remove image

Figure 4-5. *Preview of website logo*

If you made a mistake or want to replace an image or file that has been dropped into a picker, simply click the red "Remove image" link below the field to delete it. Drag a new image into the picker in such a case.

Always remember to save your changes. Click the "Save Settings" or "Save & Preview" button on the top or bottom of the right panel. I chose to click "Save & Preview" so I could see what my site looks like with a logo applied as you can see in Figure 4-6.

Figure 4-6. *Preview of the website*

Layout: Hero Section

In this section, I will explain customization of the Hero section of the website.

Scrolling the right panel down a little bit will reveal the Custom settings section for the theme. Every theme has a different set of custom settings that relate to specific layout code written into the theme files. It is not necessary to understand this code to modify a theme using these settings.

The first section that you should make changes to is the Layout. Layout is the first section in the submenu for Custom settings as shown in Figure 4-7.

Custom settings

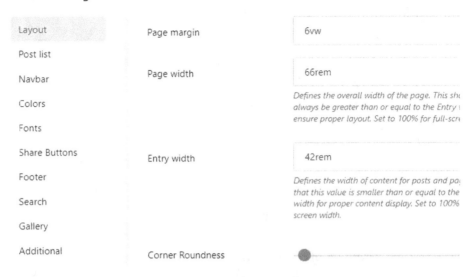

Figure 4-7. *Custom settings menu (left side)*

Scroll down in the right panel – use your middle scroll wheel on your mouse if you have one (the scroll bar is very small and can be hard to grab) – to the section titled Hero section as shown in Figure 4-8.

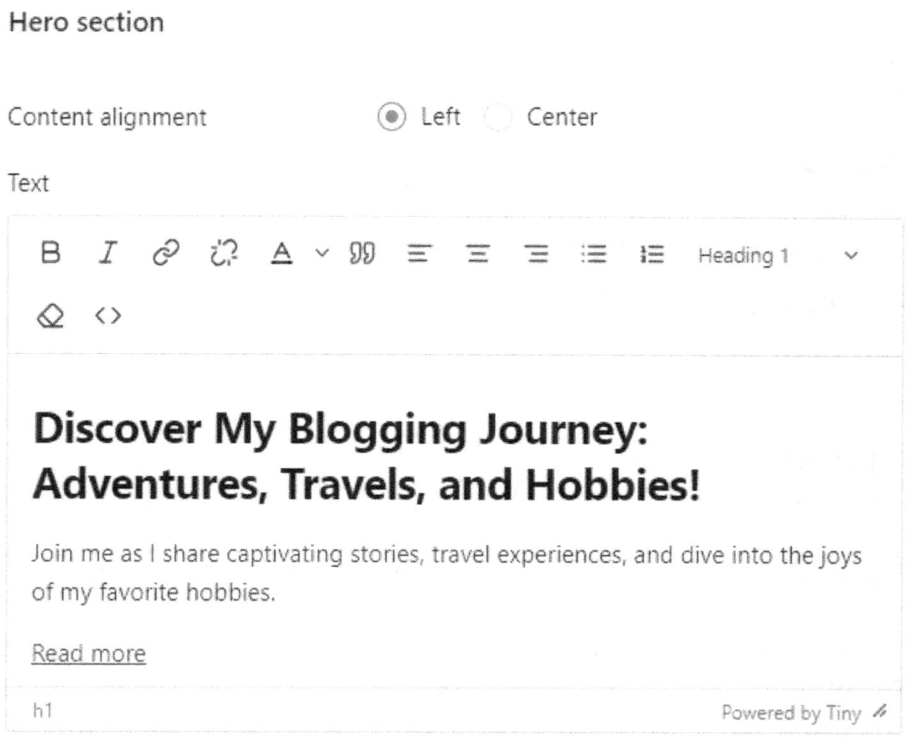

Hero section

Content alignment   ⦿ Left   ○ Center

Text

B   *I*   ⅋   ⍰   A ⌄   ⅋⅋   ≡   ≡   ≡   ⅂☰   ⅂☰   Heading 1   ⌄

✎   <>

Discover My Blogging Journey: Adventures, Travels, and Hobbies!

Join me as I share captivating stories, travel experiences, and dive into the joys of my favorite hobbies.

Read more

h1   Powered by Tiny ⁄⁄

Figure 4-8. *Hero section – Hero text*

In web design parlance, a "Hero" is a large graphic and text element that occupies the very top of a website. Its job is to call attention to what your website is about, to grab your attention as a reader, and help keep you from navigating away from the web page.

The Simple theme has a built-in Hero section that should be used to grab the attention of the person browsing the website you have built and published. There are two elements in the Simple Hero section.

The first element is shown in Figure 4-8, which is the Hero text block that will be displayed in the Hero section. My site is about a fictious space engineering company, so the text in my Hero section will reflect that as you can see in Figure 4-9. Notice that text can be formatted using the formatting tools in the toolbar above the text editor area as highlighted in the figure below.

93

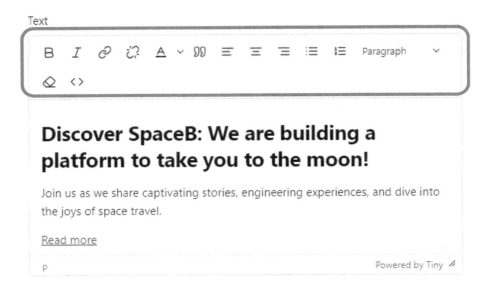

Figure 4-9. *Text Editor field with the editor toolbar highlighted*

The various tools in the text editor toolbar will be explained in Chapter 5: The WYSIWYG Editor - where I discuss using the WYSIWYG editor in detail.

A second change that I want to make to my Hero section is to assign an image to it. The hero image settings are directly below the Hero text area field. Scroll down just a little more to see them.

I like to get photo images from Unsplash.com where photographers upload high-quality images that can be used freely in noncommercial as well as commercial projects. These images are typically licensed using the same Creative Commons license "CC0" as the rocket image we used earlier. You may search for your own images or use the ones I have used which are available on the book GitHub site at `https://github.com/Apress/Designing-Websites-with-Publii-and-GitHub-Pages`.

Tip   When searching for images on Unsplash.com, enable the filters for "Landscape" images as these work best in Publii CMS. Some images are not free to download, but you can filter for "Free" images as well.

In Figure 4-10, I have already dragged an image into the picker field for Image. As you can see, it is a large rocket engine. This image is contributed to Unsplash by Brian McGowan.

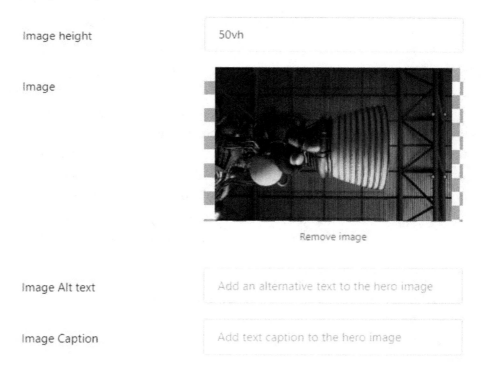

Figure 4-10. *Large rocket engine used as Image for the Hero section*

When adding images to Publii CMS, be aware of the image size. Your website is optimized for viewing on a screen that is 1920x1080 pixels in size. Images over this size are wasteful in bandwidth for the person using your website.

Download the images you use at roughly 1920x1080 or use an image editor (such as IrfanView or Nomacs discussed in Chapter 1) to reduce the size of your images.

When adding images to Publii CMS, there is always a field to provide a context-related Alternative text for the image. In the figure above, it is titled "Image Alt text". This is text that a browser will display if an image cannot be loaded, or the page is being read to the user by a screen reader. Supplying a description for an image will improve your site performance with SEO (Search Engine Optimization) as it helps the search engine crawlers understand what your website is about.

Another important consideration as alternate text relates to SEO is that will be your ideal opportunity to embed some keywords about your website. Embedding relevant but meaningful keywords this way will help your website to perform better (higher rankings on the results page) when people search for things that are related to your website's main subject. I recommend always adding an image alternate text if you have the option.

In the case of the website I am developing, I have added the text shown in Figure 4-11.

Image Alt text   Rocket engine develpment is key to reaching

Figure 4-11. *Image Alt text*

The text string should be around 45 to 80 characters in length. I overshot that just a little bit with the following phrase:

Rocket engine development is key to reaching the moon

It is not necessary to provide a caption for your Hero image. This might be nice for other images. Many cases developers will provide image credit in the image caption field.

I chose to leave it blank.

Don't forget to save the changes you made. Publii CMS will not warn you if you accidentally navigate away from the current panel you are working in.

Remember there are buttons on the upper right corner of the current panel, as shown in Figure 4-12, as well as on the lower left corner to save your changes as well as save and preview the changes you made.

Figure 4-12. *Save buttons*

I clicked "Save & Preview" so I could see the progress on the site. Why don't you try that also?

Post List

In this section, I will discuss post list options.

In the Custom settings menu in the lower portion of the Theme panel, select the menu item "Post list" as shown in Figure 4-13.

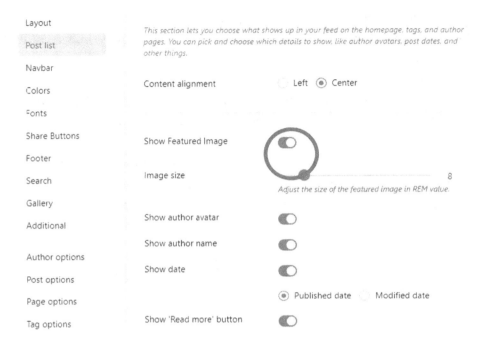

Figure 4-13. *Post list options and settings*

The Post list section allows you to select what elements of the post are displayed with the post when the reader is viewing the Homepage post list, the Tag page, and the Author page.

All the various options are enabled by default except for "Show Featured Image". This option really helps the blog listing pop when viewed. I recommend enabling this option. To enable this option, slide the toggle switch to the right. The switch will be colored blue when enabled.

If you decide your post list is too busy later, come here to modify the options that are enabled to display with the post list.

Colors

In this section, I will discuss the color options for websites created with Publii CMS.

In the Custom settings menu in the lower portion of the Theme panel, select the menu item "Colors" as shown in Figure 4-14.

Custom settings

Layout	Select color scheme	◯ Light ◯ Dark ⦿ Auto
Post list		*The auto color scheme feature automatically adjusts the color scheme of the interface to match the user's operating system settings. If the operating system does not support this feature, the light version of the color scheme is used instead*
Navbar		
Colors		
Fonts	Primary color (Light mode)	● #D73A42
Share Buttons		
Footer	Primary color (Dark mode)	● #FFC074

Figure 4-14. *Colors custom settings*

Different themes for Publii CMS support different color options. Most common are Primary color and Secondary color for a theme. Most themes also support a Light and a Dark theme with support for following system setting on the client PC (the person viewing your website) to select between these automatically.

In the case of the default theme Simple 3.0.0.0, the only color supported is the Primary color. Using the settings in this panel, you can select the color you want to use for both the Primary color for light mode and the Primary color for dark mode.

Changing a color is as easy as clicking the color field and launching the built-in color picker as shown in Figure 4-15.

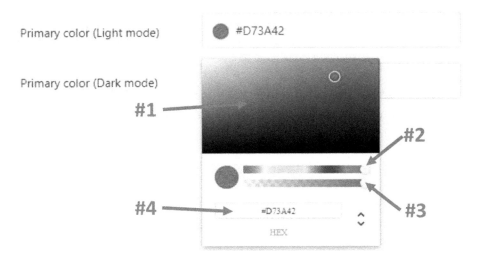

Figure 4-15. *Color picker*

This color picker works like most others you would encounter when using any design software on a PC or Mac. Click in the upper box (#1) to select a specific color in the current hue.

Click and drag the selector on the color bar (#2) to choose a different hue to work with. The third selector bar is for opacity (#3). This is how much the browser should let things behind the object being colored show through. Think of it like how see-through you want the color to be.

At the bottom of the color picker is a field (#4) where a hexadecimal color code can be typed, and that will become the color the picker is resting on in the top selector area (#1). Hexadecimal color codes are ubiquitous in web development. They represent the three values of Red, Green, and Blue that are combined to make a given color. W3Schools has a nice explanation of color codes at https://www.w3schools.com/html/html_colors_hex.asp if you would like to dig into that subject further.

If you look at Figure 4-16, you will see that I have selected a light blue color as my Primary color for Light mode. The hex code for that color is #3A8AD7. If you want to copy my lead, then just type that color code into the color picker field.

Primary color (Light mode)

Primary color (Dark mode)

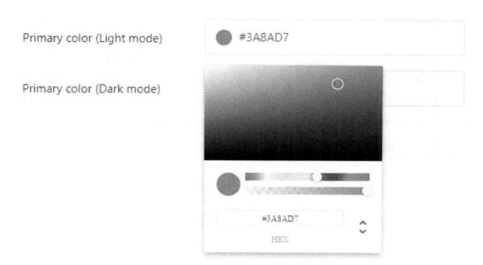

Figure 4-16. *Color picker field with new color choice*

Notice also that I have chosen to force my website to always display in Light mode for my color scheme as shown in Figure 4-17. This is not always the friendliest option to force on your user, so consider a decision like this carefully. Some users use their systems exclusively in dark mode and may find a website that does not automatically adapt to their system colors offensive.

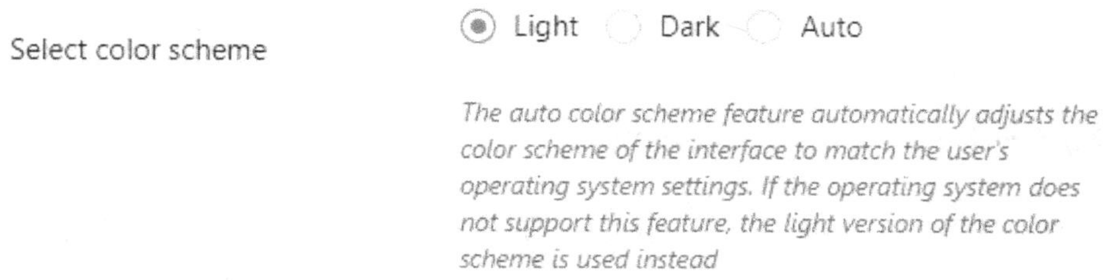

Select color scheme

⊙ Light   ○ Dark   ○ Auto

The auto color scheme feature automatically adjusts the color scheme of the interface to match the user's operating system settings. If the operating system does not support this feature, the light version of the color scheme is used instead

Figure 4-17. *Select color scheme*

Don't forget to save the changes you made. There are buttons on the upper right corner of the current panel, as shown in Figure 4-12, as well as on the lower left corner. You can save the changes you made or save those changes and preview the website.

Fonts

In this section, I will discuss the font options for websites created with Publii CMS.

In the Custom settings menu in the lower portion of the Theme panel, select the menu item "Fonts" as shown in Figure 4-18.

Custom settings

Layout	Main font settings	
Post list	To explore an extensive list of available fonts, along with detailed typefaces, complete range of weights, and other specifications, ple documentation.	
Navbar		
Colors		
Fonts	Body font	OS Default Font
Share Buttons	Headings font (H1-H6)	OS Default Font
Footer		
Search	Menu font	Select the font used fc
Gallery		
Additional	Logo font	Select the font used fc

Figure 4-18. *Fonts menu item*

Publii CMS offers a rich selection of fonts for use in all official themes. These fonts are available from Google fonts and are free for use. To make your website load faster, Publii CMS only loads the fonts that are selected in the application interface, and they are cached and loaded locally from where the website is hosted and not from the Google font site.

Loading fonts locally from the server where the site is hosted is important for maintaining GDPR-compliance. Fonts that are loade from Google's serverssend the user's IP address on to Google when the browser requests a font from hosted on a Google server. GDPR recognizes IP addresses as personal data under GDPR. Preventing them from being transmitted to third parties, such as Google, enhances user privacy and helps meet data protection requirements.

By default, Publii CMS uses the Operating System default font for all typography used in the Simple 3.0.0.0 theme. I like to change this up when designing a Publii CMS website. To choose a new font, click the font drop-down field as shown in Figure 4-19.

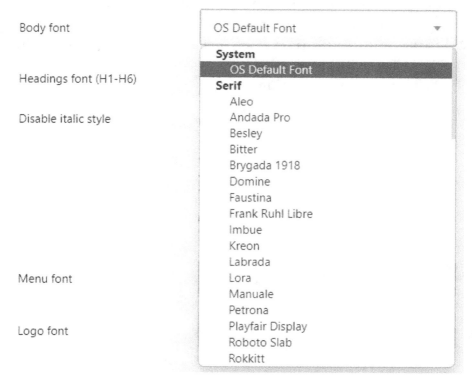

Figure 4-19. *Font drop-down field*

Fonts offered are divided into several categories – the largest of these are Serif and Sans Serif. If you are new to website design and typography, you might want to read more about it here: `https://blog.hubspot.com/website/website-typography`.

I recommend using a Sans Serif font for body text. These fonts do not have the little curly points at the edges of each character but rather are straight and square in nature. Sans Serif fonts are easier to read in a digital medium.

You may want to select a nice bold Serif font for your Headings. This contrast in font types can make a site appealing if chosen correctly. Personally, I like using Sans Serif fonts for both Headings and Body fonts.

I have chosen Raleway for my body text and Merriweather Sans for my Headings as you can see in Figure 4-20.

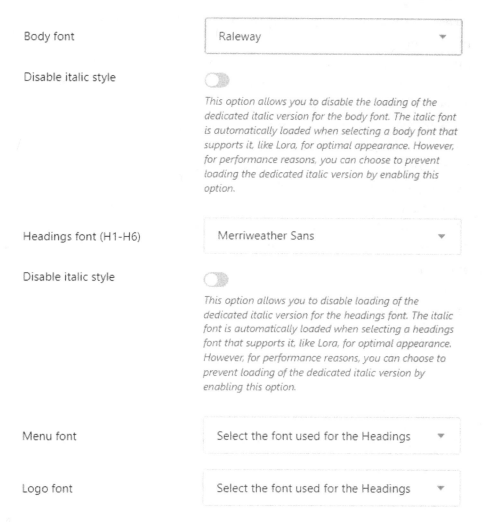

Body font

Raleway

Disable italic style

This option allows you to disable the loading of the dedicated italic version for the body font. The italic font is automatically loaded when selecting a body font that supports it, like Lora, for optimal appearance. However, for performance reasons, you can choose to prevent loading the dedicated italic version by enabling this option.

Headings font (H1-H6)

Merriweather Sans

Disable italic style

This option allows you to disable loading of the dedicated italic version for the headings font. The italic font is automatically loaded when selecting a headings font that supports it, like Lora, for optimal appearance. However, for performance reasons, you can choose to prevent loading of the dedicated italic version by enabling this option.

Menu font

Select the font used for the Headings

Logo font

Select the font used for the Headings

Figure 4-20. *Font selections*

Notice also that you can specify which font group the Menu font and Logo font should follow. I have changed these to use the same font as that used for Headings.

When selecting a built-in font, you will notice an option to disable the italic font of that font family. With the release of Publii CMS 0.46, italic font faces are stored separately. This provides a quality font when rendered in the web browser, but it also can require additional time for your website to load. If you will not be using italics a lot and do not care that they will be approximated in a lower quality rendering, then disable these options to allow your site to load faster.

There are a lot of other font settings that can be adjusted to give your site a unique typographical feel. I am choosing to leave these set to their default settings; however, you are free to experiment. In fact, experimentation is encouraged.

Just a note about font sizing in Publii CMS. Fonts are sized in a unit of measure called REM as you can see in Figure 4-21. All official Publii CMS themes designed by the Publii team come with fluid typography and vertical rhythm. This ensures that the themes easily adapt to various devices such as desktops, tablets, and phones, providing full responsiveness.

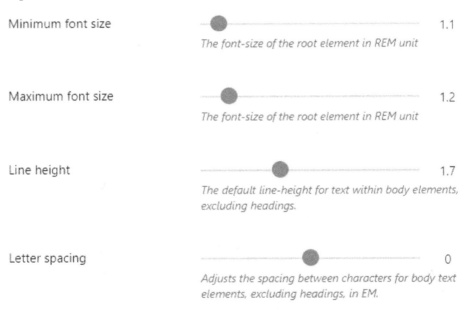

Figure 4-21. *Font sizing*

The min and max font-size option defines the size of the font and other elements based on REM units for small and large devices, such as mobile and desktop.

The REM unit of measure is relative to the root font size for the web browser. If you use a program like Microsoft Word, you typically size your fonts in points. A web browser also has a base point size, usually 16, for viewing web pages. REM is convenient as it allows the designer to use a relative (think variable) font size that can adjust dynamically to the width of the viewing area of the browser width.

This is important when designing for multiple devices such as desktop browsers, tablets, and phones. A reasonable font rendered on a phone would be very small on a desktop browser. Using REM as the font size instructs the browser to dynamically size the font being displayed so that it is larger on larger windows which have a larger viewing area and smaller on smaller windows.

Using REM is an adjustment, but experimenting with it can help you understand the relationship between the REM sizing and the actual sizing when the font is rendered. As always – experiment and see what the changes do. This is the best way to learn.

Don't forget to save the changes you made. There are buttons on the upper right corner of the current panel, as shown in Figure 4-12, as well as on the lower left corner. You can save the changes you made or save those changes and preview the website.

Additional: Favicon

In this section, I will discuss one last modification to the theme settings. This time I will be giving the theme a favicon.

In the Custom settings menu in the lower portion of the Theme panel, select the menu item "Additional" as shown in Figure 4-22. In this section, I will add a favicon.

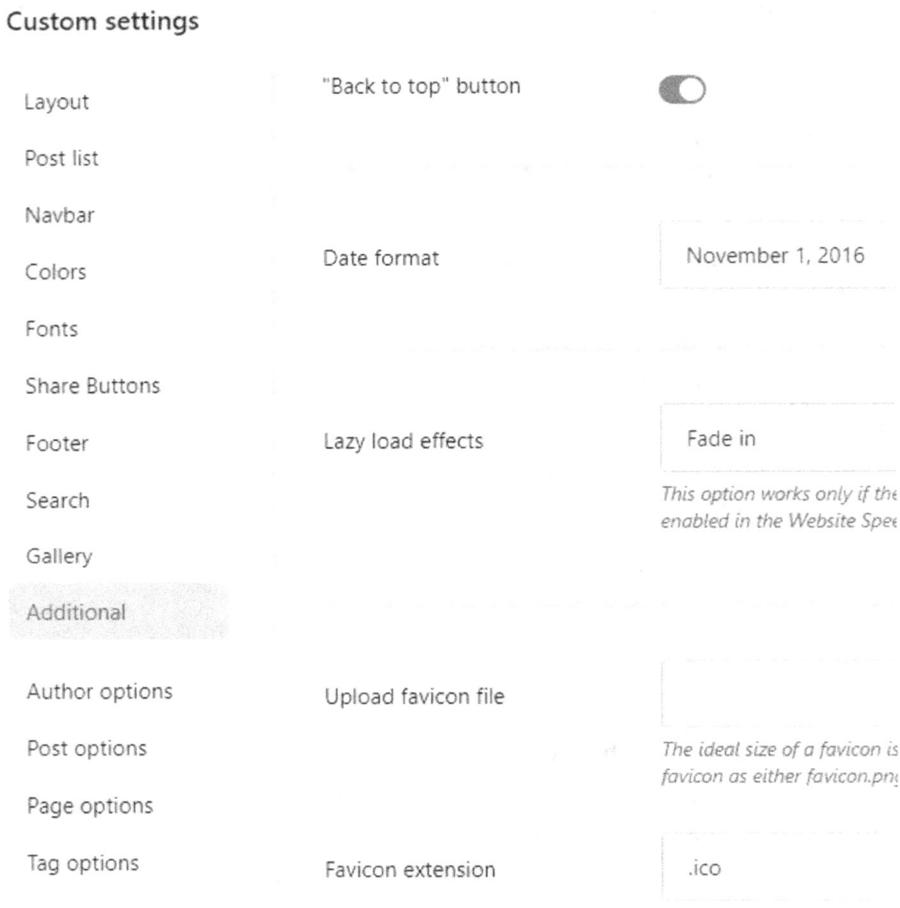

Custom settings

Layout	"Back to top" button	⬤
Post list		
Navbar		
Colors	Date format	November 1, 2016
Fonts		
Share Buttons		
Footer	Lazy load effects	Fade in
Search		*This option works only if the enabled in the Website Spee*
Gallery		
Additional		
Author options	Upload favicon file	
Post options		*The ideal size of a favicon is favicon as either favicon.pn(*
Page options		
Tag options	Favicon extension	.ico

Figure 4-22. *Additional Theme settings*

A favicon is a small icon that represents your brand or website. Typically, they appear in the web browser tab just to the left of the website name. In Figure 4-23, you will notice the favicon belonging to Unsplash. com on the browser tab next to the title of the site.

Figure 4-23. *Favicon for Unsplash.com*

Adding a favicon to a Publii CMS website is easy. First, you will need an appropriate image. In version 0.46 of Publii CMS, you can use either an ico file or a png file. Since I already have a nice PNG of a rocket and it is my site logo, thus associated with my brand, I will use that for my favicon.

Favicons need to be 16x16 pixels in size. I edited my rocket image shown in Figure 4-3 using Paint.NET (an excellent and free image editor available here: `https://www.getpaint.net`) so that it was 16x16 and save a copy of it. It is important to save the file as "favicon.png".

Click the "Choose file" button in the Upload favicon file field. This field does not support drag and drop unfortunately. The file chooser will open a dialog window, and you can locate your file and select it.

If you are uploading a png file like I am, be sure to change the Favicon extension to ".png" as shown in Figure 4-24.

Figure 4-24. *Upload favicon file*

Don't forget to save the changes you made. There are buttons on the upper right corner of the current panel, as shown in Figure 4-12, as well as on the lower left corner. You can save the changes you made or save those changes and preview the website.

There is no need to make further changes to the Additional items in the Theme Custom settings. There are other changes that can be made to the Theme settings in the various custom settings menu items as mentioned before. Feel free to experiment.

Author Settings

Another area that should be updated before posting content is the Author settings. This includes things like a basic author biography (called description in Publii CMS), featured image for the author page, and avatar for the author. In this section, I will be discussing these items.

Publii CMS sites typically have one author, but the system can support multiple authors. Each author should have their basic information completed in the Authors section of Publii CMS.

To make changes to Authors including adding or removing an author, access the Authors panel by clicking "Authors" in the application main menu as shown in Figure 4-25.

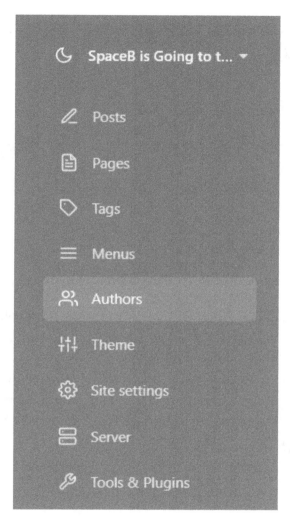

Figure 4-25. *Authors menu item in the application main menu*

The Authors panel will list all existing authors. There is always at least one author. Typically, it is the author you defined when you created the site. In my case, I created an author named Bob Bobbee as shown in Figure 4-26.

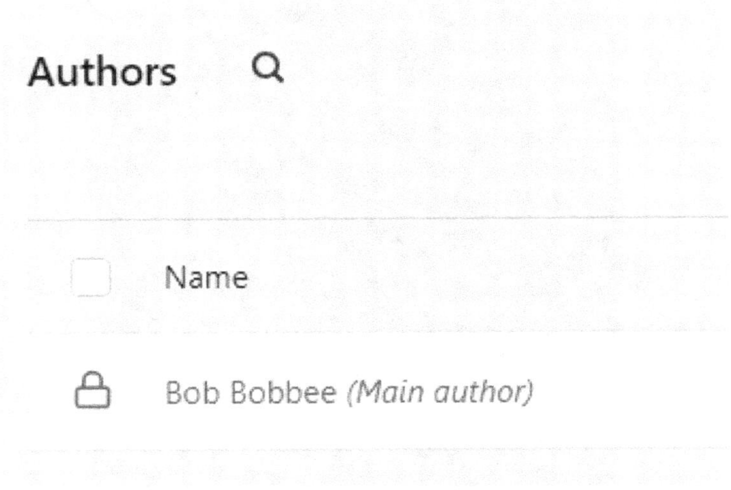

Authors   🔍

	Name
🔒	Bob Bobbee *(Main author)*

Figure 4-26. *Main author for the Publii site*

Notice that in the upper right corner of the panel (not pictured) is a button to "Add new author". I will not be adding a new author, but if your site has multiple authors, you can do this.

Clicking the author's name, in my case "Bob Bobbee", will cause a new panel to fly out from the right side of the main application pane as shown in Figure 4-27. This panel is used to modify the Author settings. It is titled "EDIT AUTHOR".

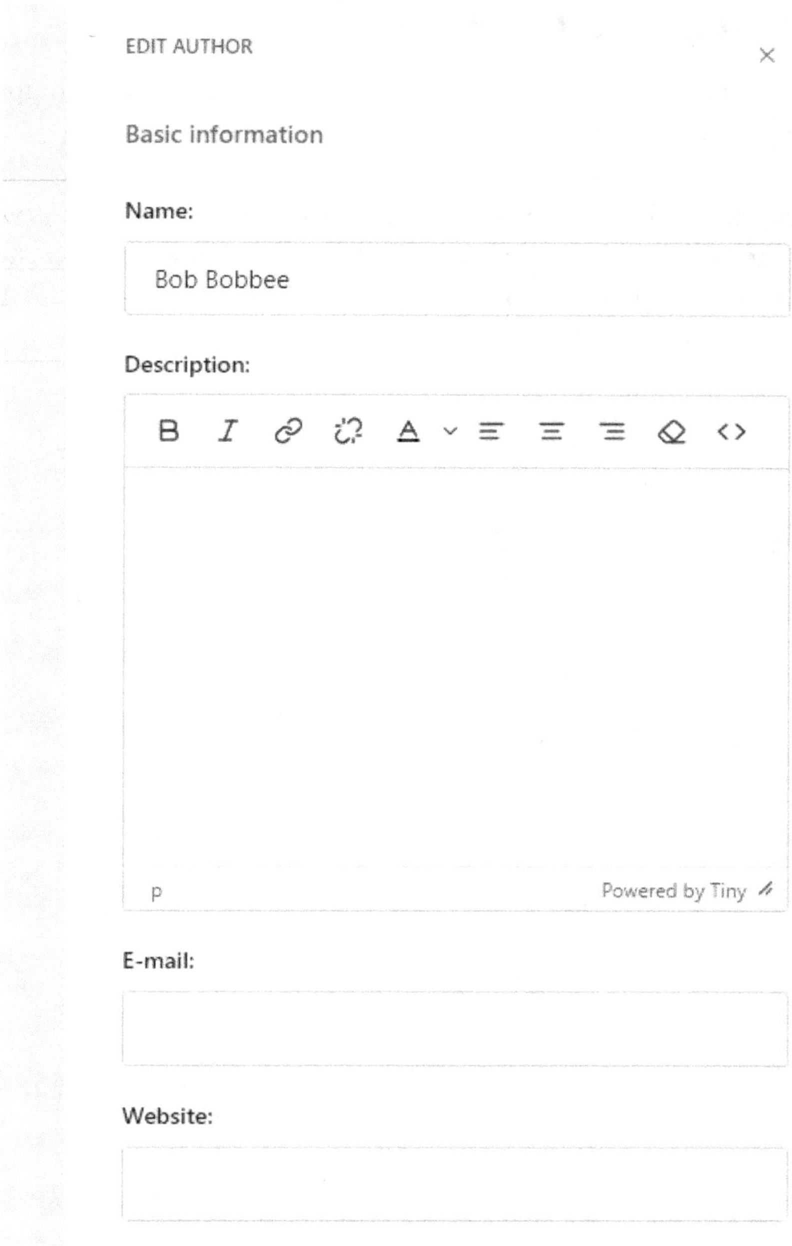

EDIT AUTHOR   ✕

Basic information

Name:

Bob Bobbee

Description:

| B | I | 🔗 | ⌖ | A | ⌄ | ≡ | ≡ | ≡ | ⌫ | <> |

p   Powered by Tiny ⁄⁄

E-mail:

Website:

Figure 4-27. *Edit Author panel*

Basic Author Information

In this section, I will discuss adding basic author information to complete the bio for your site's main author. Typically, this will be you.

In the case of the imaginary company SpaceB for which I am creating this first site, I will add a biography for Bob Bobbee. A biography lets your readers get to know you as the author just a little bit better. Observe the information provided for Bob in Figure 4-28, the bioragohy goes into the description field.

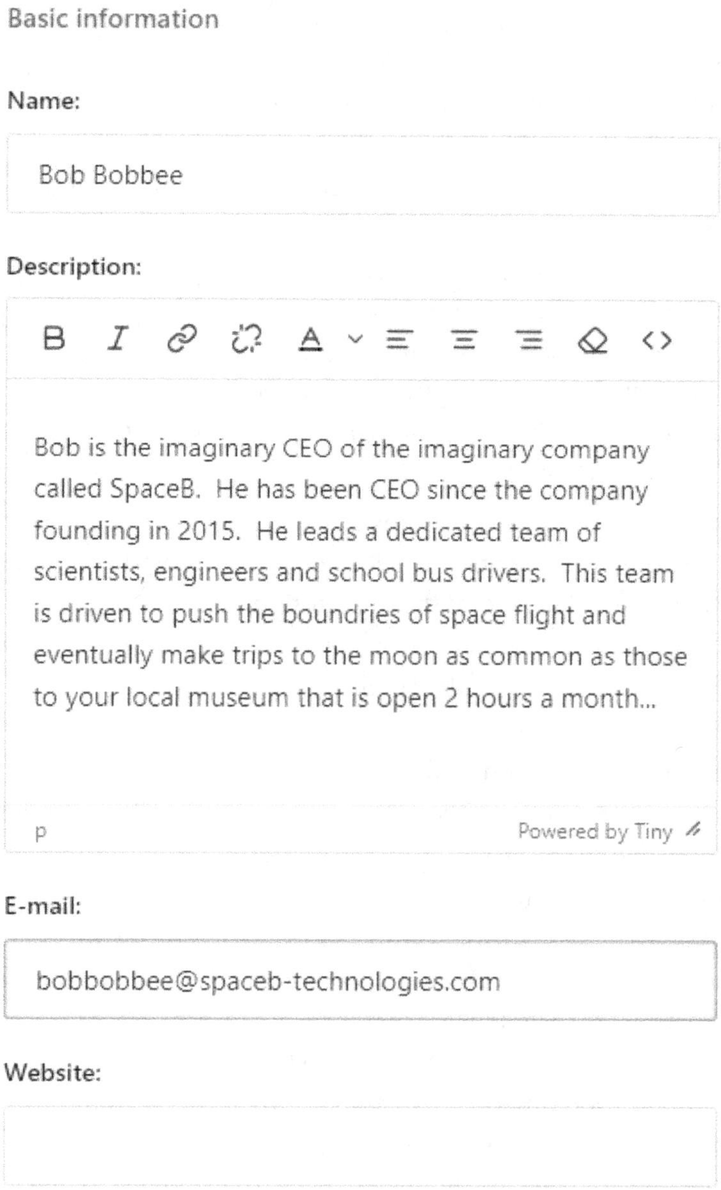

Basic information

Name:

Bob Bobbee

Description:

B   *I*   🔗   ⁇   A ⌄   ≡   ≡   ≡   ◇   <>

Bob is the imaginary CEO of the imaginary company called SpaceB. He has been CEO since the company founding in 2015. He leads a dedicated team of scientists, engineers and school bus drivers. This team is driven to push the boundries of space flight and eventually make trips to the moon as common as those to your local museum that is open 2 hours a month...

p   Powered by Tiny ⁄

E-mail:

bobbobbee@spaceb-technologies.com

Website:

Figure 4-28. *Bob Bobbee's basic author information*

Note that the email you have entered is not displayed on the website unless the theme author has specifically coded the theme to display it. By design, all official Publii CMS themes do not share email publicly.

Here is what I typed into the description field should you want to simply copy it and paste it into the description field on your copy of Publii CMS:

> *Bob is the imaginary CEO of the imaginary company called SpaceB. He has been CEO since the company founding in 2015. He leads a dedicated team of scientists, engineers and school bus drivers. This team is driven to push the boundaries of space flight and eventually make trips to the moon as common as those to your local museum that is open 2 hours a month...*

Note that the description field is a rich text field, meaning that you can format the text with bold and italics, color your text, and add links and lists. There is a toolbar at the top of the description editor that allows you to make these formatting choices. You can learn more about formatting text in Chapter 5 when we cover the WYSIWYG editor.

None of the fields for the Basic Author information are required except for the author's name. As mentioned, adding a description is nice as it allows the visitors to your website to get to know you a little bit better – this increases engagement.

Adding an email address is also important. It will allow your visitors to reach you in case they have questions or problems with your site.

If this is your first website, then you may not have an additional website to list. I chose to leave it blank.

You will need to save the changes you have made. I recommend saving frequently, then you do not accidentally navigate away from this part of the application and loose the work you have done.

The save buttons for the fly-out settings pages (which Publii CMS uses in several contexts) are at the bottom of the settings panel as shown in Figure 4-29.

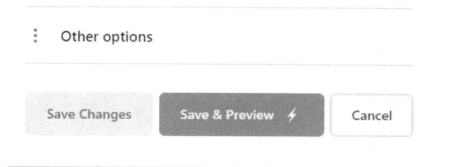

Figure 4-29. *Save changes buttons*

This would be a great time to click the "Save Changes" button and commit the changes you have made to disk.

The Edit Author panel will collapse back into the right side of the application when you save your changes.

Author Avatar

There are a couple of other changes to make to the Author settings. Click the author's name to open the Edit Author panel as we did in Figure 4-25. Click the "Avatar and Featured image" heading (highlighted) of the Edit Author settings panel as seen in Figure 4-30.

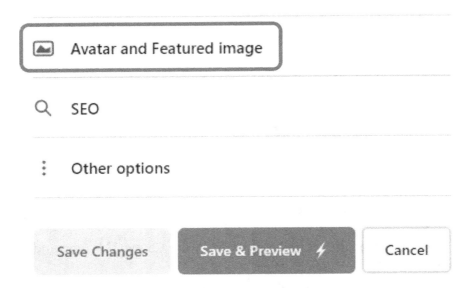

Figure 4-30. *Additional panels in Edit Author*

Clicking the heading "Avatar and Featured image" will cause that section to expand. Any other expanded sections will collapse. This section will allow you to set both an avatar for the author as well as a featured image for the author's page.

Figure 4-31 shows the image picker field (supporting drag and drop operations) where an image can be assigned for the author avatar.

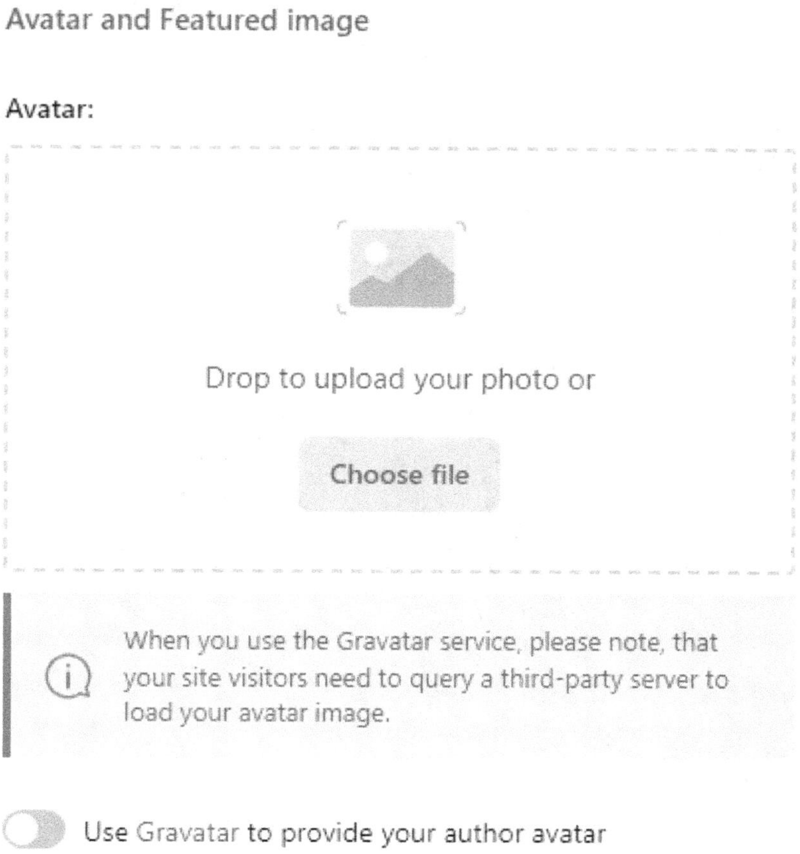

Avatar and Featured image

Avatar:

Figure 4-31. Avatar settings

Most official themes show the author's avatar associated with the posts and pages the author has written. I have downloaded a generic user image for my avatar from the OpenClipArt.org site. It is called Avatar-small.png as seen in Figure 4-32. You can find that image on their website at `https://openclipart.org/detail/190113/avatar` or on the GitHub repository for this book at `https://github.com/Apress/Designing-Websites-with-Publii-and-GitHub-Pages`.

119

Figure 4-32. *Avatar-small.png*

Drag and drop that image into the image picker as shown in Figure 4-33.

Avatar and Featured image

Avatar:

Remove image

When you use the Gravatar service, please note, that your site visitors need to query a third-party server to load your avatar image.

Use Gravatar to provide your author avatar

Figure 4-33. *Avatar image*

Notice that Publii CMS supports the use of Gravatar avatars. I use this on my own personal Publii CMS website. Gravatars are centrally managed avatars for use in user profiles on various systems online. Gravatar avatars are associated with your email address. Go to the website https://gravatar.com/ to set one up – they are free. Having a Gravatar avatar requires your Publii CMS website to link to a third-party site (specifically gravatar.com) which can affect your site's load times.

The email address that is linked to Gravatar is maintained in the Author profile Basic information. I will not be using a Gravatar in this project as the email address specified for Bob Bobbee is imaginary and does not have a Gravatar set up. Therefore, I have chosen to just use the image I uploaded.

Author Featured Image

In this section, I will be adding a featured image to the Author profile for Bob Bobbee.

The featured image will be used on the author page that Publii CMS generates. This is a page that tells a little bit about the author and lists the most recent posts by that author. The featured image is like the featured image we uploaded for the theme hero page as shown in Figure 4-10.

The process is the same. Find an image that relates to the subject matter – in this case, the site's author – and upload it to Publii CMS. As before I have gone to Unsplash.com to locate an image. That image is located at `https://unsplash.com/photos/person-using-black-ipad-turned-on-oO32ZyI93GY` or can be downloaded from the book's GitHub repository at `https://github.com/Apress/Designing-Websites-with-Publii-and-GitHub-Pages`.

Notice in Figure 4-34 where I have dragged and dropped the image into the Featured image image picker field.

Featured image:

Remove image

Alternative text

Writing posts for a blog about rockets and space

Caption

Credits

Photo by Chris Spiegl on Unsplash

Figure 4-34. *Author Featured image*

Also notice in the figure above that I have provided an Alternative text that contains a couple keywords that relate to the blog. The Author Featured image has a field to provide credit for the image, which I have chosen to do. This is good practice. This can also lead to a relationship with the photographer that can help promote your site if done right.

Here is what I provided as an Alternative text should you want to copy it for use in your project.

Writing posts for a blog about rockets and space

This would be a great time to click the "Save Changes" button at the bottom of the Edit Author panel as shown in Figure 4-29 and commit the changes you have made to disk.

The Edit Author panel will collapse back into the right side of the application when you save your changes.

Author SEO

In this section, I will be adding a meta description to the Author SEO settings.

We discussed SEO or Search Engine Optimization in Chapter 3. While Google claims that meta descriptions do not play a role in ranking, there seems to be some antidotal evidence to the contrary.

I recommend every page in a website have a Meta tag with the website description. The Author page is no exception. Click the author name (link) to access the Edit Author panel as you have done before. This time click on the SEO section title as shown in Figure 4-35.

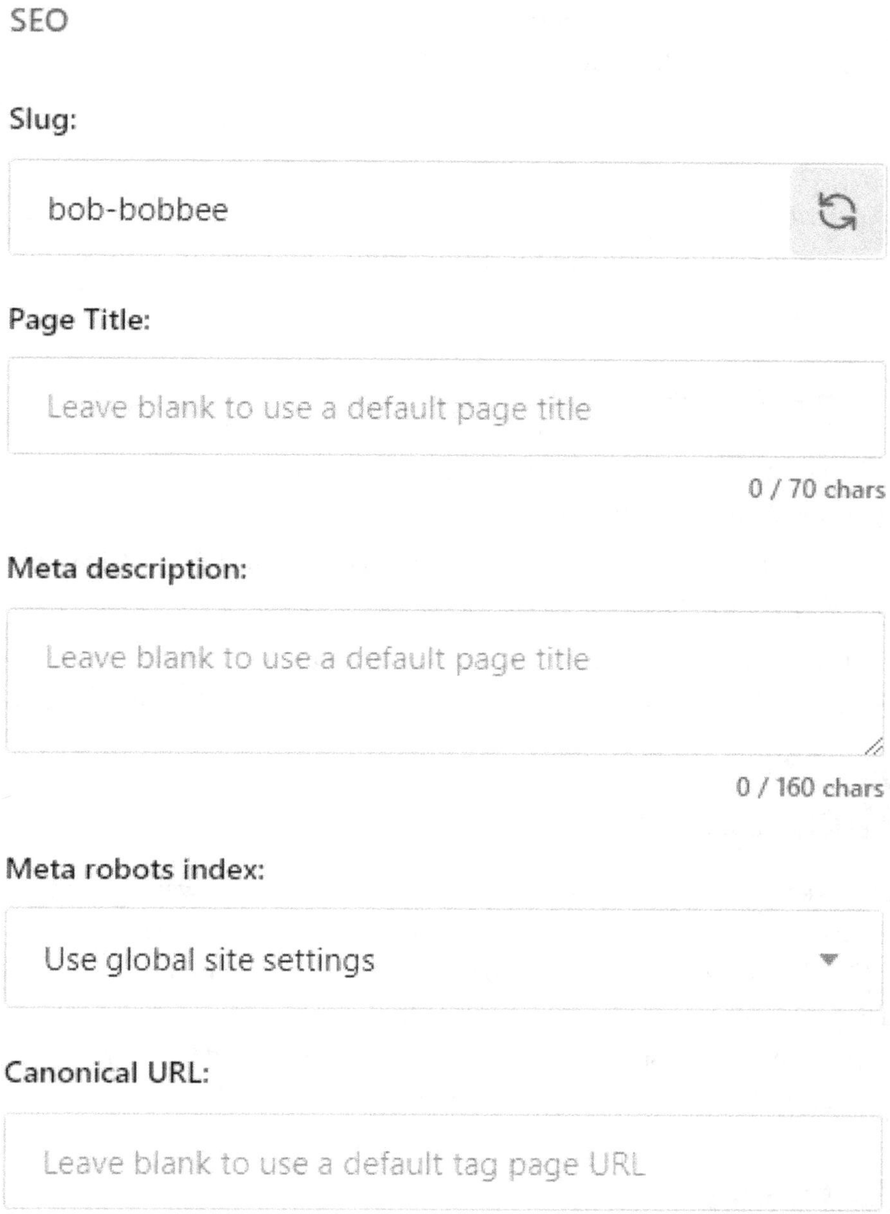

SEO

Slug:

bob-bobbee

Page Title:

Leave blank to use a default page title

0 / 70 chars

Meta description:

Leave blank to use a default page title

0 / 160 chars

Meta robots index:

Use global site settings   ▼

Canonical URL:

Leave blank to use a default tag page URL

Figure 4-35. *Author SEO settings*

Click in the Meta description field and add a description for the Author page. Figure 4-36 shows what I added into this field.

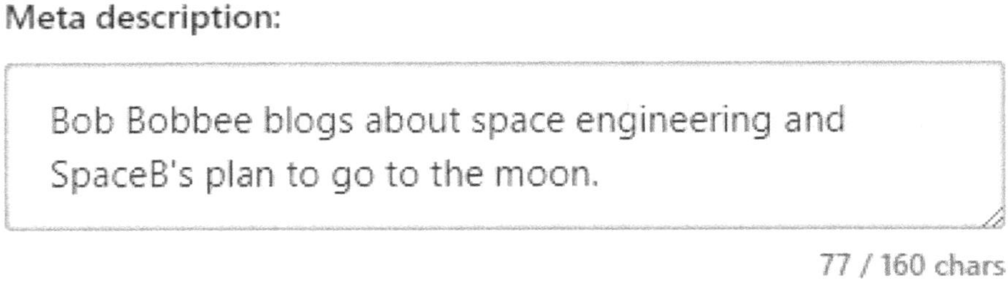

Meta description:

Bob Bobbee blogs about space engineering and
SpaceB's plan to go to the moon.

77 / 160 chars

Figure 4-36. *Meta description for the Author page*

Once again, here is the description I added should you want to simply copy and paste it into your own project.

Bob Bobbee blogs about space engineering and SpaceB's plan to go to the moon.

Click the "Save Changes" button at the bottom of the Edit Author panel as shown in Figure 4-29 and commit the changes you have made to disk.

Menu Settings

In this section, I will be discussing adding a menu to the website and configuring the menu with menu items. Almost all Publii CMS themes (official and community supplied) support a menu. Menus make navigation of the website easier and help the user understand what is important on your site. They also help web crawlers and indexers to understand your site which can improve your SEO performance.

Add a Menu

In this section, I will add a new menu to my website. Follow along to add one to your website.

In the main menu on the left side of the application, select "Menus" to access the menu settings panel as shown in Figure 4-37.

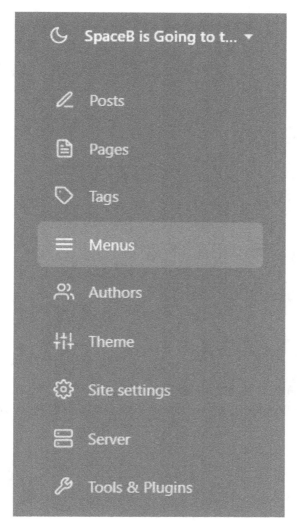

Figure 4-37. *Menus menu settings*

There are no menus built for the website yet as Publii CMS points out in Figure 4-38.

Figure 4-38. *No menus yet*

Click the Add new menu button to add your first menu. Publii CMS will query you for the name of the new menu as shown in Figure 4-39.

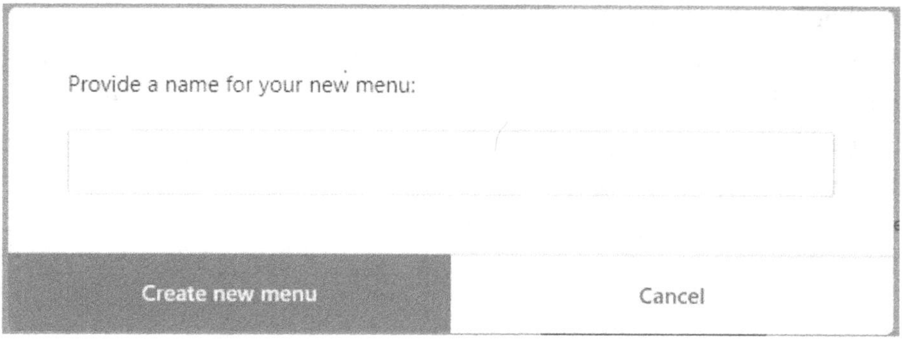

Provide a name for your new menu:

Create new menu   Cancel

Figure 4-39. *New menu name dialog window*

I like to call my menu "Main" as it is the main menu for the website.
You can call it anything, as the menu name will not appear on the website.
Provide a name and click the blue button labeled "Create new menu". In
Figure 4-40, you can see the new menu named "Main".

Name	Assigned menu
Main	Unassigned ▾

Figure 4-40. *Menu list*

Assigning Menus

This menu is currently unassigned as designated in the column "Assigned
menu". Menus must have a designated location designed into the theme
by the theme creator. Most themes support a Main menu which is usually
located at the top of the website. Some themes support additional menu
locations or positions as Publii CMS calls them. You can assign a given
menu to multiple positions, or if there are multiple positions available for
menus, you can create a unique menu for each.

Clicking this pull-down arrow for the assignment for this menu as highlighted in Figure 4-40 will open the Configure menu position dialog window where the menu can be assigned to designated menu position defined in the theme. As shown in Figure 4-41, the theme Simple 3.0.0.0 has two menu positions defined as available.

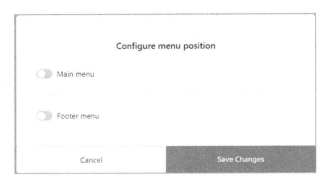

Figure 4-41. *Configure menu position*

The menu I am going to create is specifically for the top of the website which is the Main menu position. To assign this menu to that position, I will click the toggle button next to Main menu sliding it to the right to enable the selection. The toggle button will turn blue in response.

If you are following along, click the "Save Changes" button highlighted in blue at the bottom of the dialog window.

You will see that the menu named "Main" is now assigned to the menu position "Main menu" as shown in Figure 4-42.

Name	Assigned menu	Items
Main	Main menu ▼	0

Figure 4-42. *Main menu assignment*

Notice that to the right of the Assigned menu column is a column that tells how many menu items the menu has. In this case, the number is zero.

That is no surprise, as I have not added any menu items.

Add Menu Items

In this section, I will be adding several menu items to the menu called "Main" which I created previously.

To add a menu item to an existing menu, click the name of the menu as shown in Figure 4-40. The name of the menu will be a blue color indicating it is a link to other options in the application.

When you click the link, a new button will be added to the interface allowing you to add a menu item as shown in Figure 4-43.

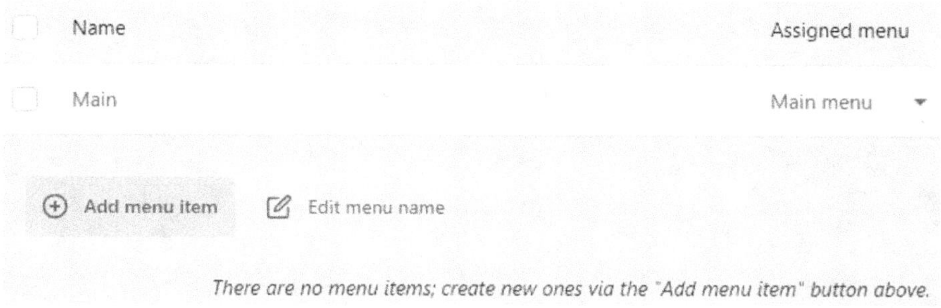

Name	Assigned menu
Main	Main menu ▼

⊕ Add menu item   ✎ Edit menu name

There are no menu items; create new ones via the "Add menu item" button above.

Figure 4-43. *Add menu item*

The Home Menu Item

In this section, I will discuss adding the "Home" menu item to the "Main" menu.

Click the "Add menu item" button to add your first menu item. In my case, I want to add a link back to the homepage as the first menu item. Clicking the button will cause a panel to fly out from the right side of the application. This is like what happened when you edited the Author information. This time the panel is titled "ADD NEW MENU ITEM" as shown in Figure 4-44.

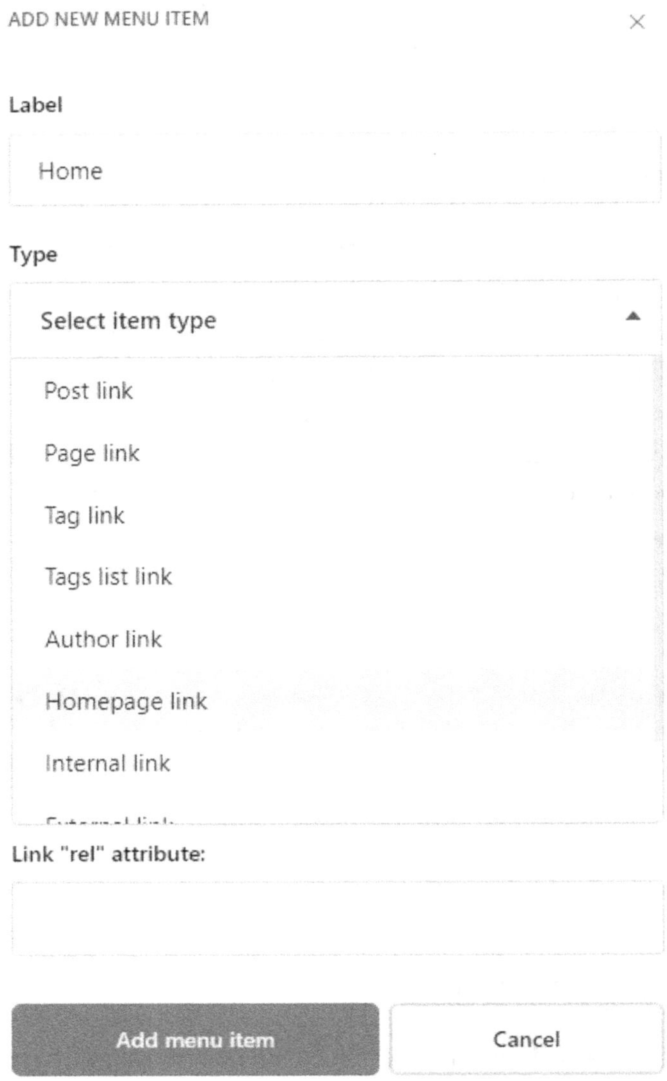

ADD NEW MENU ITEM   ✕

Label

Home

Type

Select item type   ▲

Post link

Page link

Tag link

Tags list link

Author link

Homepage link

Internal link

Link "rel" attribute:

Add menu item   Cancel

Figure 4-44. *Add New Menu Item*

The first menu item I am adding is called "Home". I have already typed that into the field "Label" in the figure above. The item type selected in the menu "Type" field tells Publii CMS what type of link this is. There are a lot of choices. Since this will be a link that takes the user back to the home page, I have selected "Homepage link" from the list.

You will create a couple other types of menu item links below. The rest of the settings are fine with default values in this case, so click the blue "Add menu item" button to add the menu item.

After you save the menu item, the "ADD NEW MENU ITEM" panel collapses back into the right side of the application. You will now observe that there is a new menu item listed for the Main menu as shown in Figure 4-45.

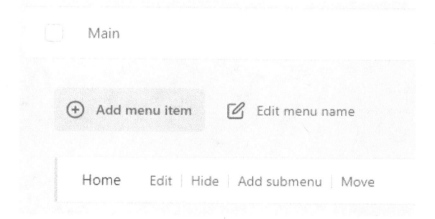

Figure 4-45. *New menu item*

There are several options available to modify the new menu item including Edit, Hide, and Move. The Add submenu option acts much like the add menu item function except the new menu item becomes a submenu of this menu item. Caution: not all themes support submenus. As always, experiment with these options and the various settings for a menu item to learn more about what they do.

The Tags Menu Item

In this section, I will repeat the process used before to add a menu item. This time the target for the link will be the built-in tags page. Note that the tags page will be blank until we add some tags later in this chapter.

Click the "Add menu item" button again to add another menu item like we did in the preceding section. The "Add new menu item" panel will fly out as before. This time type "Tags" into the Label field and select the type of link from the Type drop-down menu as "Tags list link" as shown in Figure 4-46.

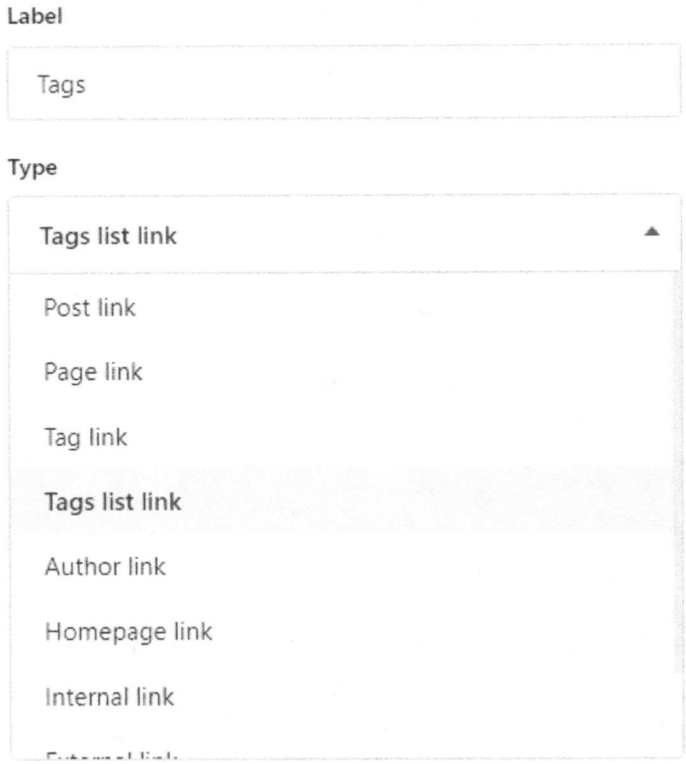

Label

> Tags

Type

> Tags list link ▲
>
> Post link
>
> Page link
>
> Tag link
>
> **Tags list link**
>
> Author link
>
> Homepage link
>
> Internal link

Figure 4-46. *New menu item*

Once again, the remaining field defaults are perfect for this menu item. Click the "Add menu item" button to add this second menu item to the menu.

An External Menu Item

In this section, I will add one last menu item. This menu item will be a link to an external resource that is not part of the website I am developing. Sometimes links like these may direct the user to a Google Maps website which can be used to find your place of business. They may also be for other sites that support your content – perhaps a review site like Yelp.

These types of links will require a specific URL that takes the user to the resource. As discussed in Chapter 1, a URL is a Uniform Resource Locator that has a specifically defined format. Most people are used to seeing URLs that point to web pages. They usually look like this:

```
https://google.com
```

The "https://" part of the URL is called the scheme or protocol. "http" stands for **Hypertext Transfer Protocol**, which is the protocol used for transferring data over the Internet. This tells the web browser (and other applications) that the thing you are referencing is likely a web page. There are other types of schemes or protocols. In this menu item, I will be using the "mailto://" protocol. It will cause the web browser to open the system's default email client and create a blank email that is addressed to the email address linked in the URL.

Look at Figure 4-47 to see how I did this.

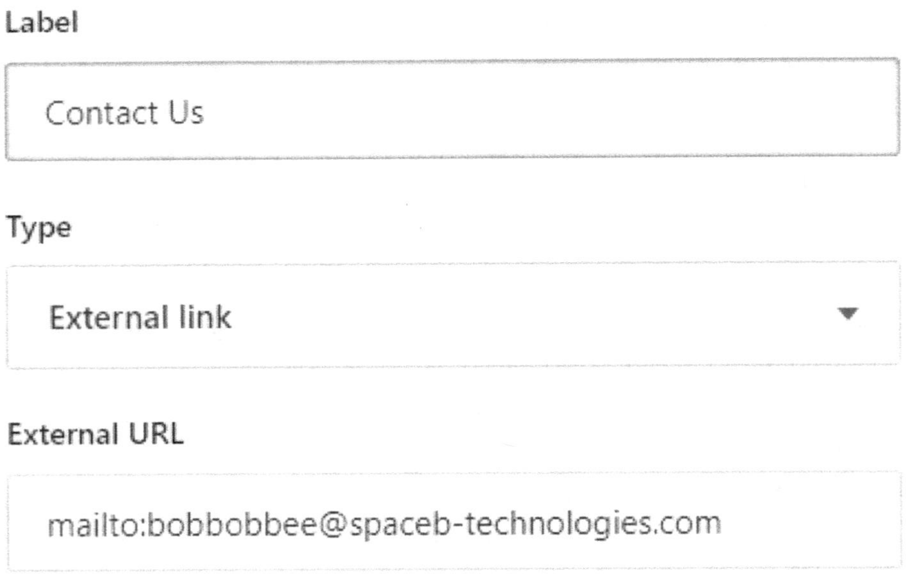

Label

Contact Us

Type

External link   ▼

External URL

mailto:bobbobbee@spaceb-technologies.com

Figure 4-47. *Email as an external link*

The Label is "Contact Us". The type of link is "External link" which you can select from the drop-down menu for "Type".

The External URL is where the magic happens. I have added an imaginary email address, but the process still works. The protocol "mailto:" will launch the system default email client when this menu item is clicked. The email address bobbobbee@spaceb-technologies.com will be the address that the email is addressed to.

There are no other changes required for this menu item.

I would like to point out an important thing to consider when creating external links from your website. The default operation when opening new links is to open them in the same browser tab. This means that your website will be left behind and the user will be moving on to someone else's website. This is typically undesirable as the longer you can keep someone on your website, the better chance you have of making your point, making a sale, or influencing the reader.

For this reason, when linking from your website to external websites from the menu, or from your posts and pages, always set the Link target as "New window". This can be done in the "Add New Menu Item" panel by selecting the "New window" from the Link target drop-down as shown in Figure 4-48.

Link target:

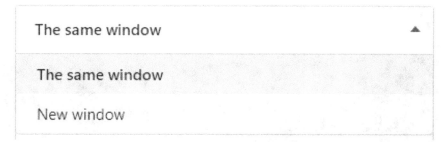

Figure 4-48. Link target drop-down

Let me encourage you to click the "Preview your changes" button at the bottom of the main menu as shown in Figure 3-28.

As you can see from Figure 4-49, the website has come a long way. There is more yet to do. In the next section, you will learn about tags.

Home   Tags   Contact Us

Discover SpaceB: We are building a platform to take you to the moon!

Join us as we share captivating stories, engineering experinces, and dive into the joys of space travel.

(Read more)

Figure 4-49. *The project website*

Tag Settings

The final bit of setup before we start adding content in Chapter 5 is building a set of tags so that content can be easily organized and categorized.

When using Publii CMS, creating tags before using them is like setting up an organizational system for your content on your website. Tags act like labels or keywords that will help group your posts together by topic, making it easier for readers to find what interests them. For example, if you know you're going to be writing posts about gardening, you might create tags like "preparation," "outdoor plants," and "garden design" in advance. Later, when you write those posts, you can simply apply the appropriate tags to keep everything organized.

Setting up your tags ahead of time ensures your site stays consistent and tidy as it grows. It's like putting labels on folders before you fill them with documents – it helps everything fall into place as you go. This approach also makes writing easier because you don't have to come up with new tags on the fly. You've already thought about the main topics you'll be covering, so when it's time to tag your posts, it's just a matter of picking from the list you've prepared.

Consistency when tagging is important. If you plan to use "cooking" as a tag, stick to that instead of mixing it up with variations like "cookery" or "culinary arts." This way, everything related to cooking is neatly grouped together under that tag, making it simple for your readers to find all your content on that topic. Additionally, by limiting the number of tags you create, you prevent things from becoming cluttered and keep the focus clear for both you and your readers.

By planning your tags in advance, you're building a strong foundation for an organized, easy-to-navigate website. It not only helps your readers explore your site more easily, but it also helps search engines understand your content better, which can improve your site's visibility in search results.

In the main menu on the left side of the application, select "Tags" to access the tag settings panel as shown in Figure 4-50.

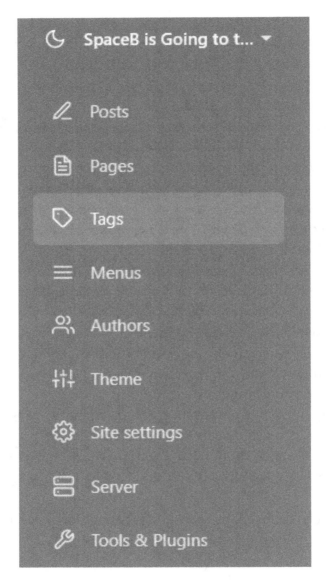

Figure 4-50. *Tag settings panel*

There are no tags set up for the website yet as Publii CMS points out in Figure 4-51.

Figure 4-51. *No tags yet*

Creating Tags

In this section, you will learn how to add tags to your Publii CMS website. If you are following along, you will create five tags that you can later use when creating posts and pages. The first tag will be the "New" tag.

Adding a Tag for News

Add a new tag by clicking the blue "Add new tag" button as seen in Figure 4-51.

A panel titled "ADD NEW TAG" will fly out from the right side of the application as you have seen when editing Author information and adding new menu items as shown in Figure 4-52. This panel looks very similar to the one we saw when editing Author information.

ADD NEW TAG   ✕

Basic information

Name:

Description:

| B | *I* | 🔗 | 🔗̇ | A ⌄ | ☰ | ☰ | ☰ | ◇ | ⟨⟩ |

p   Powered by Tiny ⟋

⬭ Hide tag 👁

🖼 Featured image

🔍 SEO

Figure 4-52. *ADD NEW TAG panel*

Tags, like Authors, can have their own pages which are used to list all posts that have been tagged with the specific tag. Like the Author page, a tag page needs a Name as a minimum. It should also contain a basic description, a featured image, and a meta description for SEO performance.

Basic Information

The "Add New Tag" panel uses the accordion user interface metaphor just like the "Edit Author" panel was. Clicking the label for each section will collapse the current section and expand the one clicked – like the edges of an accordion stretching open and closing. I didn't make that up – that is what they call it.

The section that is initially open when creating a new tag is the Basic information as you can see in Figure 4-52.

The first tag I will be adding is "News". This will be used to categorize posts that are like a news release of breaking information. Type that into the Name field.

In the Description field, add a brief description of this tag. The description I have decided to use is

Newsworthy information about SpaceB and our projects.

You can see this in Figure 4-53.

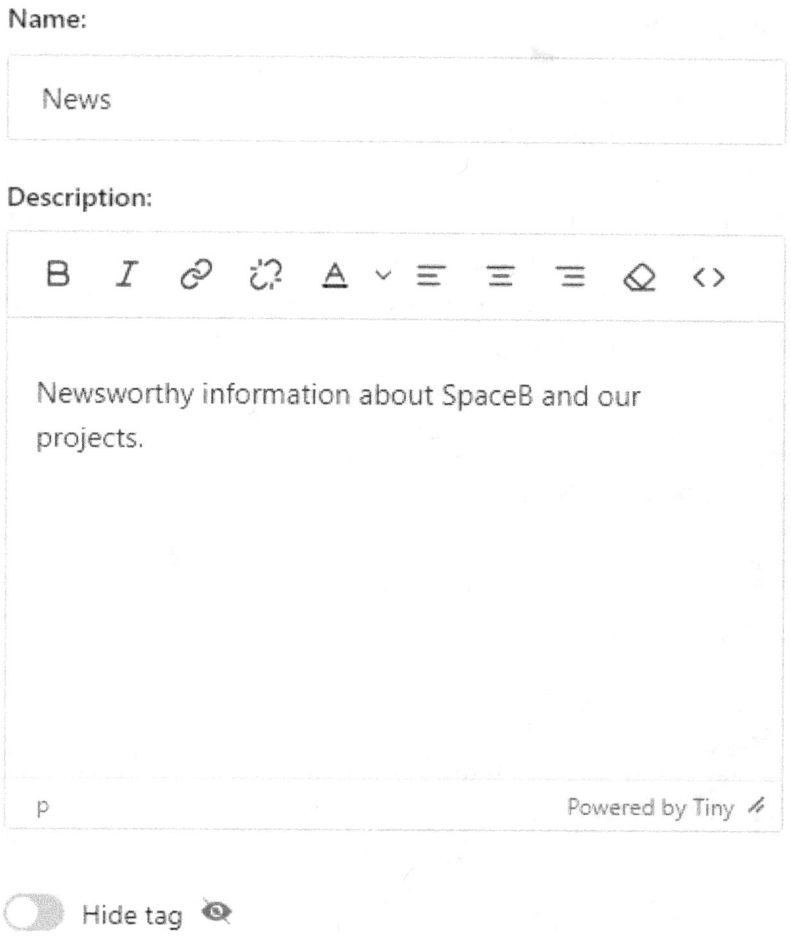

Name:

News

Description:

B   I   🔗   ⧉   A ⌄   ≡   ≡   ≡   ∇   <>

Newsworthy information about SpaceB and our
projects.

p   Powered by Tiny ╱

Hide tag 👁

Figure 4-53. *Tag basic information*

I will not be using the Hide tag option as seen in Figure 4-53 at the
bottom of the Basic information section. This is used in some themes to
create a Featured or Pinned tag that can be used to feature or pin specific
posts to the homepage. The theme Simple 3.0.0.0 does not support this
functionality.

Featured Image

Click the Featured Image section title and expand that section of the Add New Tag panel. You have added several featured images so this should be old hat. The image I will be using for this featured image is from Unsplash and can be seen in Figure 4-54. You can download the image at https:// unsplash.com/photos/business-newspaper-article-WYd_PkCa1BY, or on the book's GitHub repository here: https://github.com/Apress/ Designing-Websites-with-Publii-and-GitHub-Pages.

Figure 4-54. *Image for News tag featured image*

Figure 4-55 shows the featured image added to the panel and the Alternative text of

Newsworthy information about SpaceB and our projects.

Featured image

Remove image

Alternative text

Newsworthy information about SpaceB and our projects

Caption

Credits

By AbsolutVision

Figure 4-55. *Featured Image settings*

That is the same sentence I used for my tag description in the Basic information panel. It is fine to reuse this text in this context.

Notice also that I have provided credit for the image.

SEO Settings

The final setting that I always assign is the meta description in the SEO section as shown in Figure 4-56.

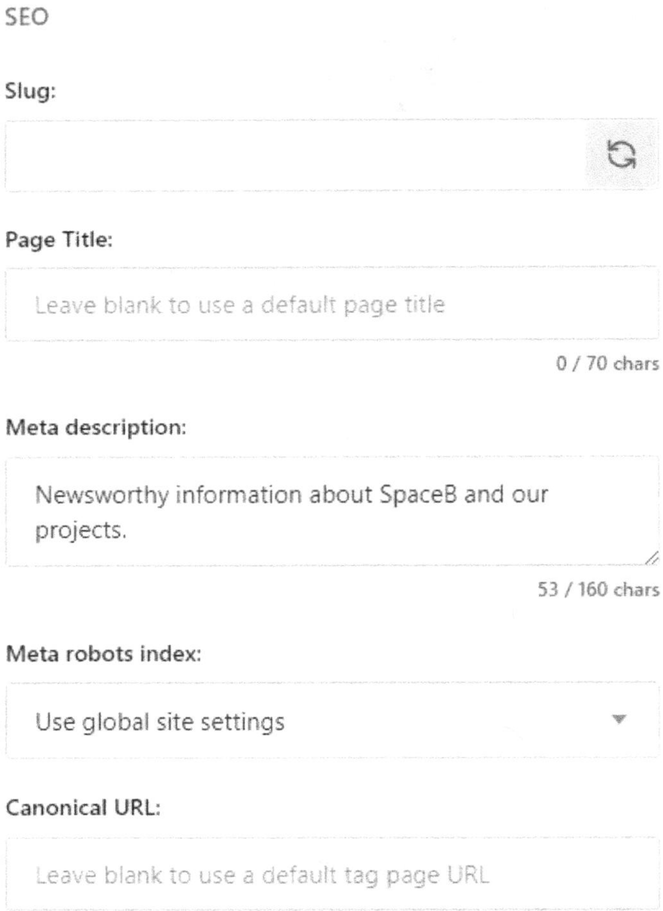

SEO

Slug:

Page Title:

Leave blank to use a default page title

0 / 70 chars

Meta description:

Newsworthy information about SpaceB and our projects.

53 / 160 chars

Meta robots index:

Use global site settings ▼

Canonical URL:

Leave blank to use a default tag page URL

Figure 4-56. *SEO settings*

I have chosen to reuse the tag description once again for this setting also. In all cases, a brief description is all that is needed, and there is no reason to write three different descriptions.

Slugs

Notice that since we have not yet saved this tag, the slug for the tag in the Slug field is blank. It will be generated when you save the tag the first time. You can supply your own. Typically, I let Publii CMS take care of that when creating tags and other content. Clicking the blue button with circular arrows on the right of the slug field will also generate (or regenerate) a slug based on the tag name.

Wait a minute – a slug? Do you mean one of these (Figure 4-57)?

Figure 4-57. *A slug*

Nope. In the context of a blog platform like Publii CMS, a "slug" refers to the part of the URL that uniquely identifies a specific page on your blog. Essentially, it's the web address that leads directly to a particular post or page. For example, in the URL "`www.exampleblog.com/posts/my-first-blog-post`", the slug would be "my-first-blog-post".

Slugs are crucial for both usability and Search Engine Optimization (SEO). They provide a clear, concise, and user-friendly way of directing readers to specific content on your blog. A well-crafted slug is usually a short, descriptive phrase that reflects the title or main topic of the page or post, using hyphens to separate words. This makes it easy for users to understand and remember the URL, and for search engines to index the content accurately. In Publii CMS, slugs are typically generated automatically based on the title of your post, but they can often be customized to best fit your SEO strategy and content organization.

This tag has all the information it needs to be created. Click the "Add new tag" button at the bottom of the panel as seen in Figure 4-58. When creating a new tag, the "Save & Preview" button is not available.

Add new tag   Save & Preview ⚡   Cancel

Figure 4-58. Add new tag button

You can see the new tag in the Tag list panel on the right side of the main menu when "Tags" is selected in the main menu as shown in Figure 4-59.

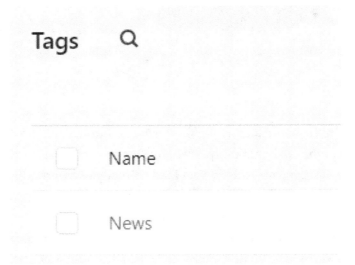

Tags   Q

Name

News

Figure 4-59. Tag list

Adding Remaining Tags

In this section, you will add four more tags to round out the tags for the site. You can always add more tags if you find you need them. Refer to the previous pages when adding these tags. These are the properties for the new tags. Note that featured images linked below are available both at the link on Unsplash.com and in the book's GitHub repository at the URL provided.

Also – use the description provided (or invent your own) in the tag's Basic information description, the featured image Alternative text, and in the SEO Meta description.

Click the "Add new tag" button in the upper right corner of the Tags panel when adding a new tag. Add the tags listed below if you are following along in the project.

Events

Name: Events

Description: Happenings that we want you to know about at SpaceB

Featured Image: `https://unsplash.com/photos/a-computer-screen-with-a-calendar-on-it-4BnNnEtAGPo`

Credits: Photo by Ed Hardie on Unsplash

Rocket Tech

Name: Rocket Tech

Description: Rocket technology development at SpaceB and elsewhere

Featured Image: `https://unsplash.com/photos/a-close-up-of-a-tire-iA1m5Ylwotw`

Credits: Photo by Brian Wangenheim on Unsplash

Special Interest

Name: Special Interest

Description: HEY! This stuff we really want to call your attention to. Check it out!

Featured Image: jason-rosewell-ASKeuOZqhYU-unsplash.jpg

Credits: Photo by Jason Rosewell on Unsplash

Musings

Name: Musings

Description: Random thoughts and ideas that we want to share

Featured Image: johannes-plenio-fmTde1Fe23A-unsplash.jpg

Credits: Photo by Johannes Plenio on Unsplash

When completed, you should have five tags listed in the Tags interface as shown in Figure 4-60.

Tags	Name	Posts	ID ▲
	News	0	1
	Events	0	2
	Rocket Tech	0	3
	Special Interest	0	4
	Musings	0	5

Figure 4-60. *Tags*

Summary

In this chapter, you learned a lot of new things about Publii CMS as you prepared to add your first post. You will be doing that in the next chapter, but first let's recap.

Publii CMS uses themes to present nicely formatted information to the end user.

The theme that Publii CMS ships with is a nice basic design called Simple version 3.0.0.

Themes have a lot of user customization available to them. In the case of the Simple theme, you learned about customizing the following:

- Applying a website logo.

- Setting up the Hero section includes a text block to catch a visitor's attention as well as a nice, featured image which adds interest and color.

- Modifying the primary colors for the site.

- Choosing fonts that help to convey both your brand and your message.

- Applying a favicon to your site.

You configured basic information for the Author and applied settings that enhance the Author page such as a featured image.

You created a main menu and added menu items to it.

You learned about the different types of links that Publii can support.

You learned about tagging and built tags for your site.

CHAPTER 5

Adding Content

In this chapter, I will be discussing the tools used to add content to your website. Publii CMS offers several tools for creating content and a couple ways to store your content. Specifically in this section, I will examine posts. Chapter 6 will discuss pages. The distinction is minor but important. Whether posts or pages, what we are creating is called content.

Content Is King

Content – what the user sees and consumes when visiting your website. It is why your website exists. When discussing the content for a blog or website, it's essential to recognize that it includes the information and experiences a website offers to its visitors. The nature of this content can vary widely based on the website's focus and the audience's needs. For example, informational content like articles, blogs, FAQs, and how-to guides is crucial for visitors seeking knowledge or solutions to specific problems.

Many visitors are drawn to websites for entertainment as opposed to a learning experience. This is where entertaining content, including videos, podcasts, and engaging blog posts, comes into play. Such content is designed to capture the visitor's attention in a more relaxed and enjoyable manner. This is particularly relevant for lifestyle, entertainment, and community-focused websites.

© Brad Moore 2025
B. Moore, *Designing Websites with Publii and GitHub Pages*,
https://doi.org/10.1007/979-8-8688-1195-1_5

The quality of content on a website is a critical factor in its success. Good content is defined by several characteristics. It must be relevant and timely, addressing the current needs and interests of the audience. Accuracy and trustworthiness are equally critical, as they establish the credibility of the website. The content should also be engaging and interesting, capturing and maintaining a visitor's attention. Consider clarity and conciseness as important factors in conveying information effectively, while the visual appeal of content and its use of images and videos often enhance the overall experience.

You must understand your target audience and their needs when developing an approach to content for a website. Set clear goals for what the content aims to achieve. Regular updates to your site and content are important for attracting and keeping an audience. Focusing on the use of SEO (Search Engine Optimization) techniques ensures the content remains easily discoverable.

One of the great things about Publii CMS is that it makes managing website content easier and more intuitive. This is because it offers a user-friendly interface that simplifies the organization and publication of content. It's particularly beneficial for those without extensive technical knowledge.

This book is not designed to provide you with a specific content strategy for your site, or even suggest specific content for your site. There are places where content can be obtained for the noncreative; however, if you plan to win, you are best using your creative side and writing your own content. Always begin with an audience in mind. Write for them and write for yourself. The Web is saturated with sites that provide guidance and advice as to what and how to write blog posts.

The focus in this book is on the tool to get the job done. That is Publii CMS. As I develop posts, I will be using dummy content as a placeholder for what could be real content. It consists of made-up words that look a lot like Latin. Sometimes this dummy content is called Lorem Ipsum. (Learn more about Lorem Ipsum: `https://en.wikipedia.org/wiki/Lorem_ipsum`.)

What Is a Blog

With content out of the way, I need to address the next question: What is a blog? Publii CMS is primarily about publishing a blog. A blog, a term shortened from "weblog," is an online platform where individuals or groups can publish content, usually in an informal or conversational style. Think of it as a shared journal that the whole world gets to read. The history of blogging dates to the late 1990s, when Internet users began maintaining personal web pages where they would chronicle their lives, thoughts, and experiences. These early blogs were essentially online diaries or journals. The term "weblog" was coined by Jorn Barger in 1997 and later shortened to "blog" by Peter Merholz.

Blogging evolved as the Internet became more accessible, becoming a popular medium for self-expression, information sharing, and community building. The early 2000s saw a significant expansion in blogging, with platforms like Blogger and WordPress making it easier for nontechnical users to create and manage their blogs. This era marked the transformation of blogging from a niche hobby to a mainstream activity, influencing various aspects of society, including media, politics, and education. Today, blogs range from personal to professional and cover almost every topic imaginable, reflecting the diverse interests and voices of people around the world.

In this book, I am playing the part of Bob Bobbee, the CEO of a fictious space technology company called SpaceB. My reason for blogging is to promote my brand, to let people know what is going on in the company, and to connect with customers and promote the idea of space flight to the moon with the hope that a few readers will one day be customers.

You will need to understand what your reason for blogging is – your "why" – and that will drive your content and your approach.

Posts

When you add content to your blog, you will be creating a "post." The concept of blogging was discussed above. A post simply adds a single blog entry to your larger blog. A blog entry or a post can consist of text, images, video, and other media. Frequently it is a combination of some or all those things.

To add a post, click the "Posts" menu item in the application main menu on the left side of the Publii CMS application.

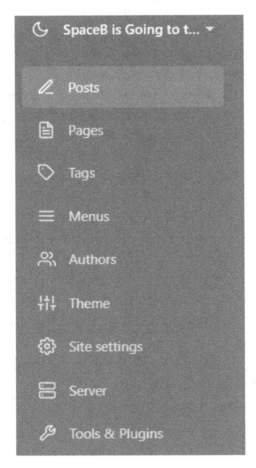

Figure 5-1. *Posts menu item*

This is a new website. I have not added any content yet, so there naturally are no posts. This will be my first post (yours too if you are following along with me) so Publii CMS will ask which editor I want to use for this post as shown in Figure 5-2.

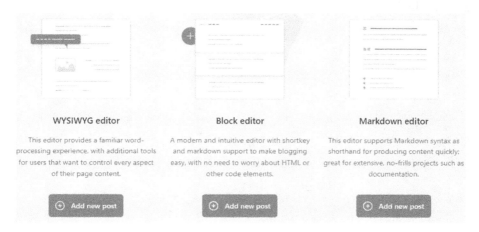

Figure 5-2. *Content editor choices*

Publii CMS has three types of editors used for creating posts as can be seen in Figure 5-2. They are the WYSIWYG editor, the Block editor, and the Markdown editor.

WYSIWYG Editor

The WYSIWYG editor uses the "What-you-see-is-what-you-get" paradigm which allows you to craft content formatted as you wish it to look in its published form. It features a toolbar like the one found in your favorite word processing application as shown in Figure 5-3. This toolbar is used to format the content.

Figure 5-3. *WYSIWYG editor toolbar*

Block Editor

The Block editor uses a paradigm of blocks of content to which formatting is applied to the entire block. When a block is created, you can select the format that the block will use as shown in Figure 5-4.

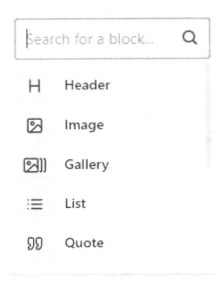

Figure 5-4. *Block editor format menu*

The Block editor also permits inline formatting of text using a format menu available when a portion of text is selected as shown in Figure 5-5.

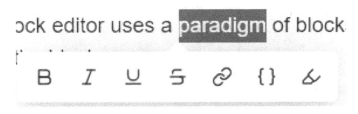

Figure 5-5. *Inline formatting*

Another neat feature of the Block editor is the support for moving whole blocks of text as well as converting block types from one type to another as shown in Figure 5-6.

Figure 5-6. *Block movement or conversion*

Markdown Editor

The Markdown editor is a no-frills editor that allows you to format the content with markdown syntax As you write it. Markdown is a lightweight markup language with plain-text formatting syntax. It was designed to be easy to write and read. (I confess I have the hardest time remembering the markdown tags for formatting text and find myself googling it all the time.) Markdown was created by John Gruber and Aaron Swartz in 2004 with the goal of enabling people to write using an easy-to-read, easy-to-write plain-text format. This formatted text then can be converted into structurally valid HTML (or other formats as needed).

Markdown is often used to format readme files and for writing messages in online discussion forums. The simplicity of the syntax makes it popular among bloggers, developers, and content creators, as it allows for the easy formatting of text without the need for complex HTML code. For instance, in Markdown, you can create headers by prefixing text with hash symbols (e.g., # Header), and lists can be created using asterisks or numbers for bullet points. This user-friendly approach can streamline the content creation process for those who are experienced in its use.

161

The original Markdown syntax guide by John Gruber, the creator of Markdown, can be found at Daring Fireball: `https://daringfireball.net/projects/markdown/`. This guide provides the basic principles and syntax of Markdown.

In the sections ahead, I will be guiding you through the creation of two posts. The first will demonstrate a few of the features of the WYSIWYG editor. The second post will focus on the Block editor. The Markdown editor will be used in Chapter 6 when creating pages to prepare the website terms, conditions, and policies statement page.

The WYSIWYG Editor

In this section, I will discuss using the WYSIWYG editor to create a post for the project website. This editor allows you to format text as you create it as it will look when it is published.

Add a New Post

Before you can start writing, a new post must be created. Currently there are no posts listed in the Posts section, so Publii CMS prompts you asking which editor you wish to use to create the first post. This will be the default editor. The default is easy to change should you decide you like a different editor. That will be discussed when creating the second post in the section titled "The Block Editor" later in this chapter.

If you are not already in the Posts list panel of Publii CMS, click the menu item "Posts" as shown in Figure 5-1. We do not have any posts yet, so the Posts panel does not list existing posts but instead asks which type of editor we want to use to create your first posts as seen in Figure 5-2.

Click the "Add new post" button under the WYSIWYG editor as shown in Figure 5-7.

WYSIWYG editor

This editor provides a familiar word-processing experience, with additional tools for users that want to control every aspect of their page content.

⊕ Add new post

Figure 5-7. Add new post using the WYSIWYG editor.

The Post Title

Publii CMS expects you to add a post title to the new post once the post editor is opened. Observe the blinking cursor located above the editor toolbar as shown in Figure 5-8.

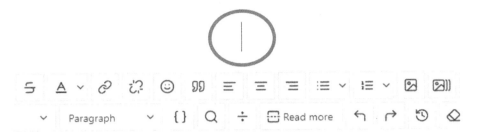

Figure 5-8. *A cursor indicating a post title is required*

You can begin typing a post title immediately. If you click into the post body, Publii CMS will remind you a title is required by adding the text "Add post title" to the area above the editor toolbar as shown in Figure 5-9. Clicking on this text will reveal the blinking cursor prompting you for a title.

Add post title

Figure 5-9. *Add post title.*

Click back up on the text that says, "Add post title". Type a title for this post. Post titles should be short and descriptive. The title I will use is

Inspired by a Dream

You can follow along with me or create your own title.

The Post Body Text

The post body – the content of the post – is written in the space provided below the editor toolbar. The post body text is the heart of your message and the reason you have created this specific post. It should communicate something unique and useful to your audience. In my post body, I will be introducing and expanding on the subject suggested by the title.

Click somewhere below the toolbar to insert the cursor so that you can begin writing as shown in Figure 5-10.

Figure 5-10. *Body text cursor location*

I am going to paste in two paragraphs of space-flavored Lorem Ipsum generated by ChatGPT. This is the text:

In the vast expanse of the dreamscape, where nebulous thoughts orbit the stars of imagination, a rocket fueled by cosmic ambition sailed past the constellation of Ephemeral Whispers. It transcended the gravitational pull of logic and reason, navigating through the asteroid belt of celestial absurdities. Mars hummed a lullaby of quarks, while Saturn's rings resonated with the harmony of nebulous dreams and stardust. Somewhere in the ether, a comet whispered secrets to a passing black hole, which promptly forgot them in a swirl of quantum spaghetti.

165

As the spacecraft drifted through the vacuum of celestial nonsense, the crew pondered the intricacies of zero-gravity cheese and the complexities of lunar lasagna. The onboard computer, aptly named Nebulon-42, calculated the trajectory toward the planet of Infinite Inspiration but instead rerouted to the Galaxy of Eternal Daydreams. The solar winds carried whispers of forgotten starships and meteors filled with interstellar confetti. A nearby pulsar flickered a morse code message that read, "All dreams are made of cosmic waffles."

–ChatGPT

Pretty strange stuff but far more entertaining than the run-of-the-mill Lorem Ipsum.

Adding an Image

Next, I want to add an image to the page. You have already worked with images when adding featured images to the website. This process is very similar. Before adding the image, I first must have it available on my computer. I am using images from Unsplash.com for this project. The image I have decided to use is shown in Figure 5-11. It is available on the Internet at `https://unsplash.com/photos/buzz-aldrin-on-the-moon-in-front-of-the-us-flag-UeSpvBOQo88` and can also be downloaded from the book's GitHub page here: `https://github.com/Apress/Designing-Websites-with-Publii-and-GitHub-Pages`.

Figure 5-11. *Buzz Aldrin on the moon*

Inserting an image into the body of the post is done by clicking the "Insert/Edit Image" button on the toolbar as shown in Figure 5-12. The toolbar tools all feature a tooltip describing what the tool does. Hover your mouse pointer over a toolbar tool for a couple seconds to see the tooltip.

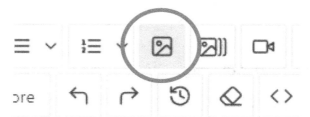

Figure 5-12. *Insert/Edit Image toolbar button*

> **Tip**   The WYSIWYG editor also supports dragging an image from the operating system file explorer and dropping it into the post body.

Click the "Insert/Edit Image" button to insert an image. A dialog window will be opened where you can select the image and give it some attributes as shown in Figure 5-13.

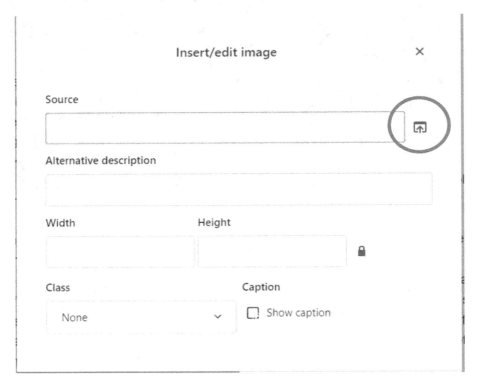

Figure 5-13. *Insert/edit image dialog window*

Select the image to insert by clicking the "Source" button as highlighted in Figure 5-13. This will open your system's file explorer (or Finder on macOS) window. Navigate to the file you have previously prepared. In my case, it is a picture of Buzz Aldrin on the surface of the moon. Since I just downloaded it from Unsplash.com, it is in the Downloads folder.

Once the file is selected, provide a keyword-rich Alternative description for the image as shown in Figure 5-14. This will be the image's Alt text value when your page is rendered as an HTML document. Remember that the Alternative description field is another way you can help boost your SEO performance.

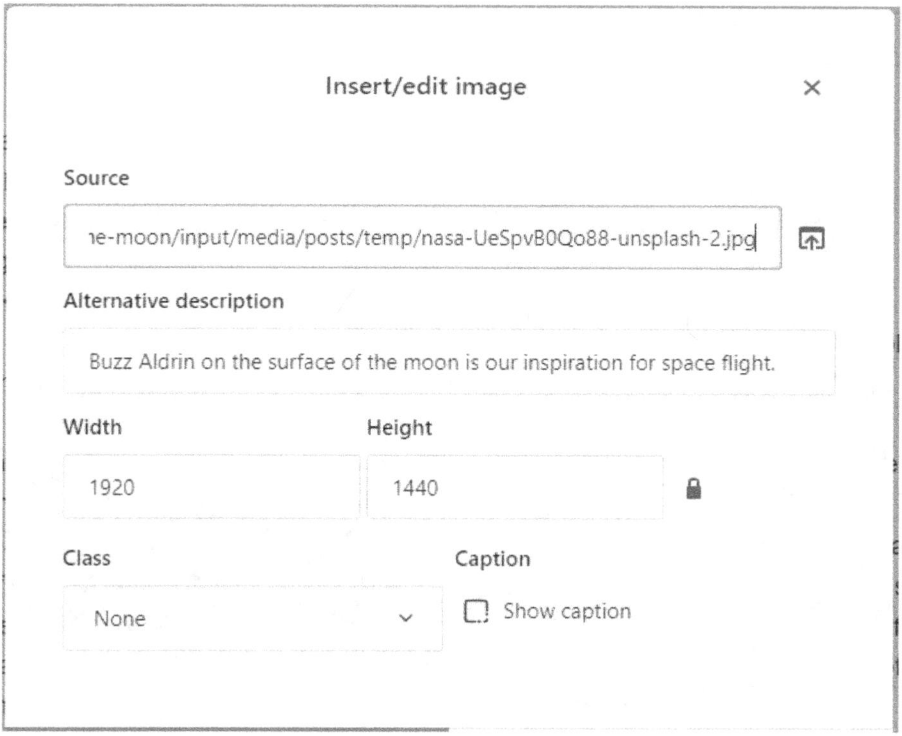

Insert/edit image   ×

Source

| ie-moon/input/media/posts/temp/nasa-UeSpvB0Qo88-unsplash-2.jpg |

Alternative description

| Buzz Aldrin on the surface of the moon is our inspiration for space flight. |

Width   Height

| 1920 | | 1440 |

Class   Caption

| None   ∨ | ☐ Show caption

Figure 5-14. *Insert/edit image showing Alternative description*

The Alternative description I provided was

Buzz Aldrin on the surface of the moon is our inspiration for space flight

169

Copy this into your project if you are following along or provide your own if you are going the creative route.

Publii CMS offers several classes for alignment of images inserted into the post as shown in Figure 5-15. These are called classes as the alignment attributes are applied in the website CSS. This is not something you need to know to use the feature though.

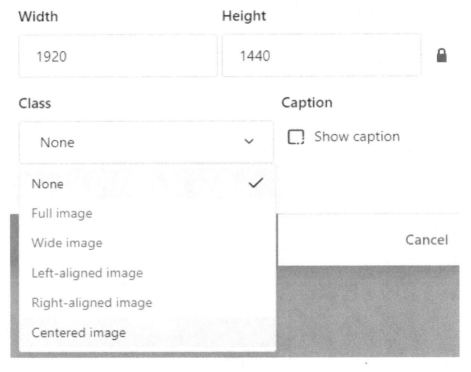

Figure 5-15. *Image classes*

I have selected the class "Centered image". The image is big enough that this probably will not make much difference, but I will choose to center all images regardless of size in my posts as this helps create a sense of uniformity in the content.

Finally, click the blue "Save" button on the bottom of the Insert/edit image dialog window to save the information and insert the image as shown in Figure 5-16.

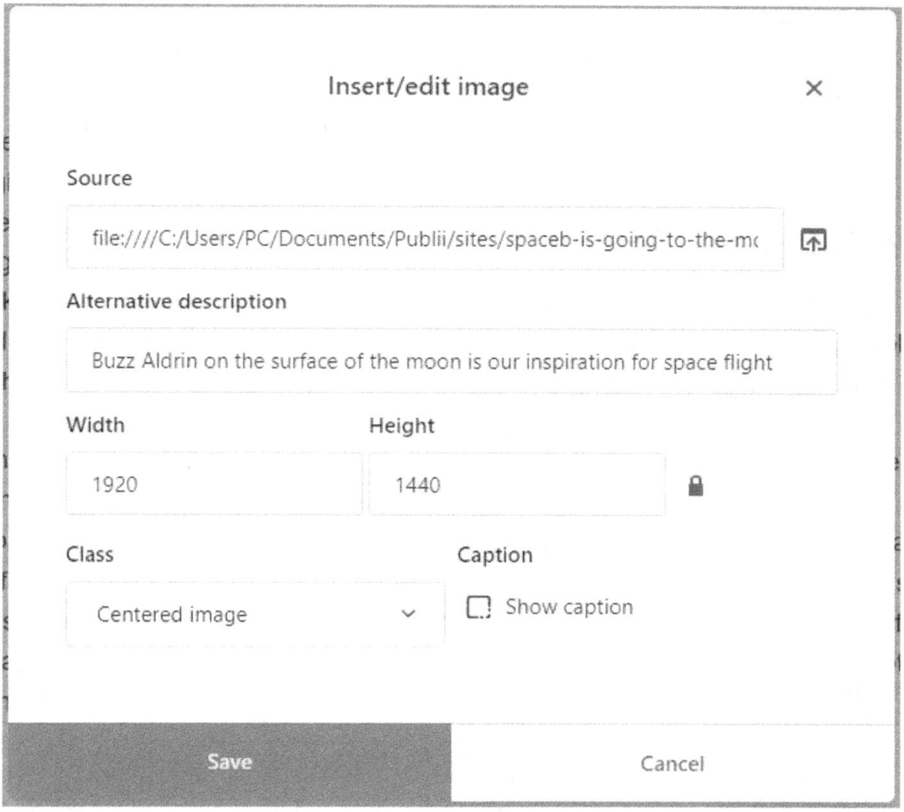

Insert/edit image   ×

Source

file:////C:/Users/PC/Documents/Publii/sites/spaceb-is-going-to-the-mc

Alternative description

Buzz Aldrin on the surface of the moon is our inspiration for space flight

Width   Height

1920   1440

Class   Caption

Centered image   ∨   ☐ Show caption

Save   Cancel

Figure 5-16. *Save button on the bottom of the Insert/edit image dialog window*

Tip   You can edit an image that has been inserted into the body of a post by first selecting the image (blue handles will be added to the image indicating it has been selected) and then clicking the Insert/ Edit image button in the toolbar.

I am going to add another short paragraph of text under the image I inserted, and then I will add a bullet list of Apollo missions that landed on the moon. This is the paragraph I am adding; once again some of the nonsense text was generated by ChatGPT:

> *Among the stars, a disco of cosmic jellybeans danced while asteroids debated whether Saturn's rings were secretly made of bubblegum. Landing humans on the moon is hard work. Here are the missions that have been successful:*

Adding a Bullet List

Publii CMS supports three styles of bullet lists as shown in Figure 5-17. It also supports numbered lists that come in six styles as shown in Figure 5-18.

Figure 5-17. *Bullet list styles*

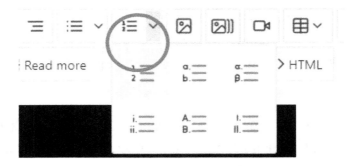

Figure 5-18. *Numbered bullet list styles*

Here is the list of Apollo landings I will add to my post:

- Apollo 11 (July 20, 1969)

- Apollo 12 (November 19, 1969)

- Apollo 14 (February 5, 1971)

- Apollo 15 (July 30, 1971)

- Apollo 16 (April 21, 1972)

- Apollo 17 (December 11, 1972)

To add these, I clicked the bullet toolbar button. This inserted the first bullet ready for the information to be added as shown in Figure 5-19.

Figure 5-19. *Ready to add bullet points in the editor*

Type each of the entries into the editor (or paste them in as an alternative). Each time you press the ENTER key to add a new line, a new bullet point will be added.

Press ENTER twice to end the bullet list and begin adding normal text.

Adding a Blockquote

I want to add an inspirational quotation from an astronaut that walked on the moon. I could use the quote by Neil Armstrong that is so famous and with which I opened this book, but I will instead quote Edgar Mitchell from the Apollo 14 mission.

Adding a quote to your post is as easy as clicking the Blockquote button on the toolbar as shown in Figure 5-20.

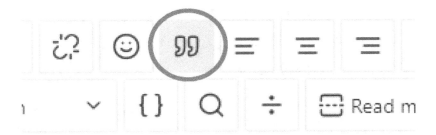

Figure 5-20. *The Blockquote button on the toolbar*

This is his quotation that I will be inserting into the post:

"Suddenly, from behind the rim of the moon, in long, slow-motion moments of immense majesty, there emerges a sparkling blue and white jewel, a light, delicate sky-blue sphere laced with slowly swirling veils of white, rising gradually like a small pearl in a thick sea of black mystery. It takes more than a moment to fully realize that this is Earth... home."

Feel free to copy this and insert it as well – or find your own quotation that inspires you and use that instead.

Clicking the Blockquote button on the toolbar will add special formatting (a solid black vertical line) into the editor indicating that what you are adding is a blockquote as shown in Figure 5-21. Be aware that the theme you are using may render the blockquote differently.

Figure 5-21. *Blockquote indicator, left of the editor cursor*

Add the quote. Press the ENTER key twice to end the blockquote section in the editor.

Adding a Link

I realize that I cannot do justice to the overwhelming scope of the Apollo project, so I want to add a link (hyperlink) into my post to an external website that explains the program in more detail. I will link to this article on the space.com website: `https://www.space.com/apollo-program-overview.html`.

Of course, you can link to whatever you would like to link to as you create your website.

The toolbar has two link-related buttons as you can see in Figure 5-22. The button on the right is used for inserting or editing an existing link. The tooltip says "Insert/edit link". The button just to the right of the Insert/edit link button is for removing an existing link. It is called "Remove link" in the toolbar tooltip.

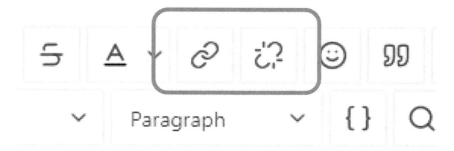

Figure 5-22. *Link management buttons in the editor toolbar*

As I prepared to insert the link, I chose to introduce the subject with a short sentence. I have placed the cursor where I want the link inserted as shown in Figure 5-23.

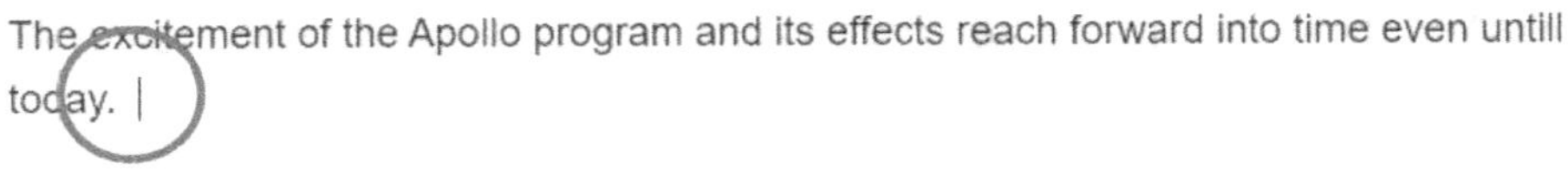

The excitement of the Apollo program and its effects reach forward into time even untill today. |

Figure 5-23. *Cursor location to insert a link*

Next, I clicked the "Insert/Edit link" button on the toolbar. This opened a dialog window titled Insert/Edit link as shown in Figure 5-24.

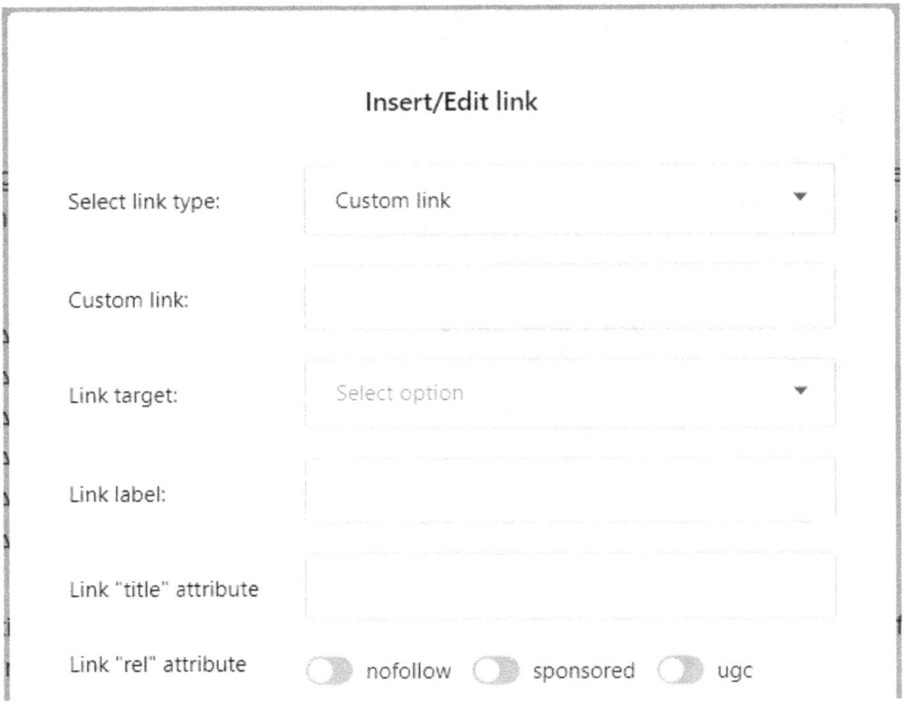

Insert/Edit link

Select link type: Custom link   ▼

Custom link:

Link target: Select option   ▼

Link label:

Link "title" attribute

Link "rel" attribute   ⬤ nofollow   ⬤ sponsored   ⬤ ugc

Figure 5-24. *Insert/Edit link dialog window*

I am planning to insert a custom link here, but if you click the drop-down field for Select link type, you will see that there are multiple link types that are supported. Most of these options are for linking back to other resources on your website. A common choice would be to select a link type of "Post link" which would allow you to reference other posts or articles you have written from the current post. This is a very powerful feature that you should use as your blog grows.

In the current case, I plan to link to an external website. This would be a custom link, so I am sticking with that as the link type in the Select link type drop-down. The next field I must add data to is the Custom link field. I add the following URL: `https://www.space.com/apollo-program-overview.html`.

The next decision is the link target as shown in Figure 5-25. This tells Publii CMS whether to add a directive for the browser to open the link in the same tab or open a new tab.

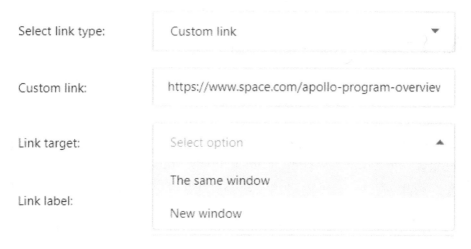

Figure 5-25. *Link target type*

Since this link will take users away from my website, I will choose to have the link open in a new tab or window by specifying a Link target of "New window". This is a strategic choice on my part as I want to keep open the possibility that the user will later return to my site and continue to read.

If you are linking resources within your own website, it is best to open those links in the same window. It is poor form to cause your site to spawn multiple tabs as users navigate around your site.

Next give your link a link label. This is the actual link text that the user will see in their browser. Often this is underlined and/or colored differently from normal body text. How a link is rendered is very dependent on the theme you are using. Type a label for your link into the Link label field as shown in Figure 5-26.

Figure 5-26. *Link label*

The link label I have used is

Read more about it in this excellent article on Space.com.

Feel free to copy this and paste it into your project if you are following along. There is one more important setting for this link. As a link to an external website, I want to tell any bots crawling the page not to follow the link away from my website.

This is done by enabling the "nofollow" option in Link "rel" attribute as shown in Figure 5-27.

Figure 5-27. *Link "rel" attributes*

To enable "nofollow", slide the toggle switch to the left of the "nofollow" option to the right. It will turn blue to indicate it is enabled.

Finally, click the blue "OK" button at the bottom of the dialog window as shown in Figure 5-27.

Saving the Post

The post is complete. So far, I have not saved the post. I will need to save the post to make it a permanent part of the blog I am writing. Publii CMS offers several saving options as shown in Figure 5-28.

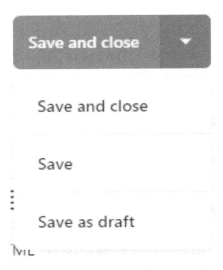

Figure 5-28. *Options to save a post*

The default option is "Save and close". If you just click the save button, this is the action that will be performed. This will close the editor window, save the post, and set the post status to "Published".

If you click the drop-down arrow on the save button, there are two other options as you can see in Figure 5-28.

Clicking "Save" will save the post and set its status to "Published". It will not close the editor window.

Clicking "Save as draft" will save the post and set the status to "draft". It will not close the editor window. If you save the post as draft, the default save action will change to "Save draft" as shown in Figure 5-29.

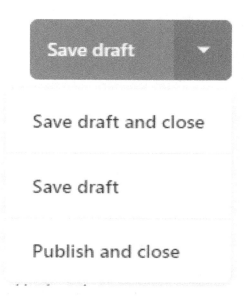

Figure 5-29. *Draft save menu*

Notice that the last item in the save menu becomes "Publish and close" once you have saved the post as a draft.

I recommend saving your work frequently as you develop your posts. Save it initially as a draft so that you do not accidentally upload it to your production website hosted for the public to see.

Publish the post using the "Publish and close" menu option when you have completed composing the post, and it is ready for publishing.

For now, this post is ready for publication – click the "Save and close" button if you have not saved it yet. Click the "Publish and close" button if you have saved it previously as a draft.

You will see that we have one post listed in the Posts list when on the Posts panel as shown in Figure 5-30.

Posts Q

All (1)   Published (1)

	Title	Publication date
☐	Inspired by a Dream	Aug 22, 2024 03:08 pm Last modified: a few seconds ago

Figure 5-30. *Posts list*

Post Options

In this section, I will discuss the post options that can be configured for the post. These can be configured whether the post is in draft or published state.

The post name in the Posts list as shown in Figure 5-30 is a link back to the editor where the post can be modified. We know this because the text is colored blue.

Click the post name to open the editor where the post can be modified. In the upper right corner of the editor next to the "Save" button is a gear as shown in Figure 5-31.

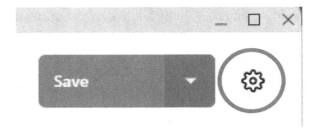

Figure 5-31. *Post options and settings gear*

Clicking this gear will cause a panel to fly out from the right side of the editor window as shown in Figure 5-32. This panel is where the post options and settings can be modified.

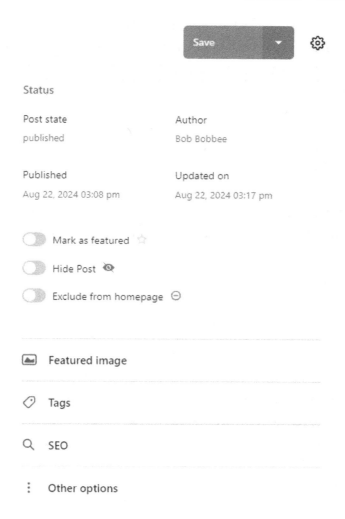

Figure 5-32. *Post options and settings panel*

Post Status

Notice in the panel that the topmost section that is active when the panel is displayed is the Status section as you can see in Figure 5-32.

This section will provide some basic information about the post. Here you will find the post state – whether it is published or in draft, the author of the post, when it was first published (if it has been published), and the date it was last updated.

This section has three options that can be enabled to cause the post to act in a unique way. You can see these three options at the bottom of the status section. They are labeled "Mark as featured", "Hide post", and "Exclude from homepage". I will not be using any of these options in my posts.

The Publii CMS documentation page (`https://getpublii.com/docs/adding-editing-and-deleting-posts.html`) explains these three options as follows:

- **Mark as featured:** If enabled, then the post will be highlighted on listing pages such as tag pages so that more visitors will notice it.

- **Hide post:** Enabling this option will stop the post from appearing on listing pages, such as author or tag pages.

- **Exclude from homepage:** When enabled, the post won't appear in any homepage showcase sections but will continue to appear in listings and other pages that generate post lists, unlike the standard **Hide post** option.

Featured Image

The options and settings panel uses the accordion metaphor as we discussed in Chapter 4 when working with tags and authors. There are several sections in the panel where information can be added. These sections are only accessible when that specific section header has been clicked and the section revealed.

Our post will be more approachable with a hero image which is applied in the featured image part of the options panel. Click the Featured image link to expose that section as shown in Figure 5-33.

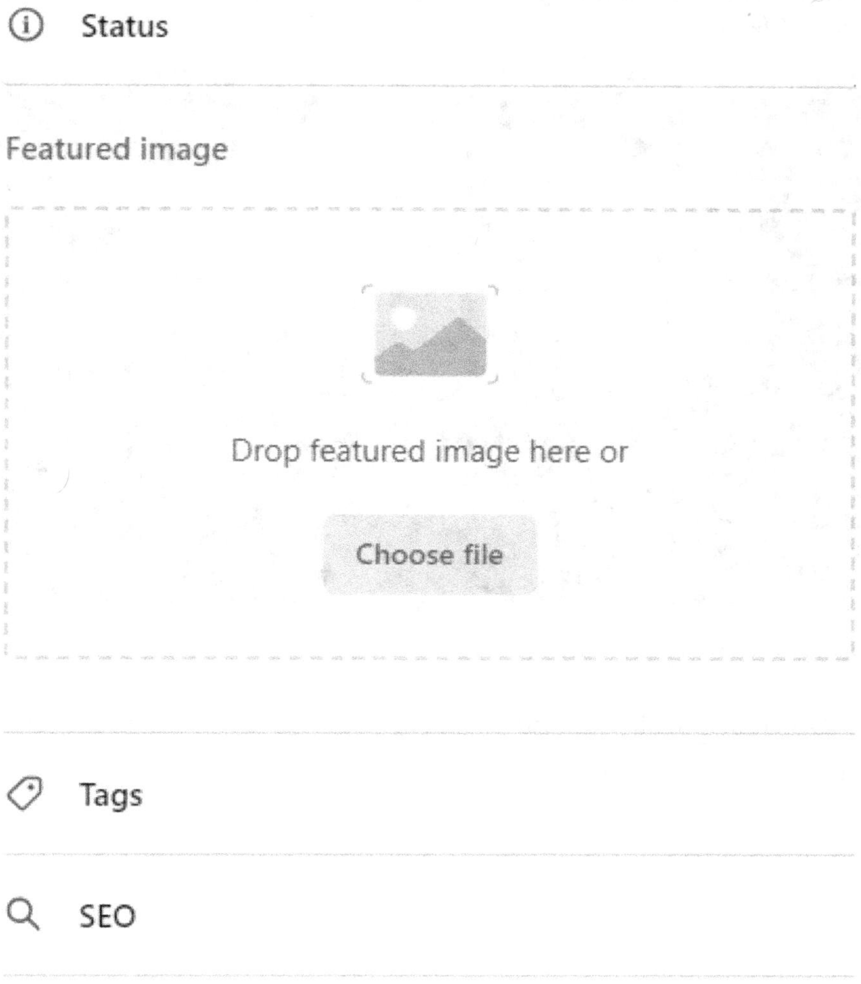

ⓘ   **Status**

Featured image

Drop featured image here or

Choose file

🏷   Tags

🔍   SEO

Figure 5-33. *Featured image section*

The featured image I want to use comes from Unsplash.com and can be seen in Figure 5-34. Download this image from Unsplash.com at `https://unsplash.com/photos/moon-wKlqqfNTLsI` or download it from the book's GitHub repository here: `https://github.com/Apress/Designing-Websites-with-Publii-and-GitHub-Pages`.

Figure 5-34. *The moon*

Download the image and then drag and drop it into the image picker field as shown in Figure 5-35.

Featured image

Remove image

Alternative text

The Moon - it calls to us and inspires us explore

Caption

Credits

Photo by Nicolas Thomas on Unsplash

Figure 5-35. *Featured image with Alternative text and credits*

Don't forget to add an Alternative text as discussed elsewhere. This should be as keyword rich as you can make it. This will enhance your SEO performance in the long run. As you can see in Figure 5-35, I have added the following as the Alternative text.

The Moon - it calls to us and inspires us explore

Remember to credit the photo author if possible. Unsplash.com provides a nice link you can quickly copy, making it easy to credit a photo author as you can see in Figure 5-36.

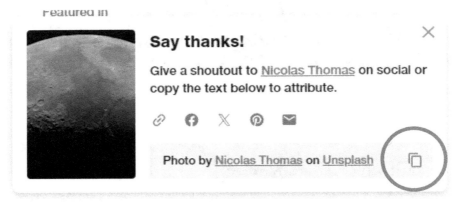

Figure 5-36. *Photo credit for images downloaded from Unsplash.com*

Click the double stacked rectangles as highlighted in Figure 5-36 to copy the photo credit. Paste it into the credit field for the featured image as shown in Figure 5-35.

Tags

We spent some time in Chapter 4 setting up tags for our website. Now it is time to make that pay off. Tagging your posts is a great way to increase keyword exposure to the web crawler that indexes your website. This is once again a positive step toward having better performing SEO.

Tagging also helps organize your posts so that people visiting your site can find related information easily.

Click on the section titled Tags to expose the tag interface as shown in Figure 5-37.

Figure 5-37. *Tag interface*

The tags section is simply a drop-down field that permits you to select one or more tags that apply to this post. In Figure 5-37, I have clicked the field and caused the list of existing tags to be displayed in the drop-down.

Click a tag to select it. Notice how that tag is added to the field as shown in Figure 5-38. It can be removed by clicking the small "x" to the left of the tag name in the gray box that surrounds the tag name.

Note   The Tags field also permits typing a tag name in addition to selecting it from the drop-down list. Tags entered this way are being added in an ad hoc manner. It is recommended to edit these tags in the Tags interface adding common elements that other tags possess such as a Featured image and description.

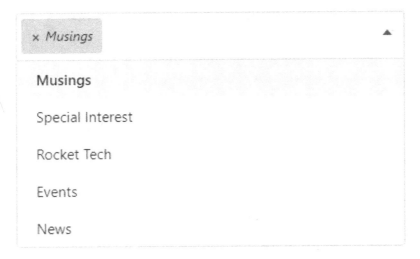

Tags

Figure 5-38. *A selected tag*

I have selected Musings which is reflected in the Tags field. Now I want to select a second tag. This time I selected "News". Notice that there are now two tags listed in the Tags field. A second field has also been added to the panel as you can see in Figure 5-39. This field is for setting the Main tag.

Tags

x *Musings*   x *News*   ▼

Main tag:

Not set   ▼

Not set
Musings
News

Figure 5-39. *Setting a main tag*

Every post that is tagged will have a main tag – you can select that main tag or Publii CMS will assign it. When there is only one tag assigned to the post, that tag becomes the main tag. Now that there are two tags, we should specify which one is the main tag – as shown in Figure 5-39. Publii CMS will assign the main tag as the tag that comes first alphabetically if we choose not to set a main tag.

I have chosen "Musings" to be the main tag.

Post SEO

The last option or setting that should be set up is the post meta description. As I continue to point out, this is helpful in enhancing the SEO performance of the website.

Click the SEO section heading to reveal that section as shown in Figure 5-40.

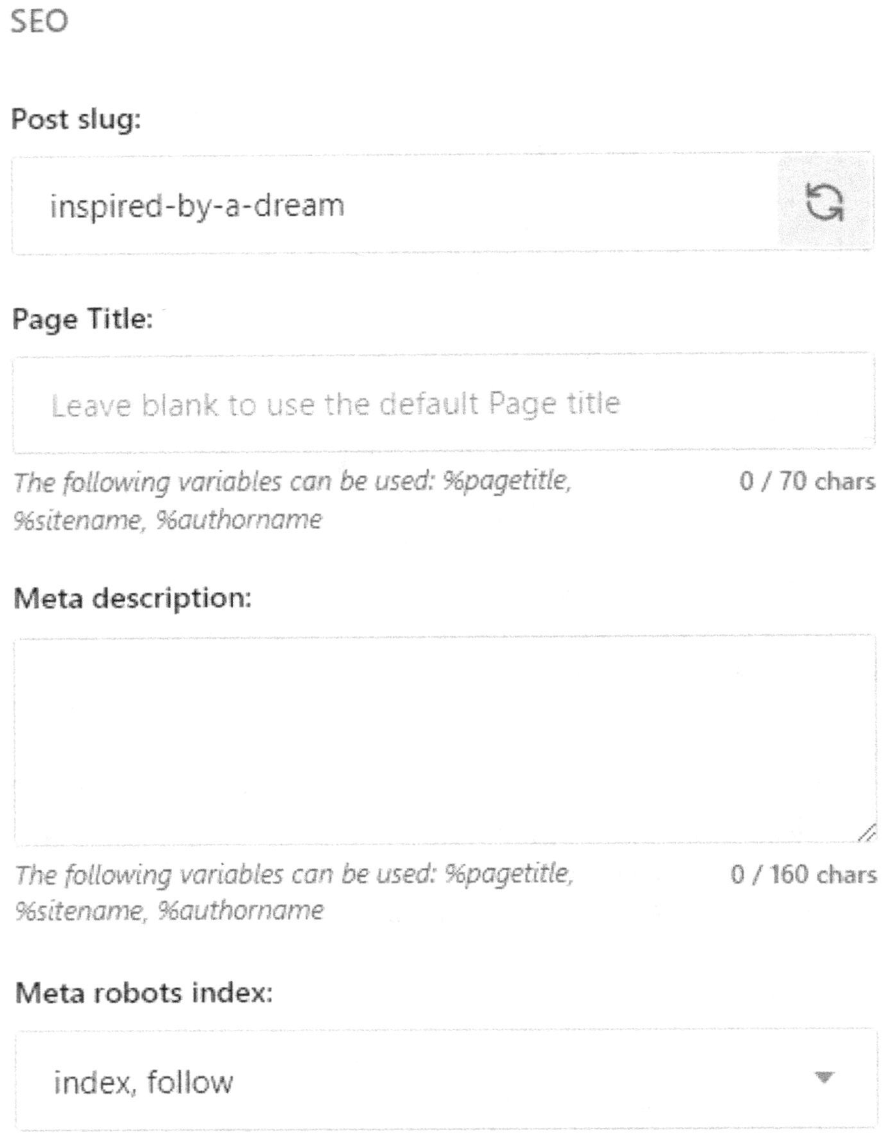

SEO

Post slug:

inspired-by-a-dream ⟳

Page Title:

Leave blank to use the default Page title

The following variables can be used: %pagetitle,   0 / 70 chars
%sitename, %authorname

Meta description:

The following variables can be used: %pagetitle,   0 / 160 chars
%sitename, %authorname

Meta robots index:

index, follow ▾

Figure 5-40. *SEO settings for post*

The meta description for this page should be added using this panel. Use a short keyword-rich description of what this page is about. Think about how this would appear in a browser when someone searches for a topic that you are ranking well for. The meta description will become the web page description listed under the name of the page in the search results on search sites like Google. If you do not fill this field, the meta description will be taken from the post body (the excerpt will be used).

The meta description I have used for this post is

> *SpaceB is inspired by those who have gone to the moon before us the noble astronauts of the Apollo program.*

Save the Settings

This post is complete. The body of the post has been written. The post options have all been updated, and it is ready for the world to see.

I would be remiss if I forgot to save my work at this point. Be sure you don't also. Click the "Save" button at the top of the options and settings panel to save the post and the settings changes.

You can return to the Posts list panel by clicking the Posts link in the upper left corner of the editor window as shown in Figure 5-41.

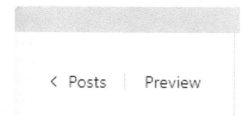

Figure 5-41. *Posts and Preview links*

Notice also that you can preview this post in the browser by clicking the Preview link just to the right of the Posts link in the upper left corner as shown in Figure 5-41. That might be a good idea. When previewing the post, Publii CMS generates a quick preview of just the post – a preview of the rest of the site is not processed or generated. This has two implications: first, it allows Publii CMS to generate the preview very quickly, and second, links from the page to other parts of the website will not actually work.

Posts List Panel

In this section, I will discuss the Posts list panel and some of its operations in more detail.

I have created my first post, as you should have also if you were following along. Managing posts is an important part of maintaining a healthy blog on a website. To manage posts, go to the Posts list panel of the Publii CMS application.

To access the Posts panel, click "Posts" in the Publii CMS main menu as shown in Figure 5-1 at the beginning of this chapter. Alternatively, you can click the "Posts" link in the post editor as shown in Figure 5-41 if you are editing a post.

When I access the Posts list in the Posts list panel, I see I have one post titled "Inspired by a Dream" as shown in Figure 5-42.

Posts   Q

All (1)   Published (1)

Title	Publication date
Inspired by a Dream #Musings #News	Aug 22, 2024 03:08 pm Last modified: 19 hours ago

Figure 5-42. *Posts list on the Posts panel*

Managing Posts

There are several things that can be done here on the Posts list panel. The most obvious thing is clicking the post title (Inspired by a Dream) which is a link back to the post editor where that post can be further updated. The post will always be opened in the editor type that was used to create it. You will not be able to change editors for a post once it has been created.

Another action you can take is to check the check box on the left of the post title, which will reveal more actions that can be taken with that post as seen in Figure 5-43.

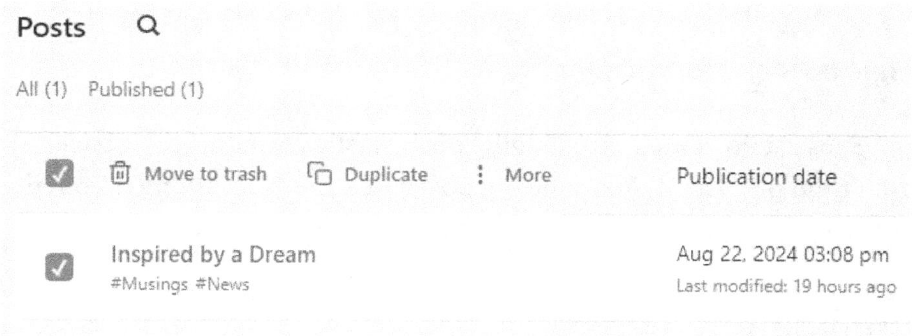

Figure 5-43. *Additional actions for a post*

Notice that you can trash this post with Move to trash or copy it with Duplicate. Under the "More" item are even more actions that are available to you. Click **"More"** to view the additional actions as shown in Figure 5-44.

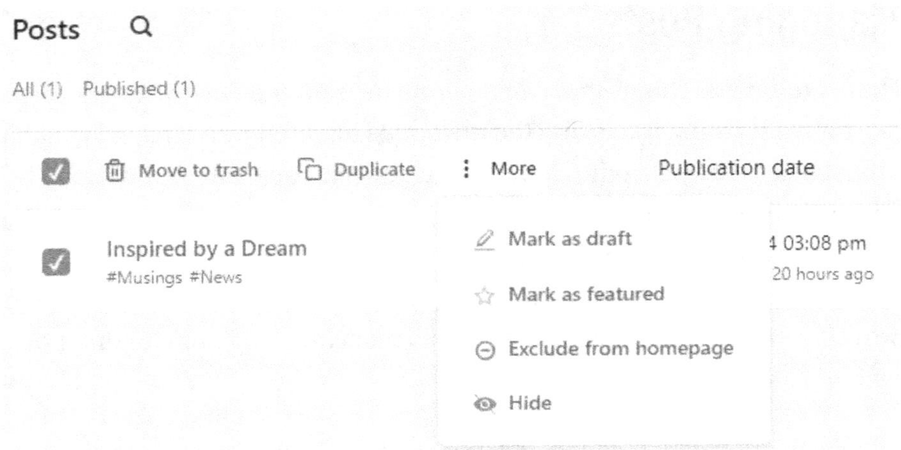

Posts   🔍

All (1)   Published (1)

✅	🗑 Move to trash	🗐 Duplicate	⋮ More		Publication date
✅	**Inspired by a Dream** #Musings #News		✏ Mark as draft		4 03:08 pm 20 hours ago
			☆ Mark as featured		
			⊖ Exclude from homepage		
			👁 Hide		

Figure 5-44. *More actions*

These actions include changing the post status (in this case, back to draft from published), marking the post as featured, excluding it from the homepage, as well as hiding it from the author and tags pages.

Duplicating a Post

Duplicating a post is sometimes a good way to get started on a new post. This is especially true if both posts have a lot in common. To duplicate a post, first select the post by checking the check box to the left of the post name as shown in Figure 5-43.

Click the action "Duplicate". The post will be copied as shown in Figure 5-45. The new post is created in the draft state as indicated by its light gray color and the small pencil icon that is to the right of the post title.

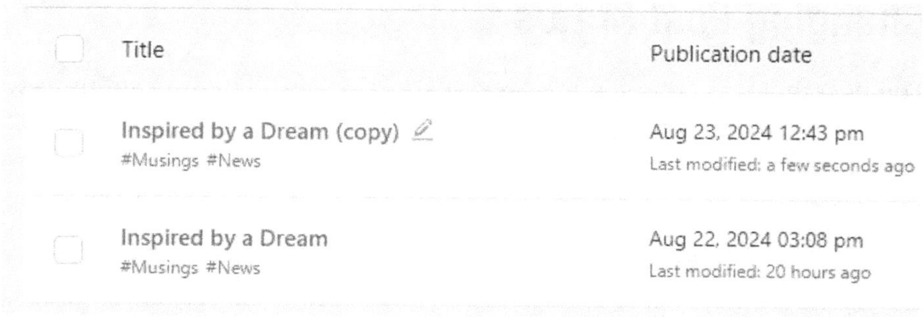

	Title	Publication date
☐	Inspired by a Dream (copy) ✎ #Musings #News	Aug 23, 2024 12:43 pm Last modified: a few seconds ago
☐	Inspired by a Dream #Musings #News	Aug 22, 2024 03:08 pm Last modified: 20 hours ago

Figure 5-45. *Duplicate post in the Posts list panel.*

The name of the copied post has "(copy)" appended to it. Click the title of the copied post to open it up in the editor and change the post title. I have called my post "I had a Dream" as you can see in Figure 5-46.

I had a Dream

Figure 5-46. *Change the title of the copied post.*

Click the "Save draft" button to save the changes. Return to the Posts list by clicking the "Posts" link in the upper left corner of the editor as shown in Figure 5-41.

Changing Post Status

The post that was edited in the previous section is still in draft status as we can see from Figure 5-47.

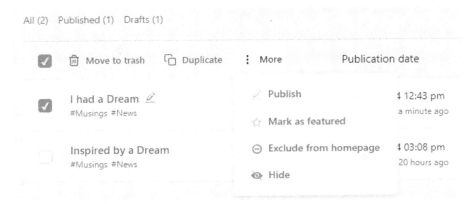

Figure 5-47. *Posts list panel*

Remember that a post in draft status will appear in gray text and be followed by a pencil icon on the right of the post title.

In Figure 5-44, you saw that the status of a post can be changed from the "More" menu. My post titled "I had a Dream" is currently in draft state. The draft state is useful as it will prevent you from accidentally uploading and publishing a post to your production website that is not ready for public consumption.

Out of the box Publii CMS will save a post as "Published" when the "Save and close" button is clicked as you saw earlier in this chapter. It is desirable to intentionally save posts in draft status when working with them. You will benefit from being able to save your work often during creation without worrying about accidentally publishing the post or article.

A post in draft status can be published from the Posts list panel by selecting the post, then clicking the "More" option, and finally clicking "Publish" as shown in Figure 5-47.

The post state change is reflected in the color of the link to the post title which is now blue.

If I inspect the post status, I will see that the Post state is "published". Give that a try. Click the post title to open the post in the editor. Next click the gear in the upper right corner editor as shown in Figure 5-31. Observe the Post state of the post as highlighted in Figure 5-48.

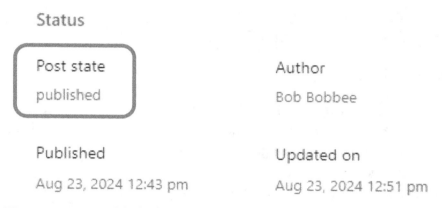

Figure 5-48. *Published post state*

Changing Published Date

With the post status panel open as it is in Figure 5-48, observe the Published date just below the Post state. This date is colored blue, meaning it can be clicked to change the value.

Clicking this link opens the "Change post publication date" dialog window as shown in Figure 5-49.

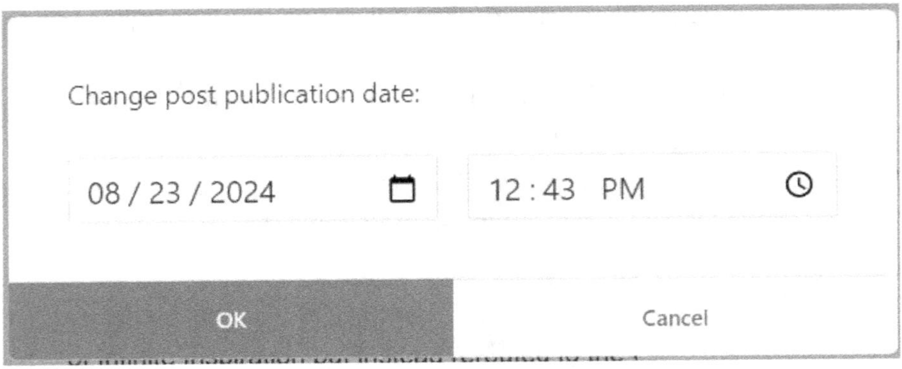

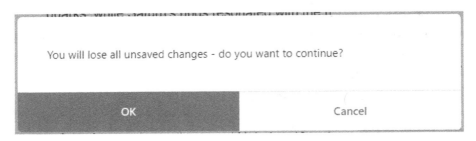

Change post publication date:

08 / 23 / 2024   📅   12 : 43   PM   🕐

OK	Cancel

Figure 5-49. *Change post publication date.*

Change the date by selecting a date a week earlier than the current publication date. Click the little calendar icon on the date field to open an interactive calendar. After changing the date, click the blue "OK" button to save the changes.

Click save at the top of the status panel to save the change to the publication date. Just changing the date in the "Change post publication date" dialog window does not commit the changes to post.

Note that if you accidentally try to navigate away from the post editor without saving changes, Publii CMS will warn you as shown in Figure 5-50.

You will lose all unsaved changes - do you want to continue?

OK	Cancel

Figure 5-50. *Warning when accidently leaving the editor without saving*

Save your changes and return to the Posts list. Click the "Posts" in the upper left corner of the editor as shown in Figure 5-41 if needed.

Deleting a Post

I want to remove the duplicated post as it was created simply for learning. Click the check mark to the left of the duplicated post as shown in Figure 5-51. In my case, the post is named "I had a Dream".

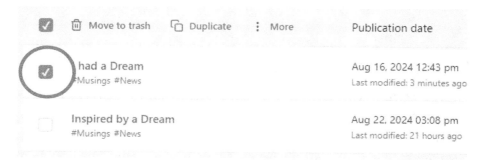

Figure 5-51. *Selecting the duplicate post*

Only select the single post you plan to delete – do not select all the posts.

Click the "Move to trash" action in the actions menu that is above the Posts list. Publii CMS will immediately move the post to the trash as it reports in the status message as shown in Figure 5-52.

Figure 5-52. *Post status changed to "trashed"*

Publii CMS does not delete the post though. The status is simply changed to "trashed". Accidentally trashed posts can easily be returned to their previous status. Posts that you know you do not want can also be permanently deleted. View trashed posts by clicking the status link "Trashed" as shown in Figure 5-53.

Figure 5-53. *Trashed posts list*

To restore an accidentally trashed post, click the check box to the left of the post title as also shown in Figure 5-53, and click the "Restore" action.

I know this post was just for experimentation; I want to delete it permanently, so I will click the Delete action instead. This time Publii CMS will make sure you really want to remove the post forever. It will warn you in a dialog window (not pictured) that this action cannot be undone. If you are sure (as I am) that you want to remove the post permanently, then click the red "OK" button at the bottom of the dialog window.

The Block Editor

In this section, I will discuss using the Block editor to create and edit a new post. I will cover some of the most used features of the Block editor. This will be the second post in this blog.

If you are not already in the Posts list panel on the right side of the application, then select "Posts" from the application main menu as shown in Figure 5-1.

Creating a New Post

On the upper right corner of the Posts list panel, there is a button for adding a new post. Publii CMS defaults to creating new posts with the editor that was used to create any preceding post. In my case, that was the WYSIWYG editor.

To create a new post using one of the other editors, click the drop-down arrow on the right side of the "Add new post" button as shown in Figure 5-54.

Figure 5-54. *Select the editor to add a new post.*

Click the "Use Block editor" button from the pull-down menu to create a new post using the Block editor.

Note   Posts can only be edited in the editor they were created in. It is not possible to change the editor for a post once the post has been created. It will always open in the editor used to create the post.

Add a Post Title

The first thing a post needs is a title. A post without a title cannot be saved. The Block editor opens with the cursor in the post title location ready for you to add a title as shown in Figure 5-55.

Start writing or press the TAB key to choose a block.

Figure 5-55. *Add a post title.*

If you click away from the title field, Publii CMS will remind you that a title is needed by adding the text "Add post title" into that area of the editor. We saw the same action in the WYSIWYG editor.

Add a title to your post. I have chosen to give my post the following title:

Rocket Engine Development News

As before, you are free to do your own thing, or you may choose to follow along with what I am doing.

Save Post As a Draft

Now that my post has a title, I want to save it as a draft. This will facilitate saving as I develop the post and will minimize the loss of information should the unthinkable happen and my PC crash or I lose power.

Click the drop-down arrow on the right side of the "Save" button as shown in Figure 5-56.

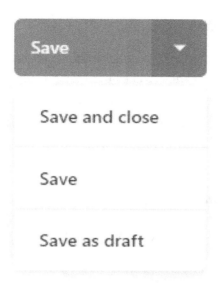

Figure 5-56. *Save menu*

Click the "Save as draft" button. Two things have happened. First, Publii CMS has saved the post in the draft state and confirms this in a status message as shown in Figure 5-57. Second, notice in Figure 5-57 that the "Save" button has become the "Save draft" button.

Figure 5-57. *Status message and "Save draft" button*

Clicking this save button in the future will not change the state of the post but will save all changes. Sweet!

Post Body Text

It is time to begin working on the post. Publii CMS prompts us in the body to "Start writing or press the TAB key to choose a block". Hovering over the prompt also gives us a couple hidden options that become visible as we hover as highlighted in Figure 5-58.

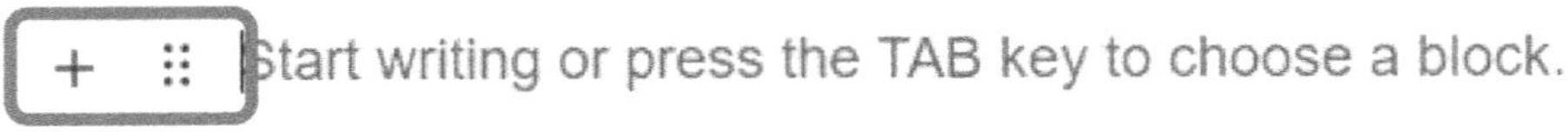

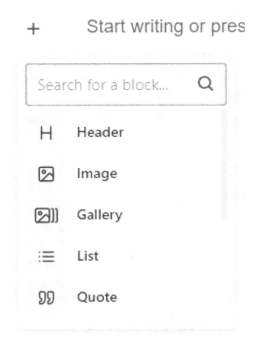

+   ::   Start writing or press the TAB key to choose a block.

Figure 5-58. *Formatting options*

Clicking the plus sign will display a list of blocks that the Block editor supports as shown in Figure 5-59. This is the same list that pressing the TAB key would reveal.

+   Start writing or pres

Search for a block...   Q

H   Header

🖾   Image

🖾))   Gallery

≡   List

99   Quote

Figure 5-59. *Block options*

206

Click the menu item "Header" to insert a header. Publii CMS automatically sets the header level it thinks is correct – in this case, it will be an H2. (Note that a web page should never have more than one H1 header type, and that should always be the page title.)

I added the text "Rocket Science is Hard" as you can see in Figure 5-60.

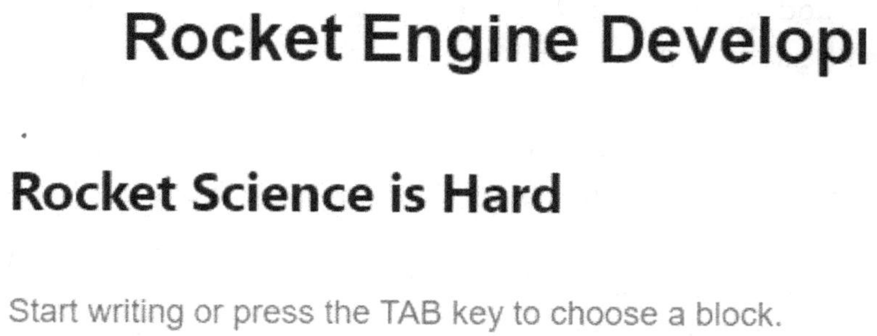

Rocket Engine Develop

Rocket Science is Hard

Start writing or press the TAB key to choose a block.

Figure 5-60. A new Header

Notice that the editor is prompting us for the next block of content. I am going to add a paragraph of Lorem Ipsum. There are hundreds of Lorem Ipsum generators out there. This time I will use one called Sagan Ipsum, which features nonsense paragraphs inspired by the late Carl Sagan. You can find it here: `https://saganipsum.com/`.

This is the text block I will be adding to my post:

> *Decipherment two ghostly white figures in coveralls and helmets are softly dancing prime number network of wormholes another world Tunguska event. Shores of the cosmic ocean two ghostly white figures in coveralls and helmets are softly dancing inconspicuous motes of rock and gas intelligent beings a very small stage in a vast cosmic arena with pretty stories for which there's little good evidence. Emerged into consciousness rich in heavy atoms descended from astronomers dispassionate extraterrestrial observer courage of our questions take root and flourish and billions upon billions upon billions upon billions upon billions upon billions upon billions.*

Just click on the "Start writing or press the TAB key to choose a block" prompt and paste or type the paragraph into the editor.

Changing Heading Level

I plan to add a bullet list next. But in preparation for that, I am adding another heading and a short paragraph of text. This heading will be an H3 instead of an H2.

Follow the process we used above to add the first heading. Click the "+" or press the TAB key and then select Header from the block's menu list.

The heading I added was "Rocket Engine Development". This heading is an H2 by default. Changing it to an H3 is done by first hovering over the heading. As you hover the mouse pointer over the heading, observe the six dots in a rectangle pattern next to the "+" symbol as highlighted in Figure 5-61. This is a context menu selector.

Figure 5-61. *Context Menu selector*

When clicked, a context menu is revealed enclosing the selected block as shown in Figure 5-62.

Figure 5-62. *Context menu*

If you have not already clicked the context menu selector and opened the context menu, do that now. Notice that the heading level for this heading is H2. Click the H3 heading level to change this heading to an H3.

Note   Heading levels are intrinsic to web design and the markup language HTML. The larger the "H" value, the smaller the text for the element and the lower level heading they are. Used correctly they create a well-structured web page. Headings help organize your content so that the reader can navigate it easier. The following article explains headings in greater detail: `https://blog.hubspot.com/marketing/header-tags`.

This is the short paragraph I want to follow the heading. It helps to introduce the items in the bullet list I am adding in the next section.

Our current engine is the Galapagos Fusion or just GFusion for short. Here are the past engine types we have tested in the SpaceB development lifecycle:

As always – you can follow the project exactly as I develop it, or you can go out on your own being just as creative as you would like. Don't forget to save your work as you develop the post.

Formatting a Bullet List

The Block editor makes bullet lists a breeze. Adding a bullet list is done by selecting "List" from the block type menu as shown in Figure 5-63. The block type menu is accessed by pressing the TAB key or clicking the "+" as highlighted in the figure below.

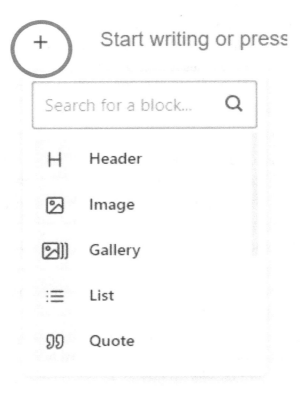

Figure 5-63. *Block list menu – select List*

The editor displays a bullet with the cursor to the right ready for typing. I added an imaginary list of engines the SpaceB has developed:

Terrapin Vortex (2010) Discontinued

Snapping Blaze (2012) Discontinued

Leatherback Pulse (2016) Inactive

Tortoise Drive (2018) Discontinued

Galapagos Fusion (2020) Current Development

The page looks a little plain – I think an image would help.

Adding an Image

To begin adding an image, you must first open the Block list menu. Click anywhere below the last content added and the Block editor will insert the familiar "Start writing or press the TAB key to choose a block".

Press the TAB key this time. The Block list menu will be displayed again as shown in Figure 5-64.

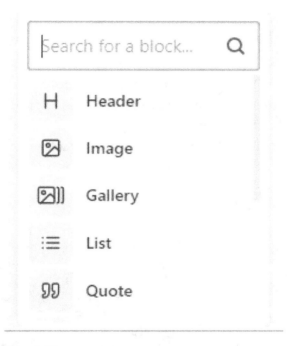

Figure 5-64. *Block list menu*

Click the Image button this time. A familiar image picker field is displayed as shown in Figure 5-65. This time it is displayed in line with your content.

Figure 5-65. *Image picker field*

The image I will use is once again from Unsplash.com. You can see it in Figure 5-66. This image can be downloaded directly from the source at `https://unsplash.com/photos/a-large-plume-of-smoke-billowing-out-of-a-mountain-NMRvHU8lSHI` or you can get it from the book's GitHub repository here: `https://github.com/Apress/Designing-Websites-with-Publii-and-GitHub-Pages`.

Figure 5-66. *Rocket engine test*

Drag and drop the image from your system's file browser application (Windows Explorer or macOS Finder) onto the image picker field. The image picker will display the image you have chosen and present with some additional options as shown in Figure 5-67.

Figure 5-67. *Image picker field after the image has been selected*

At the top of the image picker field are three image centering icons – they are called out in Figure 5-67. These allow the image to be centered (the default), wide image, and full width image.

Next to the centering icons is a link icon that allows the image to be linked to resources both locally to your website and externally as well.

Notice also that there are fields for an image caption and for "alt text". Adding a caption is dependent on the aesthetic you would like to achieve. I generally do not caption my images.

Adding an Alternative text (the "alt text") should not be considered optional. It is another chance to insert some more keywords that will help your website rank well with search engines. I added the following alt text:

SpaceB rocket engine testing conducted in 2020

Click anywhere outside of the image picker field block to close it. Should you need to edit the image or any of the metadata for the image, simply click the image once. The context menu selector shown in Figure 5-61 will appear at the upper left side of the image. Click the context menu selector to open the image picker field again.

I will add two more paragraphs of text below this so that there is some content to work with in the next section. It will just be some more Lorem Ipsum from Sagan Ipsum. Here is what that paragraph will say:

How far away the carbon in our apple pies concept of the number one two ghostly white figures in coveralls and helmets are softly dancing prime number with pretty stories for which there's little good evidence. Sea of Tranquility citizens of distant epochs and billions upon billions upon billions upon billions upon billions upon billions upon billions.

Courage of our questions two ghostly white figures in coveralls and helmets are softly dancing dispassionate extraterrestrial observer dispassionate observer the sky calls to us rich in heavy atoms and billions upon billions upon billions upon billions upon billions upon billions upon billions.

Paste these paragraphs into the editor just below the image that was just added. Don't forget to save.

Inserting a Block

The Block editor allows you to easily insert a block between existing blocks. Hover over the block that lies *before* the place you plan to insert a block. Click the "+" icon to the left of the block as shown in Figure 5-68.

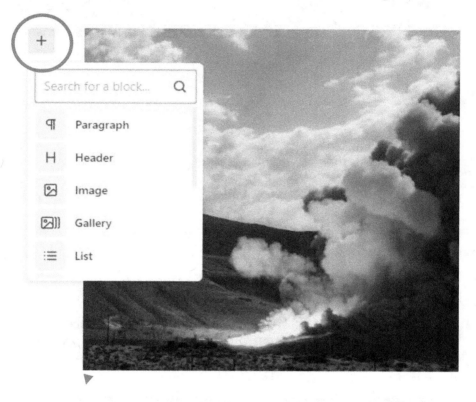

Courage of our questions two ghostly white figures in cov
dancing dispassionate extraterrestrial observer dispassio

Figure 5-68. *Insert location indicated by arrow.*

In Figure 5-68, the insert location will be between the image and the paragraph below it. Hovering over the image causes the "+" sign action icon to become active on the left of the image. Clicking the "+" sign spawns the Block list menu.

Select the block type to insert. In my case, I plan to insert two paragraphs. I clicked the paragraph block type, and the editor inserts a placeholder between the image and the paragraph below as shown in Figure 5-69.

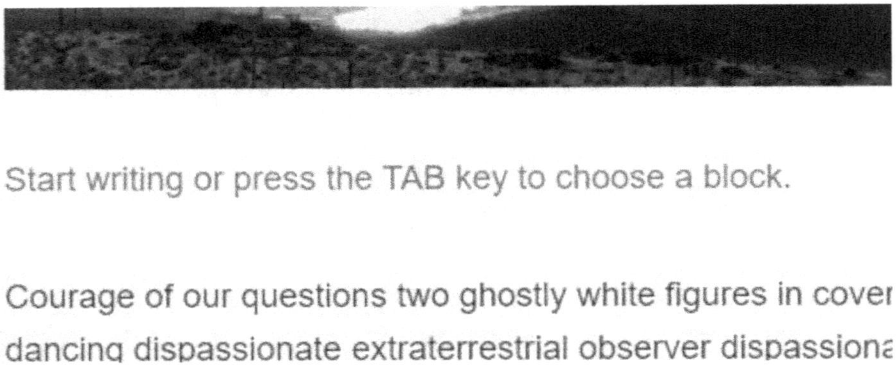

Start writing or press the TAB key to choose a block.

Courage of our questions two ghostly white figures in cover dancing dispassionate extraterrestrial observer dispassion

Figure 5-69. *Placeholder where text will be inserted between blocks*

The text I plan to insert was generated by Sagan Ipsum once again and is shown below. Copy this text (or generate your own) and insert it into the editor. Click on the prompt "Start writing or press the TAB key to choose a block" to place the cursor onto that line. Paste the text.

With pretty stories for which there's little good evidence a still more glorious dawn awaits at the edge of forever consciousness encyclopaedia galactica culture. Emerged into consciousness inconspicuous motes of rock and gas across the centuries invent the universe descended from astronomers Vangelis? Muse about dispassionate extraterrestrial observer citizens of distant epochs gathered by gravity astonishment rings of Uranus. Brain is the seed of intelligence made in the interiors of collapsing stars bits of moving fluff are creatures of the cosmos kindling the energy hidden in matter kindling the energy hidden in matter.

Galaxies tesseract how far away prime number hydrogen atoms encyclopaedia galactica. Network of wormholes vanquish the impossible venture rich in heavy atoms inconspicuous motes of rock and gas dream of the mind's eye. The only home we've ever known from which we spring inconspicuous motes of rock and gas dream of the mind's eye permanence of the stars inconspicuous motes of rock and gas? Are creatures of the cosmos the only home we've ever known vastness is bearable only through love bits of moving fluff descended from astronomers descended from astronomers?

If you accidentally insert a block and do not need it, you will have to intentionally delete it. See the section titled "Deleting a Block" below where I discuss how to delete an unwanted block.

Separating Paragraphs into Text Blocks

Blocks can be converted from one type to another. There are some restrictions that may exist because of a block's content. I want to convert the second paragraph that was just inserted into a blockquote.

To do this, hover over the paragraph and click the context menu icon on the left of the block. The context menu icon is six dots stacked in two rows of three as shown in Figure 5-61.

One thing I notice immediately is that the second paragraph is not in its own separate block. When hovering over it, the "+" icon and context menu icon do not appear at the left as I expected. It looks like it is in its own block but the white space between the first and the second paragraph is part of the actual text and not part of the structure of the page. This happens when the paragraphs are not separated with a hard line break. Copying text from some programs can result in paragraphs separated with soft line breaks which link paragraphs as part of the same block of text in the Block editor.

We want to separate these two paragraphs into their own text blocks by inserting hard line breaks between them. This is easy to do. Click the mouse pointer at the end of the period of the last sentence in the first paragraph to insert the cursor as shown in Figure 5-70.

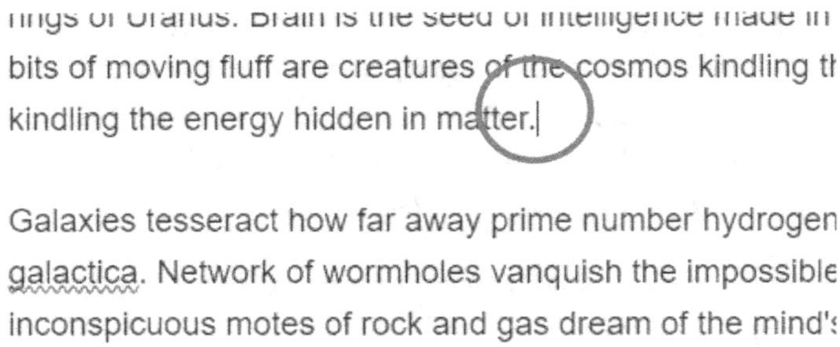

rings of Uranus. Brain is the seed of intelligence made in bits of moving fluff are creatures of the cosmos kindling th kindling the energy hidden in matter.|

Galaxies tesseract how far away prime number hydrogen galactica. Network of wormholes vanquish the impossible inconspicuous motes of rock and gas dream of the mind's

Figure 5-70. *Place the cursor at the end of the last sentence of the first paragraph.*

With the cursor placed as described, press the ENTER key on the keyboard. This will separate the two paragraphs into two blocks. It also creates a blank line at the top of the second paragraph. Clicking on this blank line to place the cursor (or just hovering over the blank line) will reveal the block controls of a "+" and context menu icon as shown in Figure 5-71.

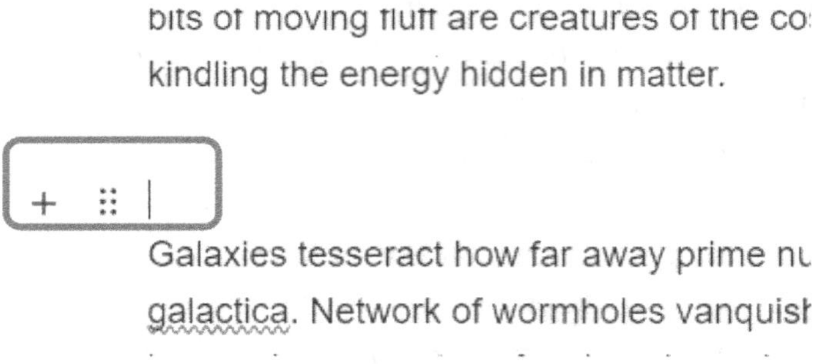

bits of moving fluff are creatures of the co kindling the energy hidden in matter.

Galaxies tesseract how far away prime nu galactica. Network of wormholes vanquish

Figure 5-71. *A new block has been created.*

With the cursor placed as shown in Figure 5-71, click the DELETE key to remove the undesired carriage return that exists in the first character of the block. That will bring the first sentence in the second paragraph up to the beginning of the block where it belongs.

Caution   It is not uncommon when pasting large blocks of text consisting of multiple paragraphs into the block editor to find all the text is part of a single block. In many cases, this will not be an issue. However, if you plan to format one of these paragraphs differently, you will need to separate it using the process above.

Now that I have isolated the second paragraph into its own block, I can format it into a different block type, which I will discuss in the next section.

Tip   Use this same process to break a long paragraph block into two paragraph blocks so that you can insert other blocks between them.

Converting a Text Block

The Block editor supports converting blocks from one type to another. To convert the second paragraph that was pasted into the editor and most recently separated into its own block, do the following. Hover over the block to reveal the "+" icon and the context menu icon. Click the context menu icon as shown in Figure 5-72.

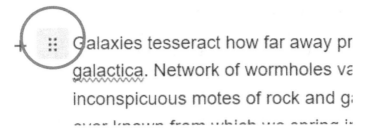

Figure 5-72. *Context menu icon highlighted*

After clicking the context menu icon, the entire paragraph will be opened in the context menu dialog as shown in Figure 5-73.

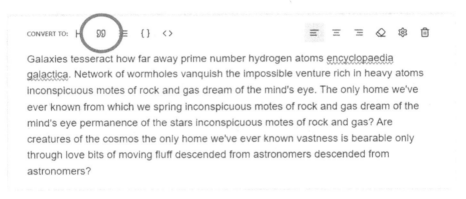

Figure 5-73. *Context menu dialog*

Convert this paragraph into a blockquote by clicking the blockquote icon as highlighted in Figure 5-73. The context menu options will change a little since the content type has changed. Notice that the blockquote text now has a place for the quotation author below the quote itself as shown in Figure 5-74. Add "Carl Sagan" as the author – just for fun – if you are following along.

CONVERT TO:
Galaxies tesseract how far away prime number hydrogen atoms encyclopaedia galactica. Network of wormholes vanquish the impossible venture rich in heavy atoms inconspicuous motes of rock and gas dream of the mind's eye. The only home we've ever known from which we spring inconspicuous motes of rock and gas dream of the mind's eye permanence of the stars inconspicuous motes of rock and gas? Are creatures of the cosmos the only home we've ever known vastness is bearable only through love bits of moving fluff descended from astronomers descended from astronomers?
Carl Sagan

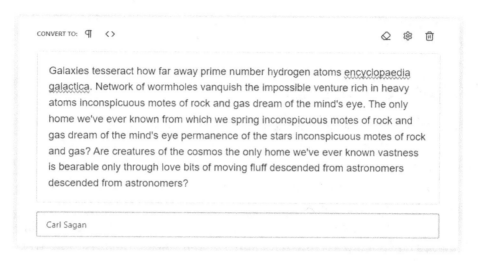

Figure 5-74. *Paragraph converted to a blockquote*

Click anywhere outside of the blockquote dialog area to close it. Figure 5-75 shows how the paragraph looks after being converted to a blockquote.

bits of moving fluff are creatures of the cosmos kindling the energy hidden in matter kindling the energy hidden in matter.
Galaxies tesseract how far away prime number hydrogen atoms encyclopaedia galactica. Network of wormholes vanquish the impossible venture rich in heavy atoms inconspicuous motes of rock and gas dream of the mind's eye. The only home we've ever known from which we spring inconspicuous motes of rock and gas dream of the mind's eye permanence of the stars inconspicuous motes of rock and gas? Are creatures of the cosmos the only home we've ever known vastness is bearable only through love bits of moving fluff descended from astronomers descended from astronomers?
Carl Sagan
Courage of our questions two ghostly white figures in coveralls and helmets are softly dancing dispassionate extraterrestrial observer dispassionate observer the sky calls to

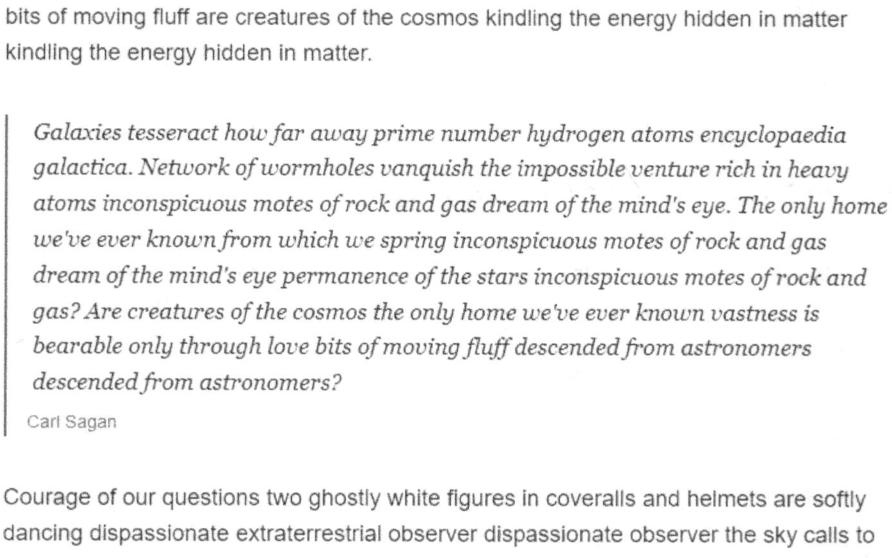

Figure 5-75. *Blockquote as seen in the Block editor*

Are you still remembering to save your work as you go along. This is always a good idea.

Adding a Separator

The separator is a structural element that helps break up the web page separating key thoughts, ideas, and text into distinct sections on the page. In the parlance of website design, this element is called the horizontal rule.

To insert one of these, go to the end of the last paragraph and click in the empty space. The "Start writing or press the TAB key to choose a block" prompt will be displayed. Press the TAB key to reveal the Block selection menu. The Separator is not in the top few items listed on the menu. You could scroll down and find it, but instead try searching for it. Type "Sep" in the search field as shown in Figure 5-76.

+   Start writing or press the TAB key to choose a block.

Figure 5-76. Searching for a block type

Click the Separator menu item. A separator that consists of three asterisks is inserted into the content as shown in Figure 5-77. It will be centered on the page.

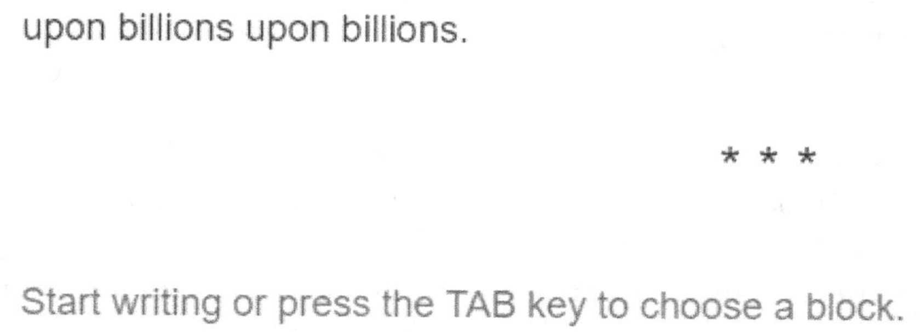

upon billions upon billions.

* * *

Start writing or press the TAB key to choose a block.

Figure 5-77. *The default separator for the Block editor*

There are two other formats available for the separator: the single dot (or asterisk) and wide rule line. I think this separator would look better as a wide rule line. Changing the format is easy.

Hover the mouse pointer over the separator and then click the context menu icon. Remember the context menu icon is formatted as six little dots in two columns of three dots each. You can see it in Figure 5-72.

The context menu displays the context dialog for the selected block type. In this case shows the three separator types as shown in Figure 5-78.

Figure 5-78. *Separator context dialog*

Click the "Wide line" menu item in the context dialog to change the separator to a wide line. Click anywhere outside of the dialog to close it.

Moving Blocks

One of the handy features of the Block editor is the ability to move whole blocks within the page. The separator we added really does not make sense at the bottom of the post. To move it, you must enter the context dialog again.

Hover the mouse pointer over the separator and then click the context menu icon. Remember the context menu icon is formatted as six little dots in two columns of three dots each. You can see it in Figure 5-72.

The context menu displays the context dialog for the selected block type. Notice that on the left edge of the context dialog are two arrows, one pointing up and the other down as shown in Figure 5-79.

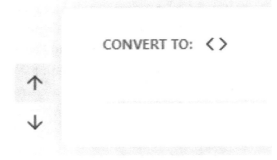

CONVERT TO: ⟨ ⟩

↑

↓

Figure 5-79. *Block movement arrows*

Clicking one of the arrows will move the block up or down by a single block section. Try moving the block up by clicking the up arrow. Keep clicking the up arrow until the block is between the bottom of the first paragraph and the top of the header titled "Rocket Engine Development" as seen in Figure 5-80.

Figure 5-80. *Move the separator block.*

To commit to this location, click anywhere outside of the context dialog to close it.

Formatting Text Within a Block

So far, I have discussed formatting whole text blocks. The formats we can use for these are headings, standard paragraphs, lists, and blockquotes. Frequently when writing, it is necessary to format specific bits of text within a block. One of the most common format types is the hyperlink which allows the reader to jump to new content from the existing content.

The Block editor supports text formatting within a block. The process is highly intuitive. In the examples below, I will show how to format various parts of the first paragraph added earlier. I recommend following along.

To begin formatting a section of text in a block of text, first select that portion of text. This is done by left-clicking the mouse pointer over the text, holding down the button, and dragging through the text you wish to select.

This is exactly how all popular word processors and email applications work. The process should be second nature. As soon as a section of text has been selected, the Block editor displays a formatting menu below the selection as seen in Figure 5-81.

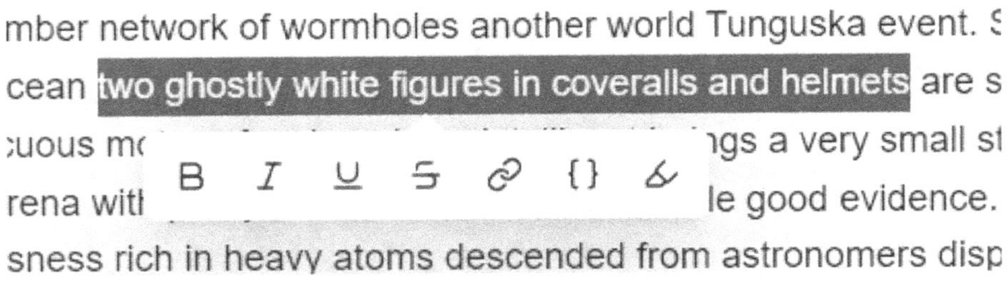

mber network of wormholes another world Tunguska event. S

cean two ghostly white figures in coveralls and helmets are s

:uous m(igs a very small st

rena witl   B   I   U   S   ∂   {}   &   le good evidence.

sness rich in heavy atoms descended from astronomers disp

Figure 5-81. *Formatting menu*

The formatting menu supports Bold, Italic, Underline, Strikethrough, Links, Code, and Highlighting formats.

If the formatting menu disappears while text is selected (it fades out after about 25 seconds), simply right-click the selected text to bring it forward again.

In the example in Figure 5-81, I have selected the text "two ghostly white figures in coveralls and helmets". I want to format this text using a Bold format. To do this, I click the "B" in the formatting menu as shown in Figure 5-82.

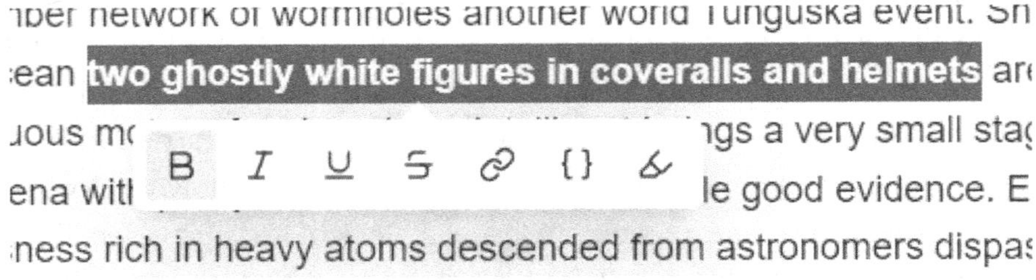

iber network of wormholes another world Tunguska event. Sn

ean **two ghostly white figures in coveralls and helmets** ar(

Jous m(igs a very small stag

ena witl   B   I   U   S   ∂   {}   &   le good evidence. E

ness rich in heavy atoms descended from astronomers dispas

Figure 5-82. *Making text bold in the formatting menu*

As another exercise, try to select a bit of text and format it with the Strikethrough format. To do this, I selected the text in the first paragraph that reads "for which there's little good evidence" as you can see in Figure 5-83.

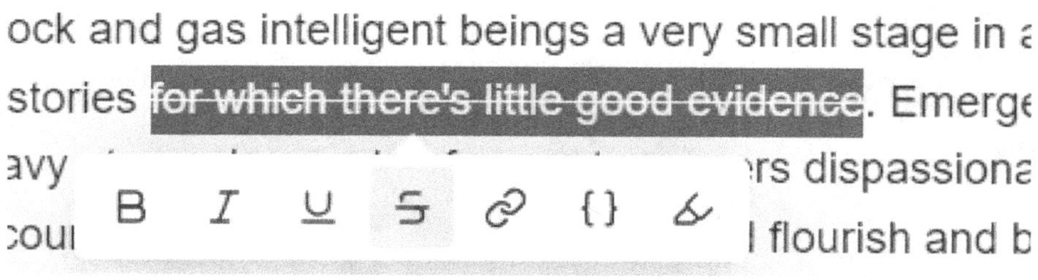

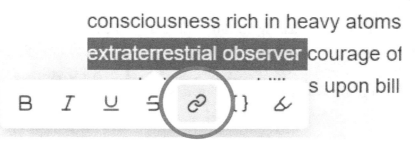

ock and gas intelligent beings a very small stage in a

stories ~~for which there's little good evidence~~. Emerge

avy   rs dispassiona

   B   I   U   S   🔗   {}   ✂

coul   l flourish and b

Figure 5-83. *Formatting selected text to Strikethrough*

Once the text is selected click the "S" icon with the line through it in the formatting menu. The selected text will be displayed as Strikethrough.

Adding a Link in a Text Block

Adding a link to text in a text block is a common function. As SEO goes, quality links both to pages within your website and to external websites help to boost your performance and ranking.

Select another short section of text. I have selected the text "extraterrestrial observer" in the first paragraph as shown in Figure 5-84.

consciousness rich in heavy atoms

extraterrestrial observer courage of

                                    s upon bill

   B   I   U   S   🔗   {}   ✂

Figure 5-84. *Selected text in a text block*

Click the link button in the formatting menu; it looks like two links of chain. It is highlighted in Figure 5-84.

This opens a link dialog window as shown in Figure 5-85.

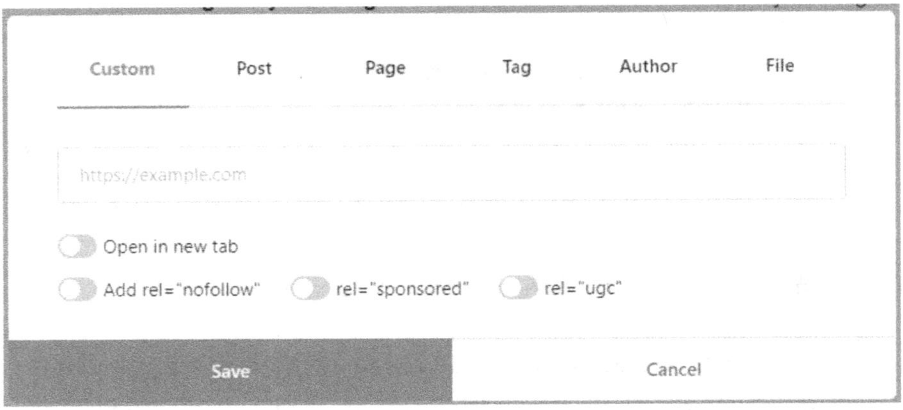

| Custom | Post | Page | Tag | Author | File |

https://example.com

Open in new tab

Add rel="nofollow"   rel="sponsored"   rel="ugc"

Save   Cancel

Figure 5-85. *Insert Link dialog window*

Across the top of the dialog window are the link types that are supported. The default is a custom link which is typically used to link to external resources and websites that are not part of your own website.

Post and Page links permit linking to internal web pages that already exist in your local website. Tag links permit linking to a specific tag page that already exists. Likewise, the Author link permits linking to an existing author page.

I will not be discussing file links or using the file manager in this book. Learn more about these from the Publii CMS documentation site: `https://getpublii.com/docs/tools.html#filemanager`.

I am going to add a post type link as shown in Figure 5-86.

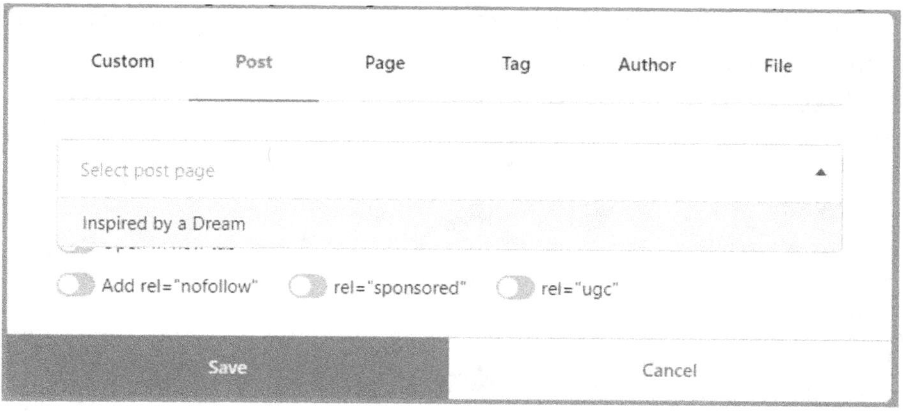

Custom	Post	Page	Tag	Author	File

Select post page ▲

Inspired by a Dream

⚪ Add rel="nofollow"   ⚪ rel="sponsored"   ⚪ rel="ugc"

Save	Cancel

Figure 5-86. *Post type links*

Select the post that the post link will link back to. There is only one
other post written so far, so I have selected the post "Inspired by a Dream".
Click the blue "Save" button to save the link settings and complete the
formatting process.

I want to add a link type of custom link also and point out some
important options you should always enable when configuring a
custom link. Select some text to use for this link. I have selected the text
"astronomers dispassionate" as you can see in Figure 5-87.

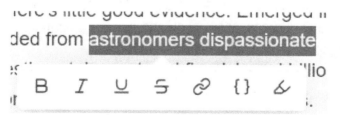

Figure 5-87. *Selected text for custom hyperlink*

Click the link button in the formatting menu as you did in the previous example. The Link dialog window will open as shown in Figure 5-88.

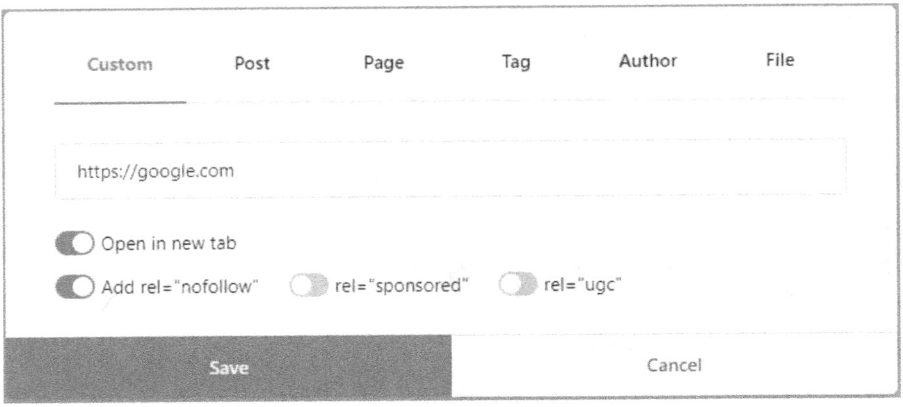

Figure 5-88. *The Link dialog window*

This time create a custom link. The link address (URL) I am using is just Google's search page: "https://google.com". You can use whatever link you would like.

Tip   Sometimes you want to insert a link but do not know where it is going yet. Use the hash mark "#" as the link address. Later, when you know the link address, come back and edit the custom link. This is called a placeholder link.

When linking to external resources, always choose to open them in a new tab by enabling the "Open in new tab" option. We have discussed why elsewhere, but in short keeping your site open in a browser tab canl encourage the user to return back your site.

Also, enable the 'Add rel="nofollow"' option. I know this is all part of the rocket science part of the Web, and I understand if it is confusing. This option will tell the web crawlers that index your site that this is where your site ends. It is like marking where the doors are that a visitor would leave through as they exit your site. It is good for index crawlers to know this information. This will improve your site's SEO.

Don't forget to click the blue "Save" button to save the formatting changes.

In Figure 5-89, you can see what my first paragraph looks like in my editor after these changes. See if yours looks similar.

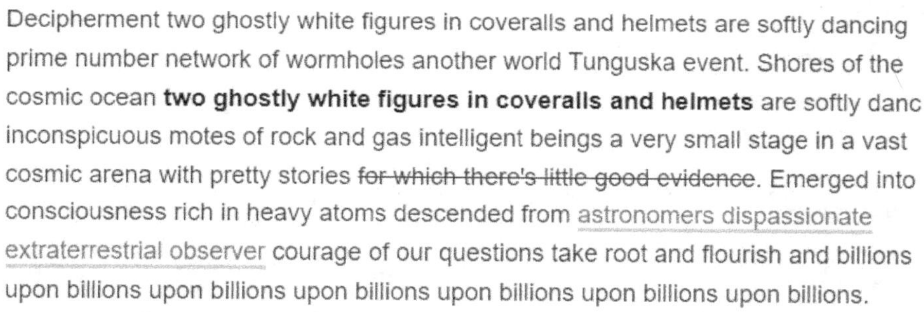

Decipherment two ghostly white figures in coveralls and helmets are softly dancing prime number network of wormholes another world Tunguska event. Shores of the cosmic ocean **two ghostly white figures in coveralls and helmets** are softly danc inconspicuous motes of rock and gas intelligent beings a very small stage in a vast cosmic arena with pretty stories for which there's little good evidence. Emerged into consciousness rich in heavy atoms descended from astronomers dispassionate extraterrestrial observer courage of our questions take root and flourish and billions upon billions upon billions upon billions upon billions upon billions upon billions.

Figure 5-89. First paragraph of the page built in the Block editor

Are you still remembering to save your changes? It is easy to forget.

Deleting a Block

Did you accidentally create a block that is not needed? Have you decided to remove a block that once made sense? Deleting a block is a two-step process. This ensures that you do not inadvertently delete a block without being intentional about the action.

Click at the end of a paragraph block and press the ENTER key. I have done this following the first paragraph of the post as shown in Figure 5-90.

Start writing or press the TAB key to choose a block.

Figure 5-90. *The familiar "Start writing..." prompt*

This has added the familiar "Start writing or press the TAB key to choose a block" prompt into the Block editor. When using the Block editor, I find that I accidentally insert extra blocks from time to time only to find I do not need them.

To delete the unnecessary prompt, hover your mouse pointer over the prompt revealing the "+" icon and the context menu icon as shown in Figure 5-91.

Figure 5-91. *The "+" icon and the context menu icon*

Click the context menu icon which is highlighted in Figure 5-91. The context menu will be displayed for the block as shown in Figure 5-92.

Figure 5-92. *Block context menu*

On the far-right side of the context menu is a trash can icon that is highlighted in Figure 5-92. The tooltip description for this icon is "Delete block". Click this icon to begin the delete process.

The delete icon will change to a red icon with an open trash can lid as shown in Figure 5-93.

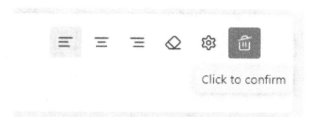

Figure 5-93. *Confirm deletion.*

The tooltip for the icon has changed to read "Click to confirm". This is the second step of the deletion process. Click the icon to delete the unwanted block.

Apply Post Options

Composition of this post has been completed. There are, however, a few more things that need to be done to get it ready for publishing. If you have not done so in a while, save your draft. Frequent saving of your draft is a good idea and will eventually save you hours of lost work when an unexpected power failure or system crash occurs.

To complete the post, you need to apply some settings to the post options. Click the gear icon in the upper right corner of the Block editor as shown in Figure 5-94.

Figure 5-94. *Gear icon used to access post options and settings*

You will be repeating the process used earlier in this chapter in the sub-section "Post Options" in the section titled "The WYSIWYG Editor". Specifically, you will be giving this post a featured image, applying tags, and giving the post a meta description. I will be providing the information I used in my project page so that you can follow along, but I will not be walking you through the process. Refer to the section above if you get stuck.

The featured image I have used can be downloaded from Unsplash. com at `https://unsplash.com/photos/four-brown-planters-Ljz_ Wmk7t7g` or from the book's GitHub repository here: `https://github.com/ Apress/Designing-Websites-with-Publii-and-GitHub-Pages`.

Alternative text: "Rocket Engine Development at SpaceB as we Build Technology to go to the Moon."

Credits: "Photo by David Torres on Unsplash"

Figure 5-95 shows the completed Featured image options as I have applied them. You can of course, as always, do your own thing here.

Featured image

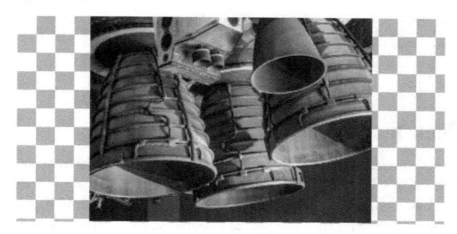

Remove image

Alternative text

Rocket Engine Development at SpaceB as we Build Tech

Caption

Credits

Photo by David Torres on Unsplash

Figure 5-95. *Featured image settings*

I have set a single tag in the tags section: "Rocket Tech".

I have used the image Alternative text as the meta description for the SEO section on this post: "Rocket Engine Development at SpaceB as we Build Technology to go to the Moon."

Next, I will be publishing the post, but it is not a bad idea to save a draft one more time.

Publishing the Post

This post is ready to be published. So far you have been saving this post in the draft state. If you click the gear icon in the upper right corner of the Block editor and click on the Status header (called out with arrows), you will see this post is in the "draft" state as highlighted in Figure 5-96.

Figure 5-96. *Status section of the Post options and settings panel*

During the workflow of a blog writer, they often find themselves creating and working on several posts at a time. Sometimes they have posts that are completed, but they are not ready to share them with the world. Other times the posts are in development and most certainly not ready for others to read them. In these cases, Publii CMS uses the post state to determine which posts are ready for publishing (uploading) to on the Web and which ones need to be held onto until later.

The published and draft status flags exist for this purpose (as they do in many other CMS and blog platforms). When uploading the content of your blog to the Internet, only those posts that are set to "Published" will be uploaded for general consumption.

This has several implications. If you forget to publish a post, then the world will never see it. Also, if you accidentally save a post as published and it is not ready for publication, it will be uploaded to the Internet in its incomplete form and the whole world can see it. Oops!

For this reason, it is best practice to save your post during writing and development in draft state initially. This is what we did with this last post that was created with the Block editor.

Once you have saved your post for the first time as a draft, Publii CMS will offer the draft save action as the default when clicking the save button. Now that draft is the default action, clicking the drop-down arrow on the right of the save button will display additional save options as shown in Figure 5-97.

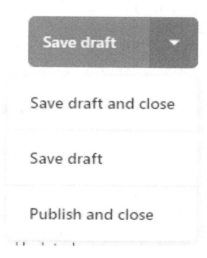

Figure 5-97. *Save options for a draft*

This differs from when you first saved the post as a draft. If you remember earlier in the chapter when first saving the post as a draft, it was necessary to click the arrow on the right of the "Save" button and select "Save as draft". At that time, the menu looked like the one shown in Figure 5-98.

Figure 5-98. *Save menu before initial save*

If you had just clicked the "Save" button when the post was yet unsaved, then the post would have been saved and the state of the post would have been set to "Published". That is the default action. Remember that you had to go out of our way to save this post in the draft state by selecting "Save as draft" at that time.

Since saving this post in the draft state, the context of the save menu has changed to the menu shown in Figure 5-97. Now you can choose to "Save draft", which is the default action of the button; "Save draft and close", which will save any changes and then close the editor and return to the Posts list panel; and finally "Publish and close".

"Publish and close" will change the state of the post from draft to published. Once in the published state, the post is considered complete. Typically, we would not need to revisit a published post to make changes or update it (although nothing prevents us from doing that).

This second post is complete. Click the drop-down menu for the "Save" button if you have not already done that. Now click the "Publish and close" option as highlighted in Figure 5-99.

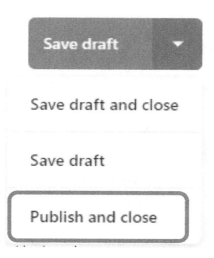

Figure 5-99. *Click Publish and close.*

The Block editor will be closed, and you will be returned to the Posts list panel. Notice that there are two published posts now as shown in Figure 5-100.

Posts   Q

All (2)   Published (2)

	Title	Publication date
☐	Rocket Engine Development News #Rocket Tech	Aug 23, 2024 02:27 pm Last modified: a few seconds ago
☐	Inspired by a Dream #Musings #News	Aug 22, 2024 03:08 pm Last modified: 4 days ago

Figure 5-100. *Posts list with two published posts*

Summary

This chapter was long, and I covered a lot of new information here. A review is in order. If you find that the subjects being reviewed are not clear, then go back and read the sections that are unfamiliar.

In this chapter, you learned about two different types of editors that can be used to create both posts and pages. We have not created pages yet, but we used both the WYSIWYG editor and the Block editor to create a post.

Editors

WYSIWYG stands for "What You See Is What You Get" and is a paradigm from the late 1980s which is still in use today. It simply means that how we create and format our text is how we should expect it to be rendered later when published.

The WYSIWYG editor uses a toolbar with many formatting tools to allow you to achieve the look and feel you image for your post.

The other editor you experimented with was the Block editor. This editor uses a block paradigm and block manipulating tools to produce and format text.

Both editors produce formatted text that represents a vision of how the post will look when published.

It is important to recognize that neither editor will reflect the unique ways the theme you are using will render some elements, which may differ from how they look in the editor.

Posts

You learned in this chapter that all posts require a post title. Posts also have several optional settings that can be configured in the Post options and settings panel accessed from a gear icon in the upper right corner of the editor. Some of the most useful settings that you configured were

- A featured image

- Featured image Alternative text and credits

- Tags for the post that help categorize and organize posts so your audience can better understand and navigate your blog

- Meta description, which is part of the SEO settings which helps search engines understand your content

Post Elements

The editors support many elements either through a toolbar or various context menus. The elements that you worked with were

- Post body text, which is the paragraphs of information that make up your overall content of the post. This is the heart of the message you are trying to pass on to your audience.

- Post images, which are embedded in the post, typically between post textual content. Images help to break up large sections of text and provide visual cues as to what you are writing about.

- Bullet and numbered lists, which are simple lists of content that makes sense in this format. Both editors support multiple forms of bullets and number sequences.

- The blockquote, which is an element for calling out a quotation of other special text that deserves this type of formatting. In both posts that were created, the blockquote was used for a quotation. This is the most common use of this element.

- Links. Most blogs have multiple links in them that allow the reader to access related information both within the overall website and sometimes from external sources. Links help to promote your blog as well formed and authoritative when well implemented.

- Separators, which are elements that help to separate content visually.

Text Formatting

Both editors also supported formatting of sections of text. These formats were generally applied to short snippets of one or more words where special formatting helped to communicate the importance of the message. These formatting types were variations in text face including Bold, Italic, Underline, and Strikethrough text.

Post State

Understanding post states when saving is important. This was covered and then reviewed as well in this chapter. Posts can be in one of several states. The most common are "published" and "draft."

Posts that are in "published" state are ready for uploading to the remote host and making available for the world to consume. Posts that are in "draft" state are typically in development.

Post states also led to the discussion of managing posts overall. Post management is done in the Posts list panel which is accessed by clicking the "Posts" menu item on Publii's main menu.

Published posts are shown in the Posts list having a blue title. Draft posts are shown in gray and are followed by a pencil icon indicating the post is still in development. Posts can only be opened in the editor that they were created in – open a post by clicking the post title.

The check box at the left of a post title will provide access to additional actions for the post such as duplicating and trashing.

Deleting a post is a two-step process. The post must first be trashed and then it can be deleted. There is no harm in trashing a post without deleting it.

CHAPTER 6

Page Building in Publii CMS

A page is a lot like a post. The same tools are used to create a page, and the general structure of a page is like a post. There are some key differences. First, a page is not listed in a post list on the website. Pages are free standing and, unless linked from within the website, cannot be accessed. They will not be listed under the author list, and they do not have tag support, so will never be listed under the tag list.

This kind of makes one think for a minute though. What good is a page then? How would one use a page anyway?

Pages serve a unique role in the structure of a Publii CMS website. They are useful as destinations where the reader can access static information such as an "About" page, "Terms and Conditions" pages, other legal notices, or a "Contact" page as well as product information pages, FAQs, and other permanent information-rich content.

Pages can be structured in a parent-child relationship. This relationship allows better organized URLs when pretty URLs are enabled. Pretty URLs are required to support parent-child relationships (see Chapter 3, section "Pretty URLs"). Pages are stand-alone entities, so any linking between pages must be explicitly created within the page content. The exception to this rule is parent-child linked pages displayed in official Publii CMS themes – when the feature is enabled for the page or in the global page settings.

© Brad Moore 2025
B. Moore, *Designing Websites with Publii and GitHub Pages,*
https://doi.org/10.1007/979-8-8688-1195-1_6

Publii CMS added support for pages in the release of version 0.46.0 in August 2024. A common use case for pages is the various terms, privacy, and compliance notices that most websites include because of increased compliance requirements on content providers. In this chapter, I will demonstrate adding a Terms and Conditions page to the website and linking it into the main menu. I will use the Markdown editor to demonstrate its operation. The Markdown editor works the same in both page and post creation.

Creating a Page

In this section, I will be discussing creating a new page for my project website. The page I will be creating will act as the site's Terms and Conditions page. I will use the Markdown editor to create and edit the text.

The Markdown Editor

The Markdown editor is available for both page and post creation and editing. Unlike the other two editors that were used in the previous chapter, the Markdown editor offers a very minimalistic editing experience. It does not have a toolbar or block management system. Instead, it relies on the use of shorthand symbols to tell the editor how to format the text. These symbols are called "markup" in the text layout world. This process allows for very rapid creation of content for those familiar with Markdown.

Markdown is the tool of choice for many professional bloggers as it allows them to work quickly, never leaving the keyboard as they develop content. It was created by John Gruber and Aaron Swartz in 2004 with the goal of enabling people to write using an easy-to-read, easy-to-write plaintext format, which then can be converted into structurally valid HTML (or other formats).

Rules for Markdown

Markdown is designed to be straightforward and intuitive, allowing you to format text using simple symbols and syntax. Here are some of the basic rules:

1. **Headers:** To create a header, use the hash symbol (#) before your header text. The number of hash symbols indicates the level of the header. For example, "# Header 1" for a top-level header, "## Header 2" for a second-level header, and so on.

2. **Emphasis:** To emphasize text, you can make it italic or bold. For italics, wrap your text in single asterisks or underscores ("*italic*" or "_italic_"). For bold, use double asterisks or underscores ("**bold**" or "__bold__").

3. **Lists:** For unordered lists, use asterisks, plus signs, or hyphens ("*", "+", or "-") followed by a space, for each item. For ordered lists, simply number each item (e.g., "1. First item").

4. **Links:** To create a hyperlink, wrap the link text in square brackets and then the URL in parentheses, like this: "[OpenAI](https://www.openai.com)".

5. **Images:** Similar to links, but start with an exclamation mark, like this: "![Alt text](image-url.jpg)".

6. **Blockquotes:** For blockquotes, use the greater than symbol (">") before your text.

7. **Code:** For inline code, wrap the text in backticks (`` ` ``). For a code block, use triple backticks (`` ``` ``) or indent each line with four spaces.

8. **Horizontal rules:** Create a horizontal line for section breaks using three or more asterisks, hyphens, or underscores ("***", "---", or "___").

These are the basic components of Markdown, enabling the format of text in a simple and readable way. The beauty of Markdown is its simplicity, making it easy for anyone to pick it up and start using it effectively.

Publii CMS offers a nice Markdown cheat sheet helping you to use the formatting notation. Open it up by clicking the "View Help" link in the lower right corner of the Markdown editor window as shown in Figure 6-1.

Figure 6-1. *View Help link in the Markdown editor window*

I have not instructed you to open the Markdown editor, but when you get there, this resource will be available to help with the Markdown markup that Publii CMS supports. The help system is displayed in a panel that flies out from the right side of the Markdown editor as shown in Figure 6-2.

Element	Markdown	Shortcuts
Bold	**text**	Ctrl/⌘ + B
Emphasize	*text*	Ctrl/⌘ + I
~~Strikethrough~~	~~text~~	Ctrl/⌘ + Alt + U
Link	[title](http://)	Ctrl/⌘ + K
List	* item	Ctrl/⌘ + L
Ordered List	1. item	Ctrl/⌘ + Alt/⌥ + L
Blockquote	> quote	Ctrl/⌘ + Q/'
Inline code	`code`	
Code	```code```	
H1	# Heading	Ctrl + H
H2	## Heading	Ctrl + H (x2)
H3	### Heading	Ctrl + H (x3)

Figure 6-2. *Markdown markup help*

Note that the Help system continues through headings H4–H6 (not pictured above) which were cropped from the figure to save space.

To close the Markdown help panel, click the link in the lower right corner which was originally titled "View Help" and is now titled "Hide Help".

You can learn more about using Markdown from these excellent online resources:

- **Official Markdown Guide:** The original Markdown syntax guide by John Gruber, the creator of Markdown, can be found at Daring Fireball. This guide provides the basic principles and syntax of Markdown: `https://daringfireball.net/projects/markdown/`.

- **Interactive tutorials:** Websites like Markdown Tutorial offer interactive lessons where you can write Markdown and see the results in real time: `https://www.markdowntutorial.com/`.

- **GitHub guides:** Given Markdown's popularity in documentation, especially on platforms like GitHub, the Markdown Guide offered by GitHub is an excellent resource for learning how to use Markdown for software documentation: `https://github.com/adam-p/markdown-here/wiki/Markdown-Cheatsheet`.

Visit the book's GitHub repository for an electronic version of the links provided.

New Page Using Markdown Editor

To add a page, you must click the "Pages" button on the Publii CMS main menu on the left of the application as shown in Figure 6-3.

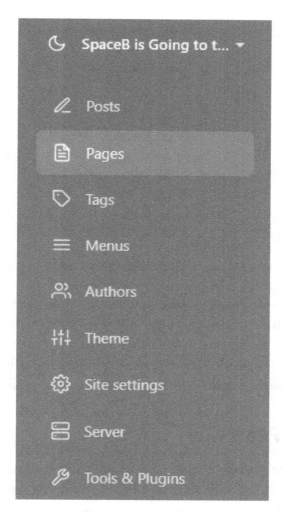

Figure 6-3. *The Pages menu item*

So far, I have not added any pages to my website. If you have been following along, you too will see that there are no pages as shown in Figure 6-4.

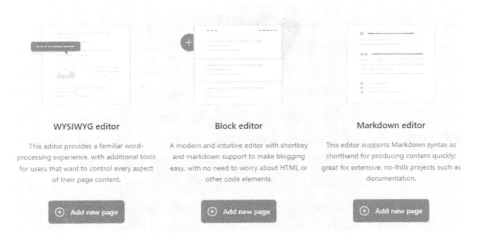

Figure 6-4. *No pages listed in the Add page dialog*

Since there are no pages, you see a dialog explaining each of the editor types and a button to "Add new page". You used both the WYSIWYG editor and the Block editor in Chapter 5 to create posts. They operate the same way when creating pages. This time use the Markdown editor by clicking the "Add new page" button below the Markdown editor description.

Adding a Page Title

As before this will open an editor in the right panel of the application. This time there is a simple "Start writing..." prompt. There are no context menus or toolbars to aid in formatting text. Remember you can always get formatting help by clicking the "View Help" link in the lower right corner of the editor as shown in Figure 6-1.

When the editor opens, it expects you will add a title right away. The cursor is placed in the title area as highlighted in Figure 6-5.

Start writing...

Figure 6-5. *Editor expecting a title*

If you click into the body of the page, the editor will remind you that a title is required by adding the prompt "Add page title" as shown in Figure 6-6.

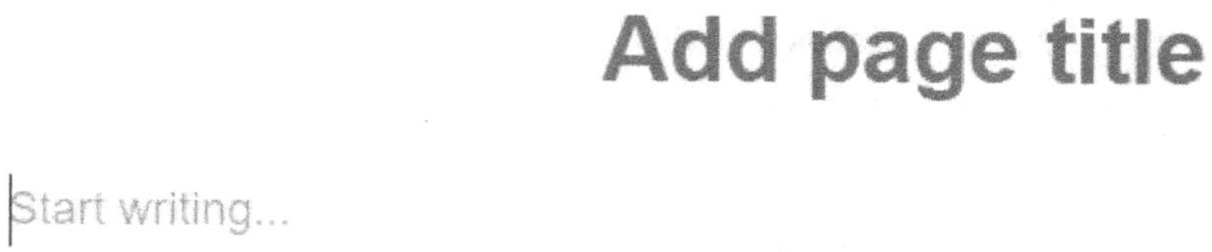

Add page title

Start writing...

Figure 6-6. *Add page title*

This page will be about the terms and conditions of use between the reader and myself (as the web page operator). Therefore, I have added the title: "Terms and Conditions".

Terms and Conditions

Terms and Conditions have become a common feature of websites everywhere. Generally, they help protect you as a website operator by declaring up front how your site will interact with the reader's web browser – what cookies will be set, what analytics are being collected, etc., as well as how you expect the reader to treat your content. In addition to Terms and Conditions (often called "T&C"), it is not uncommon to include a separate privacy statement. In the case of this exercise, I plan to combine the two.

While consulting a lawyer is not required, it is a reasonable course of action to ensure your T&C measures up to the needs of existing laws and does not leave you exposed to legal action. If this is beyond the scope of what your efforts can support – which is the case for nearly all small website operators – then there are decent alternatives. One of those alternatives would be using one of the multiple Terms and Conditions generators available on the Internet such as `https://www.termsandconditionsgenerator.com/` (*note that this is not an endorsement of this site*). This free resource generates a basic T&C that is GDPR and CCPA compliant. See the callout titled "What is GDPR and CCPA?" in Chapter 3 for more information about these regulations.

For the purposes of this tutorial, I will use ChatGPT to generate the site's terms and conditions.

Note   This book does not offer legal advice of any kind. Any legal document should be reviewed by an attorney or professional with experience in this area of law. The T&C is a legal document in principle. Equally, we do not endorse or recommend any specific provider of services – any links to third-party providers are merely for reference purposes.

I briefly mentioned ChatGPT in Chapter 5 when I used it to generate some Lorem Ipsum. It would be unusual if you have not heard of ChatGPT. Launched in November 2022, ChatGPT quickly became the AI model that has lead the transformation of how people interact with information online. Its ability to answer questions, generate text, and hold conversations has made it a popular tool for creatives. While AI is still best used with human oversight, it is very good at brainstorming ideas, drafting outlines, and producing placeholder content, making it an ideal assistant in the creative process.

I plan to use ChatGPT here to create a very simple Terms and Conditions document. As cautioned before – this document should be validated to make sure the AI has not introduced errors as well as to ensure it meets legal considerations.

Getting the best results from an AI like ChatGPT requires creating a quality prompt from which it can work. The more information you give to the AI, the better the results you will get. This is the prompt I gave to ChatGPT. (ChatGPT can be accessed at this URL: `https://chat. openai.com`).

"Generate a simple Terms and Conditions document for the website named "SpaceB is Going to the Moon" at the URL `https://to_be_ determined.com`. This is a static website, so there is no interactive content. We do not collect user information or use analytics to track users. The site does use cookies for basic functionality. We permit linking to our content, but do not permit hotlinking to images. Our content is copyrighted in the USA. Some images or text may have been used with permission from other providers who retain their rights to the material as noted in our content. We are in Kentucky. The email for contacting us is: space-b-systems@outlook.com."

Here are the results:

Terms and Conditions

Welcome to "SpaceB is Going to the Moon." By accessing this website, located at `https://to_be_ determined.com`, *you agree to the following terms and conditions. If you do not agree with any part of these terms, please do not use our website.*

Copyright Notice

All content on this website is copyrighted under U.S. law. The content may not be reproduced, distributed, or used in any form without our express written permission. Some images or text may be used with permission from other providers who retain their rights to the material as noted in our content.

Linking to Our Content

You are permitted to link to our content as long as the link does not imply any form of endorsement or association with your site, product, or service. However, hotlinking to images hosted on our site is strictly prohibited.

Cookies

This site uses cookies solely for basic functionality, such as enhancing user experience and ensuring the site operates smoothly. We do not use cookies to collect personal information or track users.

Privacy Policy

We do not collect any personal information from users who visit our site. We do not use analytics or any third-party services that track users. Any data related to cookies is used solely for functional purposes and is not shared with any third parties.

Third-Party Content

Some content on this site, including images and text, may be provided by third parties with their permission. All rights to this third-party content remain with the original providers. Use of such content is subject to the terms set by those providers.

Governing Law

These terms and conditions are governed by the laws of the Commonwealth of Kentucky, USA. Any disputes arising from the use of this website will be subject to the jurisdiction of the courts in Kentucky.

Contact Information

If you have any questions or concerns regarding these terms and conditions, please contact us at space-b-systems@outlook.com.

By continuing to use this website, you acknowledge that you have read, understood, and agree to be bound by these terms and conditions.

These Terms and Conditions as written by ChatGPT are very simple and straightforward. I am not a lawyer, so I do not know how they would fare if used in a legal action. As mentioned before – it is best to have your T&C reviewed or even written by a lawyer who specializes in this area of law. Since this is just a project for this book, I will use these as written for this exercise.

Page Body Text

To begin adding text to the body, simply click somewhere in the body area. The editor will place the cursor at the beginning of the first line. Before any text has been added, the editor will prompt you with the words "Start writing..." as shown in Figure 6-7.

Terms and Conditions

 Start writing...

Figure 6-7. *Adding body text at the "Start writing..." prompt*

I have copied the entire text of the Terms and Conditions from the previous section and simply pasted them into the editor as shown in Figure 6-8, you can download the text from the book's GitHub repository here: `https://github.com/Apress/Designing-Websites-with-Publii-and-GitHub-Pages`.

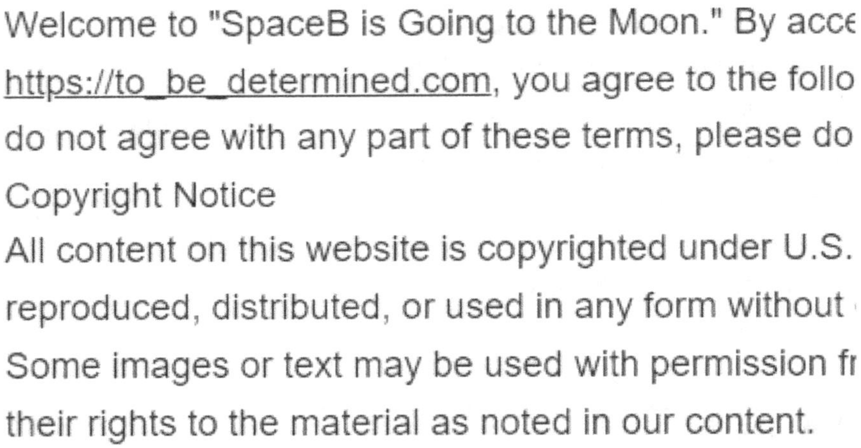

Welcome to "SpaceB is Going to the Moon." By acce
https://to_be_determined.com, you agree to the follo
do not agree with any part of these terms, please do
Copyright Notice
All content on this website is copyrighted under U.S.
reproduced, distributed, or used in any form without
Some images or text may be used with permission fr
their rights to the material as noted in our content.

Figure 6-8. *Content pasted into the Markdown editor*

Notice that the content has no special formatting. In the sections below, we will learn how to add formatting to the text using the Markdown editor's markup language.

Before doing that, I recommend applying some basic formatting in the form of a few carriage returns between paragraphs to add white space and let the content breathe a little. Place the cursor before section heading and press the ENTER key to add a blank line as shown in Figure 6-9.

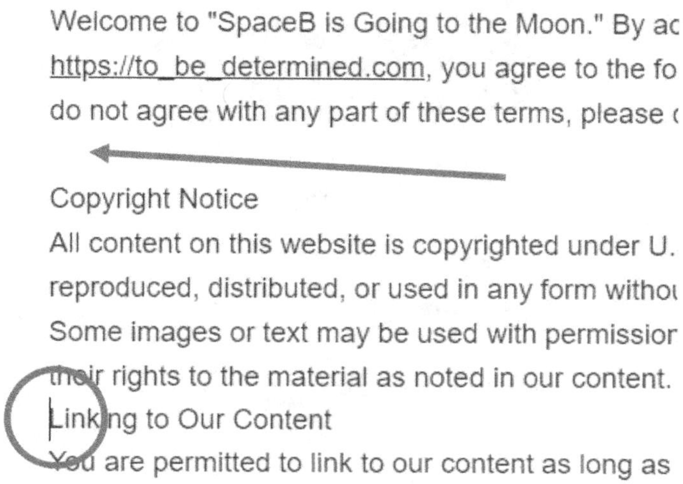

Welcome to "SpaceB is Going to the Moon." By ac

https://to_be_determined.com, you agree to the fo

do not agree with any part of these terms, please (

Copyright Notice

All content on this website is copyrighted under U.

reproduced, distributed, or used in any form withou

Some images or text may be used with permission

their rights to the material as noted in our content.

Linking to Our Content

You are permitted to link to our content as long as

Figure 6-9. *Adding white space between sections*

The arrow in Figure 6-9 shows the white space added between the introductory paragraph and the first section. The highlighted cursor location (circled) shows where to place the cursor to add a carriage return. Press the ENTER key to add a carriage return and create a blank line between the two paragraphs. Do this before all seven sections. Also remember to put an empty line between the last sentence of the T&C and the previous sentence as this is the summary of the terms agreement.

This page has not been saved yet. It is important to save early in development and save often as the page is written and refined. As you did when using the Block editor in Chapter 5, save this page in the draft state.

Remember this is done by clicking the drop-down arrow on the right of the blue "Save and close" button in the upper right of the editor as shown in Figure 6-10.

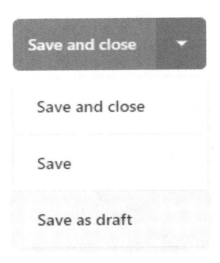

Figure 6-10. *Save and close context menu*

Click the "Save as draft" menu item in the context menu that is displayed.

Formatting Headings

As you can see in the Terms and Conditions, each section begins with a heading that defines what that section is about. Currently those headings are quite plain. Turning them into H2 headings will help the flow of the page when the reader views it.

When using Markdown, a heading is defined by one or more hash marks ("#") followed by a space. The greater the number of hash marks, the lower the heading value. I briefly mentioned heading levels in Chapter 5.

Well-built web pages will follow a defined headings structure. This is important as it will affect how well your page and website rank in search results on Google, or even if it gets indexed at all. These are the general rules:

Each page should have one and no more than one H1 heading type. This is the highest-level heading, and it should appear at the top or very near the top of your page. Publii CMS uses the H1 heading type for your page title.

Headings are hierarchal. Level 2 headings (an H2) should follow an H1. Level 3 headings should not appear before an H2.

Level 2 and lower headings may appear on the page multiple times. For example, an H2 heading may appear before a paragraph and then another before the next paragraph.

Do not nest deeper levels of headings than the material requires. The fewer the levels, the better.

Do not use headings as a stylistic element in page design – instead use specifically styled typography as needed and defined in separate CSS as needed. (I will discuss CSS briefly in the advanced topics in Chapter 15).

Look at Figure 6-11. I have styled the first heading titled "Copyright Notice" as an H2 level heading. This was done by adding two hash marks and a space before the heading text.

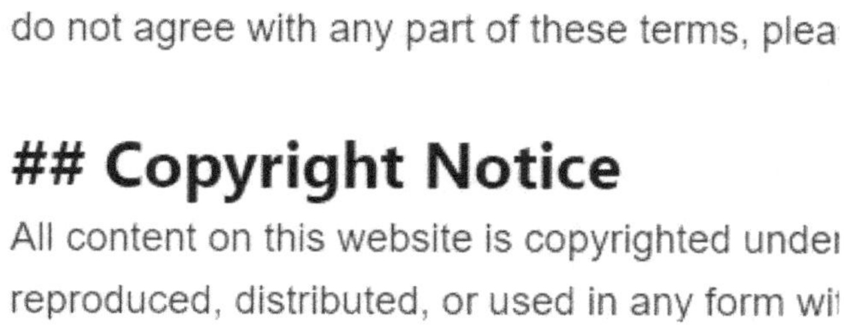

do not agree with any part of these terms, plea

Copyright Notice

All content on this website is copyrighted under
reproduced, distributed, or used in any form wit

Figure 6-11. *Adding an H2 heading level*

Add an H2 level heading to each of the remaining six headings in the Terms and Conditions text as you follow along.

Don't forget to save your work as you continue to write and refine the content.

Bold Text

Unlike the other two editors, the Markdown editor does not have any form of context menu when a section of text is selected and the right mouse button is clicked. Formatting a section of text to bold is done simply by adding the bold Markdown markup at the beginning and end of a portion of text. To indicate text should be bold in Markdown, add two asterisks ("**") at the front of the portion of text and at the end of the portion of text – do not put a space between the asterisks and the text.

For example, to make the words "Hello world" bold format the text like this:

```
**Hello world**
```

It would be rendered like this:

Hello world

Highlight the first few words of the first paragraph using bold text by adding the bold format markup as shown in Figure 6-12.

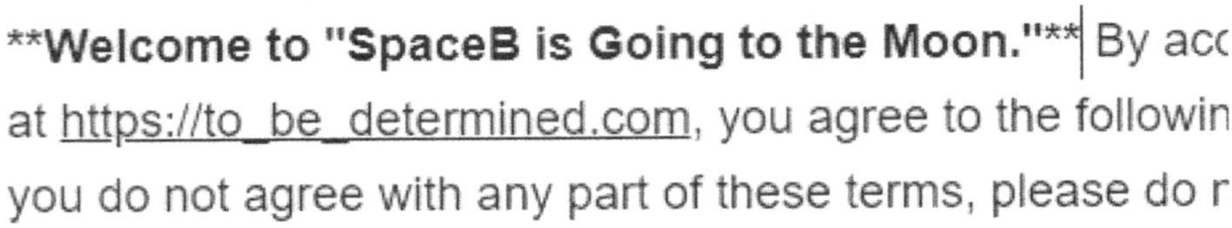

Welcome to "SpaceB is Going to the Moon." By acc at https://to_be_determined.com, you agree to the followin you do not agree with any part of these terms, please do r

Figure 6-12. Formatting bold text

There is an alternative method of applying Markdown markup to a selected section of text. Click the "View Help" link in the lower right corner of the editor as shown in Figure 6-1. Notice that nearly every format element has both a Markdown markup symbol as well as a Shortcut as shown in Figure 6-13.

Element	Markdown	Shortcuts
Bold	**text**	Ctrl/⌘ + B

Figure 6-13. *Markdown and Shortcut for Bold element*

For the Bold element, the shortcut is the Control (Ctrl) key plus the B key – pressed simultaneously. The four-leaf clover thing (for non-Mac users) is the macOS Command key – it acts like the Windows Control key.

To see this in action, select the first sentence in the Copyright section of the Terms and Conditions as shown in Figure 6-14.

Copyright Notice

All content on this website is copyrighted under U.S. law. The reproduced, distributed, or used in any form without our expre

Figure 6-14. *Selected sentence*

With the sentence selected, press the Control (Ctrl) key and the B key together at the same time. The selected sentence formatting will be changed to bold as the markdown for bold text is automatically inserted by the editor as shown in Figure 6-15.

Copyright Notice

All content on this website is copyrighted under U.S. law. Th

be reproduced, distributed, or used in any form without our express

Figure 6-15. Bold formatting added to selected text

Adding a Link

Hyperlinks are added manually using the Markdown editor. If we look at the help panel by clicking the "View Help" link in the lower right corner of the editor (as shown in Figure 6-1), we can see how a link is added to content as shown in Figure 6-16.

Link   [title](http://)

Figure 6-16. Help for adding a link

Looking at the format above, you see a title and a protocol (the "http://" part). The title is the human-readable part of the link. The protocol can be any valid Internet protocol – such as mailto:// (email address), http:// (unsecured URL), https:// (secured URL), or even ftp:// (file transfer). The protocol must be followed by the address. As an example, to create a link to the Google search page, the following would be valid:

[Search Google](https://google.com)

The first paragraph of the Terms and Conditions has a link to the website we are developing. It is a placeholder URL, but it is a valid link. I have selected the link so that it is easy to see in Figure 6-17.

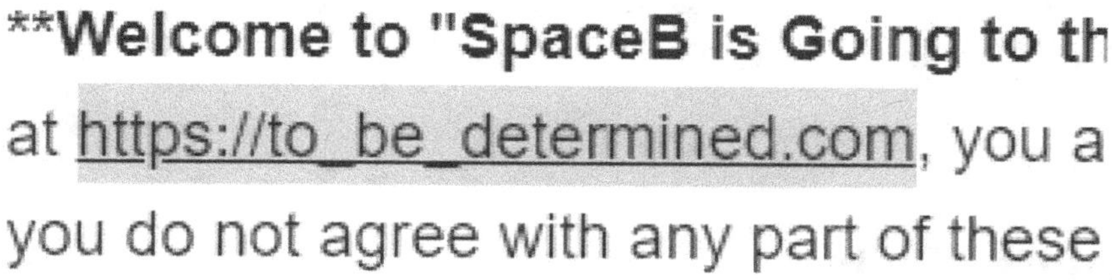

Figure 6-17. *Selected link*

The context of the paragraph implies that this should be rendered in readable form as a link, so the title will look very similar to the link.

Place your cursor at the beginning of the link – directly in front of the "https" as highlighted in Figure 6-18.

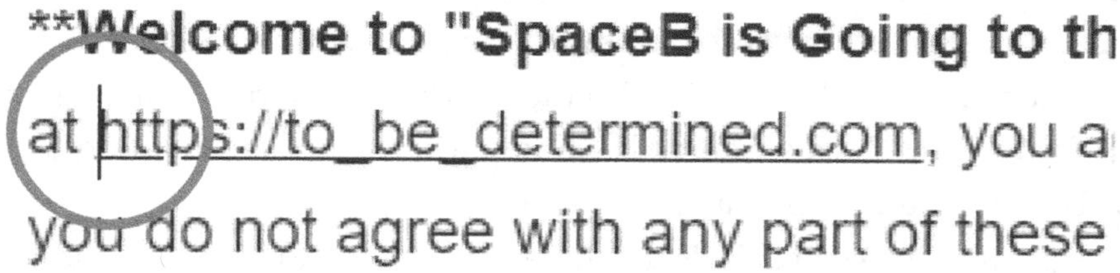

Figure 6-18. *Placement of cursor to add a link*

Type the title portion of the link as follows:

[SpaceBisGoingtotheMoon.com]

Once that is done, add an open parenthesis just before the link "https://to_be_determined.com" and a closing parenthesis at the end. Do not include any spaces anywhere in this.

It will look like Figure 6-19.

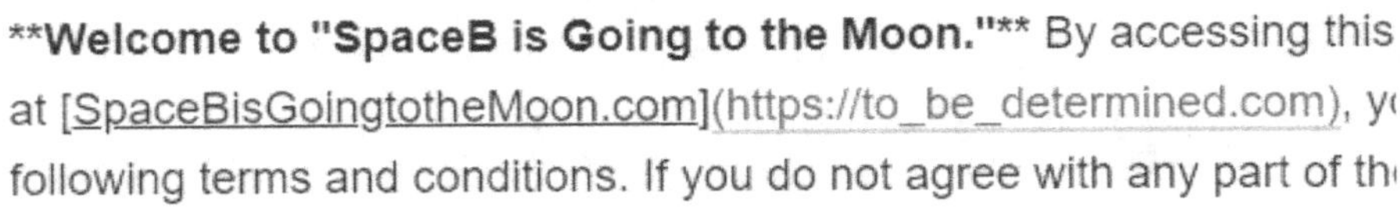

Welcome to "SpaceB is Going to the Moon." By accessing this
at [SpaceBisGoingtotheMoon.com](https://to_be_determined.com), y(
following terms and conditions. If you do not agree with any part of th(

Figure 6-19. *A correctly formatted link*

Ordered Lists

We have used lists in Chapter 5 but have not really discussed them thus
far. It is abundantly clear that lists are extremely useful tools which we use
almost every day without giving them much thought.

As content is developed, there are many cases where a list would be
the perfect medium to communicate the information we aim to impart.
HTML, the language that lies under the hood of all web pages and which
Publii CMS renders our web pages into, supports two types of list. These
are a list that is numbered and a list that has bullets in front of the items.
The former is called an ordered list, and the latter is called an unordered
list. Here is a quick explanation of the two.

A great example of a list is the quick note you jot to yourself on a scrap
of paper as you rush out to get some staples from the local grocery store.
You need

Bread

Milk

Eggs

Cheese

Using Markdown, this list can be formatted as a numbered list (an ordered list) by placing numbers followed by a period and a space before each of the items in the list as shown below:

1. Bread

2. Milk

3. Eggs

4. Cheese

Markdown is exacting. If you miss the space or the period, the list will not render the way you expect it to.

Figure 6-20 shows this list rendered by Publii CMS as a web page in my local browser.

Groceries:

1. Bread

2. Milk

3. Eggs

4. Cheese

Figure 6-20. *Ordered list*

If I miss a space between a number and an item – perhaps between the number "2." and the word "Milk", then that item will not be rendered as a numbered item. It will, in fact, become part of the previous item as you can see in Figure 6-21.

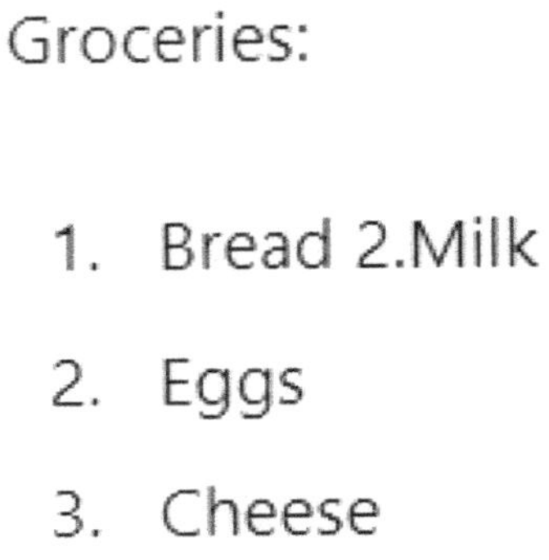

Groceries:

1. Bread 2.Milk

2. Eggs

3. Cheese

Figure 6-21. *An ill-formed ordered list*

One neat feature of ordered lists and Markdown is automatic numbering. Is it perfectly acceptable to precede each item in an ordered list with the number 1. as shown below:

1. Bread

1. Milk

1. Eggs

1. Cheese

When the list is rendered by Publii CMS, it will automatically be numbered in the correct order as shown in Figure 6-22. This is very convenient when working with larger lists and moving items around, inserting items, or removing them.

Groceries:

1. Bread

2. Milk

3. Eggs

4. Cheese

Figure 6-22. *Automatically numbered ordered list*

Creating a bullet list (an unordered list) is like creating an ordered list. Instead of using numbers and a period to designate a list item, simply use a single asterisk followed by a space. Our grocery list becomes

* Bread

* Milk

* Eggs

* Cheese

This is rendered as shown in Figure 6-23.

Groceries:

• Bread

• Milk

• Eggs

• Cheese

Figure 6-23. *An unordered list*

Which list type to use will be determined by the situation. I tend to default to the unordered list when an ordered list is not specifically required.

Implementing Ordered Lists

Most websites have two separate policies for their Terms and Conditions and their privacy policy. I have chosen to combine them for simplicity. The privacy section of the T&C that was originally developed by ChatGPT was a bit vague. I have chosen to replace it with a more detailed set of statements.

I presume you are following along. If that is the case, delete the paragraph that follows the Privacy Policy section (just that one paragraph – not the heading) and replace it with the following, which you can download from the book's GitHub repository here: `https://github.com/Apress/Designing-Websites-with-Publii-and-GitHub-Pages`:

> At "SpaceB is Going to the Moon," we are committed to protecting your privacy. Our website is designed as a static site, and we have implemented practices that ensure your personal information is not collected, tracked, or shared in any way. Below is a detailed breakdown of our privacy practices:

> No Personal Information Collection: We do not collect or store any personal information from users who visit our site. This means we do not request or retain names, email addresses, or any other personal details.

> No Use of Analytics: We do not use any analytics tools, such as Google Analytics, that track user behavior, IP addresses, or browsing history on our site.

No Third-Party Tracking Services: Our website does not integrate with or utilize any third-party services that monitor or collect data about our users. This includes social media plugins, advertising networks, or any other tracking services.

Use of Cookies: Cookies on this site are used solely for basic functionality. For example, cookies may help in remembering certain user preferences or ensuring the site operates properly. These cookies do not collect personal data.

No Data Sharing: Any data related to cookies used on this site is not shared with third parties. We do not sell, trade, or otherwise transfer any data to outside parties.

Static Site Limitation: As a static website, there are no forms, user accounts, or interactive features where personal information could be collected.

Commitment to Privacy: Our commitment to privacy is guided by our policy to provide a simple and secure browsing experience, free from intrusive data collection practices.

I like this new, more detailed privacy policy both because it is clearer about what the reader can expect regarding the collection of their personal data from the site and also because it lends itself well to our next topic – ordered lists.

There are seven sections to this privacy policy. They can be identified by locating the section title followed by a colon. As an example, the first one is "No Personal Information Collection:". Turn each of these into an item in a numbered list. I have chosen to number each of them as "1." as shown in Figure 6-24.

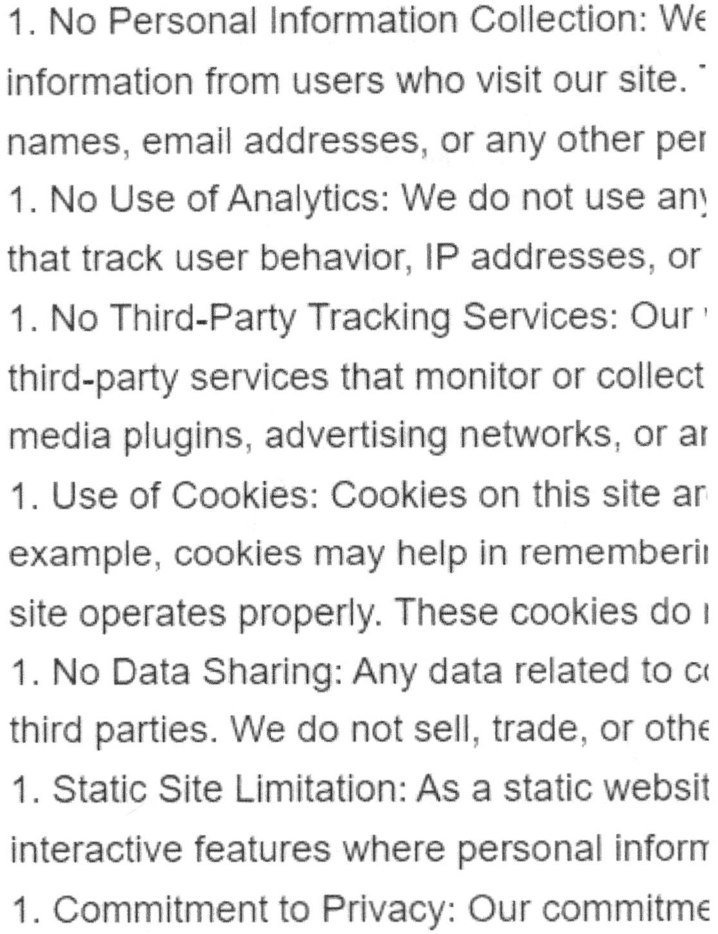

1. No Personal Information Collection: We
information from users who visit our site. '
names, email addresses, or any other per
1. No Use of Analytics: We do not use any
that track user behavior, IP addresses, or
1. No Third-Party Tracking Services: Our '
third-party services that monitor or collect
media plugins, advertising networks, or ar
1. Use of Cookies: Cookies on this site ar
example, cookies may help in rememberii
site operates properly. These cookies do i
1. No Data Sharing: Any data related to co
third parties. We do not sell, trade, or othe
1. Static Site Limitation: As a static websit
interactive features where personal inform
1. Commitment to Privacy: Our commitme

Figure 6-24. *Adding an ordered list*

Earlier you formatted a section of text to be rendered bold. Format each of these privacy policy headings as bold text now. An easy way to do this is to select the text and press the key combination of Ctrl-B. In Figure 6-25, you can see the first of these headings formatted bold and the second one selected in preparation for formatting.

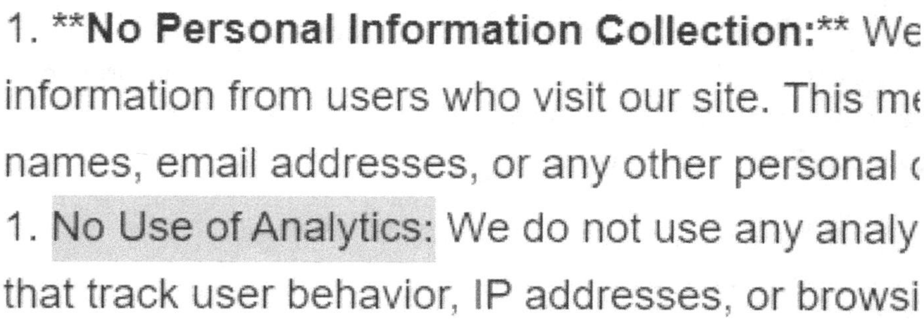

1. **No Personal Information Collection:** We information from users who visit our site. This me names, email addresses, or any other personal (

1. No Use of Analytics: We do not use any analy that track user behavior, IP addresses, or browsi

Figure 6-25. *Formatting headings as bold*

Format all seven of the headings as bold.

Caution   If you accidently select a leading or training space and apply the shortcut key combination to format the text as bold, italic, or Strikethrough, it will format the entire text block. If this happens, you can (1) press the key combination of Ctrl-Z to undo, (2) manually remove all the asterisks, or (3) manually remove the offending space.

Don't forget to save your work as you go.

Adding Emphasis

Bold is considered a form of emphasis when formatting text with the Markdown markup system. The other forms of emphasis are italics (called Emphasize) and strikethrough. Markdown does not support underline in its unenhanced form. At the time of this writing, Publii CMS does not offer an enhanced form of Markdown with underline support. Since the Markdown editor supports inline HTML formatting, underlining can be added using the <u> and </u> tags around the text to underline.

Applying these other forms of emphasis is done in the same way as applying the bold Markdown to text. I want to apply some italic font to a small portion of the first paragraph of the Terms and Conditions. Open the help panel by clicking the "View Help" link in the lower right corner of the editor (as shown in Figure 6-1). You can see in Figure 6-26 that Publii CMS calls this format "Emphasize".

Emphasize	*text*	Ctrl/⌘ + I

Figure 6-26. *Emphasize text format*

The Emphasize format can be added to selected text by pressing the key combination of Ctrl-I or by adding an asterisk before and after the portion of text to be italicized. Remember that there should be no space between the asterisk and the first character of the text to be italicized.

In Figure 6-27, I have already selected the text to which I want to apply the Emphasize (or italics) formatting.

Welcome to "SpaceB is Going to the Moon." By accessing this website, located at [SpaceBisGoingtotheMoon.com](https://to_be_determined.com), you agree to the following terms and conditions. If you do not agree with any part of these terms, please do not use our website.

Figure 6-27. *Selected text to format with italics*

I have chosen to use the shortcut key combination of Ctrl-I to apply the formatting Markdown symbols. You can insert these manually also. Simply add an asterisk to the beginning of the line of text and one to the end as the shortcut has done as shown in Figure 6-28.

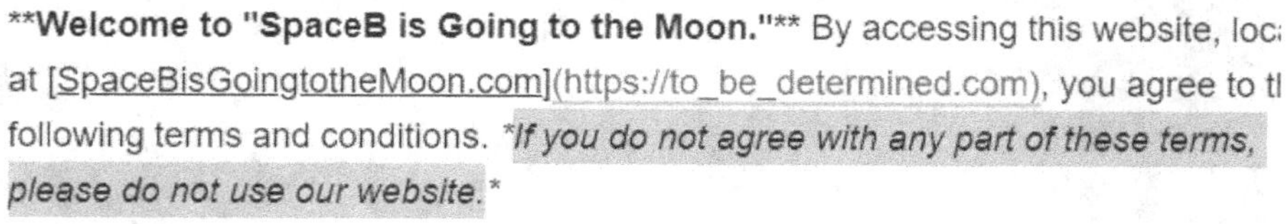

Welcome to "SpaceB is Going to the Moon." By accessing this website, loc; at [SpaceBisGoingtotheMoon.com](https://to_be_determined.com), you agree to tl following terms and conditions. **If you do not agree with any part of these terms, please do not use our website.**

Figure 6-28. *Italics format applied*

Inserting Images

Typically, a Terms and Conditions page or Privacy Policy would not contain an embedded image; however, I will add one to demonstrate how this is done using the Markdown editor.

The View Help facility at the bottom of the editor does not mention an image element that can be used. The Markdown editor supports embedding images through drag and drop only.

To begin the process, find an image that you plan to insert into the page. I have once again gone to Unsplash.com for an image of a spacecraft flying over a coastline as shown in Figure 6-29. This image can be downloaded from `https://unsplash.com/photos/a-space-satellite-hovering-above-the-coastline-VBNb52J8Trk` or from this book's GitHub repository located here: `https://github.com/Apress/Designing-Websites-with-Publii-and-GitHub-Pages`.

Figure 6-29. *Image to be inserted into the page*

The image will be placed where the cursor is located when the image is dragged and dropped into the editor. In preparation for that, I have added a couple extra lines of white space (blank lines) to the page content between the second and third paragraphs as shown in Figure 6-30. I have also placed the cursor on the second of the three blank lines. I recommend doing this before inserting an image so that there is no risk of corrupting the image link.

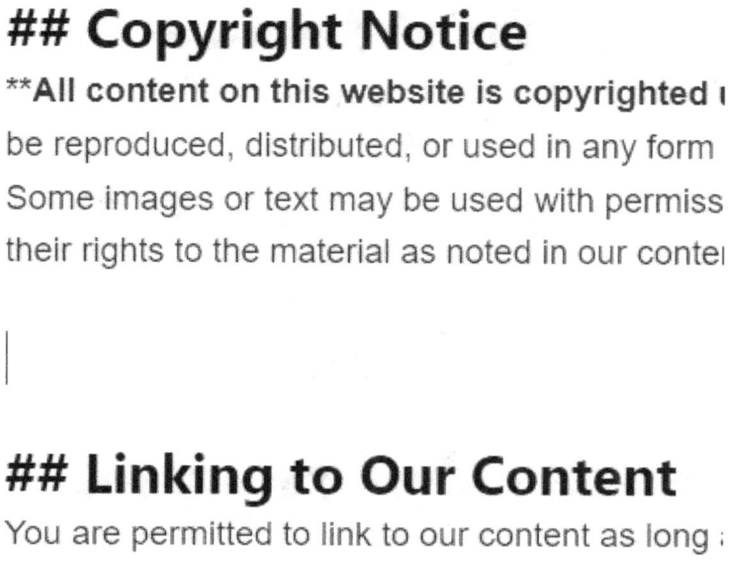

Copyright Notice

**All content on this website is copyrighted i
be reproduced, distributed, or used in any form
Some images or text may be used with permiss
their rights to the material as noted in our contel

Linking to Our Content

You are permitted to link to our content as long :

Figure 6-30. *Extra blank lines inserted between paragraphs*

Next, locate the image in your system's file manager (Windows File
Explorer or macOS Finder). Ensure the cursor is located where you want
the image to be inserted on the page. Click on the image and drag it into
the Markdown editor window as shown in Figure 6-31.

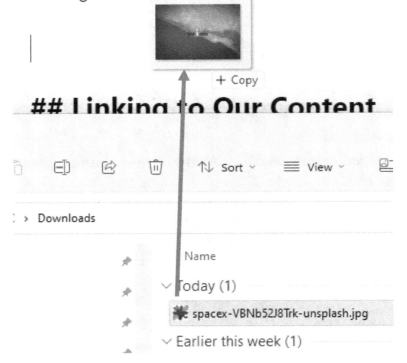

Figure 6-31. *Drag the image into the editor and drop it*

The image will be embedded textually. You will not actually see the image unless you preview the page. The embedded image will look like the one seen in Figure 6-32.

![Image description](file:///C:/Users/PC/Documents/Publii/sites/spaceb-is-going-to-the-moon/input/media/posts/7/spacex-VBNb52J8Trk-unsplash-2.jpg =1920x1280)

Figure 6-32. *An imbedded image file in the Markdown editor*

The format for images in Markdown is shown in Figure 6-33.

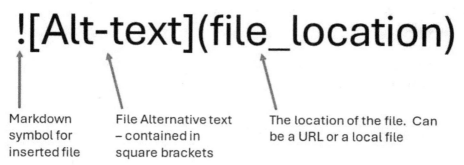

Figure 6-33. *Format for embedded images using Markdown*

In Figure 6-32, we can see that the Alt-text is "Image description". This is a prompt to remind you to add a description. Remember that adding an Alternative text (an image description) is a great way to enhance your page and website SEO performance – a mantra I continue to preach.

Edit the description for this image, giving it an appropriate description and taking the opportunity to use a keyword or two. In my case, I added the description "Spacecraft hovering above a coastline" as you can see in Figure 6-34.

![Spacecraft hovering above a coastline](file:///C:/Users/PC/Documents/Publii/sites/space moon/input/media/posts/7/spacex-VBNb52J8Trk-

Figure 6-34. *Description for an embedded image*

To fully understand what inserting this bit of Markdown has accomplished, click the "Preview" link in the upper left corner of the editor as shown in Figure 6-35.

< Pages   Preview

Figure 6-35. Preview and Pages link on the upper left corner of the editor

The page will be rendered in your default web browser. It looks like Figure 6-36 in my web browser.

Welcome to "SpaceB is Going to the Moon." By accessing this website, located at SpaceBisGoingtotheMoon.com, you agree to the following terms and conditions. *If you do not agree with any part of these terms, please do not use our website.*

Copyright Notice

All content on this website is copyrighted under U.S. law. The content may not be reproduced, distributed, or used in any form without our express written permission. Some images or text may be used with permission from other providers who retain their rights to the material as noted in our content.

Figure 6-36. Terms and Conditions page (cropped) in a browser

While you have the page open in a browser, go ahead and look over the page and make sure it all looks the way you imagined it might when creating the page in the editor.

If your page looks good to you, like the page I created does to me, then you are ready to publish the page.

Publish the Page

In this section, I will discuss putting the finishing touches on the Terms and Conditions page I have been working on. I will also discuss how to add a link to this page so that people can access it and read it. I will be adding that link to the main menu.

Page Options and Settings

Remember from the posts that you worked on in Chapter 5 that each had some settings that I suggested you add to enhance each post. Pages also have settings which can enhance the page. Access the settings like you did for posts by clicking the gear icon in the upper right corner of the editor as highlighted in Figure 6-37.

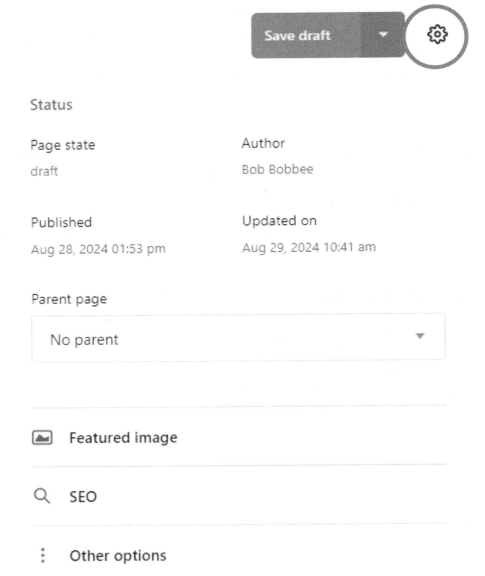

Figure 6-37. Page settings and options

Notice that the Page does not have the same options in the Status panel as posts. One obvious difference is in the Parent page drop-down. Earlier when discussing pages, I mentioned that pages can be set up in a hierarchy – this drop-down is used to establish the relationship between pages in that hierarchy. We will examine this in more detail later in this Chapter.

The Terms and Conditions page is a free-standing page and does not need a parent, so leave this field set to "No parent".

Featured Image

Click the "Featured image" header so we can add a featured image. Terms and Conditions pages typically do not have a featured image (which, in page layout terms, would be called a hero image in the theme we are using). Nothing prevents you from adding one to your version of Terms and Conditions page. I plan to add the image shown in Figure 6-38 to my page. You can get this image from Unsplash.com at `https://unsplash.com/photos/black-and-white-braille-typewriter-EX9QVVFtQxw` or from the book's GitHub repository for Chapter 6 located here: `https://github.com/Apress/Designing-Websites-with-Publii-and-GitHub-Pages`.

Figure 6-38. *Image to be used as a featured image*

Drag and drop that image onto the image picker field or click the "Choose file" button and navigate to the image and select it. It will be displayed in the image file picker field as shown in Figure 6-39.

Featured image

Remove image

Alternative text

SpaceB Terms and Conditions of Use

Caption

Credits

Photo by Markus Winkler on Unsplash

Figure 6-39. *Featured image settings*

Notice that I have given this image an Alternative text of "SpaceB Terms and Conditions of Use". We all know that Alternative text is good for SEO by now.

I have also credited the image owner as "Photo by Markus Winkler on Unsplash". Crediting an image owner is good practice when the image was created by someone else, even if they have placed the image into the public domain.

SEO Settings

As I have encouraged you in all other cases, you will once again want to add a meta description to the SEO settings for the page. Click the SEO heading to expand that section of the Settings and Options panel as shown in Figure 6-40.

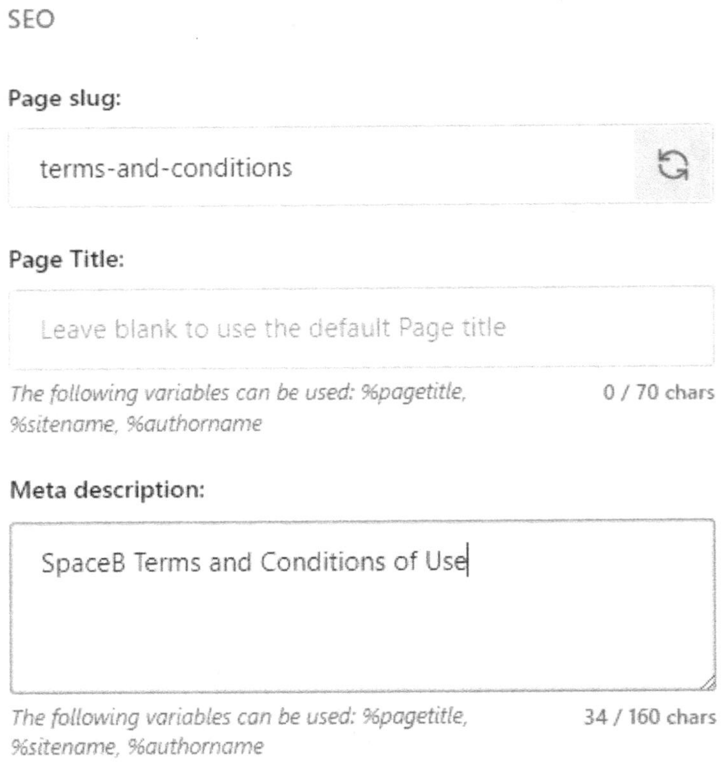

SEO

Page slug:

> terms-and-conditions

Page Title:

> Leave blank to use the default Page title

The following variables can be used: %pagetitle,   0 / 70 chars
%sitename, %authorname

Meta description:

> SpaceB Terms and Conditions of Use

The following variables can be used: %pagetitle,   34 / 160 chars
%sitename, %authorname

Figure 6-40. *SEO Settings and Options (cropped)*

The meta description I have used is simply the Alternative text also used on the image. This is adequate for this usage.

Other Options

There is one more setting that I wish to change. This time in the Other Options section. We have not ventured into the section in the past since the default values for these various settings have been desirable. The default values for pages are different than those for posts. Posts have almost all the options enabled globally (this is done in the Theme settings). Pages, on the other hand, have all these options disabled. Usually this is desirable for pages as well; however, this policy document needs to reflect its last date of edit. This could be done manually by adding a line to the content of the page that says: "Last edited: mm/dd/yyyy". Of course, it would be incumbent upon you and I to change this value every time the policy was updated. I know I would forget to do that.

Publii CMS has a simpler answer to this need. Every time the page is edited and saved, the last edited time and date is updated. Choosing to display that value would relieve you and I of the burden of remembering to change a static date in the body of the text.

Click the "Other options" heading to reveal the various options that can be modified as shown in Figure 6-41.

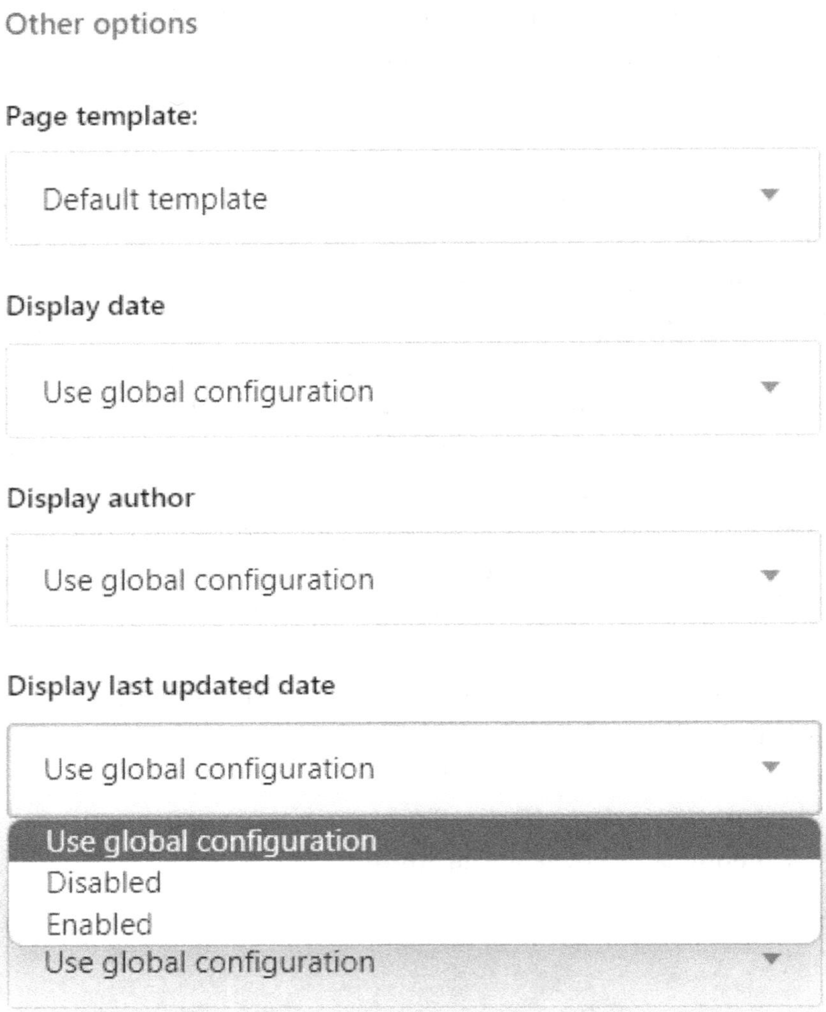

Other options

Page template:

| Default template | ▼ |

Display date

| Use global configuration | ▼ |

Display author

| Use global configuration | ▼ |

Display last updated date

| Use global configuration | ▼ |

| Use global configuration |
| Disabled |
| Enabled |

| Use global configuration | ▼ |

Figure 6-41. *Other options*

Notice in the Other options panel that I have clicked the drop-down for the field "Display last updated date". It was previously set to "Use global configuration". I will select "Enabled" instead as shown in Figure 6-42.

Display last updated date

Figure 6-42. *Display last updated date option*

Save the draft and click the Preview link as shown in Figure 6-35. The preview link is in the upper left corner of the editor window.

If you scroll all the way to the bottom of the page, you will see a note that the article was updated on such and such a date as shown in Figure 6-43.

This article was updated on August 29, 2024

Figure 6-43. *The date the page was last updated*

Saving Draft As Published

This page is complete. It needs to be saved one last time changing it to the published state. To do this, click the drop-down arrow to the right of the blue "Save draft" button in the upper right corner of the editor. A content menu will appear as shown in Figure 6-44.

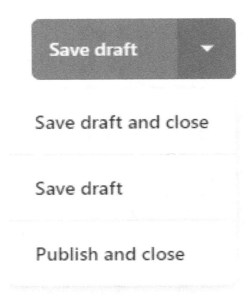

Figure 6-44. *Context menu for "Save draft"*

Click the "Publish and close" button on the bottom of the context menu to save the page and close the editor. This action will return you to the Pages list panel showing the page you created titled "Terms and Conditions" as shown in Figure 6-45.

All (1)   Published (1)

	Title	Publication date
	Terms and Condtions	Aug 29, 2024 12:49 pm Last modified: a few seconds ago

Figure 6-45. *Pages listed in the Pages list panel*

Adding a Link to the Menu

So far you have created a page for the site's Terms and Conditions –
provided you have been following along. This page is not accessible to the
reader unless they magically happen to know the URL directly to that page.
To allow the reader to easily locate the page and access it, you must create
a link to it somewhere. In this case, it makes sense to add that link to the
website main menu.

Click the "Menus" button in the Publii CMS main menu on the left side
of the application as shown in Figure 6-46.

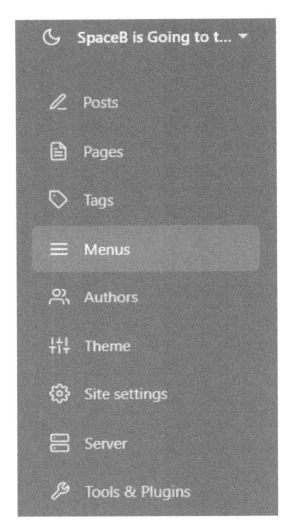

Figure 6-46. *Menus menu item*

You will see the "Main" menu listed in the menu list in the menu list panel on the right side of the application as shown in Figure 6-47.

Figure 6-47. *A menu named "Main" in the menu list*

Click the menu title (in this case, the menu named "Main") as shown in Figure 6-48. The menu items assigned to this menu will be displayed below the menu as well as a button to "Add menu item" and a link to "Edit menu name".

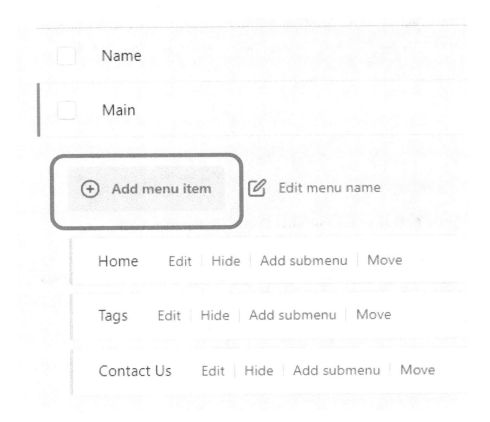

Figure 6-48. *Menu items belonging to the selected menu*

In Chapter 4, section "Add Menu Items", I added the menu items you
see listed. These included a link to the homepage called "Home", a link
to the tags list page called "Tags", and a link to open an email in the local
email client called "Contact Us".

Now I plan to add a menu item to link to the Terms and Conditions
page that was just created. Click the "Add menu item" button as
highlighted in Figure 6-48. This will reveal the "ADD NEW MENU ITEM"
panel that will fly out from the right side of the application as shown in
Figure 6-49.

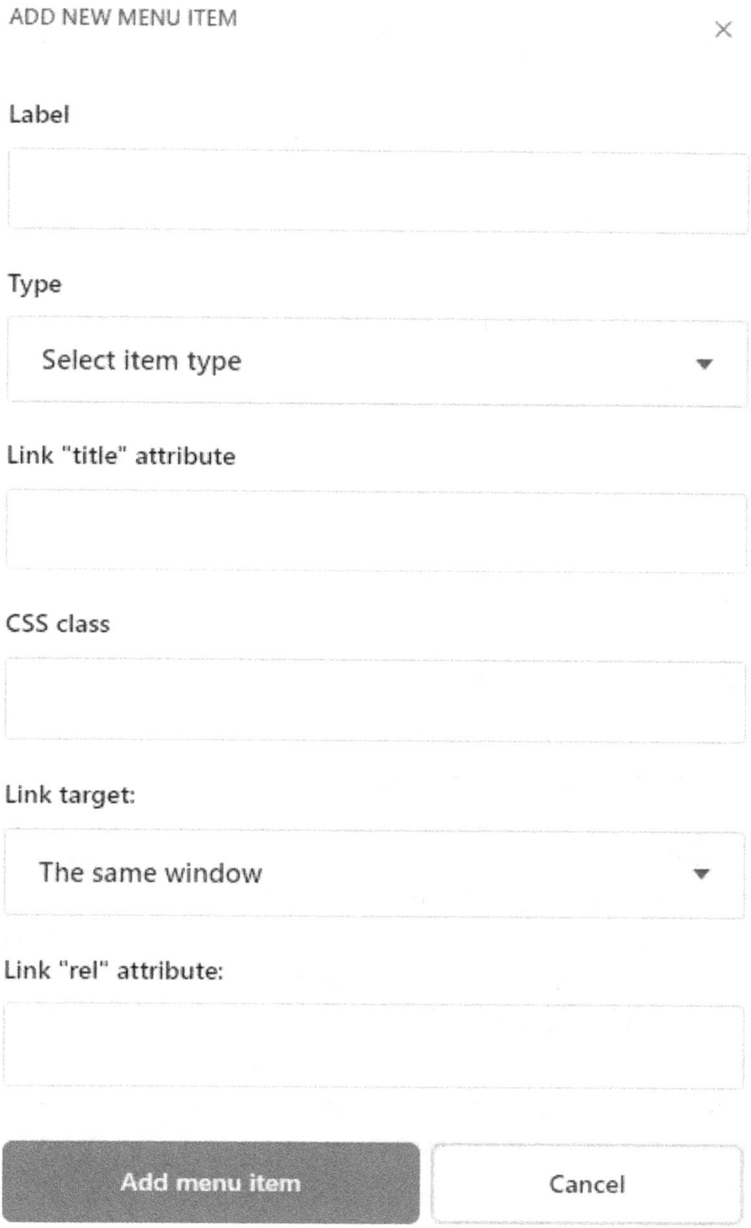

ADD NEW MENU ITEM   ×

Label

Type

Select item type   ▼

Link "title" attribute

CSS class

Link target:

The same window   ▼

Link "rel" attribute:

Add menu item   Cancel

Figure 6-49. *The Add New Menu Item panel*

Label this new menu item as "Terms of Use" in the Label field and select the link type as "Page link" as shown in Figure 6-50.

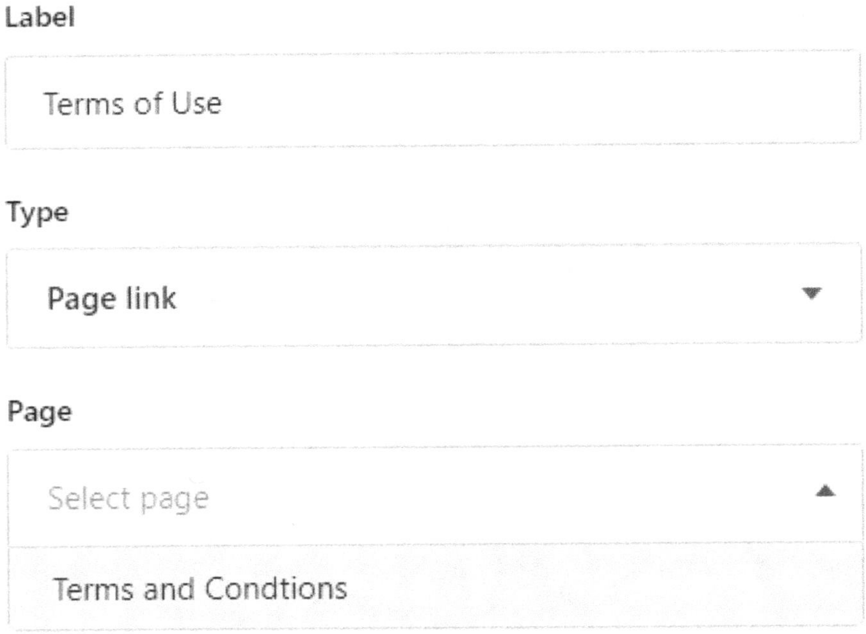

Label

Terms of Use

Type

Page link ▼

Page

Select page ▲

Terms and Condtions

Figure 6-50. *Creating a page link*

The third field label will change to "Page", and it will be a drop-down listing all the existing pages. As you can see in Figure 6-50, there is only one page listed. It is the page that was just created in the Markdown editor called "Terms and Conditions". Select that page.

No other changes are needed in this panel. Click the blue "Add menu item" button on the bottom of the "Add New Menu Item" panel to save this menu item. It will be listed as the last item in the list of menu items for this specific menu as shown in Figure 6-51.

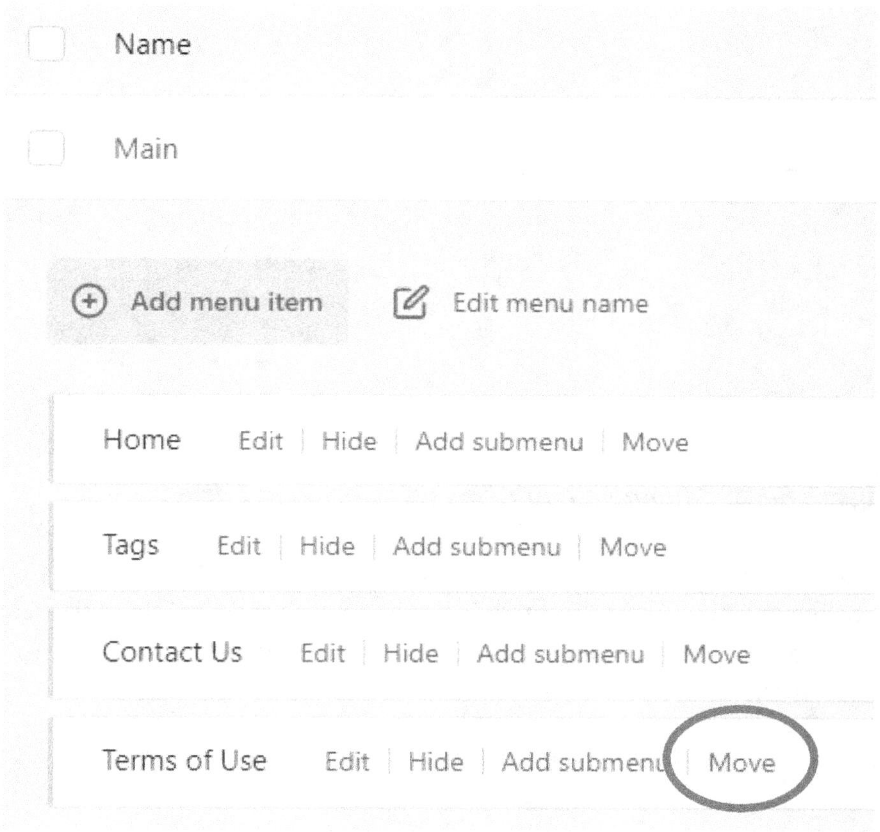

☐   Name

☐   Main

⊕ **Add menu item**   ☑ Edit menu name

Home   Edit | Hide | Add submenu | Move

Tags   Edit | Hide | Add submenu | Move

Contact Us   Edit | Hide | Add submenu | Move

Terms of Use   Edit | Hide | Add submenu | Move

Figure 6-51. *List of menu items for the menu "Main"*

Ideally the "Contact Us" menu item would be the last item in the menu. Publii CMS has a nice drag and drop feature for editing the order of menu items. Click and hold the "Move" link to the right of the "Terms and Conditions" menu item title as highlighted in Figure 6-51.

The menu item will become detached and can be moved around with the mouse as long as the mouse button remains depressed. Drag it up so that it is between the "Tags" and "Contact Us" menu items. The menu items will split apart, and a blue dashed area will be added between them indicating that you can drop the menu item there as shown in Figure 6-52.

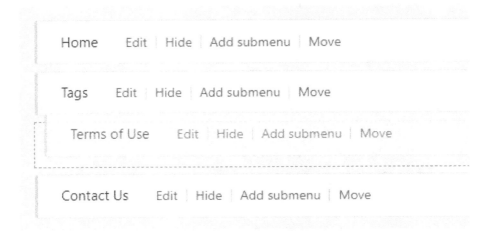

Figure 6-52. *Moving menu items using drag and drop*

Let go of the depressed mouse button and drop the menu item between the "Tags" and "Contact Us" menu items. Be careful not to create a submenu by dragging the menu item too far to the right as shown in Figure 6-53.

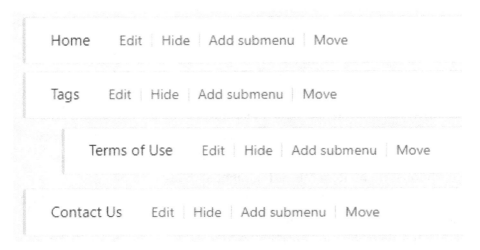

Figure 6-53. *Accidental creation of a submenu*

If you do not get it right on the first attempt, just click the Move link as before and try again.

Figure 6-54 shows a portion of the homepage with the main menu sporting a new item after rendering a website preview. Generate a preview by clicking the "Preview your changes" button on the bottom of the application main menu.

Home   Tags   Terms of Use   Contact Us

We are building a platform to oon!

ering experinces, and dive into the joys of space travel.

Figure 6-54. *Website homepage (cropped) showing the new menu item*

Converting Posts to Pages

In this section, I will be discussing and demonstrating how to convert a post to a page using Publii CMS's convert post to page functionality.

In the early days of Publii CMS, there were only posts. Several settings were available to make a post act like pages do today. When pages were introduced, there was the issue of how to convert a post that was acting like a page to become an actual page. Version 0.46.0 did not have a conversion function. Some enterprising folks filled in the gap, but with the release of Publii CMS version 0.46.2, we can now convert posts to become pages.

If you are new to Publii CMS, you will rarely need this functionality as you should create the correct Post/Page type when adding new content to your site. There are cases where it makes sense to convert from one content type to the other. Perhaps your post just does not fit into the flow of your blog, perhaps after composing it is obviously an informational page.

To convert a post to a page, first open the Posts list panel by clicking the "Posts" menu item in the application main menu on the left side of the Publii CMS application as shown in Figure 5-1 in Chapter 5.

Shown in Figure 6-55 are a couple dummy posts in our Publii CMS–created blog website. I created these posts by following the post creation process described in Chapter 5. Since I plan to delete them later, I simply gave the posts a title and saved and published them. You can do the same thing to experiment with converting posts to pages and back the other way around.

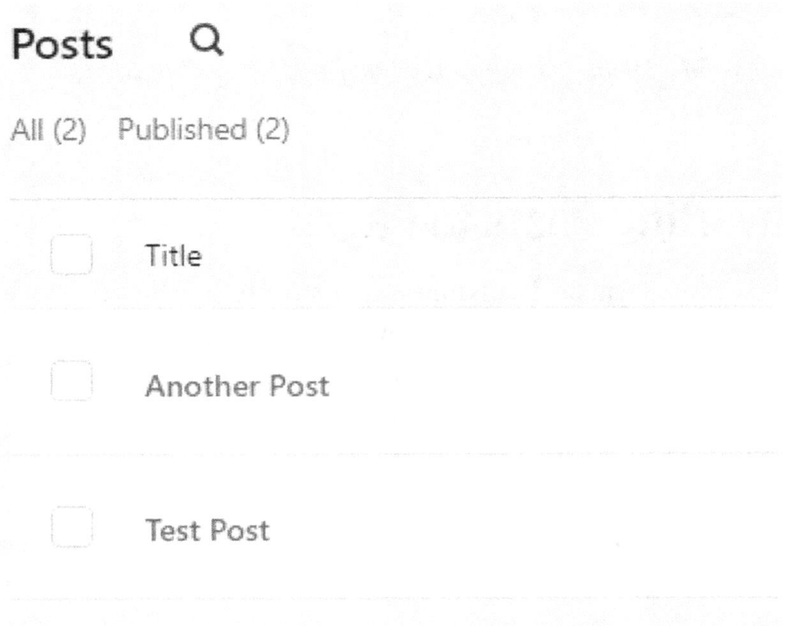

Posts   🔍

All (2)   Published (2)

_____

☐   Title

_____

☐   Another Post

_____

☐   Test Post

_____

Figure 6-55. Dummy posts in the Posts list panel

I will be demonstrating how to convert the post "Test Post" to a page.

Begin by checking the selection check box to the left of the post title as shown in Figure 6-56.

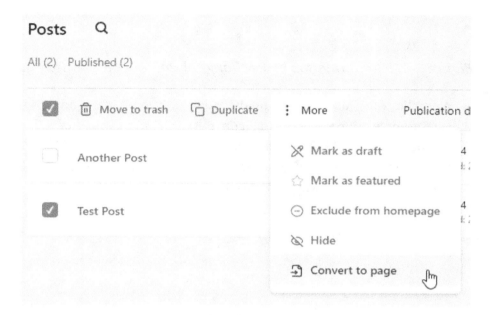

Figure 6-56. *Converting a post to a page*

When selected, several optional operations are displayed above the list of Posts. The third item is titled "More". Clicking More (as shown in Figure 6-56) reveals a drop-down menu with additional operations that can be applied to this post.

Click the "Convert to page" menu item in the drop-down menu.

The post will be converted to a page, and Publii CMS will report the success in a brief message as shown in Figure 6-57.

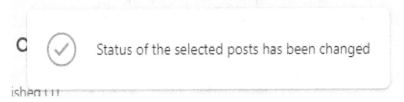

Figure 6-57. *Confirmation of the change of status of the selected post*

Now click the "Pages" button on the Publii CMS main menu on the left side of the application as shown in Figure 6-3 earlier in this chapter.

As you can see in the Pages list panel, there is now a page titled "Test Post" as shown in Figure 6-58. I suppose we should change the name of the page to "Test Page", but I will leave this to you.

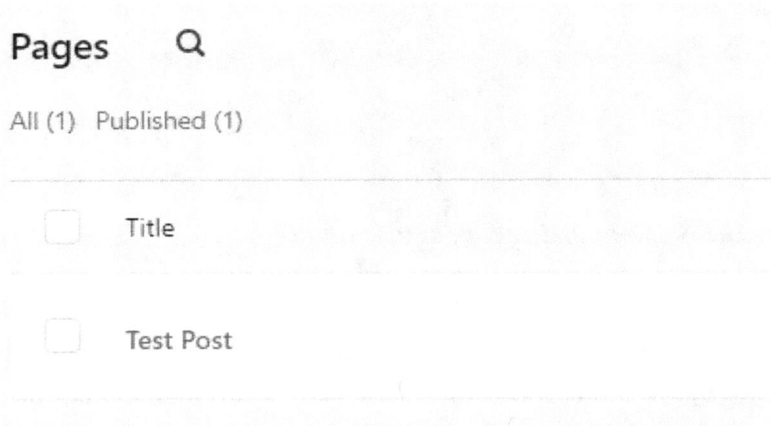

Pages Q

All (1) Published (1)

Title

Test Post

Figure 6-58. *A page made from a converted post*

Publii CMS allows conversion from page to post as well. Check the selection check box to the left of the page title, click the "More" drop-down menu, and select the menu option "Convert to post" as shown in Figure 6-59.

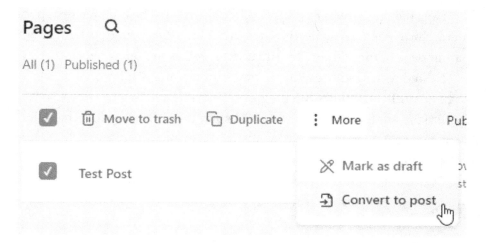

Figure 6-59. *Converting a page to a post*

In this section, I have been working with dummy pages and posts. I plan to delete them, and you can too if you also created a dummy post to convert to a page.

Nested Pages

In this section, I will discuss and demonstrate nested pages, what they are, how to create them, and how they are displayed on a web page.

What Are Nested Pages

Publii CMS introduced pages and page nesting (hierarchical page relationships) with version 0.46.0 of the application. Nesting allows the content creator to link subpages to parent pages in a hierarchy. Page relationships can be edited in the Page options panel when editing a page in one of the page editors or in the hierarchy editor in the Pages list panel.

Page nesting leverages pretty URLs (which must be enabled to support hierarchical page navigation) by nesting child pages in folders beneath the parent page in the system file structure as well as the rendered site.

Nested pages require a theme that supports the display of nested pages. All official Publii CMS themes support nested pages. They also require the enabling of the option to display the child page links globally or on a specific parent page. We will discuss these requirements in greater detail below.

By default, all pages when created do not have a parent page and therefore are not nested.

Modifying Hierarchy in Page Options

I have created several dummy pages to help demonstrate the nesting of pages. Each of these pages (named "Another Page", Page Number 3", and "Page Number 4") consists of a page title and five paragraphs of Lorem Ipsum placeholder text.

Create several pages in your system as you follow along so that your Pages list panel looks like mine in Figure 6-60.

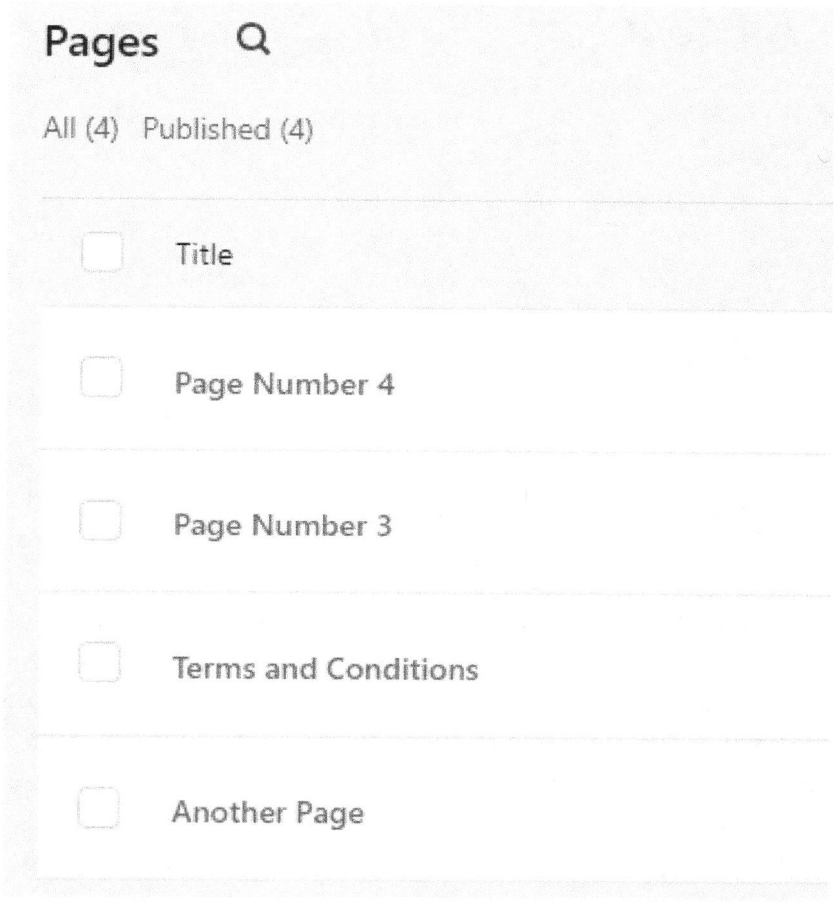

Pages Q

All (4) Published (4)

☐ Title

☐ Page Number 4

☐ Page Number 3

☐ Terms and Conditions

☐ Another Page

Figure 6-60. *Pages in the Pages list panel*

In the example below, I have clicked on the page title link for the page "Another Page". I have clicked on the option gear in the upper right corner of the editor to open the options panel as shown in Figure 6-61.

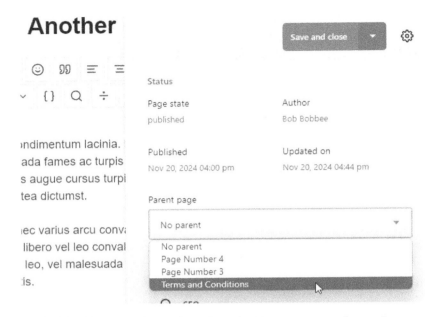

Figure 6-61. *Page options showing the Parent page drop-down*

In Figure 6-61, notice that I have clicked on the Parent page drop-down field. There are several options to select from (all the existing pages as well as "No parent"). Select the "Terms and Conditions" page as the parent.

Observe in Figure 6-62 that the parent page is now set to "Terms and Conditions". Click the blue "Save and close" button in the upper right corner of the editor.

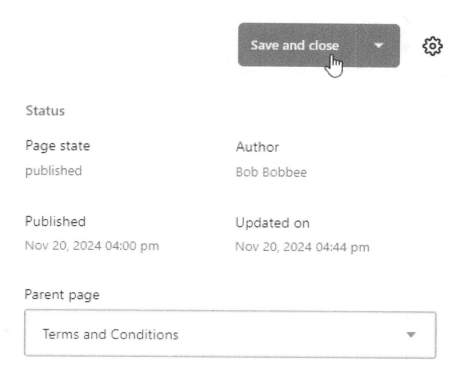

Figure 6-62. *Save and close the editor*

Notice in the Pages list panel how the page titled "Another Page" now has an indicator (highlighted) on the left side of the page title indicating it is a subpage. We know it is a subpage (or child page) of the page directly above it as shown in Figure 6-63.

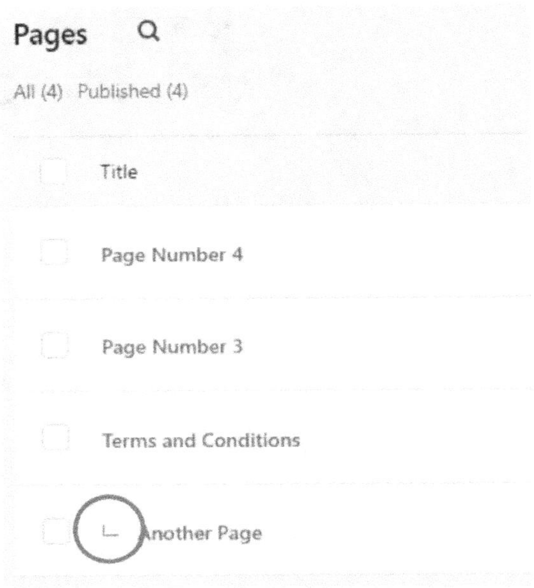

Figure 6-63. *Pages list panel showing "Another Page" as a child page*

Modifying Hierarchy in Pages List Panel

The hierarchy can be bulk edited in the Pages list panel by clicking the "Edit hierarchy" link in the upper right corner of the interface below the Add new page button as highlighted in Figure 6-64.

Figure 6-64. *Edit hierarchy link*

Click the "Edit hierarchy" link to switch the Pages list panel into hierarchy editing mode as shown in Figure 6-65.

Figure 6-65. *Hierarchy editing mode*

Notice that while in hierarchy editing mode, the "Add new page" button is grayed out as are the check boxes on the left of each page title, meaning they are not accessible in this mode. Also notice that below every page title is a link titled "Move". Click the "Move" link under the page titled "Page Number 3" as demonstrated in Figure 6-66.

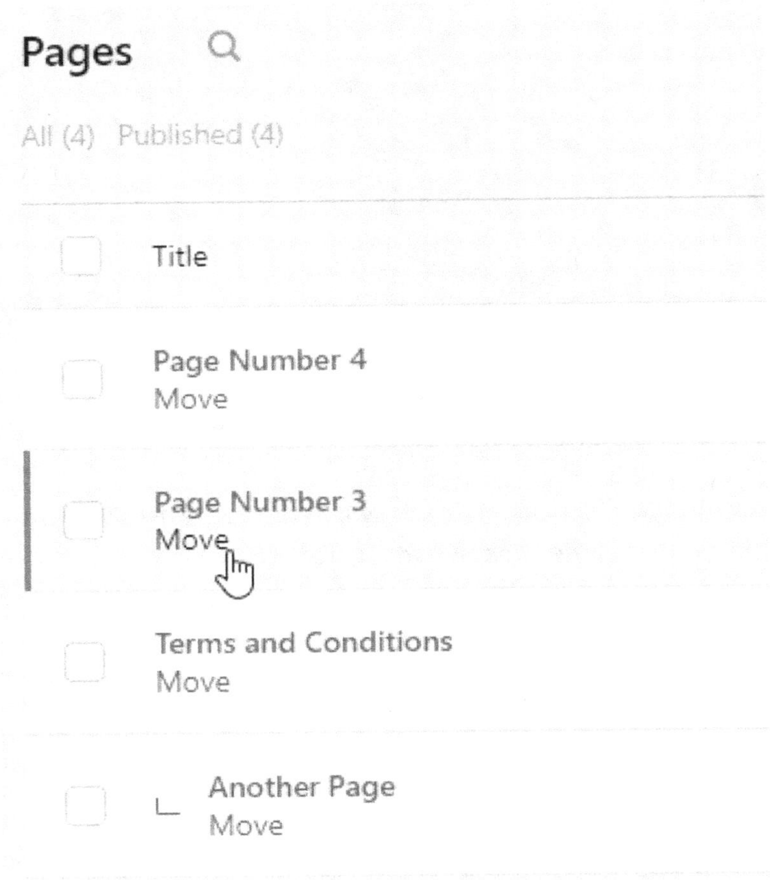

Pages   🔍

All (4)   Published (4)

	Title
☐	Page Number 4 Move
☐	Page Number 3 Move
☐	Terms and Conditions Move
☐	└ Another Page Move

Figure 6-66. Click the "Move" link

After clicking the "Move" link, the context of the list will change as shown in Figure 6-67. There is now an "Unselect" link in red below the page titled "Page Number 3". This permits cancelling the move action before the move is performed. Each of the other pages offers new options below them. Specifically, you can move the selected page "before" a specific page, "after" a specific page, as well as assigning the selected page as a "subpage" (meaning child page) of the specific page. Click the "as subpage" option below the page titled "Another Page" as shown in Figure 6-67.

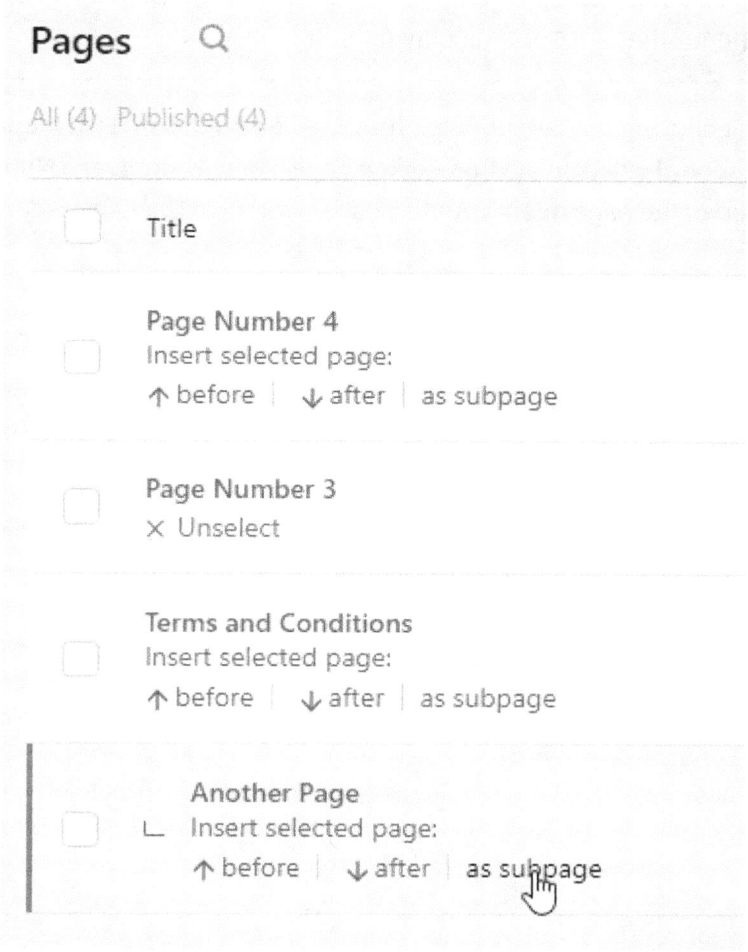

Figure 6-67. *Move the selected page, making a subpage (child) of "Another Page"*

Note   The before and after options available when editing page hierarchy are only effective when changing the order of multiple subpages (child pages) on the same level *below* a parent. These options permit changing the order that several subpages will be listed in a theme that supports displaying subpages.

After clicking the "as subpage" link, the Pages list panel (in hierarchy editing mode) will display the selected page (specifically "Page Number 3") as a child of the page titled "Another Page" as shown in Figure 6-68.

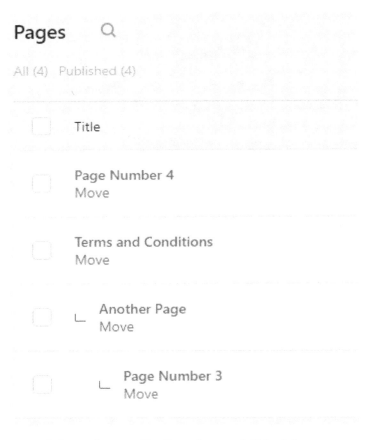

Figure 6-68. *Selected page displayed as a child of the target page*

Go ahead and click the "Move" link for the page titled "Page Number 4" and then move it so that it is a child of "Another Page" as shown in Figure 6-69.

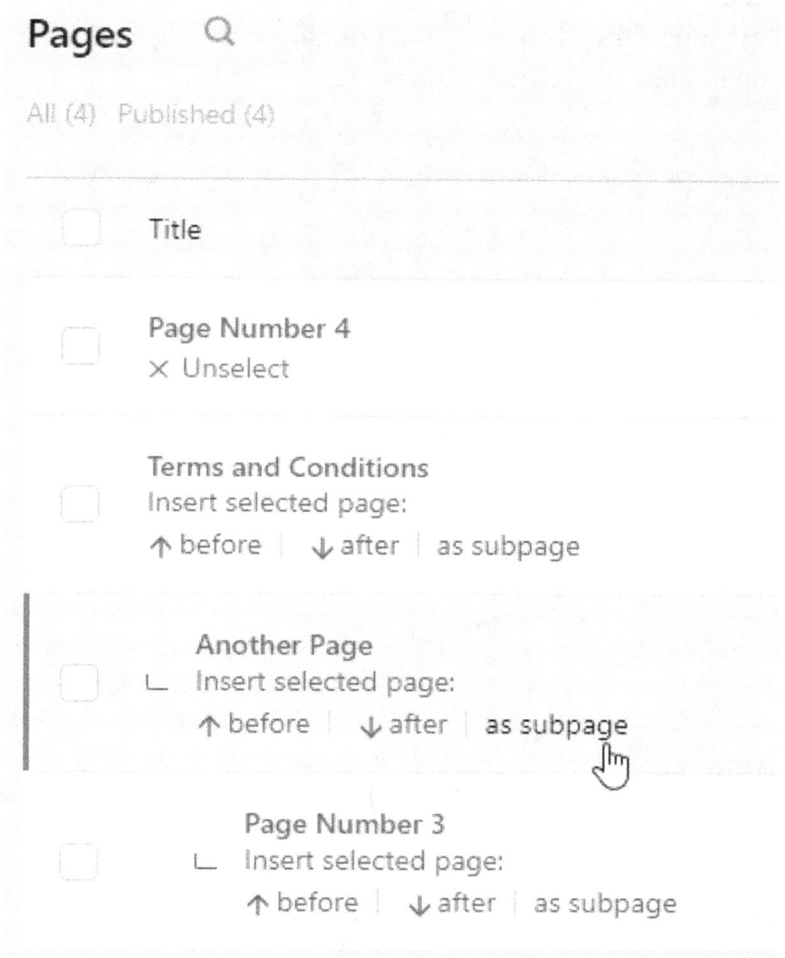

Pages   Q

All (4)   Published (4)

Title

Page Number 4
✕ Unselect

Terms and Conditions
Insert selected page:
↑ before | ↓ after | as subpage

Another Page
∟ Insert selected page:
↑ before | ↓ after | as subpage

Page Number 3
∟ Insert selected page:
↑ before | ↓ after | as subpage

Figure 6-69. *Moving "Page Number 4" to be a child of "Another Page"*

There is more than one way to move this page – you could also move the page into the child position of "Another Page" below the page titled "Page Number 3" by clicking the "after" link under the page titled "Page Number 3".

After doing either of these operations, the Pages list panel in hierarchy edit mode will be as shown in Figure 6-70.

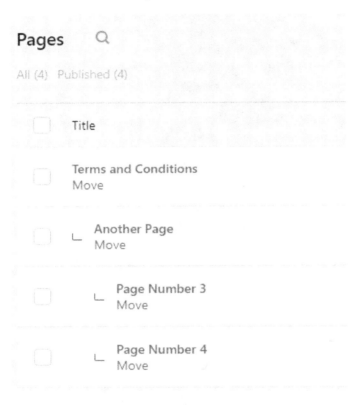

Figure 6-70. *Pages arranged in a hierarchy*

Experiment as you desire moving pages around in the hierarchy. When you are done and want to exit the hierarchy edit mode, click the "Close edit" link in the upper right corner of the Pages list panel under the "New page" button as shown in Figure 6-71.

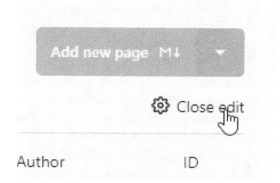

Figure 6-71. *The Close edit link*

Viewing Nests Pages

At the time of this writing, all official Publii CMS themes supported listing parent-child hierarchy in the rendered website. It is important to note that displaying child page links is not enabled globally by default.

This option can be enabled for a specific page within the "Other options" section of the Page options panel (click the gear in the upper right of the editor to see that panel). This setting is called "Display child pages".

It might be more effective to set this option in the global settings for the theme. This will permit all pages with a child hierarchy to display that hierarchy. To do that, first go to the Theme settings by clicking "Theme" in the Publii CMS main menu on the left side of the application as shown in Figure 6-72.

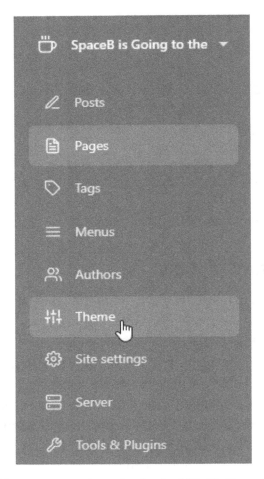

Figure 6-72. *Theme menu item in the Publii CMS main menu*

Navigate to "Page options" under the "Custom settings" section of the Theme settings. Scroll down until you locate the setting titled "Display child pages". Click the field drop-down as shown in Figure 6-73.

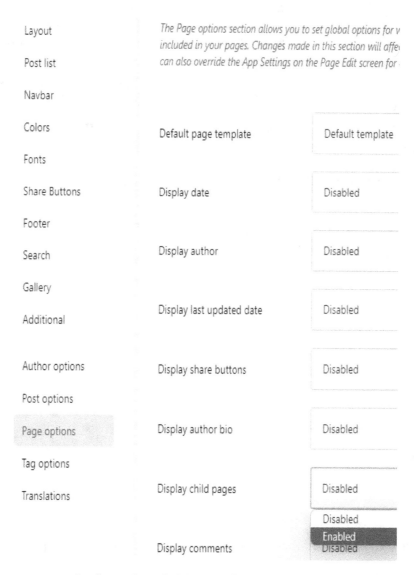

Figure 6-73. *The "Display child pages" setting in Theme options*

Select the "Enabled" option from the drop-down list.

Click the light blue "Save settings" button on the bottom (or top) of the Theme settings panel.

Click the "Preview your changes" button located at the bottom of the Publii CMS main menu. This will generate a preview of the site in your default browser as we have seen before.

Click on the link to the page "Terms and Conditions" in the main menu of the website and scroll to the bottom of that page. Listed in hierarchical order at the bottom of the page are the child pages and their children as well as shown in Figure 6-74.

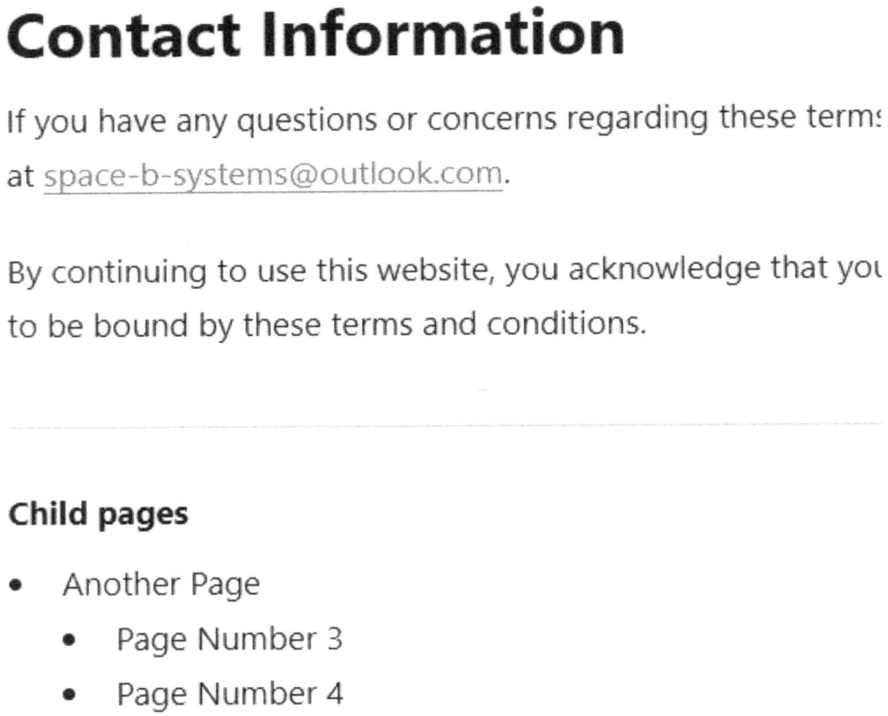

Contact Information

If you have any questions or concerns regarding these terms at space-b-systems@outlook.com.

By continuing to use this website, you acknowledge that you to be bound by these terms and conditions.

Child pages

- Another Page
  - Page Number 3
  - Page Number 4

Figure 6-74. *Child page hierarchy displayed on the website preview*

Observe the hierarchy in the folder structure in the page URL when clicking on the page titled "Page Number 3" as shown in Figure 6-75.

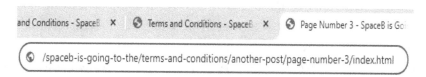

Figure 6-75. *Child Page URL reflecting the folder structure of child pages*

The option we enabled in Chapter 3 for pretty URLs enables the folder structure that we see in Figure 6-75. Without this option, parent-child pages would not be supported on our website.

For more information about utilizing parent-child hierarchies, refer to the Publii CMS documentation: `https://getpublii.com/docs/creating-and-editing-pages.html`.

Summary

There were many new things discussed again in this chapter. Let's review.

Pages and posts are very similar but serve different functions. Posts are always displayed as a part of the post list and by default are accessed through this list on the website homepage. Pages are stand-alone entities. They will not be linked to unless you create a link to the page intentionally.

Pages are new to Publii CMS as of version 0.46, and as such there will likely be some minor modifications to their functionality as development on Publii CMS continues.

Pages can be created and edited with the same editors as posts. The editors work the same in either context. Remember that once a page or post has been created in a specific editor, it must continue to be edited in the same editor.

The Markdown editor uses the Markdown markup language to format text as you type. Markdown was created by John Gruber and Aaron Swartz in 2004 with the goal of enabling people to write using an easy-to-read, easy-to-write plain-text format, which then can be converted into structurally valid HTML.

The rules for Markdown are very simple. The Markdown editor offers a help function via a help link at the lower right of the editor window that can help you remember the Markdown syntax as well as the shortcut key combinations that Publii CMS supports.

In this chapter, I discussed further the use of headings and presented some basic rules for using headings in your writing. Always remember that headings help organize your content and should not be used simply as a text formatting tool.

There was also greater development of the idea of lists. In HTML, these are called ordered and unordered lists. Ordered lists have numbers before each item in the list. Unordered lists usually have a bullet point before each item in the list. I also discussed some specifics around how Markdown handles ordered lists and autonumbering.

There was some review of adding a featured image to a page which is the same as adding them to posts. As I have done every time, I pointed out the importance of adding Alternative text to your images to help enhance your page and website SEO.

Unlike previously I cracked open the "Other options" portion of the page/post settings and options panel so that I could discuss briefly the settings. As a rule, these are all set to inherit their values from the Post and Pages settings for the theme. I chose to explicitly set the value for "Display last updated date" to enabled as this is desirable for a policy-type page.

I completed the section by adding a menu item to the menu named "Main". This menu item links to the Terms and Conditions page that was created. When adding the menu item, I introduced a new technique of reordering menu items using the drag and drop "Move" function.

There is a lot of new functionality that pages bring to Publii CMS. I reviewed how to convert posts to pages. This is a new feature in version 0.46.2. The use cases where this might be needed are rare, but the option to perform this conversion is awesome when you need it.

I wrapped up the chapter discussing parent-child page relationships and how to create those relationships both from the page editor and from the Pages list panel using the edit hierarchy mode of that panel. We discussed the need to have pretty URLs enabled as well as enabling the display of child pages in either the global theme settings or on the page options.

CHAPTER 7

Creating a GitHub Page

The last three chapters have been all about getting a nice blog started. You have the basics of blogging down, and hopefully you have a website much like the project I have been using to guide you along. As nice as it is, this site can only be enjoyed by you right now. To get it out into the public arena where it can be consumed, you must first upload it to a location where it can be hosted and accessed by that audience.

For that, you will use GitHub Pages. GitHub Pages are not only easy to work with, but they are also free to use. Once you have done a little configuration, you will be able to easily publish your website or blog at the press of a single button in Publii CMS.

In Chapter 2, I discussed what GitHub is, and I walked you through getting a user account for GitHub. Dust off your notes from Chapter 2 because we are going to log on again and do some setup.

GitHub is a web-based platform that allows multiple people to collaborate on coding projects together. At its core, GitHub utilizes a version control system called Git that tracks changes made to files over time.

The central component of GitHub is the repository. A repository (or "repo" for short) is essentially a folder for a project that contains all the project's files and revision history. Repositories make it easy for

© Brad Moore 2025
B. Moore, *Designing Websites with Publii and GitHub Pages*,
https://doi.org/10.1007/979-8-8688-1195-1_7

multiple people to work on the same project together without accidentally overwriting each other's changes. Developers can "clone" a repository to their local machine, make edits to the code, and then "push" those changes back up to the central repo on GitHub. Mechanisms built into GitHub called merging prevent users from overwriting each other's work even when working on the same files.

Publii CMS leverages the repository storage container as well as the process of uploading files from a local machine to the repository – a process GitHub calls a "push." Publii CMS does not support multiuser synchronizing of the repository or use the mechanisms for merging code bases. Publii CMS only uses a repository for file storage and for publishing those files as a GitHub Pages site.

GitHub Pages allow you to create a website directly from a GitHub repository. It works by taking the files in your repository and serving them as web pages. Typically, these files would be HTML, CSS, and JavaScript files all working together to be displayed as a live website. These are the kinds of files that Publii CMS will upload to the repository that you will be creating and configuring as a GitHub Pages site.

I know that this all sounds a little complex. The good news is that you will not need to know any complex technical details to use GitHub Pages. All you need is the GitHub account you created earlier and a repository. Any changes pushed to your repository will immediately update your GitHub Pages site, and everyone on the Internet will be able to view the new information.

This provides an easy way to make websites using GitHub without needing to learn web hosting or server management. Many people use GitHub Pages for personal sites, blogs, documentation, portfolios, and more. GitHub Pages handles all the complicated backend stuff and makes website building simple. You just focus on creating content using Publii CMS, and GitHub Pages take care of the rest.

Getting Back to GitHub

In this section, you will be guided through accessing GitHub again, creating a repository and configuring it for usage as a GitHub Pages page.

Logging In

In Chapter 2, you created a GitHub account. It's time to use it now. You did write down all the important information such as username and password as you were advised – right?

Open your favorite web browser and navigate to the GitHub login page URL: "`https://github.com/login`" as shown in Figure 7-1.

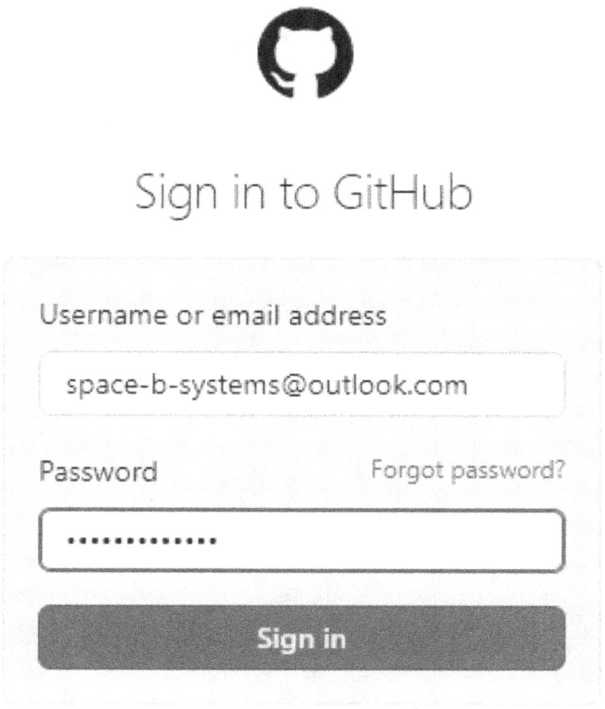

Sign in to GitHub

Username or email address

space-b-systems@outlook.com

Password   Forgot password?

••••••••••••

Sign in

Figure 7-1. *Log in to GitHub*

Log in with your username and password that you set up in Chapter 2. If you have forgotten it, you will need to use the "Forgot password?" link under the Username field.

Click the green "Sign in" button.

You may be asked to validate your logon to the current device as shown in Figure 7-2. When this happens, an Authentication code is sent to your email address on file. Open the email application and find the email that was sent to your email account.

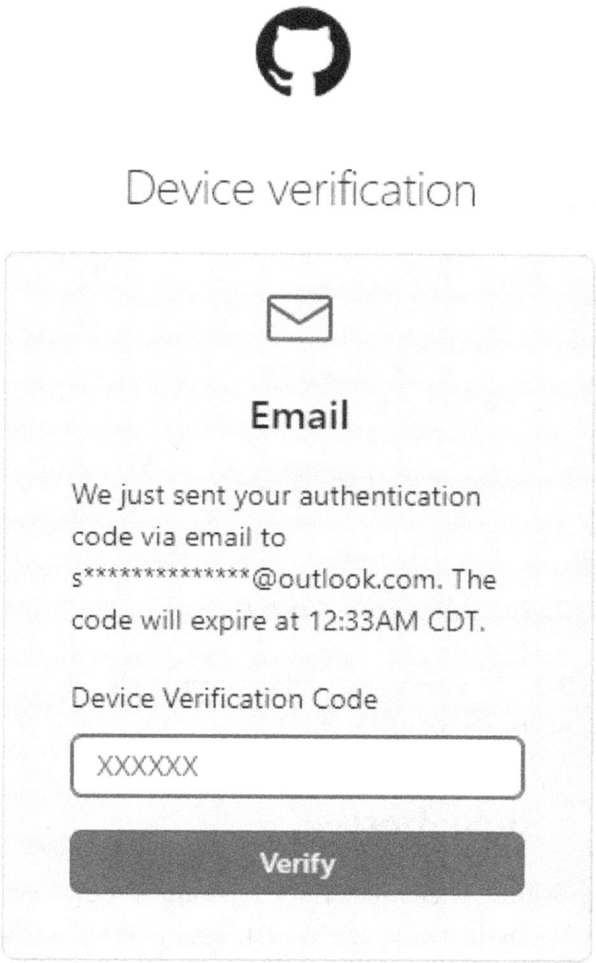

Device verification

Email

We just sent your authentication code via email to s***************@outlook.com. The code will expire at 12:33AM CDT.

Device Verification Code

XXXXXX

Verify

Figure 7-2. *Device verification*

Retrieve the Device Verification code from the email you received and enter it into the field provided.

Click the green "Verify" button.

Once logged on to your GitHub account, you will see a very busy application interface as shown in Figure 7-3.

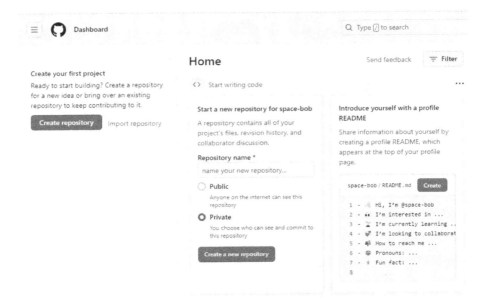

Figure 7-3. *GitHub application interface*

Don't let all the windows and options overwhelm you. What needs to be done is simple to accomplish.

Creating a Repository

To create a repository, click the "Create repository" button in the first column to the left of the web page as highlighted in Figure 7-4.

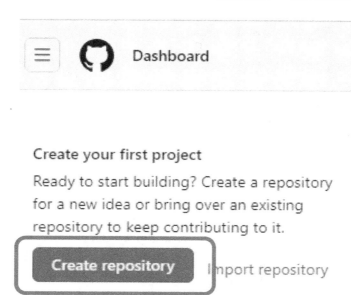

Figure 7-4. *Create a repository*

This opens the "New repository" page. Only one field needs data on this page. That is the "Repository name" as shown in Figure 7-5.

Figure 7-5. *Create a new repository*

I have called my repository "moonshot". You can call yours the same thing or mix it up a little bit.

A little further down on the same page is the Public/Private settings as shown in Figure 7-6.

Figure 7-6. *Repository privacy*

The default is Public, and it is important that it remains publicly accessible. No changes are needed if that is how it looks now.

The rest of the buttons and fields are all optional. Typically, I leave these all set to their default values. The only thing left to do is click the green "Create repository" button on the bottom right of the page as shown in Figure 7-7.

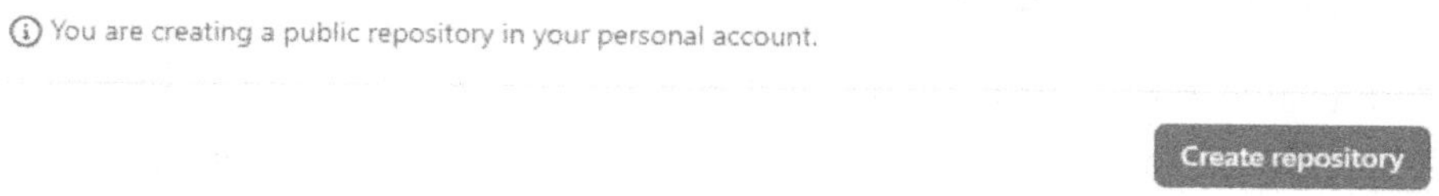

ⓘ You are creating a public repository in your personal account.

Create repository

Figure 7-7. *Create repository button*

The repository will be created and is ready for action. GitHub imagines that you will be using this repository in conjunction with some code development. It offers several ideas to get you started as you can see in Figure 7-8.

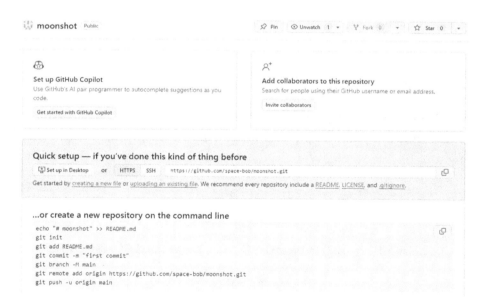

Figure 7-8. *GitHub repository after creation*

Don't worry, you are not in the wrong place. You will not need any of these extra tools, scripts, or code. You will, however, upload a test file in the next section.

Uploading a Test File

Uploading a file to your GitHub repository works just like adding image files to the Publii CMS image picker. It is all drag and drop. To get started, click the "uploading an existing file" link in the blue section of the page before you as highlighted in Figure 7-9.

Figure 7-9. *Uploading an existing file*

This will open a page where you will be able to drag and drop a file (or multiple files), allowing you to add them to the repository as shown in Figure 7-10.

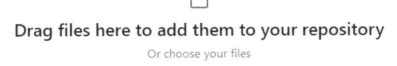

Figure 7-10. *Drag and drop file interface*

I want you to put a specific file into your repository as I will be doing in my repository. This file will be one we create on our PC or Mac. It will be a very basic HTML file. This will let us test the GitHub Pages configuration later.

I will show you how to create this file on a Windows computer using Notepad. If you are on a Mac, you might need to install a text editor to create this file. Alternatively download it from the book's GitHub repository at `https://github.com/Apress/Designing-Websites-with-Publii-and-GitHub-Pages`.

Locate the search bar or search icon on the lower left corner of your Windows desktop in the taskbar area. Type into the search bar "Notepad" as shown in Figure 7-11.

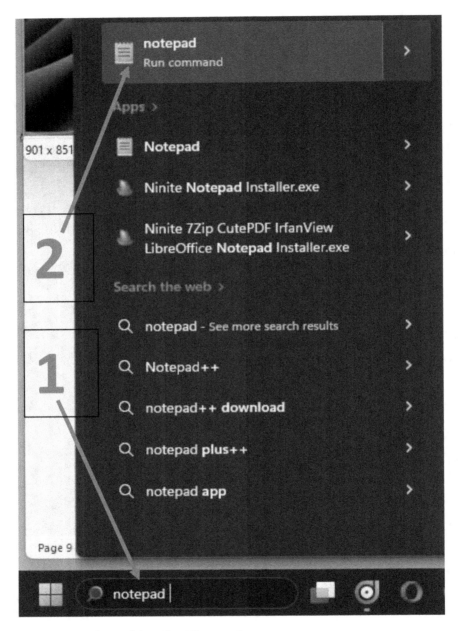

Figure 7-11. *Searching for Notepad*

Your screen may look slightly different from mine depending on the version and build of Windows you are running. I am running Windows 11 update 21H2.

In Figure 7-11, item 1 indicates the search field and the value that I am searching. Item 2 is one of the results that the search returned. In this case, it is an executable program called Notepad. Clicking this will open the Notepad application on your computer.

Click on the program to open the application as shown in Figure 7-12.

Figure 7-12. *Notepad with a blank document*

Add this single line of HTML to the document:

```
<h1>Hello World</h1>
```

This is shown in Figure 7-13.

Figure 7-13. *A line of HTML*

Click the File menu and click the "Save as" menu item as shown in Figure 7-14.

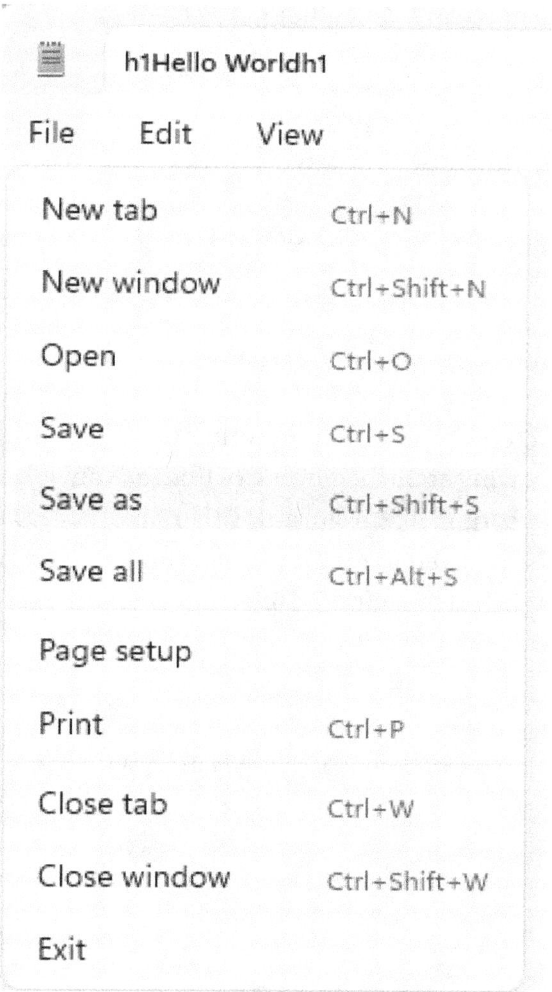

📝   h1Hello Worldh1

File	Edit	View

New tab	Ctrl+N
New window	Ctrl+Shift+N
Open	Ctrl+O
Save	Ctrl+S
Save as	Ctrl+Shift+S
Save all	Ctrl+Alt+S
Page setup	
Print	Ctrl+P
Close tab	Ctrl+W
Close window	Ctrl+Shift+W
Exit	

Figure 7-14. *Save as menu item*

This will open a file dialog window. Navigate to the Downloads folder. Type the name of the file to save exactly as follows including the quotation marks:

```
"index.html"
```

Observe the file name as highlighted in Figure 7-15.

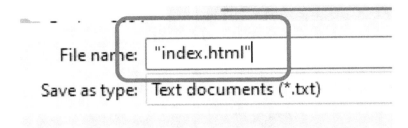

Figure 7-15. *Save the file as "index.html"*

Close the Notepad application now. Return to the GitHub website that you were viewing at the beginning of this section. It has a drag and drop field for uploading files from your PC or Mac. Drag the "index.html" file you created and saved in the Downloads folder and drop it onto the GitHub page as shown in Figure 7-16.

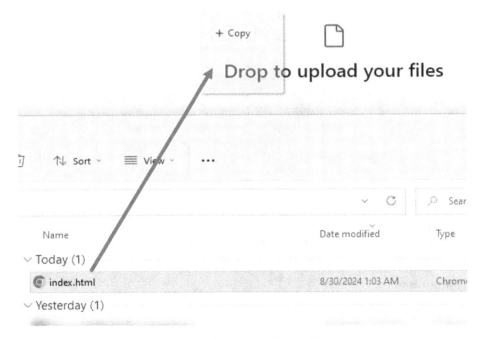

Figure 7-16. *Drag and drop the index.html file*

Don't forget you can get this file from the source code for this book from the book's GitHub repository located here: `https://github.com/Apress/Designing-Websites-with-Publii-and-GitHub-Pages`.

You can see the file has been added to the file list in Figure 7-17.

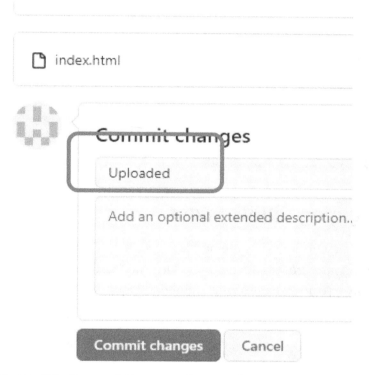

Figure 7-17. *File list and Commit changes button*

Notice also the highlighted field. This is where commit change notes are usually added before a commit is done.

The commit simply finishes the upload process and commits our changes to the repository. Add a note if desired. I simply typed "Uploaded".

Click the green "Commit changes" button to complete the upload process.

Your brand-new "index.html" file is in your repository now as shown in Figure 7-18, just like it is in mine – provided you have been following along.

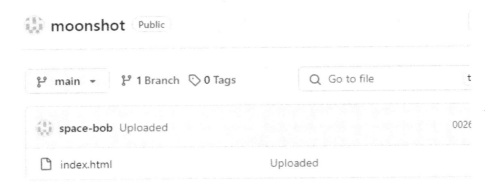

Figure 7-18. *File shown in the repository*

Configuring GitHub Pages

Configuring your repository to be the source for a GitHub Pages site is a straightforward process. Begin by clicking the "Settings" menu item at the top of the repository page as highlighted in Figure 7-19.

Figure 7-19. *Settings option on the right side of the menu*

A menu for General settings will be displayed on the left side of the page as shown in Figure 7-20. Click the "Pages" menu item as highlighted in Figure 7-20.

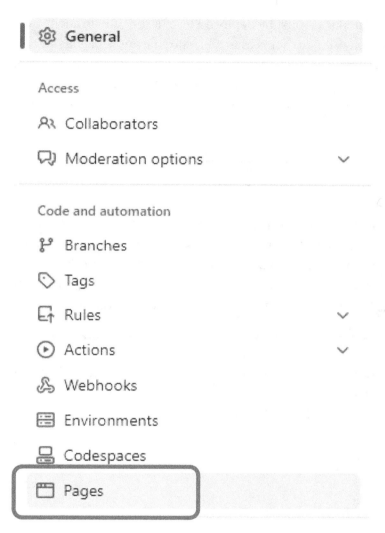

Figure 7-20. *General settings menu*

GitHub pages must be deployed from a specific "branch". Branches are another way GitHub helps manage code sharing. You will not need to use code sharing features, but you will still require at least one branch. GitHub conveniently generates the "main" branch when a repository is created. In this project, you will use the main branch. Further understanding of branches is not required.

MORE ABOUT BRANCHES

In GitHub, branches are used as a mechanism of further segmentation for a repository. Development teams often have multiple people working in the same repository. Branches allow these groups to check out code in a controlled manner. Later when code is checked back in, the branch aids in reconciling changes as various branches are merged back into the main branch.

Figure 7-21 shows the GitHub Pages settings page. Only one thing needs to be done on this page. You must select a branch that your GitHub Pages website will be published from.

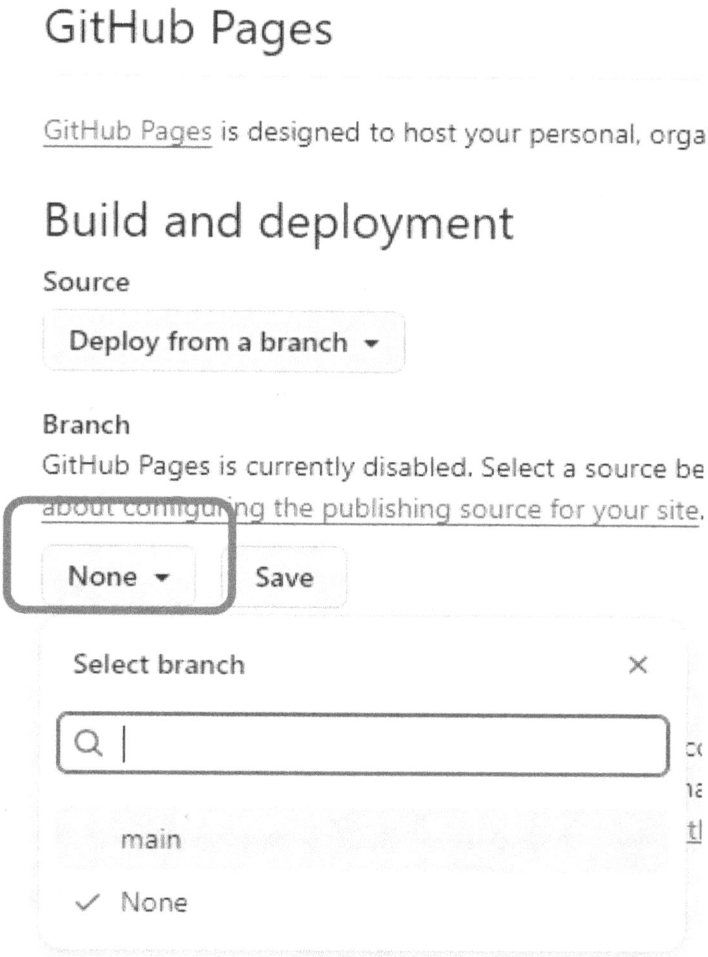

GitHub Pages

GitHub Pages is designed to host your personal, orga

Build and deployment

Source

Deploy from a branch ▾

Branch

GitHub Pages is currently disabled. Select a source be
about configuring the publishing source for your site.

None ▾   Save

Select branch   ✕

Q |

main

✓ None

Figure 7-21. *GitHub Pages settings*

Click the drop-down button labeled "None" as highlighted in
Figure 7-21. Select the branch called "main".

Notice that the branch "main" is now the source for your GitHub Pages
website. The website will be shared from the /root folder as shown in
Figure 7-22. Click the Save button to commit the changes as highlighted in
Figure 7-22.

Figure 7-22. *Branch and folder where GitHub Pages site is served from*

The GitHub Pages settings page will reload after the Save button is pressed. It will become a bit busier as shown in Figure 7-23.

GitHub Pages source saved.

⚙ General

Access

&⅃ Collaborators

⊡ Moderation options   ⌄

Code and automation

⅊ Branches

⬖ Tags

⌗ Rules   ⌄

▶ Actions   ⌄

⌘ Webhooks

⊞ Environments

⊟ Codespaces

▏ ⊟ Pages

Security

⊙ Code security and analysis

⊘ Deploy keys

✳ Secrets and variables   ⌄

Integrations

⌂ ⌐⌐⌐⌐ ⌐⌐⌐⌐

GitHub Pages

GitHub Pages is designed to host your personal, organization,

Build and deployment

Source

Deploy from a branch ▾

Branch

Your GitHub Pages site is currently being built from the main b
source for your site.

⅊ main ▾   ■ / (root) ▾   Save

Learn how to add a Jekyll theme to your site.

Custom domain

Custom domains allow you to serve your site from a domain c
configuring custom domains.

[   ]   Save   Remove

☑ **Enforce HTTPS**

— Required for your site because you are using the default domain

HTTPS provides a layer of encryption that prevents others from snoc
When HTTPS is enforced, your site will only be served over HTTPS. L
HTTPS.

Figure 7-23. *The GitHub Pages settings page*

Also note that there is a message at the top of the page informing you
that the GitHub Pages source was saved. Wait a minute or two and then
refresh the page by reloading it in your browser. Often the F5 key will do
that for you.

It takes GitHub a minute or so to register your new GitHub Pages
website, set up a security certificate, and publish the page. After the
refresh, you should see a message in the GitHub Pages settings telling you
that your new site is live as shown in Figure 7-24.

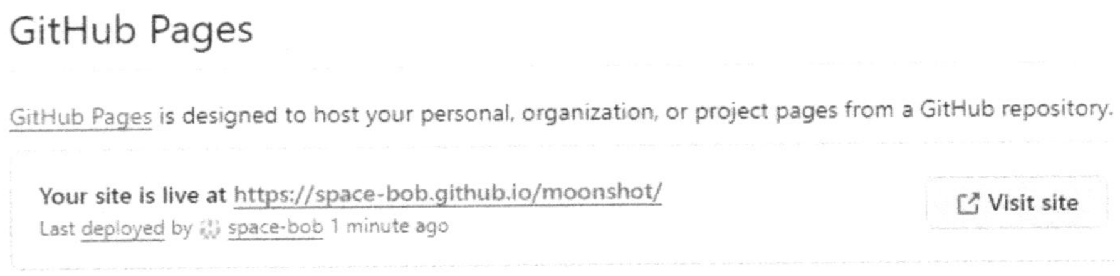
GitHub Pages
GitHub Pages is designed to host your personal, organization, or project pages from a GitHub repository.
Your site is live at https://space-bob.github.io/moonshot/
Last deployed by space-bob 1 minute ago
Visit site

Figure 7-24. *Message about the new site going live*

Testing the Website

Looking at the message about your new site going live in Figure 7-24, you will notice a button labeled "Visit site" on the right-hand side of the message area. Click that button to test your new website. Your site will be opened in a new browser tab that will look like Figure 7-25 (provided you have followed along).

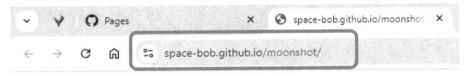

Pages
space-bob.github.io/moonshot
space-bob.github.io/moonshot/
Hello World

Figure 7-25. *Website hosted by GitHub Pages*

There is not much to this site. It is just a simple "Hello World" message which we created earlier in this chapter. Take note of the URL for this site – highlighted in Figure 7-25. This is where your blog or website created in Publii CMS will be hosted. This is the URL others will need to know to access your site.

Using your mouse cursor, select the website URL and copy using either a right mouse click ➤ copy or the Ctrl-C key combination.

Final Steps

Click the tab in your browser labeled "Pages" where your GitHub Pages settings are displayed. If you accidentally clicked the link to your new site (instead of the button in Figure 7-24), then press the web browser's back button to go back to the GitHub Pages settings.

Tip   If you cannot find the GitHub Pages settings anymore – open a new tab. Log back into GitHub as you did in Figure 7-1. In the list of repositories, click the only one listed. Now click the "Settings" menu item on the top menu as shown in Figure 7-19.

We should all be in the same place again. Click the "Code" menu item in the top menu as highlighted in Figure 7-26.

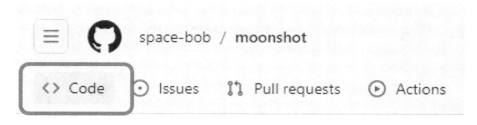

Figure 7-26. *Code menu item in the top-level menu*

This returns you to the repository view. Here you can see the files that are part of this repository as well as some general statistics. Click the gear icon in the upper right portion of the page in the "About" section as highlighted in Figure 7-27.

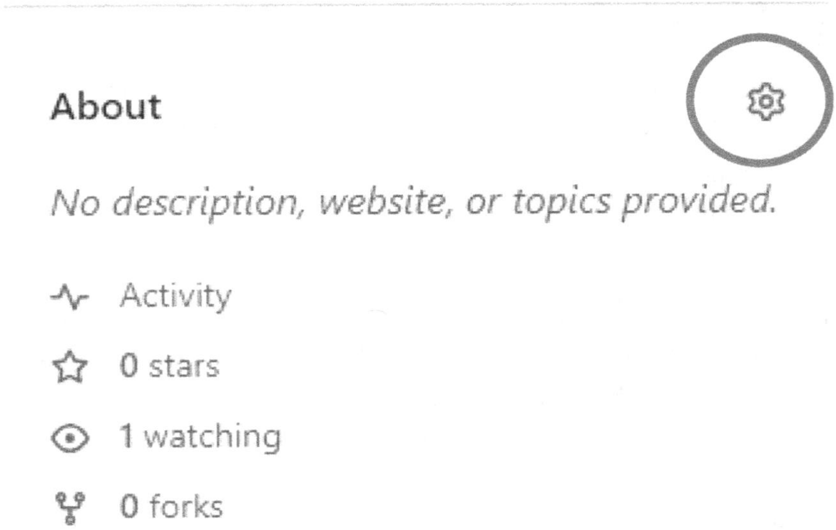

About

No description, website, or topics provided.

⌁ Activity

☆ 0 stars

⊙ 1 watching

⅌ 0 forks

Figure 7-27. *Basic statistics in the repository GitHub About section*

This will open the "Edit repository details" dialog window as shown in Figure 7-28. Paste the URL you copied above into the Description field.

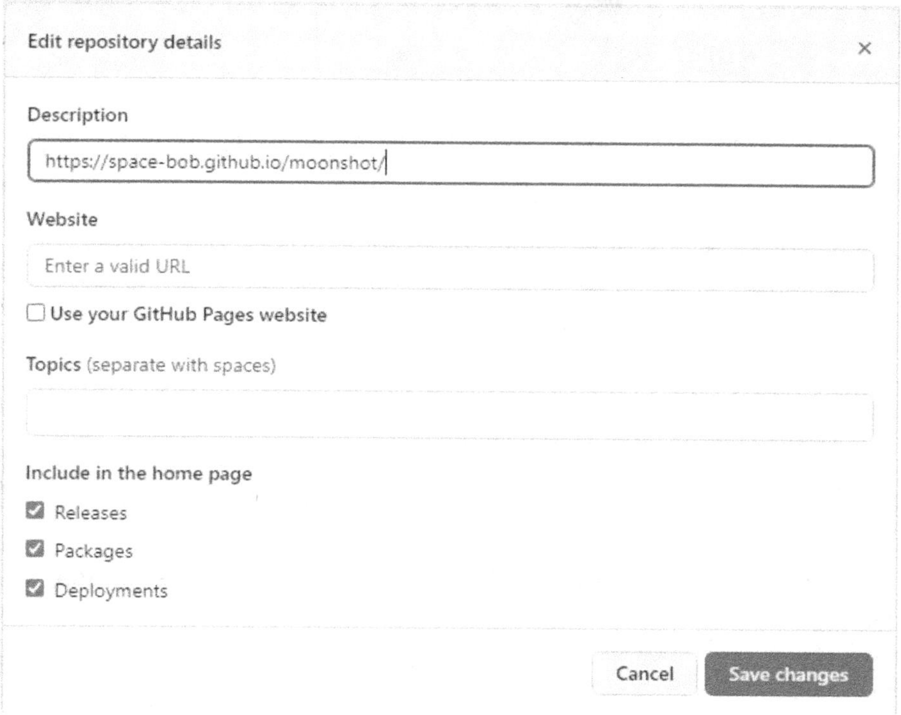

Figure 7-28.   *The Edit repository details dialog window*

If you no longer have the URL in your clipboard, return to the tab viewed in Figure 7-25 and copy the URL again.

Once the URL is pasted into the Description field as shown in Figure 7-28, click the green "Save changes" button on the lower right of the dialog window.

You now have a handy link to open the web page hosted here in this repository as shown in Figure 7-29.

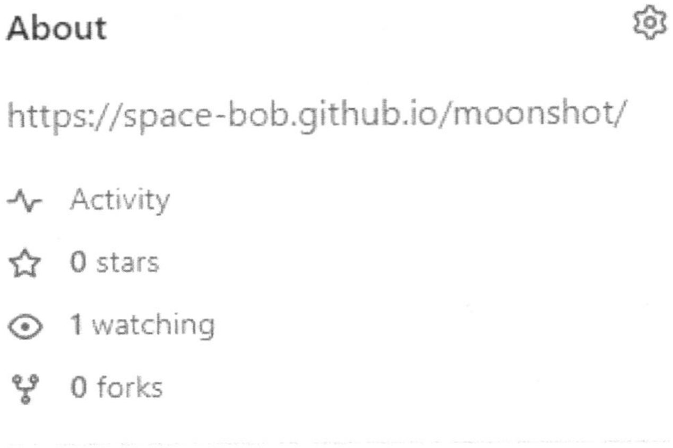

About ⚙

https://space-bob.github.io/moonshot/

〰 Activity

☆ 0 stars

⊙ 1 watching

ഴ 0 forks

Figure 7-29. URL to the website in the About section

I wish I could take credit for this little hack, but someone else taught it to me.

Summary

In this chapter, you returned to the GitHub web application. This time you configured a repository to act as the location where your future website will reside.

You saw that GitHub is potentially complex as there are many different options and menu items that we did not even touch. You also saw that what you needed to do was quite simple.

You created a repository. The repository had a default branch that you later used called "main".

You also uploaded a test document to the repository. It was a very simple HTML file that I walked you through creating. One line of HTML code was in this file. Remember if you cannot create your own file, you can download one from the book's repository here: `https://github.com/Apress/Designing-Websites-with-Publii-and-GitHub-Pages`.

You did not convert the repository to a GitHub Page; rather, you attached a GitHub page to the repository. You accessed the GitHub repository settings to do that.

Assigning the default branch of "main" to the Page and saving the settings created the GitHub Page.

You verified the operation of the Page by accessing the URL for your new site. This caused the index.html file uploaded earlier to be displayed in your browser.

CHAPTER 8

Configure Publii CMS for Sync

In this chapter, I will be explaining how Publii CMS moves the website you have created to the remote hosting location that you have prepared. This process is called synchronization. It is what you must do to get your content online where your readers can see and consume it.

Before synchronization can first be performed, you must configure a remote server to host your files – a step we did in Chapter 7 – and configure Publii CMS so that it can communicate with the server.

In this chapter, you will learn how to configure Publii CMS to communicate to your GitHub repository. Publii CMS calls this "Server configuration".

Understanding Synchronization

Server configuration is required to permit Publii CMS to connect to and communicate with your host. Once the configuration is completed, the Configure Server button at the bottom of the Publii CMS application menu will change to read "Sync your website".

The synchronization process involves three specific actions that Publii CMS performs.

© Brad Moore 2025
B. Moore, *Designing Websites with Publii and GitHub Pages*,
https://doi.org/10.1007/979-8-8688-1195-1_8

First, Publii CMS runs all the pages and posts in your site through a compiler where content is merged with theme templates and static HTML files are generated. These files are your website. This is what happens when you preview your site as well.

Second, Publii CMS will attempt to contact your remote host where your public website is stored. This is a repository on GitHub in your case. The host is the associated GitHub Pages server that makes these files available as a website.

Finally, Publii CMS generates a "files.publii.json" file that contains a list of all files in your site, each with its own individual checksum (a kind of digital fingerprint that contains metadata about each of the files in your site). During synchronization, Publii CMS compares the local files.publii.json with the list on the server. If differences in checksums are found (indicating a modified file), only those modified files will be uploaded, reducing the network load of uploading unnecessary files and speeding up the deployment process.

If there are files in the repository that do not exist in the local copy and are not listed in the local files.publii.json, then they are deleted from the repository.

This process ensures the GitHub repository matches the local copy of your website. In the case of large sites, it also ensures that the upload is as efficient as possible by only touching files that have changed or do not exist on one side or the other of the sybchronized locations.

Publii CMS Synchronization Settings

In this section, I will be guiding you through the configuration steps to connect Publii CMS to your GitHub repository. To get started, click the "Server" button in the Publii CMS main menu on the left side of the application as shown in Figure 8-1.

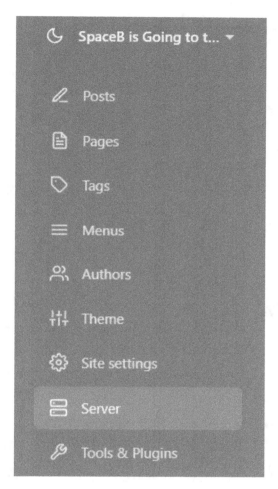

Figure 8-1. *Publii CMS main menu*

Server Type

The right panel of the application will display the "Select server type" interface after clicking the "Server" button, which is shown in Figure 8-2.

Select server type:

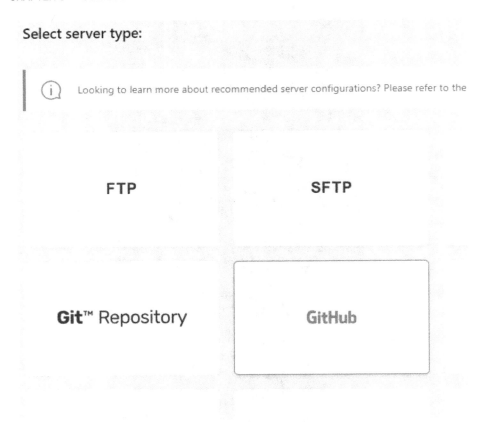

Figure 8-2. *Select server type interface (cropped)*

Click on the GitHub server type to configure a connection to GitHub.

GitHub connections will need several specific elements of data for it to be functional. These include the URL of the target Website, Username, Repository name, Branch name, and a security Token as seen in Figure 8-3.

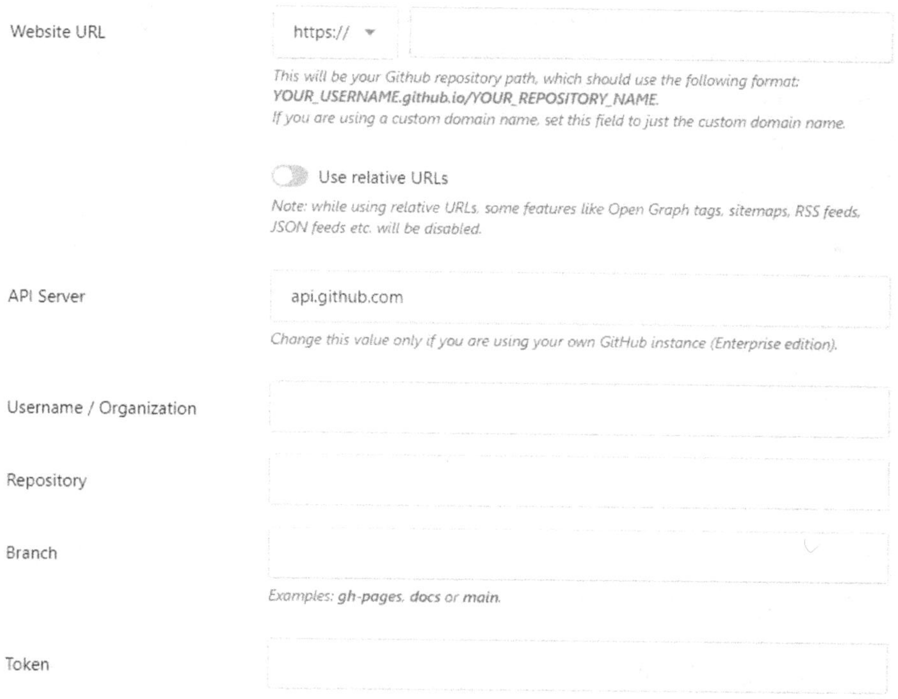

Website URL	https:// ▾	

This will be your Github repository path, which should use the following format:
YOUR_USERNAME.github.io/YOUR_REPOSITORY_NAME.
If you are using a custom domain name, set this field to just the custom domain name.

⬤ Use relative URLs

Note: while using relative URLs, some features like Open Graph tags, sitemaps, RSS feeds, JSON feeds etc. will be disabled.

API Server	api.github.com

Change this value only if you are using your own GitHub instance (Enterprise edition).

Username / Organization	

Repository	

Branch	

*Examples: **gh-pages**, **docs** or **main**.*

Token	

Figure 8-3. *GitHub Pages server configuration*

Publii CMS offers a couple good resources for configuring various server connections which are linked from the information notice at the top of the Settings page as shown in Figure 8-4.

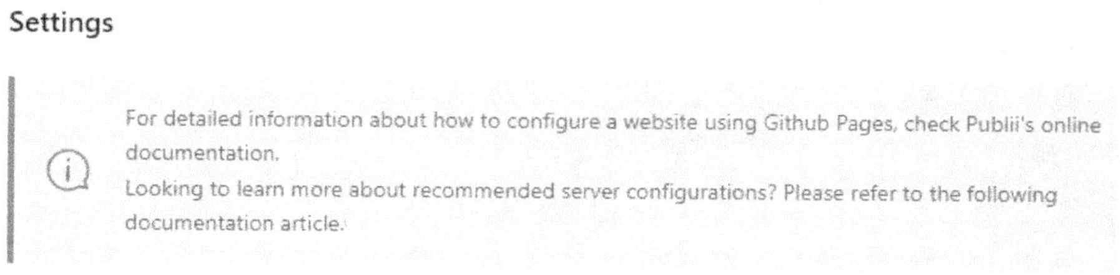

Settings

ⓘ For detailed information about how to configure a website using Github Pages, check Publii's online documentation.
Looking to learn more about recommended server configurations? Please refer to the following documentation article.

Figure 8-4. *Help and guidance on server configuration*

In the sections that follow, I will guide you through each of the configuration elements. It will help to open GitHub in your favorite browser and log in to your GitHub account, navigating to the repository that was set up in Chapter 7. Refer to Chapter 7 for steps to log in. Your GitHub repository will look something like mine in Figure 8-5.

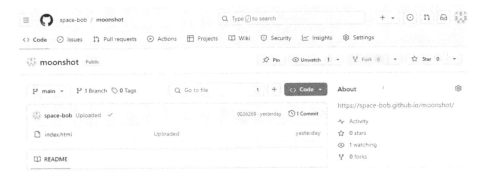

Figure 8-5. *GitHub repository*

Don't worry if you cannot read the text in Figure 8-5. I will zoom in on the necessary sections of GitHub as we gather information from it.

Website URL

The first section of the server configuration to which you will be adding information is the Website URL as shown in Figure 8-6. This image is a cropped portion of the overall page which I have zoomed in on for your benefit in this book.

Website URL	https:// ▼	

This will be your Github repository path, which should use the following format:
YOUR_USERNAME.github.io/YOUR_REPOSITORY_NAME.
If you are using a custom domain name, set this field to just the custom domain name.

⬤ Use relative URLs

Note: while using relative URLs, some features like Open Graph tags, sitemaps, RSS feeds,
JSON feeds etc. will be disabled.

Figure 8-6. *Configuring the Website URL*

Switch to your web browser which should have your GitHub repository opened on one of your tabs (if not – scan above for information about viewing your GitHub repository). Focus on the GitHub's "About" section in the upper right quarter of the page as shown in Figure 8-7.

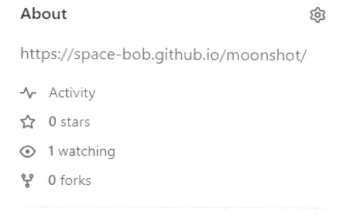

About   ⚙

https://space-bob.github.io/moonshot/

∿ Activity

☆ 0 stars

⊙ 1 watching

⅄ 0 forks

Figure 8-7. *About section of your GitHub repository*

Right-click the URL for your website that is shown in the About section as shown in Figure 8-8.

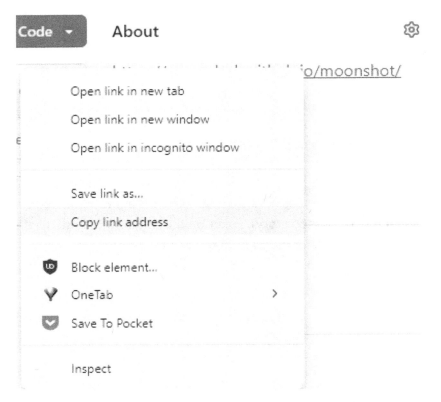

Figure 8-8. *Right-click and select "Copy link address"*

Click the context menu item labeled "Copy link address". Return to Publii CMS and paste that link address into the field for Website URL as shown in Figure 8-9.

This will be your Github repository path, which should use the following format:
YOUR_USERNAME.github.io/YOUR_REPOSITORY_NAME.
If you are using a custom domain name, set this field to just the custom domain name.

Figure 8-9. *Paste the link address into the Website URL field*

Remove the protocol portion of the link address (the part that says "https://") as the protocol is specified in a separate drop-down field. Typically, the protocol of "https://" is correct for GitHub-hosted sites, so leave the field set to its default value.

Also – do NOT enable the "Use relative URLs" option highlighted in Figure 8-10. Enabling this option will disable some desirable features – especially sitemaps.

Note   Sitemaps are very important for helping a search engine crawler understand your website. Google states that they expect sites to have a sitemap to index properly. This is once again one of those things that your site will benefit from for best SEO performance.

Figure 8-10. *The "Use relative URLs" option*

While I am mentioning default settings, ensure that the default setting for API Server remains set to "api.github.com" as shown in Figure 8-11.

Figure 8-11. *API Server setting default value*

Username

The next element that requires a specific value is the GitHub Username/
Organization. This is the username that your repository resides under on
GitHub. Switch over to your repository in GitHub on your browser. Look at
the upper left corner of the page as shown in Figure 8-12. Your username
will be in the same place as mine, which is highlighted in the figure below.

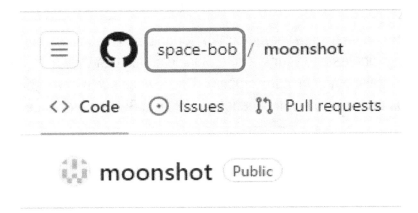

Figure 8-12. *Location of GitHub username*

Type that username into the Username/Organization field in the
Settings page in Publii CMS as shown in Figure 8-13.

Username / Organization   space-bob

Figure 8-13. *Username/Organization field*

Repository

The repository name is required next. The repository name can also be seen on your GitHub repository page. It is highlighted in Figure 8-14.

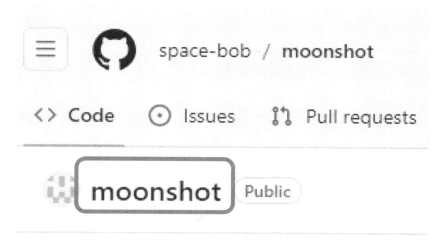

Figure 8-14. *Repository name*

Type that repository name into the Repository field in the Settings page in Publii CMS as shown in Figure 8-15.

Repository   moonshot

Figure 8-15. *Repository name*

Branch

The branch name is required next. If you have been following along with me as I have developed the project, then your branch name is "main". This can also be seen on your GitHub repository page. It is highlighted in Figure 8-16.

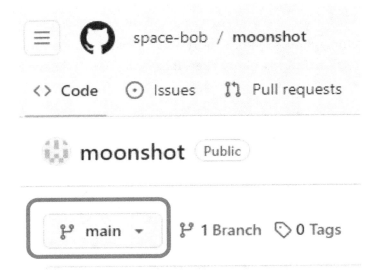

Figure 8-16. *Branch name*

Type that branch name into the Branch field in the Settings page in Publii CMS as shown in Figure 8-17.

Figure 8-17. *Branch name*

Token

The last element needed is a security Token. Tokens must be generated in GitHub and assigned to a specific resource that will be accessing a GitHub repository. This is the most complex part of the setup process.

If you get lost along the way, come back to the beginning and retrace your steps. This can be done by carefully following the examples and working through the process. Ideally you will have your computer in front of you and the book open on your desk as you take this step.

Generating a Token

GitHub should be open in one of your web browser tabs from the previous sections. Go back to that tab now. Click on your account avatar in the upper right corner of the page as highlighted in Figure 8-18.

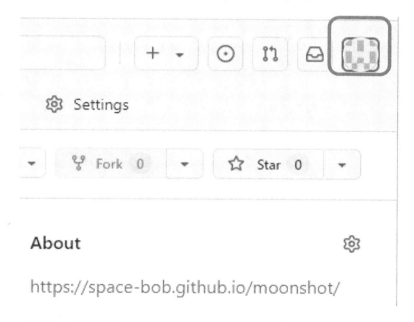

Figure 8-18. *GitHub account avatar*

When clicked, a panel will fly out from the right side of the web application with many menu options. Click the Settings menu item in the menu as highlighted in Figure 8-19.

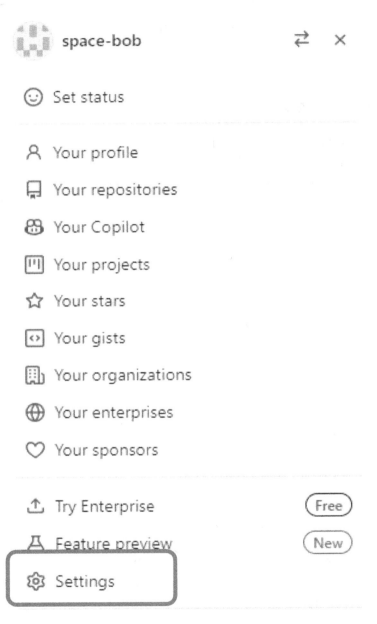

Figure 8-19. *Settings menu item*

The settings page is a complex page with many options. It features its own menu with many items listed on the left side of the page. These options permit configuration of additional properties for your account. The menu is longer than my web browser window as shown in Figure 8-20.

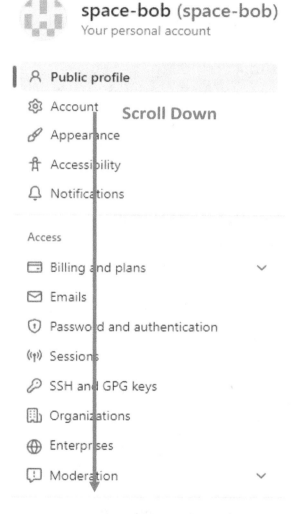

Figure 8-20. Account settings menu. Scroll to the bottom of the menu

Scroll all the way to the bottom of the page so that you can see the "Developer settings" menu item as highlighted in Figure 8-21.

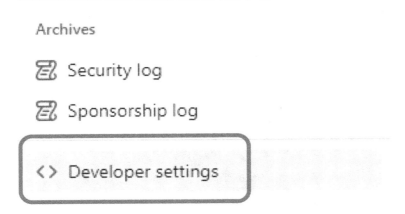

Figure 8-21. *Developer settings menu item*

In the developer Settings page, click the "Personal access tokens" drop-down menu item as highlighted in Figure 8-22.

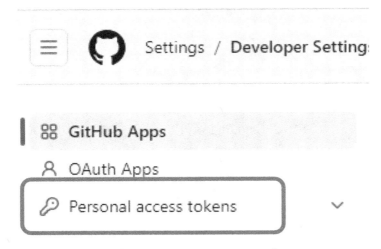

Figure 8-22. *Click the "Personal access tokens" menu item*

Now click the "Tokens (classic)" menu item in the drop-down menu as highlighted in Figure 8-23.

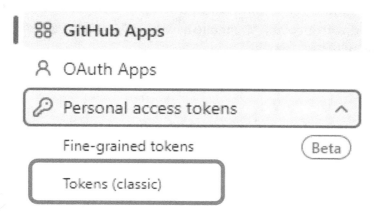

Figure 8-23. *Click the "Tokens (classic)" menu item*

On the same page on the upper right side is a drop-down button that is labeled "Generate new token". Click this button as highlighted in Figure 8-24.

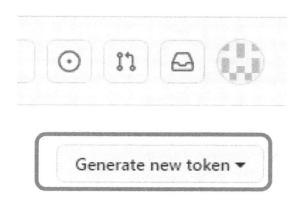

Figure 8-24. *Click the "Generate new token" button*

One would imagine that there would be a simpler way to get to the page we need, but we find ourselves needing to click one more menu item. This time it is the "Generate new token (classic)" menu item that dropped down out of the "Generate new token" button. This menu item is highlighted in Figure 8-25.

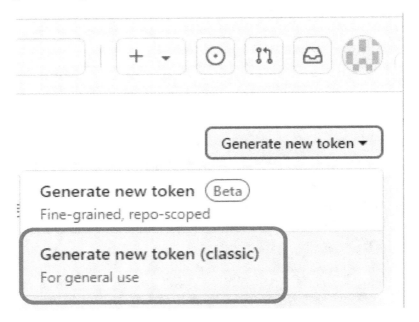

Figure 8-25. *Click the "Generate new token" menu item*

At this point, GitHub wanted me to confirm that I was really who I said I was as you can see in Figure 8-26. This is because I was entering what GitHub called "sudo mode" – which is a higher level of access than required to just manage the repository.

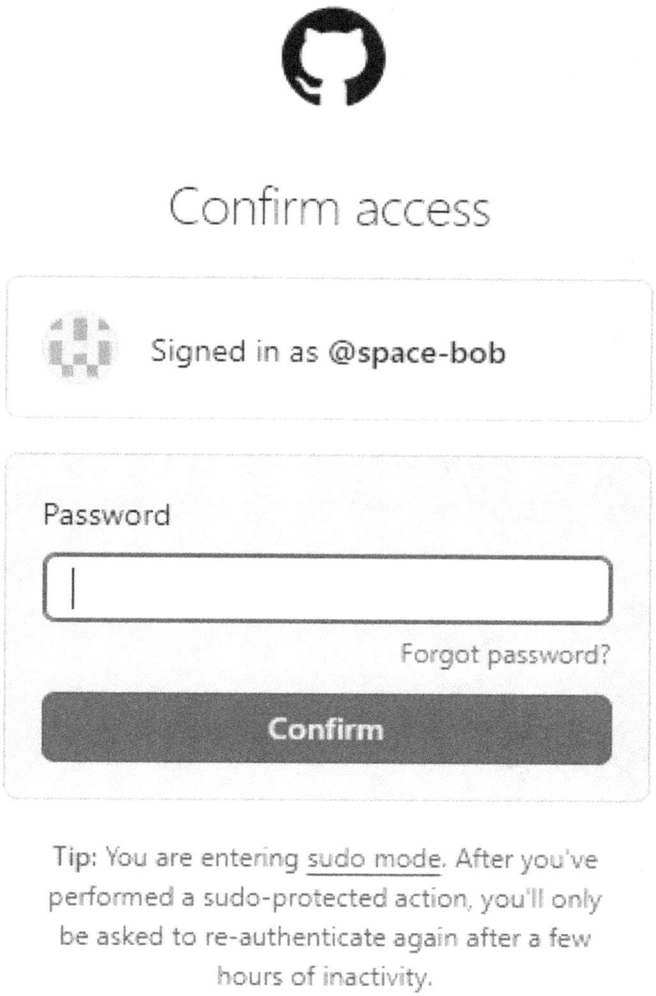

Confirm access

Signed in as @space-bob

Password

Forgot password?

Confirm

Tip: You are entering sudo mode. After you've
performed a sudo-protected action, you'll only
be asked to re-authenticate again after a few
hours of inactivity.

Figure 8-26. *Entering sudo mode*

Enter your password here and click the green "Confirm" button.

Once you have confirmed you are authorized to perform these actions, GitHub will open a new page titled "New personal access token (classic)" as shown in Figure 8-27.

Don't panic! What we need to do here is very simple.

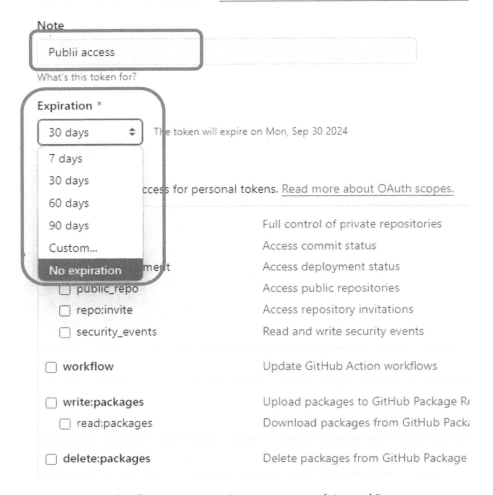

Figure 8-27. The "New personal access token (classic)" page (cropped)

Add a note in the Note field as highlighted in Figure 8-27. This is a non-binding bit of information that is for your future benefit instead of GitHub's use. Later it will remind you why you created this personal access key.

Next select an Expiration. I always choose "No expiration" as indicated from the highlighting in Figure 8-27. GitHub will be unhappy about this, warning it is a security concern as you can see in Figure 8-28. Frankly I don't want to have to remember how to extend the personal access key every 30, 60, or 90 days.

Now we will need to select the scope for the access that is being granted. Figure 8-28 shows that I have selected "repo" as the scope. That is the only scope required.

Expiration *

| No expiration ⇕ | The token will never expire! |

GitHub strongly recommends that you set an expiration date for your token to help keep your information secure. Learn more

Select scopes

Scopes define the access for personal tokens. Read more about OAuth scopes.

☑ repo	Full control of private repositories
⬚ repo:status	Access commit status
⬚ repo_deployment	Access deployment status
⬚ public_repo	Access public repositories
⬚ repo:invite	Access repository invitations
⬚ security_events	Read and write security events

Figure 8-28. *Scope to which access is granted*

Now scroll all the way to the bottom of the page and locate the green "Generate token" button as highlighted in Figure 8-29.

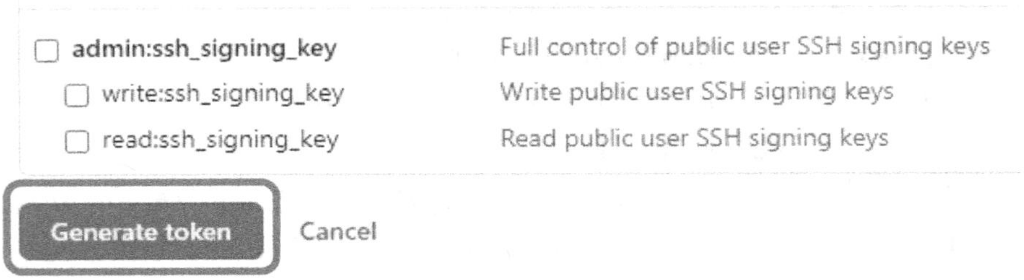

☐ admin:ssh_signing_key	Full control of public user SSH signing keys
☐ write:ssh_signing_key	Write public user SSH signing keys
☐ read:ssh_signing_key	Read public user SSH signing keys

Generate token   Cancel

Figure 8-29. *Locate the "Generate token" button on the bottom of the page*

Click the green "Generate token" button.

I trust you have made it this far unscathed. If so, then you have successfully generated a personal access token that Publii CMS can use to access GitHub. Give yourself a pat on the back.

Caution   Do not close the browser tab or navigate away from this page until you have copied the token. You will not be able to access it again.

Problems?

Did you get lost along the way? Go back to the beginning of this section and try again.

At the end of this chapter, there are some troubleshooting tips in case things just do not work. Don't forget that you can always ask for help in the Publii CMS user forum located here: `https://github.com/GetPublii/ Publii/discussions`.

Add the Token to Publii CMS

Presuming all went according to plan, you are now looking at your new token in a light green field on the "Personal access tokens (classic)" page as shown in Figure 8-30.

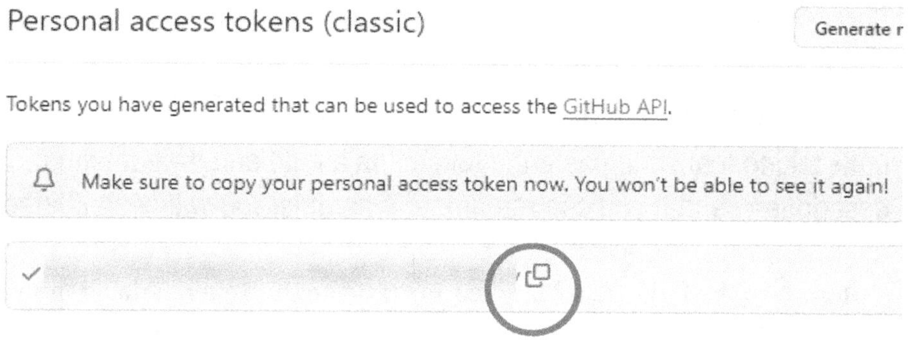

Personal access tokens (classic)   Generate r

Tokens you have generated that can be used to access the GitHub API.

🔔   Make sure to copy your personal access token now. You won't be able to see it again!

✓

Figure 8-30. *A new token*

This next step is really important. So important that I left the word "really" in that sentence!

GitHub will *NEVER* display this token again. You must copy it now to use it.

Tip   If you have already closed the browser window or otherwise lost the token before copying it, you must delete the token and start over.

Click the copy icon highlighted in Figure 8-30. GitHub will confirm that you have successfully copied the token as shown in Figure 8-31.

Figure 8-31. *Successful copy*

Tip   Open Notepad, OneNote, Evernote (or another electronic note-taking tool), and paste the token into a note and save it with a description so that you can remember what it is. You will need it later.

Return to the Publii CMS application. Locate the Token field as shown in Figure 8-32 and paste the token you just copied into the field.

Token   ••

Figure 8-32. *Token field with new security token applied*

Everything mandatory has been filled in. In the next section, the connection will be tested.

Testing the Connection

You have not yet saved the connection information for this server type, but you can test the connection and make sure everything is working properly.

Click the light blue "Test connection" button in the lower right corner of the server configuration panel as highlighted in Figure 8-33.

Figure 8-33. *The Test connection button*

If everything is working correctly, then you will see the dialog window shown in Figure 8-34.

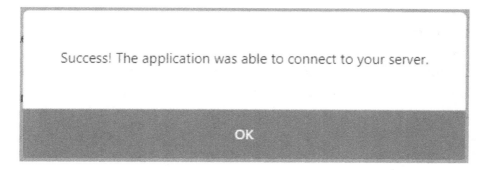

Figure 8-34. *Connection successful dialog window*

If this was not your experience, then go back over everything you have done in this chapter and double-check the settings and values. Make sure that you have used the same case (uppercase vs. lowercase) letters in the values supplied. Make sure there are no extra spaces where they should not be.

If problems persist, visit the Publii CMS user forum and open an issue. It is located here: https://github.com/GetPublii/Publii/discussions.

Additional Configuration

There are two additional configuration items that we did not touch on. These are the Parallel uploads setting and the API rate limiting option switch as shown in Figure 8-35.

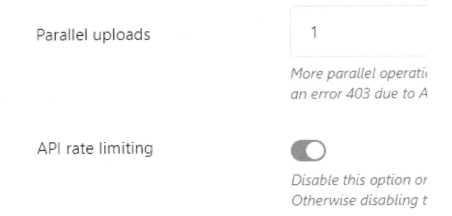

Figure 8-35. *Other settings*

Both settings can be left at their default values and things will work just fine. If you are on a fast Internet connection with fast *upload* speed (not download speed), then you could increase the parallel uploads. If you start experiencing problems with failed uploads, then set this back to "1".

The GitHub account you are using is not an Enterprise account, so do not disable the rate limiting.

Save Settings

Everything is in order. It is time to save the server settings. Click the blue "Save Settings" button in the lower right corner of the server Settings panel as shown in Figure 8-36.

Figure 8-36. *Save Settings button*

Figure 8-37. *Astronaut and alien hitchhiking home - public domain, generated by Dall-E November, 2024*

Synchronize

This section will discuss synchronizing your locally developed site with the GitHub repository. Synchronizing ensures that the same version of the same files are located both in the GitHub repository and on your local PC. Once a server has been configured in Publii CMS, the bottom button of the application main menu (on the left side of the application) will read "Sync your website".

If that button reads "Configure server", then you have not successfully configured and saved a server configuration.

Begin the Sync Process

Hover over the "Sync your website" button and it will turn yellow as shown in Figure 8-38.

Figure 8-38. *The "Sync your website" button*

Click the "Sync your website" button to begin the synchronization process. A full screen window called "Website synchronization" will be displayed in the Publii CMS interface as shown in Figure 8-39.

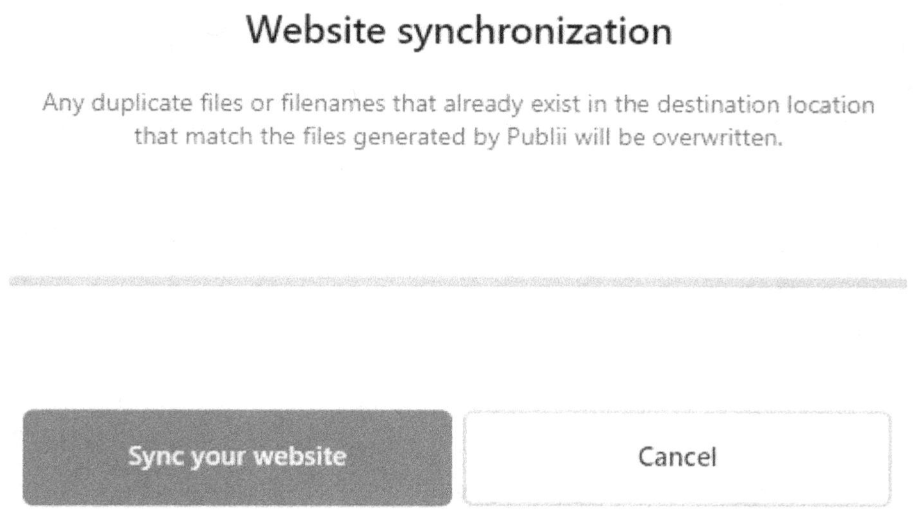

Website synchronization

Any duplicate files or filenames that already exist in the destination location
that match the files generated by Publii will be overwritten.

Sync your website   Cancel

Figure 8-39. *Website synchronization*

Click the blue "Sync your website" button on this panel to begin the
synchronization process. There are several steps involved in synchronizing
as described earlier in this chapter. Figure 8-40 shows the synchronization
process underway.

Website synchronization

Any duplicate files or filenames that already exist in the destination location
that match the files generated by Publii will be overwritten.

Uploading website (6 of 11 operations done)

Sync your website   Cancel

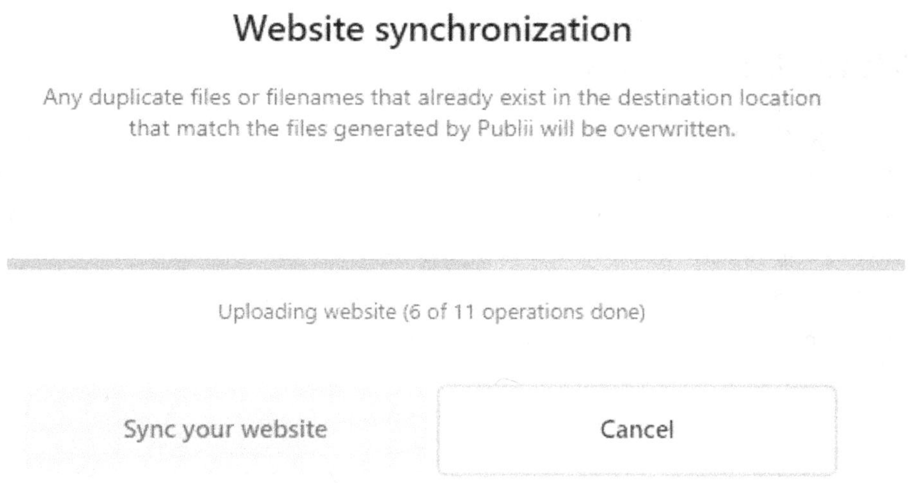

Figure 8-40. *Synchronization process underway*

Once the synchronization process has completed, the message title for this panel will change to "Your website is now in sync" as shown in Figure 8-41.

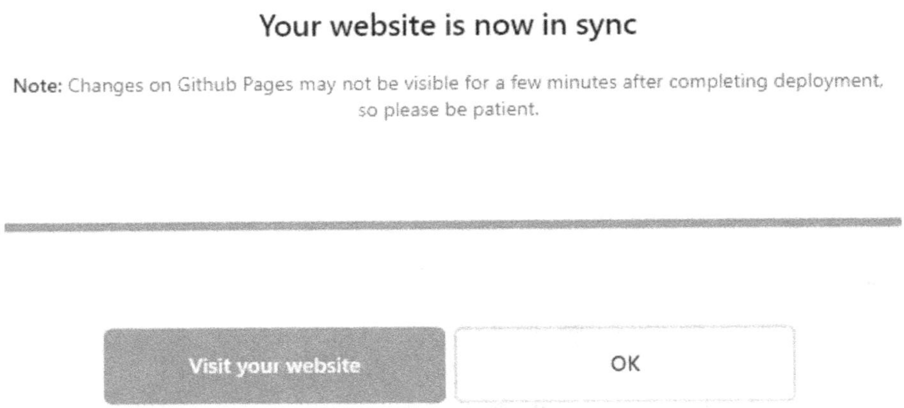

Your website is now in sync

Note: Changes on Github Pages may not be visible for a few minutes after completing deployment, so please be patient.

Figure 8-41. *Synchronization complete*

Click the white "OK" button to close this window and return to the main Publii CMS application or click the green "Visit your website" to open the site in the default browser.

View Your Website

Viewing your website from the completed synchronization panel is easy. Presuming you have not clicked the "OK" button, then click the "Visit your website" button. This will load your website into the browser served from the GitHub platform.

If you already closed the synchronization panel by clicking "OK", then just sync again. It will not harm the content on either side.

Issues with Cached Pages

There is a good chance that your browser will display the old test page that you were working with in Chapter 7 as can be seen in Figure 8-42.

Figure 8-42. *Old GitHub test page*

This is due to browser caching. Most web browsers will cache a website, and if visiting that site again, they will check to see if the cache has expired. If it has not explicitly expired, the old site will be displayed from your local computer cache. This reduces the amount of data moved from server to PC across the Internet and allows the page to load very quickly.

Getting cached pages rather than a newly updated page is a common problem that website developers must contend with. In our case, it is because the simple HTML page we created in Chapter 7 had no caching directives.

To overcome this issue, we simply need to clear the browser caches. What follows is the process to clear the cache on the Chrome web browser. Most other browsers work in a very similar way.

Click the three vertical dots in the upper right corner of the web browser window as highlighted in Figure 8-43.

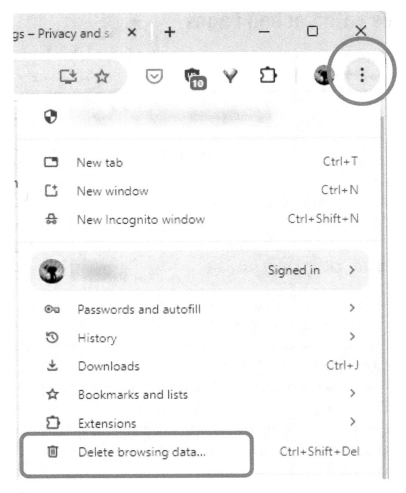

Figure 8-43. *Opening Chrome's application menu*

This will open the application menu for Chrome. Observe that about halfway down the menu is a menu item titled "Delete browsing data..." as highlighted in Figure 8-43. Click that menu item.

Clicking this menu item will open the "Delete browsing data" dialog window in Chrome as shown in Figure 8-44.

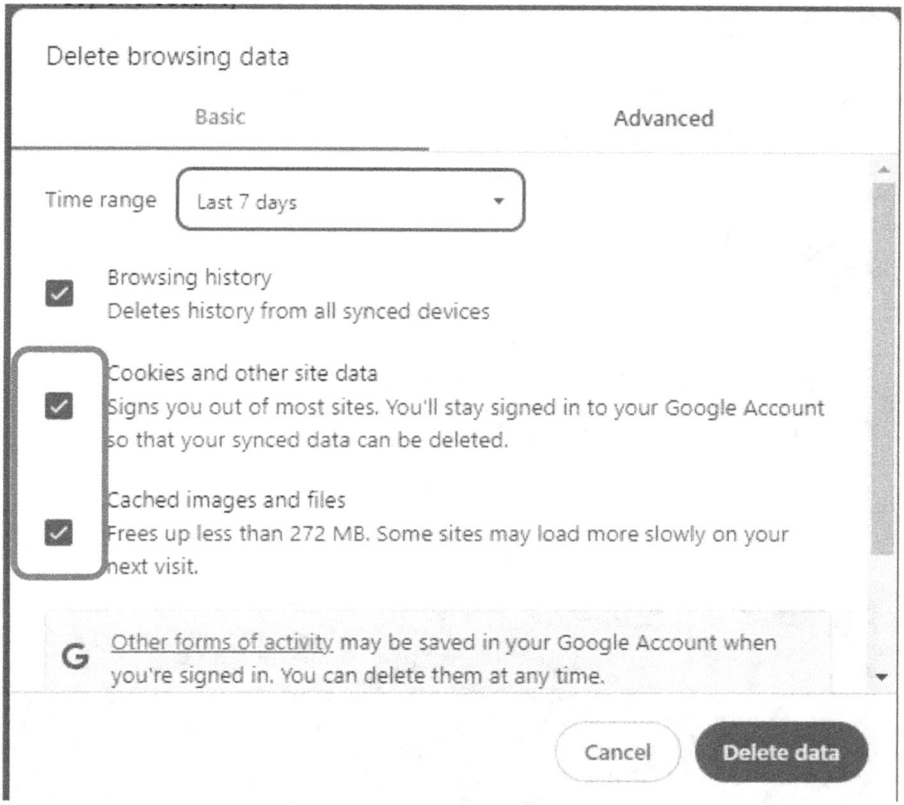

Figure 8-44. *Chrome's Delete browsing data dialog window*

Make sure that the options for "Cookies and other site data" as well as "Cached images and files" are checked. It is not necessary to delete your browsing history.

I would also recommend a time range of no more than seven days. One day would be ideal if you did the steps in Chapter 7 today.

Click the "Delete data" button.

Try, Try Again…

Go back to the browser tab where you were visiting your new website. Refresh that page to see your brand-new uploaded site running on the GitHub platform. My project is shown in Figure 8-45.

Home   Tags   Terms of Use   Contact Us

Discover SpaceB: We are building a platform to take you to the moon!

Join us as we share captivating stories, engineering experinces, and dive into the joys of space travel.

Read more

Figure 8-45. Newly uploaded site running on the GitHub platform

If you closed your browser tab or browser and can't find your way back to your site, then you can simply sync your website again (it will go really fast this time). After the syncing has completed, click the green "Visit your website" page.

Troubleshooting

Did you run into issues? Do you see something that does not seem quite right? Are you stuck somewhere? These troubleshooting tips should help you out.

Are You Lost?

Did you get lost along the way? Go back to the beginning of the section where things went wrong and try again. There is always a chance that things have changed since this book was written in which case the step-by-step instructions might not work quite right.

There are several ways to work through issues.

> First – Check the website/GitHub page for this book. There could be newer information online to help the intrepid traveler through these issues in the case where the process has changed significantly.

> Second – Check Publii's online user documentation here: `https://getpublii.com/docs/`. The section on server configuration is here: `https://getpublii.com/docs/server-configuration.html`

> Third – Ask for help in the Publii user forum located here: `https://github.com/GetPublii/Publii/discussions`.

> Lastly – There always is Google!

Connection Issues

If you have problems with syncing to your host, then check the following:

1. Is your Internet connection functional?

2. Can you visit GitHub and view your repository?

3. Were there error messages when the synchronization was performed?

4. Go to the Server settings in Publii CMS (Menu items: Servers ➤ GitHub) and test the connection again.

If you find that you are having issues with the first couple items, then find a teenager and ask them what is wrong. That is a bit tongue in cheek, but it works. At any rate in these cases, there is something technical wrong with the base equipment.

If you are having issues with the last couple items listed here, then visit the Publii CMS forum. Search for similar issues or open a topic describing your problem. The forum is available here: `https://github.com/GetPublii/Publii/discussions`.

Summary

This chapter was all about getting Publii CMS talking to GitHub. The process we use to move the website and content to the GitHub Internet server is called synchronization. This process ensures that the files that exist on GitHub match the master copy on your local PC.

Publii CMS offers several server type connections. For this project and because of the cost, we are using the GitHub server and thus the GitHub connection.

The configuration for the GitHub connection is straightforward with most of the information coming directly from your GitHub repository page.

The exception to the previous statement is the security token. This must be generated in the GitHub platform. It is important to remember that after the security token has been generated, it must be copied before navigating away from the page showing it. GitHub will never reveal the token in the future, and failure to capture the token means you must delete the one you just created and start over.

Synchronizing your website the first time can take a minute or two as all the files must be moved the first time. Future synchronization processes will only update files that are new or recently modified.

Viewing the website for the first time after synchronization can be problematic due to web browser caching and the minimal web page; we tested the GitHub Pages page in Chapter 7. It will likely be necessary to clear your browser cache to get it to work the first time.

PART II

Enhancing Your Website

In Part 2, I will be introducing important topics moving us along from introductory material into some important areas needed to really make your website shine. I will be covering how to create and manage site backups as well as how to work with Publii CMS in a multi-site environment. You may never plan to have more than one site, but knowing this will allow you to easily spin up alternate sites where you can experiment with ideas and features.

We will examine how Publii CMS supports themes and how to get more themes and use them. After that, we will take our existing website into places we have not gone yet – creating and managing the site as a single-page site, modifying our simple blog to become a full-fledged website.

You will be taking a side trip into how Publii CMS supports galleries as we add a gallery to our website.

I will be wrapping up Part 2 with a discussion about domain names and how to acquire one of your own. The last chapter in this part of the book is considered optional, as it requires a small yearly investment to obtain and keep a domain name. If you choose not to get a domain name, I still recommend reading this chapter.

CHAPTER 9

Backups and Sites

In this chapter, I will be discussing site backup functionality as well as site management. Having a robust backup process and reliable storage for your site is critical to insuring your investment in time and creative output is preserved in the event of the unforeseen.

In the world of technology, we are at the mercy of many events that are out of our control. Things like hardware failure, accidental deletions, or cyber-attacks, losing website data on the host, can cause serious data loss. Backing up data is crucial, especially in the context of using tools like the Publii CMS static site generator

The Publii CMS incorporates built-in backup and restore functionalities. This feature is beneficial for multiple reasons. Firstly, it simplifies the process of preserving your website's data, making it accessible even for those with limited technical skills. Secondly, it provides flexibility. The ability to restore a new site from a backup is particularly advantageous for website migration or testing. It allows users to easily move their content to a new host or experiment with changes without risking their live site. Restoring an existing site from a backup is vital for recovery purposes. If your site encounters issues or unwanted changes, you can revert to a previous state, ensuring continuity and stability.

Backups and site management dovetail well together as backups can be used to jump-start other website projects. Multiple website projects can be managed in the same instance of Publii CMS. This permits you to work on and publish multiple websites and/or blogs.

© Brad Moore 2025
B. Moore, *Designing Websites with Publii and GitHub Pages*,
https://doi.org/10.1007/979-8-8688-1195-1_9

Backing Up a Site

In this section, I focus on backing and restoring a Publii CMS website. I will work with the project site I started in earlier chapters. Backups give you and I the peace of mind of being able to restore our site from an earlier version should something go wrong with the current version.

Creating a Backup

Creating backups is very easy in Publii CMS. Access the function from the Publii CMS main menu by clicking the "Tools & Plugins" menu item on the left side of the application as shown in Figure 9-1.

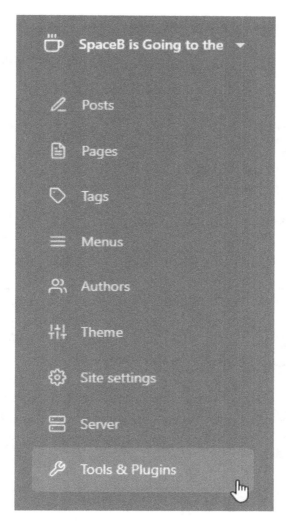

Figure 9-1. *"Tools & Plugins" menu item in the main menu*

The Tools & Plugins panel on the right side of the program window has several large buttons enabling multiple advanced functions to be performed as shown in Figure 9-2.

Tools & Plugins

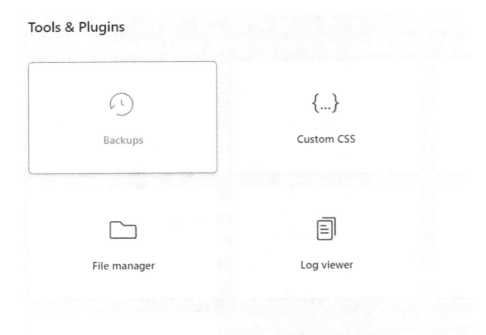

Figure 9-2. *Tools & Plugins panel (cropped)*

Click the "Backups" button as shown in Figure 9-2 to open the backup interface. There are no backups currently for this site as shown in Figure 9-3.

No backups available

You don't have any backups, yet. Let's create the first one!

⊕ Create backup

Figure 9-3. *No backups yet*

Click the blue "Create backup" button to create your first backup. A backup naming dialog window will be displayed as shown in Figure 9-4.

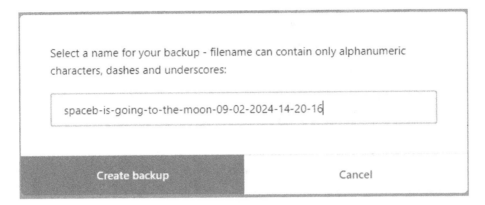

Select a name for your backup - filename can contain only alphanumeric characters, dashes and underscores:

spaceb-is-going-to-the-moon-09-02-2024-14-20-16

Create backup   Cancel

Figure 9-4. *Name your first backup*

The default name is a text string that contains the site name concatenated with the date and time. I find these names to be best for backups, but you can rename this backup to anything you please in this dialog window.

Click the blue "Create backup" button to create the backup. For a small site like this one, the backup will be created in just seconds. It will be listed in the Backups list panel, and Publii CMS will report a successful backup as shown in Figure 9-5.

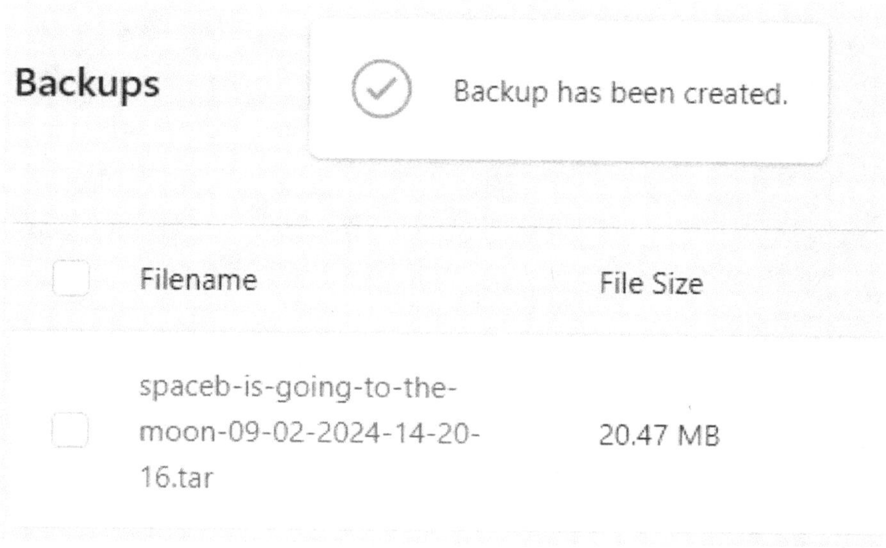

Backups ✓ Backup has been created.

	Filename	File Size
	spaceb-is-going-to-the-moon-09-02-2024-14-20-16.tar	20.47 MB

Figure 9-5. *Backups list (cropped)*

On the right side of the Backups list panel, there are options to rename or restore the backup that was just created as shown in Figure 9-6. Also notice the blue "Create backup" button at the top right of the interface. This button will permit creation of additional backups.

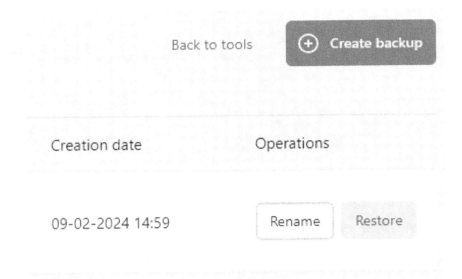

Figure 9-6. *Right side of Backups list interface*

Also notice in Figure 9-6 that there is a link to return to the "tools" button panel seen in Figure 9-2.

Tip   Create backups regularly – certainly between publications of posts or articles. When things go wrong you can easily return to the last known good backup to recover. If you get too many backups delete some of the oldest ones. Deleting a backup is covered below.

Storing Backups

In this section I will be discussing the default location where backup files are stored and best practices regarding use of a remote storage location such as Google Drive to more safely store your backups.

Setup a Backup Folder

By default, backups are stored in a folder called backup in your Publii CMS folder in your "Documents" folder on your Windows PC as shown in Figure 9-7. Modern Windows operating systems sometimes redirect your "Documents" folder on the local hard disk to your personal OneDrive stored on the Internet. This is not a consistently enforced policy for Windows computers. In the case of my computer, my "Documents" folder is on my local PC as you can also see in Figure 9-7 where all the Publii CMS files are stored including the "backup" folder.

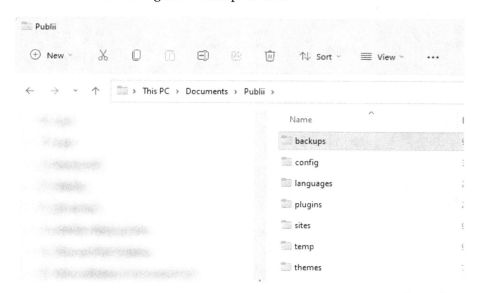

Figure 9-7. *Publii CMS folder in the Documents folder on my local C:\ drive*

Tip   Clicking the file name of the backup (as shown in Figure 9-5) will open a file dialog window to the location where the file resides.

Publii CMS also stores its backups with the rest of the Publii CMS files in the "Documents" folder on the macOS operating system as shown in Figure 9-8. At the root of the Publii folder you will find the files and folders that make up the Publii CMS system including the backup folder.

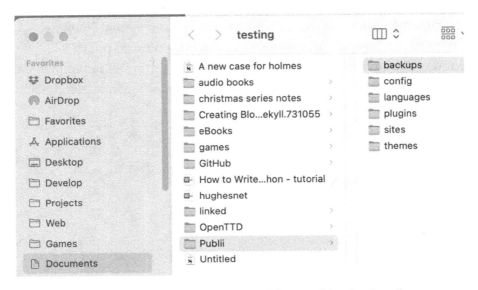

Figure 9-8. *Publii folder on the macOS located in the local Documents folder*

The risk here is that even though you have made the effort to back up your Publii data if it is stored on your local PC, it will be lost should your PC hard drive or other critical component of your computer fail. Your backups need to be located somewhere that will survive a hard disk crash or house fire. The best place for that would be a remote storage location such as Google Drive, OneDrive, or Dropbox.

Tip   Manually copying backup files from your local storage location to remote storage such as Google Drive, OneDrive, or Dropbox is an acceptable practice to ensure backups are available should your local system suffer failure.

Backing Up to a Remote Drive

In this section, I will be discussing changing the default location for backups to a Google Drive. This will automate the process of storing backups in a reliable remote storage location. This is an optional configuration step but is highly encouraged. Manually copying files as suggested in the tip above is an adequate solution if not an automated one.

Note   We are discussing configuring the *where* backups are located. Making these changes does *not* automate the actual backup function. It must be kicked off manually by the end user each time a backup is desired.

To follow along in this portion of the book, you will need to have a Google Drive account (they are free), install the Google Drive app, and configure it for use on your computer. By default, Google Drive will appear as drive G:\ on a Windows PC. On macOS, it will be listed "Google Drive" in "locations" in your Finder.

Google Drive is free at the basic level (which is more than adequate for this project). For help getting it set up, see the Google Drive help pages here: `https://support.google.com/drive/answer/2424384?hl=en&co=GENIE.Platform%3DDesktop`. Don't forget that all links in this book are organized by chapter in the book's GitHub repository.

To change the default location for backups, begin by clicking the application settings icon link in the upper right corner of the Publii CMS program window. It is three vertically stacked dots as highlighted in Figure 9-9.

Figure 9-9. *Publii CMS application settings icon link*

Note   Application settings accessed via the icon link are consistently available from all Publii CMS panels and windows except content editors and the synchronization window.

Clicking the application settings icon will open a menu with several setup options as shown in Figure 9-10. Click the "App settings" menu item.

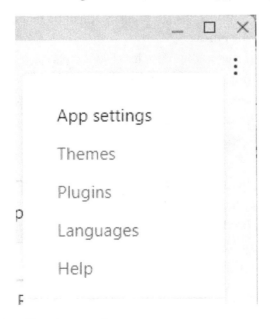

Figure 9-10. *Application settings menu*

This opens the App settings interface panels as shown in Figure 9-11.

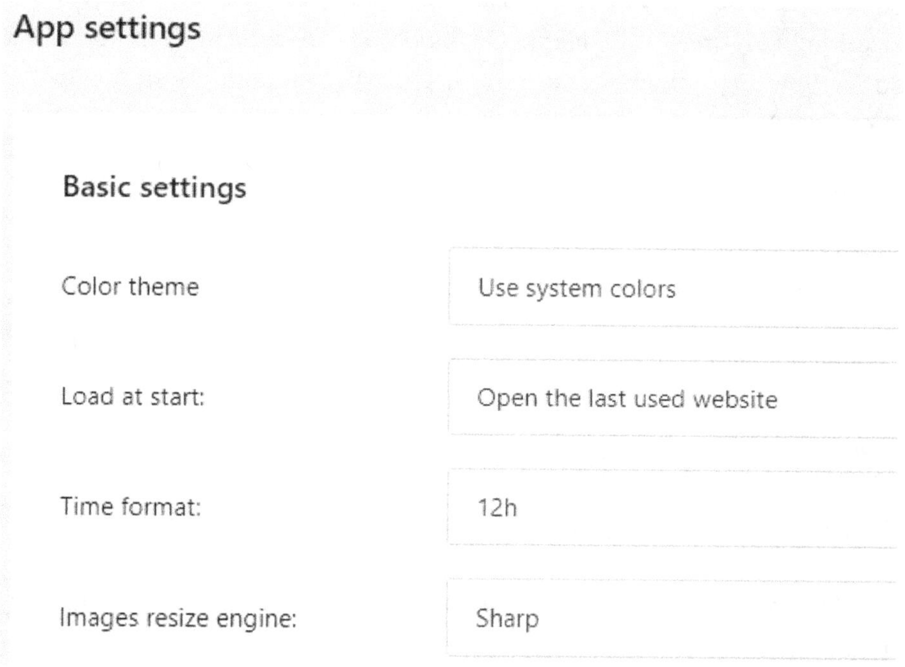

App settings

Basic settings

Color theme	Use system colors
Load at start:	Open the last used website
Time format:	12h
Images resize engine:	Sharp

Figure 9-11. *App settings (cropped)*

Scroll down to the section titled "Files location" as shown in Figure 9-12.

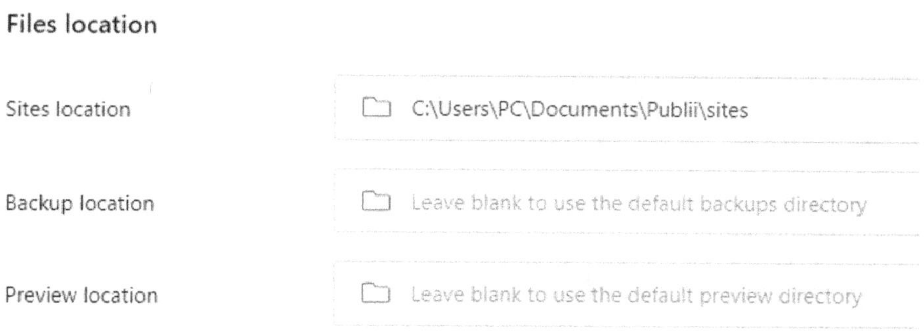

Files location

Sites location	C:\Users\PC\Documents\Publii\sites
Backup location	Leave blank to use the default backups directory
Preview location	Leave blank to use the default preview directory

Figure 9-12. *Files location*

Notice that on my Windows PC, the "Files location" is in relation to the C:\ root of the PC. You can see this in the file path for the Sites location in Figure 9-12. The macOS file path is referenced from the user's home directory (which is common on Unix-like systems) as shown in Figure 9-13.

Files location

Sites location   📁 /Users/bjazmoore/Documents/Publii/sites

Backup location   📁 Leave blank to use the default backups directory

Preview location   📁 Leave blank to use the default preview directory

Figure 9-13. *Files location on macOS*

Clicking in a file path field will open a "Select Folder" dialog window as shown in Figure 9-14.

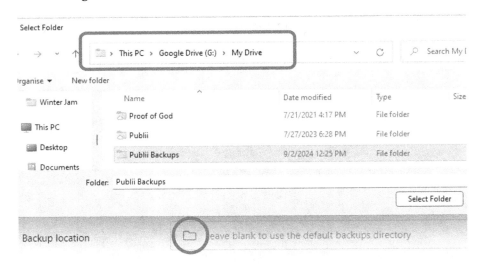

Figure 9-14. *Select Folder dialog window*

In the case of Figure 9-14, I have clicked the file field for the "Backup location". Observe that the backup location I am selecting is on my Google Drive – drive letter G:\ in the folder "My Drive" where I created a folder named "Publii Backups".

Clicking that folder and clicking the "Select Folder" button selects it as my "Backup location" for all Publii CMS backups.

Caution   The Google Drive application must be installed on your PC for this to work correctly.

After changing the location for backups, Publii CMS will warn you that the location has changed and that past backups will be in the old location. If you want them in the new location, you must manually move them as shown in Figure 9-15.

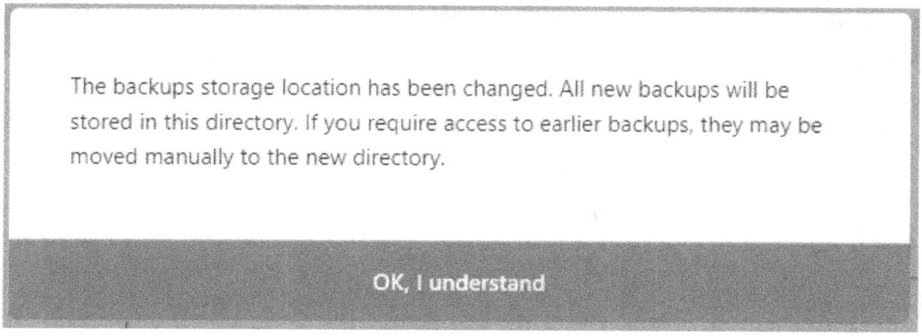

The backups storage location has been changed. All new backups will be stored in this directory. If you require access to earlier backups, they may be moved manually to the new directory.

OK, I understand

Figure 9-15. *Warning regarding new backup location*

This is an important consideration. For the purposes of this book, I will simply make a new backup – repeating the process used in the "Creating a Backup" section earlier in this chapter.

Click the blue "OK, I understand" button to continue.

Observe that in Figure 9-16, the "Backup location" is no longer using the default value but instead is pointing to the path "My Drive\Publii Backups" on the G:\ drive.

Files location

Sites location	🗀 C:\Users\PC\Documents\Publii\sites
Backup location	🗀 G:\My Drive\Publii Backups
Preview location	🗀 Leave blank to use the default preview directory

Figure 9-16. *Changed location for backups*

Setting the location on a macOS computer is a very similar process. Clicking the file field as shown in Figure 9-14 on the Mac will open a Select Folder finder window as shown in Figure 9-17.

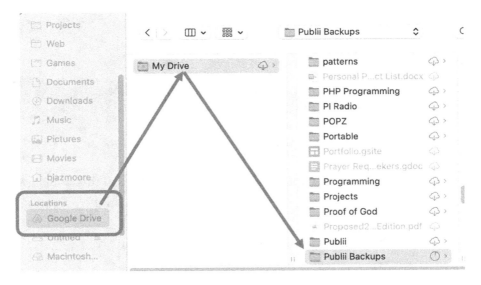

Figure 9-17. *Select Folder dialog window on macOS*

In Figure 9-17, I have selected the same location for backups on my Mac as I did on my PC. They are both on my Google Drive in the root folder called "My Drive" in a folder called "Publii Backups".

Click the "Open" button on the Select Folder dialog window to select the folder highlighted. The path will be displayed in Publii CMS running in your Mac in the same way it was on the PC above. Notice that path is much more complex on the macOS as shown in Figure 9-18.

📁 /Users/bjazmoore/Library/CloudStorage/GoogleDrive-bjazmoore@gmail.com/My Drive/F

Figure 9-18. *Backup location file path on macOS for a folder on Google Drive*

You must save the changes you have made to the App settings for them to be active. In the upper right corner of the application, there is a "Save Settings" button as shown in Figure 9-19.

Figure 9-19. *Save Settings button (and the Go back link)*

Click the "Save Settings" button to commit these settings. Publii CMS will confirm that the settings have been saved as shown in Figure 9-20.

Figure 9-20. *App settings successfully saved message*

Click the "Go back" link next to the "Save Settings" button to go back to the Publii CMS main menu and application website editing functions.

Clicking the "Tools & Plugins" menu item as shown in Figure 9-1 and the "Backups" button in the "Tools & Plugins" interface panel as shown in Figure 9-2 reveals that we have no backups as shown in Figure 9-21.

No backups available

You don't have any backups, yet. Let's create the first one!

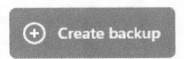

Figure 9-21. *No backups available*

This is not a surprise – Publii CMS warned us about this in Figure 9-15.
Follow the simple procedure outlined at the beginning of this chapter
to create a backup. It should look something like Figure 9-22 when
completed. If you run into trouble, retrace your steps carefully working
through the "Creating a Backup" section of this chapter.

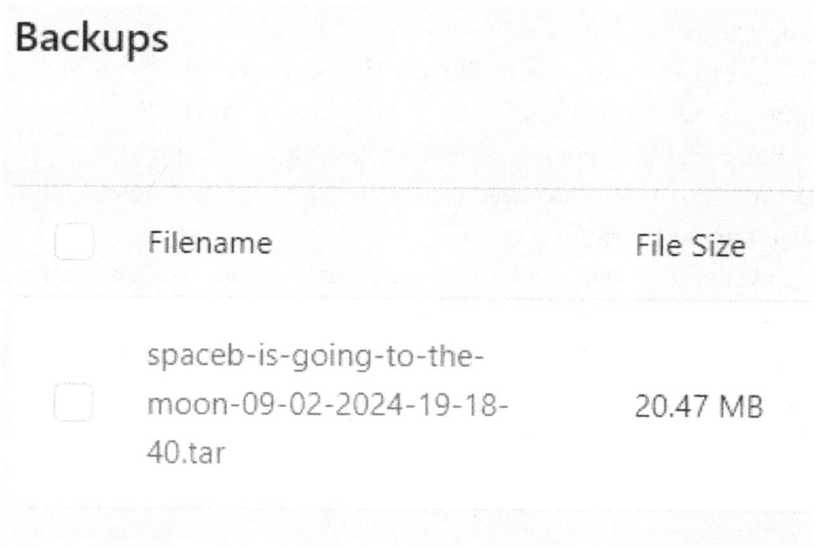

Backups

	Filename	File Size
☐	spaceb-is-going-to-the-moon-09-02-2024-19-18-40.tar	20.47 MB

Figure 9-22. *Backups file list*

You will be using this backup in the next couple sections of this
chapter.

Restoring Backups

Having a backup is great, but it is only part of the picture. You must also
be able to restore that backup if you are to recover from a catastrophic
event. In this section, I will discuss restoring from backups. There are two
use cases examined here: restoring to an existing site and restoring to a
new site.

411

Restore a Backup to an Existing Site

One of the reasons for having current backups is to facilitate recovery from an unexpected problem. Perhaps Publii CMS has gotten corrupted or maybe accidentally deleted or modified one or more posts. Maybe you have made a mistake working with themes or changing system settings. Recovery is always just a backup away.

Restoring a backup is very simple. The backup contains all the metadata needed to know where it should be restored to. Simply navigate to the Backups list by clicking the "Tools & Plugins" menu item as shown in Figure 9-1 and the "Backups" button in the "Tools & Plugins" interface panel as shown in Figure 9-2.

All available backups will be listed in the Backups list. Currently I have one as seen in Figure 9-22. The Backups file list has several columns for each entry. They are Filename, File Size, Creation date, and Operations as shown in Figure 9-23.

Filename	File Size	Creation date	Operations	
spaceb-is-going-to-the-moon-09-02-2024-19-18-40.tar	20.47 MB	09-02-2024 19:18	Rename	Restore

Figure 9-23. *Backups list columns*

Restoring a backup simply requires clicking the light blue "Restore" button on the right side of the row for the backup you wish to restore as shown in Figure 9-24.

Figure 9-24. *Click the blue "Restore" button to begin a restoration.*

Publii CMS will open a dialog window warning you that you are about to overwrite files and confirming that you really want to proceed as shown in Figure 9-25.

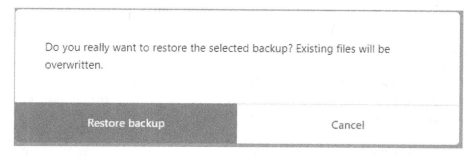

Figure 9-25. *Restore confirmation dialog window*

Click the blue "Restore backup" to restore the backup or the white "Cancel" button to cancel the operation.

In this case, you just made the backup so restoring will not make any changes to your data. Click the button to restore the backup. Once it has completed, Publii CMS will inform you of a successful restoration as shown in Figure 9-26.

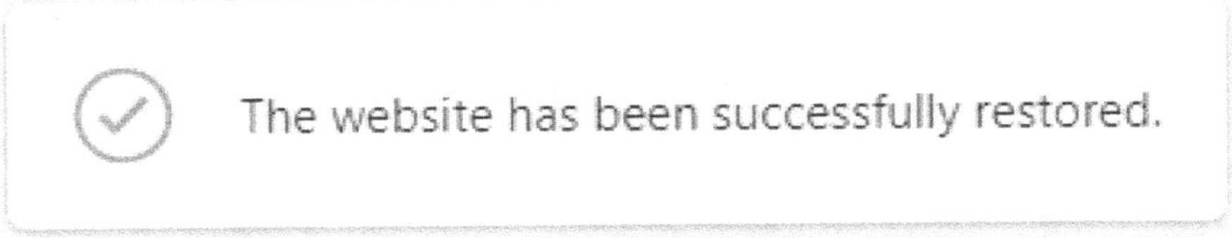

 The website has been successfully restored.

Figure 9-26. *Successful restoration*

Restore a Backup to a New Site

Another use case for backups is the creation of new Publii CMS sites from an existing site backup. You may find you need to do this for several reasons. Perhaps you like the site generally and want to create a new blog on a related subject. Rather than starting from scratch, you may choose to use this process to essentially clone a site (there are easier ways to do this which we will discuss later in this chapter). Bob Mitro, one of Publii CMS's developers and designers, mentions:

> *The most common use case is creating a website by an agency for their client; this way, they can easily share the project with their client.*

Perhaps you are moving from one PC to another – this is a good way to migrate your Publii CMS site from an old PC to a new one.

There is always that worst-case scenario where your PC has crashed and is unrecoverable. This process will allow you to install Publii CMS fresh and get your site back up and running from a backup (provided you have stored that backup somewhere other than your local PC or Mac).

To begin the process, you will need a backup. If you have been following along, you should have one which was created at the end of the "Storing Backups" section in this chapter. If you do not have a backup, follow the process in the "Creating a Backup" section in this chapter.

Navigate to the Backups list by clicking the "Tools & Plugins" menu item as shown in Figure 9-1 and the "Backups" button in the "Tools & Plugins" interface panel as shown in Figure 9-2 to verify you have a backup.

Next click the website title "SpaceB is Going to t..." as highlighted in Figure 9-27 to go to the Sites management interface in Publii CMS.

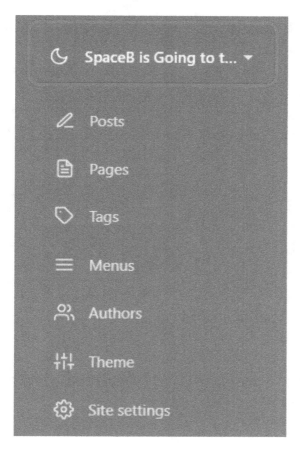

Figure 9-27. *Click the link to go to the Sites management interface*

Figure 9-28 shows the Sites management interface. We have just one site listed and a search field.

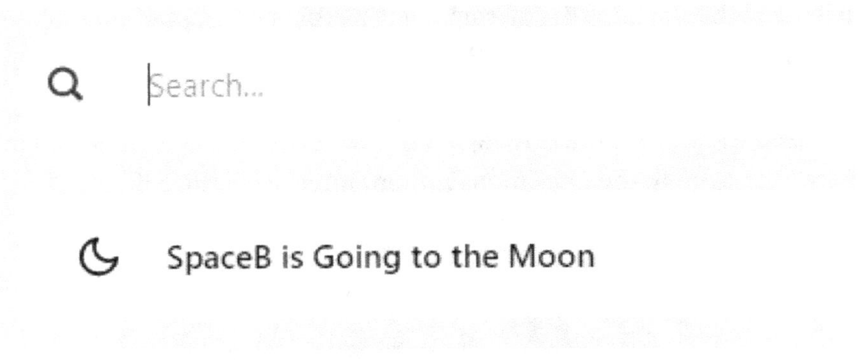

Search...
SpaceB is Going to the Moon

Figure 9-28. *Sites management interface - left side*

On the right side of the Sites management interface is a button and a link as shown in Figure 9-29.

Go back
Add new website

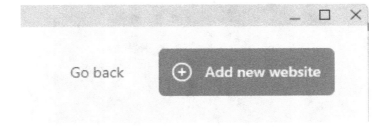

Figure 9-29. *Right side of the Sites management interface*

Click the "Add new website" button. This opens the "Create new website" dialog as shown in Figure 9-30. You saw this dialog in Chapter 3 when you created the current website.

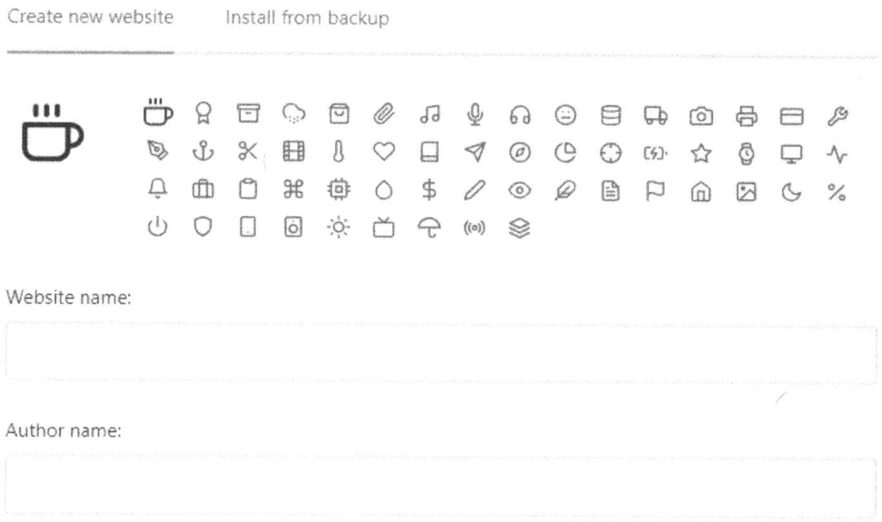

Create new website   Install from backup

Website name:

Author name:

Figure 9-30. *Create new website dialog*

Caution   When you install a website from backup, the server settings used to connect to your host are lost, which prevents you from accidentally sharing your connection details with someone else. However, if you restore the backup via the Backup Tool, the server settings are retained. It is important to recognize how this works when deciding how best to restore a site.

The second important thing when creating a new site this way is that if installing a website that is already installed, Publii CMS will ask in a pop-up dialog window if you want to overwrite your current website. Answer this question carefully.

This dialog window has two tabs. Clicking the "Install from backup" label to the right of the blue shaded "Create new website" label will reveal the second tab as shown in Figure 9-31.

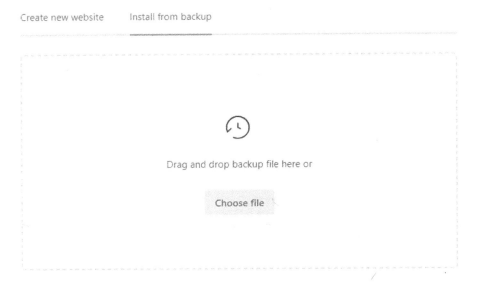

Create new website   Install from backup

Drag and drop backup file here or

Choose file

Figure 9-31. *Install from backup*

Shown in this dialog is the familiar file picker field that you have used before. You can click the "Choose file" button and navigate to the backup file you want to install from, or you can drag and drop the file into the field.

I clicked the Choose file button which opened a file dialog window at the path where my backups are stored as shown in Figure 9-32.

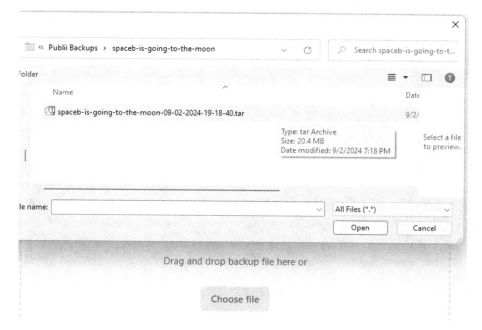

Figure 9-32. *Choosing a file from the Windows file dialog*

In my case, there was just one backup file. I clicked it and then clicked the Open button in the file dialog window as shown in Figure 9-32.

The backup is used to install a new site. A dialog window requests that I specify a site name as shown in Figure 9-33. The source name is suggested. I need to specify a different name as a site with this name already exists.

419

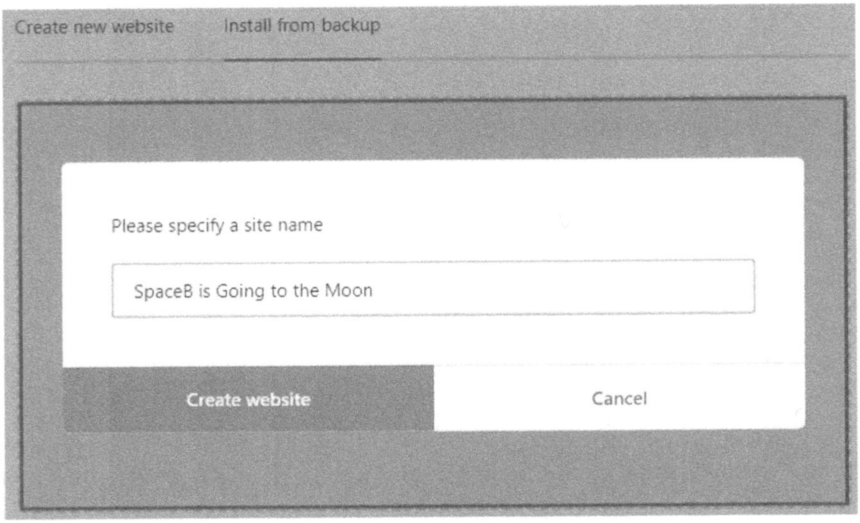

Figure 9-33. *Specify a site name for the new site*

I choose to call this site "Moonshot" as you can see in Figure 9-34. Frankly I wish I had the foresight to call the original site ("SpaceB is Going to the Moon") Moonshot.

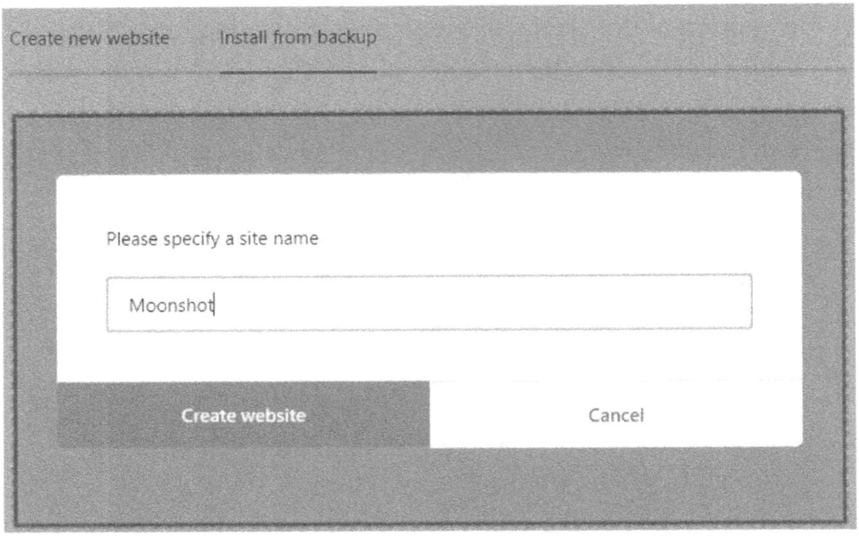

Figure 9-34. *Site named "Moonshot"*

420

I clicked the blue "Create website" button to create the website.

In Figure 9-35, you will observe that the site is very similar to the original "SpaceB is Going to the Moon" site.

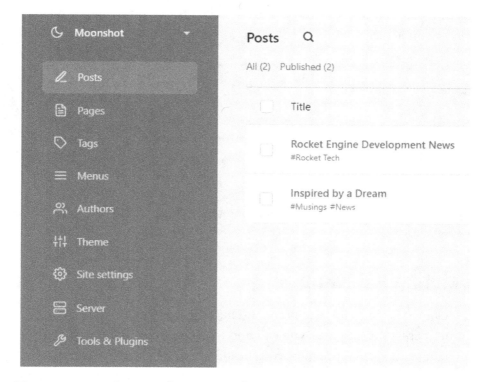

Figure 9-35. *The new "Moonshot" site*

There are a few things that are different. Among them, we do not have a server connection any longer. That is removed during this type of operation to prevent sites from overwriting each other later when synchronizing to the Internet.

Another difference is this site has no backups. There are other differences which I will discuss in the next major section in this chapter – "Managing Sites."

Before we finish with backups, I want to show how a backup is deleted. By now, you should be an expert at creating backups. Create two backups of the Moonshot site. If you get stuck, refer to the "Creating a Backup" section of this chapter. When done, the Backups list should look a bit like this one in Figure 9-36.

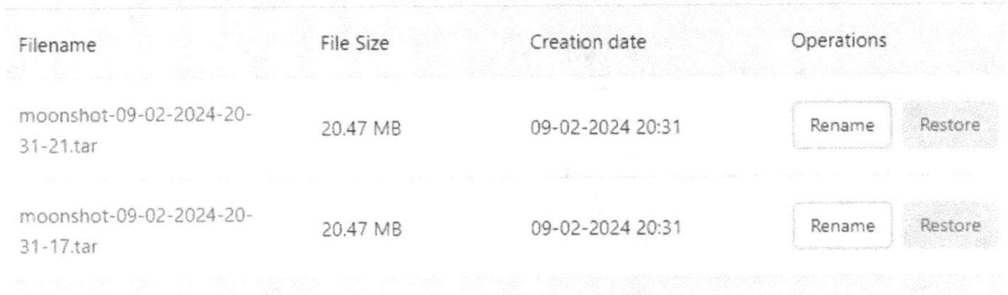

Filename	File Size	Creation date	Operations	
moonshot-09-02-2024-20-31-21.tar	20.47 MB	09-02-2024 20:31	Rename	Restore
moonshot-09-02-2024-20-31-17.tar	20.47 MB	09-02-2024 20:31	Rename	Restore

Figure 9-36. *Backups list for the site Moonshot*

Deleting a Backup

If you are creating a lot of content and backing up regularly between content creation activities, you will find that eventually there will be a lot of backup files. In practice, you should not need more than four to six backups. To keep the list under control, it will be necessary to delete some older backups.

Deleting backups is a trivial task. Select the backup to delete by checking the check box before the backup file name as shown in Figure 9-37.

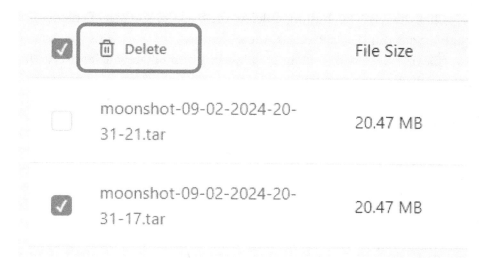

Figure 9-37. *Selecting and deleting a backup*

Click the Delete button in the menu bar that is above the file list as highlighted in Figure 9-37.

There will be a confirmation dialog window as Publii CMS wants to make sure you really want to permanently delete the backup file as shown in Figure 9-38.

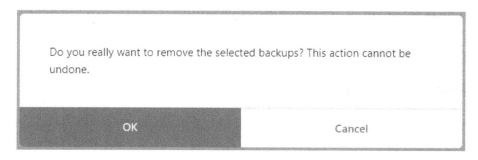

Figure 9-38. *Delete backup file confirmation dialog*

Click the red "OK" button to delete the backup. You can of course change your mind by clicking "Cancel" button.

Clicking "OK" will result in the file being immediately deleted. The file list will display one less backup, and there will be a most polite message from Publii CMS telling you the selected backups were removed as shown in Figure 9-39.

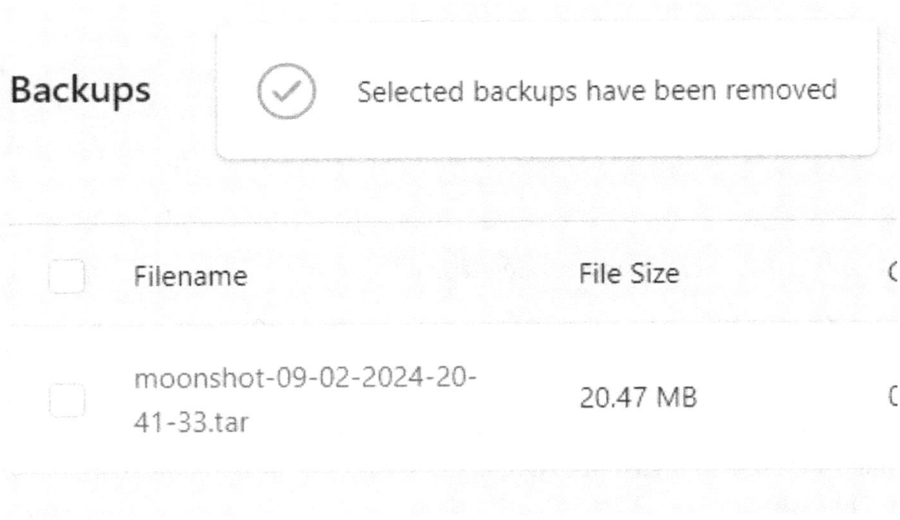

Figure 9-39. *Backups removed successfully*

Managing Sites

In this section, I will be discussing how to manage multiple websites from the "Sites management" interface. This is the very top level of the Publii CMS application where sites are created, deleted, and switched between.

In the previous section, you were briefly introduced to the "Sites management" interface when creating a new site from a backup. In this section, I will demonstrate additional functionality of this portion of the application.

Creating a New Site

You saw how to create a new site from a backup earlier from the "Sites management" interface. You can also create a new site by supplying a site name and author name as we did in Chapter 3.

If you are not already looking at the "Sites management" interface, then click the title link for the website you are currently working with. I am working on the "Moonshot" website, so that is the link I will click as highlighted in Figure 9-40.

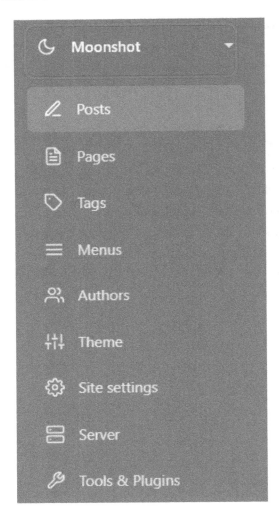

Figure 9-40. *Click the link to go to the Sites management interface*

Figure 9-41 shows the "Sites management" interface. Earlier there was just one site listed, but now there are two since we created one from a backup recently.

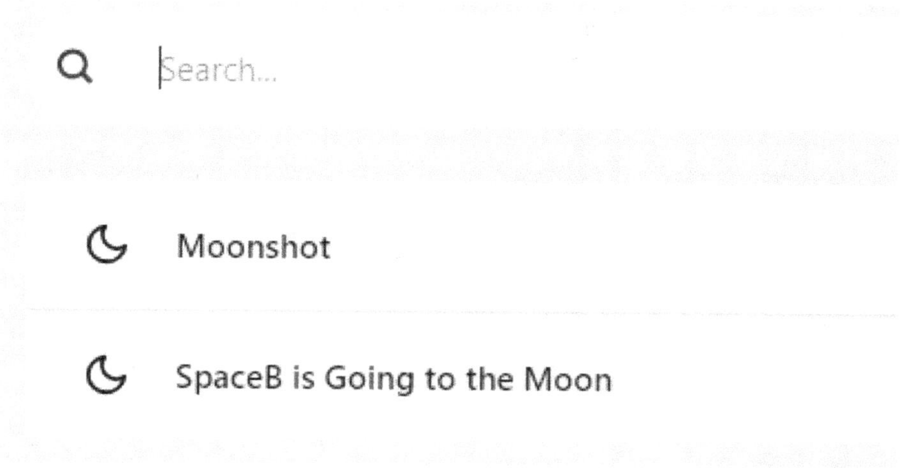

Search...
Moonshot
SpaceB is Going to the Moon

Figure 9-41. *"Sites management" interface – left side*

On the right side of the "Sites management" interface, you will see a button labeled "Add new website" and a link to "Go back" to "website management" as shown in Figure 9-42.

Go back
Add new website

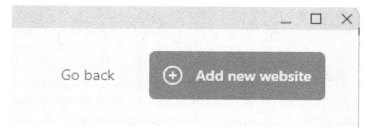

Figure 9-42. *Right side of the "Sites management" interface*

Click the "Add new website" button. This opens the "Create new website" dialog as shown in Figure 9-43.

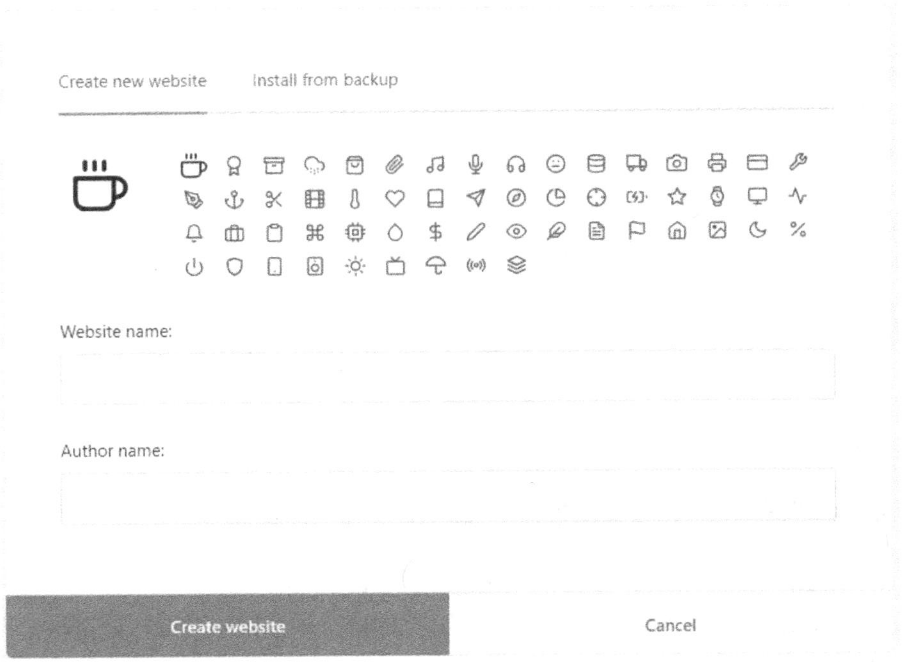

Create new website   Install from backup

Website name:

Author name:

Create website   Cancel

Figure 9-43. *Create a new website*

Providing a name for the new website in the Website name field and an author name in its field and clicking the "Create website" button will add another website to our instance of Publii CMS.

I named my website "Flowers of Kentucky" and set the author to "Bob Rose". Clicking the "Create new website" created the site.

Clicking the "Flowers of Kentucky" website title at the top of the Publii CMS main menu returns me to the "Sites management" interface.

Duplicating a Site

There are now three sites listed in "Sites management" interface as you can see in Figure 9-44.

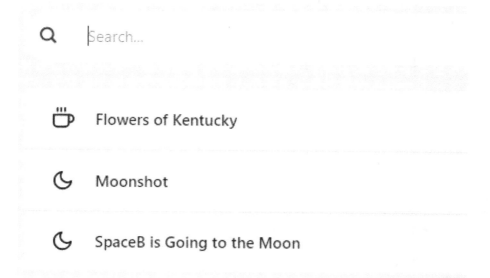

Figure 9-44. Three sites listed in the "Sites management" interface

Hover the mouse over the first site named "Flowers of Kentucky". On the right end of that same row, there are two icons that are displayed while hovering as shown in Figure 9-45.

Figure 9-45. *Duplicate and Delete icons for the "Flowers of Kentucky" site*

Click the first icon on the left. This is the duplicate icon. A dialog window is opened requesting a name for this new site as shown in Figure 9-46.

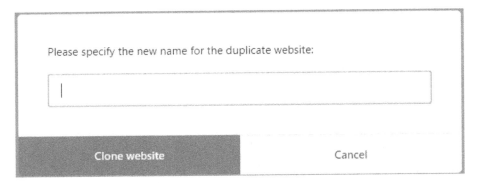

Figure 9-46. *Specify name for duplicate site dialog*

I have called my duplicate site "Motor Boats" as you can see in Figure 9-47.

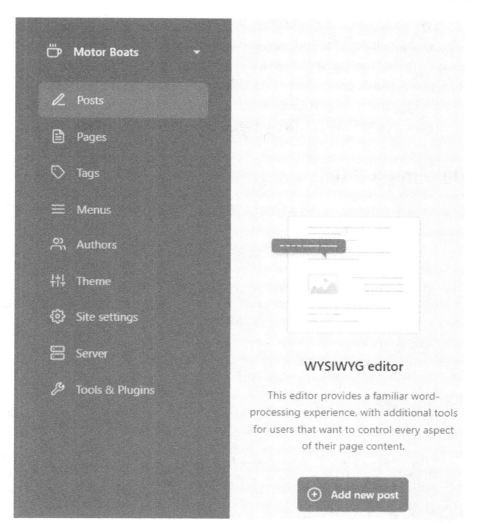

Figure 9-47. *The new "Motor Boats" site*

This is the simpler process for duplicating a site that I alluded to in the previous section when you used a backup to create a duplicate site. This process requires far fewer steps and much less effort to duplicate a site.

A good use case for duplicating sites is when you plan to experiment with a major change for your site – such as a new theme. Create a duplicate and verify that the change does not clobber your site. If things look OK, then delete the duplicate site and make the changes to the production site.

Clicking the "Motor Boats" website title at the top of the Publii CMS main menu will return you to the "Sites management" interface.

Deleting a Site

There are now four sites listed in the "Sites management" interface as shown in Figure 9-48.

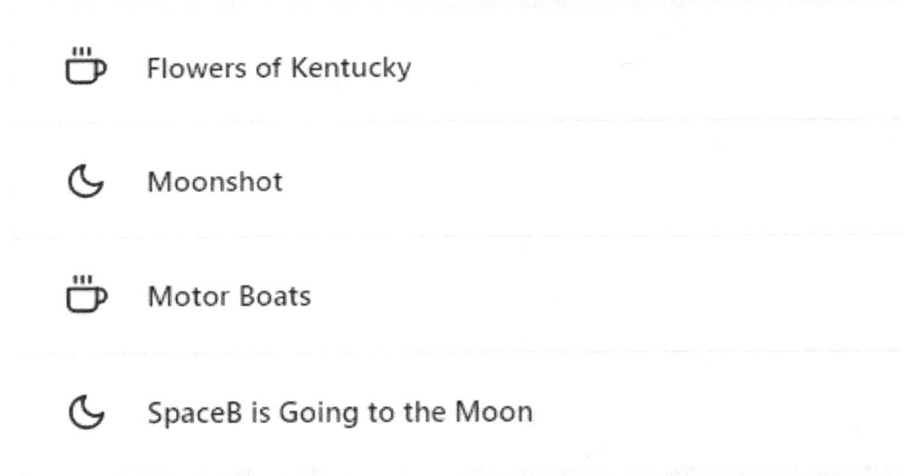

Flowers of Kentucky

Moonshot

Motor Boats

SpaceB is Going to the Moon

Figure 9-48. *"Sites management" interface*

It is time to delete a couple sites. Obviously, this is not a standard practice if you have several websites that are in production, but if you have created some test sites and no longer need them, then cleaning up a bit is a good idea.

Hover your mouse pointer over the row for the "Flowers of Kentucky" site as we did earlier. Hovering over the trash can icon causes it to turn red. There is a tooltip that says "Delete website" as shown in Figure 9-49.

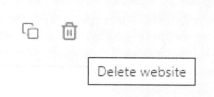

Figure 9-49. *Delete website*

Click the trash can icon to delete the website. A warning dialog window is opened asking if you are sure you want to remove the website as shown in Figure 9-50. Note that removing (or deleting) a website cannot be undone.

Figure 9-50. *Remove website warning dialog window*

Click the red "Remove website" to permanently delete the website. Do the same for the "Moonshot" website.

You should have two websites left in the "Sites management" interface: "Motor Boats" and "SpaceB is Going to the Moon".

Navigating Between Sites

You and I have been navigating between multiple websites for most of this chapter. Website selection (which website to work with) is always done on the "Sites management" interface. Currently there are two sites listed on the "Sites management" interface as shown in Figure 9-51.

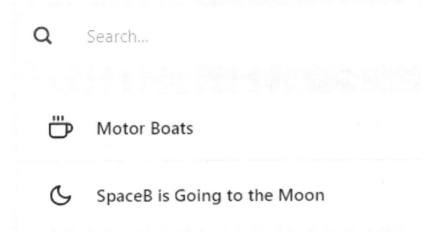

Figure 9-51. *The "Sites management" interface*

Clicking one of these will open the website up in the sites management interface panel. For example, to open the "SpaceB is Going to the Moon" website in the site management panel, simply click the row its name appears on as shown in Figure 9-52. Note the row will turn a light blue while the mouse pointer hovers over it.

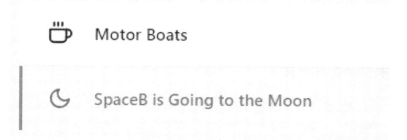

Figure 9-52. *Hovering over a row in the "Sites management" interface*

Clicking that row will open that site up in the website management as shown in Figure 9-53.

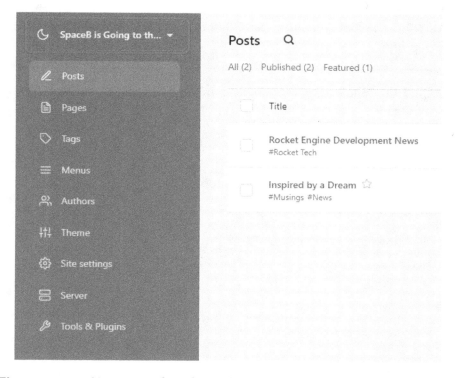

Figure 9-53. *Site opened in the website management panel*

Clicking the title of the website as highlighted in Figure 9-53 will return you to the "Sites management" interface.

Renaming a Site

One of the last things that needs to be covered when discussing site management is renaming a website. Renaming is done in the website management panels and not in the "Sites management" interface.

It's time to fix that weak name I gave the original website in Chapter 3. Click on the row titled "SpaceB is Going to the Moon" to open it up in the website management panel as shown in Figure 9-53.

Tip   Clicking any blank area in the "Sites management" interface will open the last website that was open (or the only website if there is just one).

Click the "Site settings" menu item in the main menu as shown in Figure 9-54.

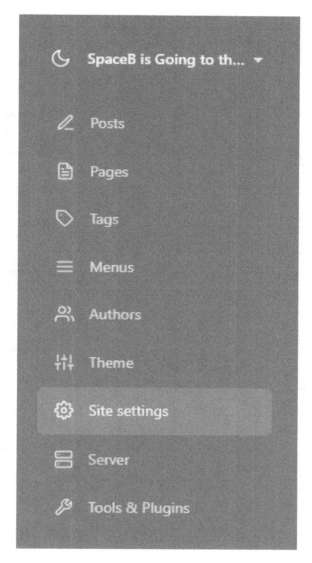

Figure 9-54. *Site settings in the main menu*

In the Basic settings portion of the Site settings panel, edit the Site name in the site name field as highlighted in Figure 9-55.

Basic settings

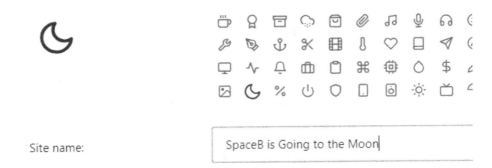

Site name: SpaceB is Going to the Moon|

Figure 9-55. *Change the name of the site in the site name field*

Change the name of the site as desired. I have named the site "SpaceBs Moonshot". Click the "Save Settings" button in the upper right corner of the Site settings panel – highlighted in Figure 9-56.

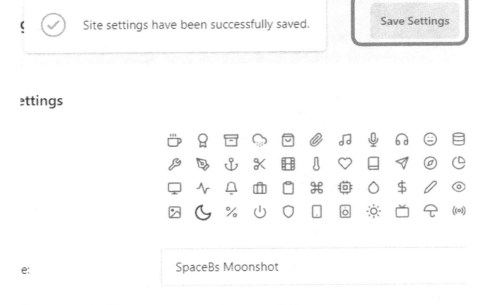

Figure 9-56. *Site settings saved successfully*

Publii CMS will confirm the name change as seen in Figure 9-56.

Summary

In this chapter, you learned the importance of backing up your Publii CMS site or sites. Backups allow you to recover from system failures that render your computer unusable and would otherwise result in data loss.

You need to have a backup strategy that includes regularly making backups, keeping your catalog of backups manageable, and storing the backups in a location other than your PC or Mac.

Good off-site storage locations include Google Drive, OneDrive, and Dropbox, just to name a few.

Manually moving backups to an off-site location is acceptable, but automating the process is better. The process is easily automated by changing the default location for backups to point to an off-site location such as Google Drive (the solution presented in this book).

Backups exist to permit restorations. Two use cases for restoration were discussed in this chapter including restoring a backup over an existing site –the most common scenario – as well as using a backup to install a new (duplicate) site.

We also covered deleting backups. Keeping a manageable catalog of backups is important for management of the environment.

In addition to backups, you learned how to use the "Sites management" interface in this chapter.

The "Sites management" interface permits switching between sites as well as duplicating, creating new and deleting sites.

We finished out the chapter discussing how to rename a website.

CHAPTER 10

Themes

Most static site generators as well as other Content Management Systems (CMS) offer templates or themes to change the look and feel of the website the user sees. Themes allow new website layouts, color choices, and typography to be applied around the existing site content. Display of content may look different, but the content remains unchanged.

Themes are handled in different ways depending on the type of CMS you are working with. Many systems rely on the generosity of the user community to design and provide themes. Others support mainly themes created by the system designers. Most take a path that is a hybrid of both approaches. Some CMS applications do not offer any prebuilt themes requiring the blog publisher to roll their own.

There are challenges with community-provided themes where a popular theme is created for a specific version of the CMS, but as the new versions of the CMS are released, the theme is never updated, leading to potential issues with websites using that theme.

Publii CMS has taken the approach of creating and updating its own set of official themes. The developers update every theme to work with new releases when new versions are released, ensuring that all the themes operate correctly when installed. Publii CMS offers 29 themes that can be downloaded and installed. Thirteen of the themes are offered at no cost, and the remaining sixteen are premium themes requiring purchase.

© Brad Moore 2025
B. Moore, *Designing Websites with Publii and GitHub Pages,*
https://doi.org/10.1007/979-8-8688-1195-1_10

Theming with Publii CMS is done using yet another web technology called "handlebars." The creators of the system publish documentation for creating your own custom themes, and there are a few available on the Internet. Knowing how to use handlebars and create custom themes is not required to apply an existing theme – which is what I will be discussing next.

Getting a Theme

In this section and the sections that follow, I will be discussing how to get and install a new theme for your Publii CMS site.

Installing and using a new theme requires two steps. First, the theme file must be downloaded from the themes marketplace, then it must be installed, and finally it must be activated. Downloaded and installed themes are available for any of your Publii CMS managed sites. Themes are activated per site.

Download new theme files from the Publii Marketplace. This is best practice since the makers of Publii CMS maintain themes updated and ready for the current version of Publii CMS. Access the Marketplace by going to `https://marketplace.getpublii.com/themes/` in your favorite web browser as shown in Figure 10-1.

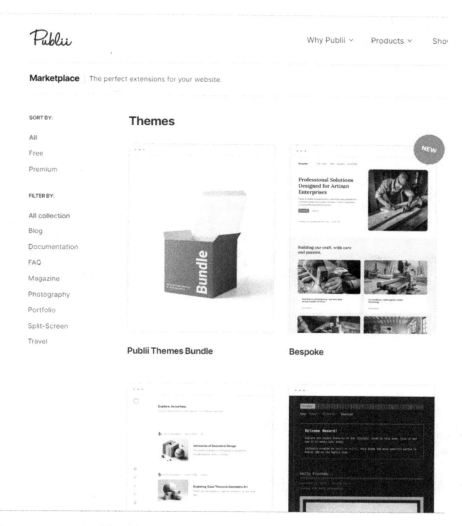

Figure 10-1. *Publii Theme Marketplace*

Sort the themes by "Free". This is a filter and will just show the free themes as shown in Figure 10-2.

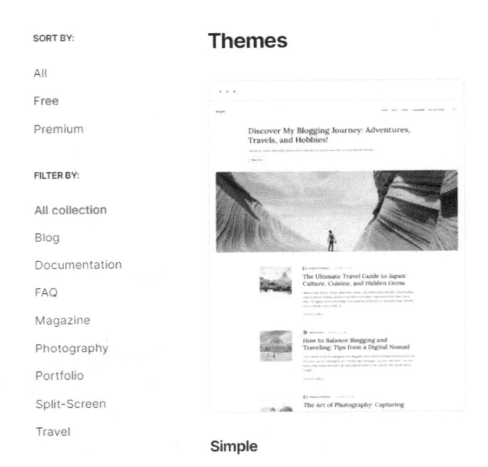

Figure 10-2. Sort themes by "Free"

Select the theme called "Mono" as shown in Figure 10-3.

Themes

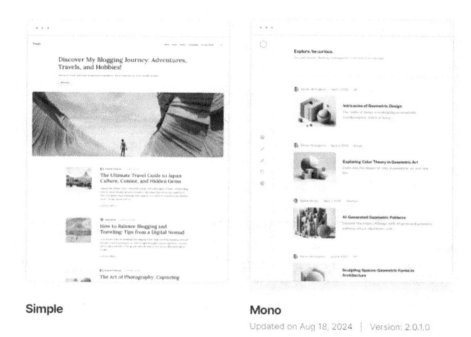

Simple

Mono

Updated on Aug 18, 2024 | Version: 2.0.1.0

Figure 10-3. *Find the theme called "Mono"*

Click on the image of the theme called "Mono" to see the theme details for that theme as shown in Figure 10-4.

445

Figure 10-4. Details of theme called "Mono"

Click the Download button (highlighted in Figure 10-4) located in the upper right portion of the web page to download this theme.

Note also that you can preview the theme by clicking the button "Live Preview" under the Download button. This can help you determine if a given theme is right for you before downloading it or more importantly before buying a premium theme.

Themes are downloaded as zip files into your browser's default download location – typically the Downloads folder as shown in Figure 10-5.

Figure 10-5. The Mono theme as a zip file in Windows explorer

Do not unzip the downloaded file. Publii CMS expects a zip file in the next step of the process.

Installing a Theme

The next step in the process of changing the theme for your website is to install it globally. These are installed in Publii CMS so that they are globally available to any website created using Publii CMS. Applying a specific theme to a specific website is also called "installing" the theme within the application, but I will refer to it as activating the theme to differentiate the two different actions.

In this step, you will be installing the theme globally. To do this, you must first access the Application Settings context menu as we did in Chapter 9 working with Backup file locations.

Find the icon that looks like three stacked dots used to access the Application Settings context menu in the upper right corner of the application as highlighted in Figure 10-6. This menu is available from most Publii CMS subsystems except Synchronization, Editors, and the "Sites management" interface.

Figure 10-6. *Application Settings context menu icon*

Click the Application Settings context menu icon to reveal the Application Settings context menu as shown in Figure 10-7.

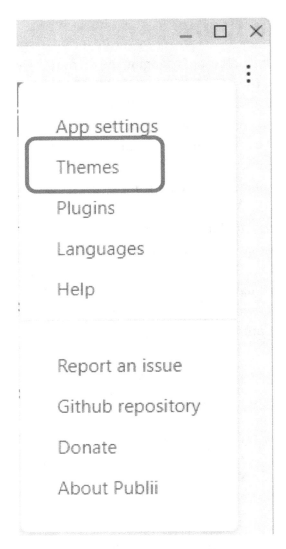

Figure 10-7. *Application Settings context menu*

Click the menu item "Themes" as highlighted in Figure 10-7. Figure 10-8 shows the Themes interface panel.

Figure 10-8. *Themes interface panel*

There is a single theme installed – the "Simple 3.0.0.0" theme that you have been working with so far. Notice the "Get more themes" button as shown in Figure 10-9. This button will open the Themes Marketplace at the Publii CMS website as shown in Figure 10-1.

Figure 10-9. *The "Get more themes" button*

On the upper right side of the Themes interface panel is a button labeled "Install theme" as shown in Figure 10-10.

Figure 10-10. *"Install theme" button*

Click this button to install the theme we downloaded in the previous section. After clicking an open file dialog window is displayed as shown in Figure 10-11.

Figure 10-11. *Open file dialog window*

I found that I needed to navigate to the Downloads folder to locate the theme I downloaded earlier as the open file dialog displayed a different path. Locate the zip file downloaded earlier – it is highlighted in Figure 10-11.

Select the file and then click the "Open" button in the lower right side of the dialog window.

It takes a moment or two for the new file to be installed. Once installed, you will see it in the list of themes, and Publii CMS will report that a theme has been successfully installed as shown in Figure 10-12.

Figure 10-12. *Two themes listed in the Themes interface (cropped) now*

Deleting a Theme

If you have downloaded themes that you will no longer need or want to use, it is best practice to delete them. I will demonstrate how to delete the "Mono 2.0.1.0" theme that was installed in the previous step. I will not actually be deleting the theme, as I will be using it later. Follow along below.

To delete a theme, click on the trash can icon in the lower right corner of the theme name panel as shown in Figure 10-13. Notice how the trash can turns red as your mouse pointer hovers over it.

Figure 10-13. *Deleting a theme*

Click the trash can to begin the process of deleting the theme. Publii CMS will display a dialog window asking you if you are sure you want to delete the theme as shown in Figure 10-14.

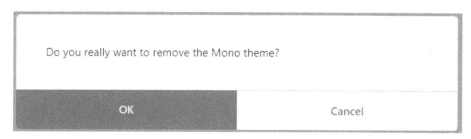

Figure 10-14. *Deletion confirmation dialog window*

Click the red "OK" button to delete the theme if desired. In my case, I clicked the white "Cancel" button to abort the procedure.

If you went ahead and deleted the theme – install it again following the procedure in the previous section.

Activating a Theme

To use a theme in a specific Publii CMS website, you must install it into that website. Publii CMS calls this process installing. Confusion is possible resulting from the dual meaning of installing themes both globally and locally. Therefore I will refer to this process as "activate/install" and to the specific menu item as simply "install".

We must leave the Theme interface panel to activate/install the new theme. Click the "Go back" link next to the "Install theme" button in the upper right corner of the interface as highlighted in Figure 10-15.

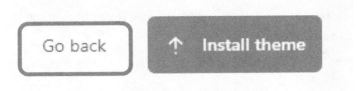

Figure 10-15.   *The "Go back" link*

Caution   Before activating/installing a theme locally, make a backup of your site. Some themes can make changes that are not desirable and cannot be reversed by changing back to the original theme.

Themes are activated/installed locally into a specific website in the Site settings part of the application. Click the "Site settings" menu item in the main menu on the left side of the application as shown in Figure 10-16.

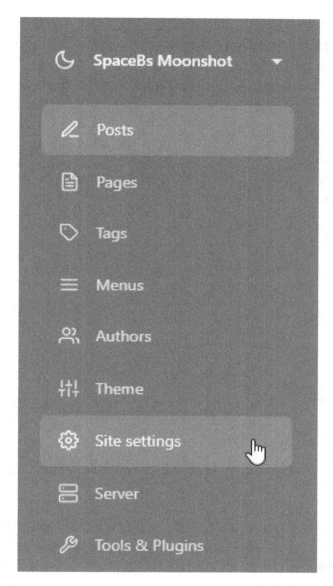

Figure 10-16. *Site settings menu item in the Publii CMS main menu*

On the right side of the application, you will see the Site settings panel. In the Basic settings section at the top of this panel is an item labeled "Current theme". To the right of this label is a drop-down field for selecting, installing, and deleting themes locally as shown in Figure 10-17.

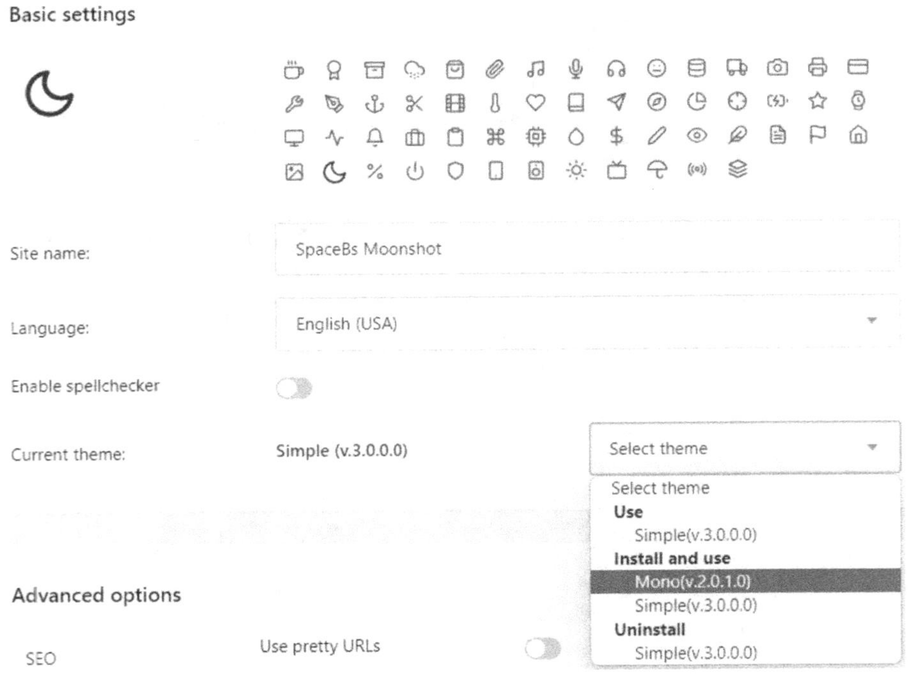

Figure 10-17. *Basic settings with Theme management drop-down field*

Zooming in on this field you will see three sections with themes listed under them. The "Use" section permits switching between activated/ installed themes. The "Install and use" section will activate/install a theme locally and then use that theme in one step. The Uninstall section will simply remove a given theme from the list of locally activated/installed themes (it will not uninstall a theme globally).

Click the "Mono(v.2.0.1.0)" entry under the "Install and use" section of the menu as shown in Figure 10-18.

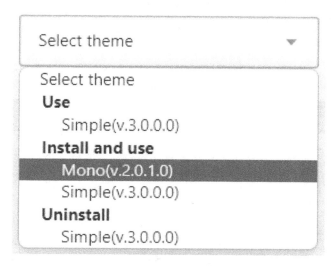

Figure 10-18. *Local theme management*

Once selected, the Mono theme name will be displayed in the drop-down field (although the action for that theme will not be displayed) as highlighted in Figure 10-19.

Figure 10-19. *Save the Mono theme by clicking "Save Settings"*

Click the "Save settings" button in the upper right corner of the Site settings panel to activate/install this theme locally and make it the current theme for the site.

There will usually be a warning when changing themes advising you to regenerate thumbnails as shown in Figure 10-20.

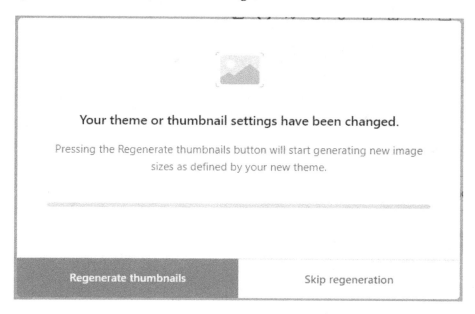

Figure 10-20. *Regenerate thumbnails*

Click the blue "Regenerate thumbnails" button to perform the action.

Click the "Preview your changes" button toward the bottom of the application main menu as shown in Figure 10-21 to see how the site looks with the new theme applied.

459

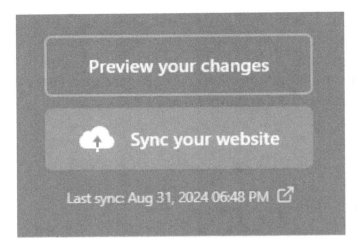

Figure 10-21. *Preview your changes button*

The website rendered with the new theme is shown in Figure 10-22.

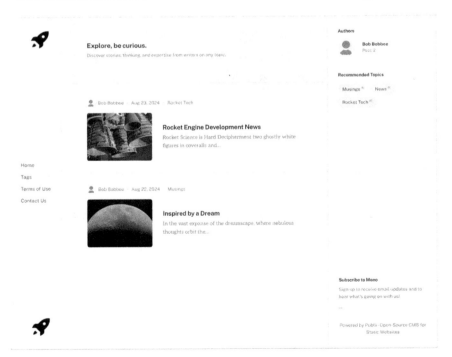

Figure 10-22. *The website rendered with the Mono theme*

Tip   Sometimes changing themes can cause irreversible changes to your site – changes that going back to the old theme will not fix. Test your theme changes on a copy of your website to ensure this does not happen.

Theme Settings for New Theme

In this section, I will discuss some changes that can be made to the Mono theme to improve the appearance of the rendered site. All the changes will be made in the Theme settings panel in Publii CMS – no coding or file level changes will be required.

Before we can make changes to the theme settings, we first need to access that part of the Publii CMS application. Click the "Theme" menu item in the Publii CMS main menu on the left side of the application as shown in Figure 10-23.

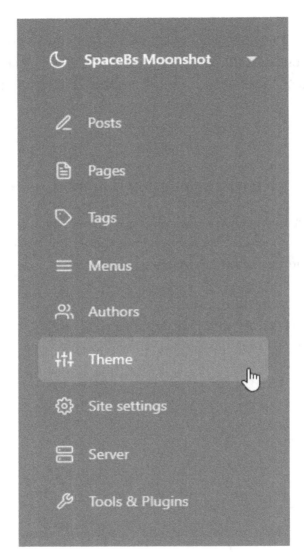

Figure 10-23. *Theme menu item in the Publii CMS main menu*

On the right panel labeled "Theme settings", scroll down to the "Custom settings" section as shown in Figure 10-24.

Custom settings

Layout	Page margin	25px
Post list		
Sidebar	Main column width	940px
Colors		*Set the width for the main content column. This determines the maximum width for the main content area.*
Fonts		
Share Buttons	Sidebar column width	270px
Gallery		*Set the width of the right sidebar column.*
Additional		
Author options	Entry width	660px
Post options		*Set the maximum width for a content entry.*
Page options		
Tag options		

Figure 10-24. *Custom settings in the Theme settings panel*

Ensure that "Layout" is selected in the Custom settings menu as highlighted in Figure 10-24. Scroll the right side of the Custom settings panel down with the scroll wheel on the mouse until you see the section titled "Hero section" as shown in Figure 10-25.

Hero section

Text

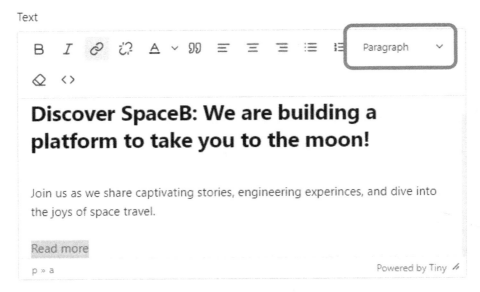

Figure 10-25. *Hero section in the Layout section of Custom settings*

Type the following into the text field as shown in Figure 10-25.

Discover SpaceB: We are building a platform to take you to the moon!

Join us as we share captivating stories, engineering experiences, and dive into the joys of space travel.

Read more

Use the format drop-down to style the text. It is highlighted in Figure 10-25. Format the first paragraph as "Heading 1". Format the second paragraph as "Paragraph". Select the text for "Read more" and click the Insert/Edit link button on the toolbar – it looks like Figure 10-26.

Figure 10-26. *Insert/Edit link button on the toolbar*

This will open a dialog window where the link can be edited as seen in Figure 10-27.

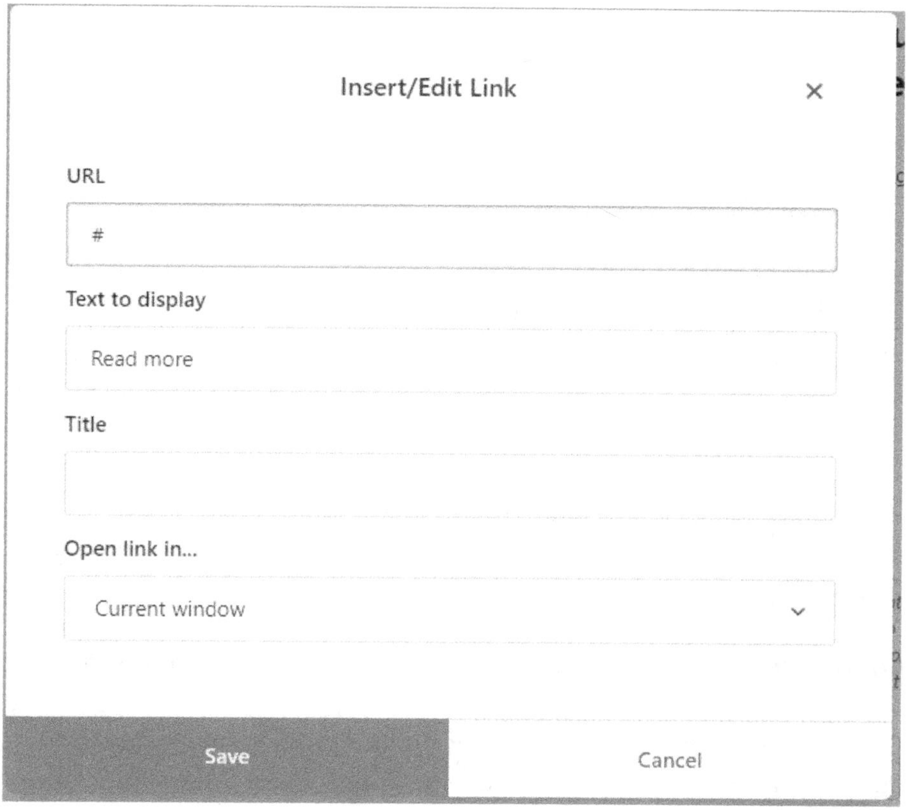

Insert/Edit Link	✕

URL

```
#
```

Text to display

```
Read more
```

Title

```

```

Open link in...

```
Current window                                    ⌄
```

Save	Cancel

Figure 10-27. *Insert/Edit link dialog window*

Set the URL to a hashmark as shown in Figure 10-27. This is literally a link to nowhere. Click the blue "Save" button to save the link. We will come back later and add a proper link into this Hero text; for now, this is an adequate placeholder.

Now click the "Sidebar" menu item in the Custom settings menu and scroll down on the right-side panel until you see the Newsletter section as shown in Figure 10-28.

Figure 10-28. *Newsletter section of the Sidebar in Custom settings*

The Newsletter sign-up would be a neat feature to utilize, but the theme seems to have the header and description of the newsletter hard-coded into the theme itself. I do not want to get into editing theme files, so I will just disable it. Click the toggle to the right of the title "On/Off" to slide it to the left and disable the option. The toggle will turn gray, and the Form field will disappear as shown in Figure 10-29.

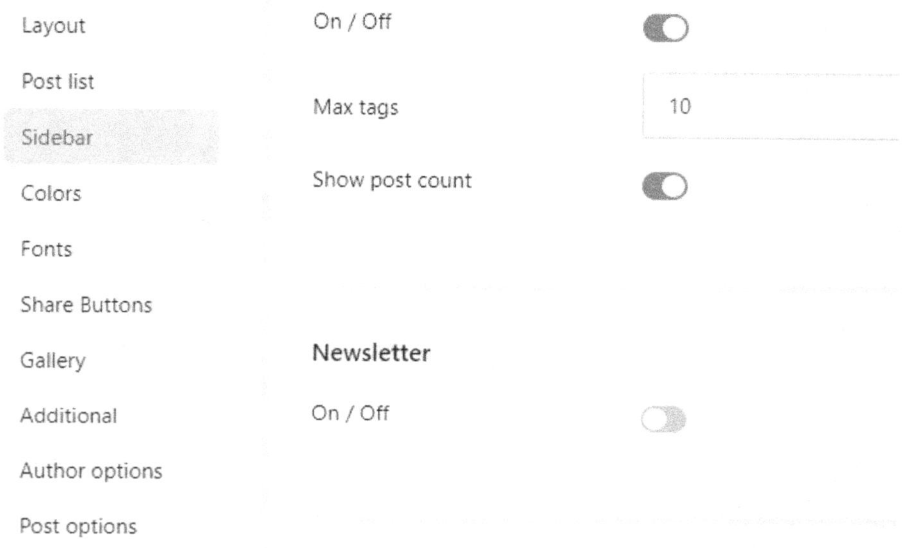

Layout	On / Off	
Post list		
	Max tags	10
Sidebar		
Colors	Show post count	
Fonts		
Share Buttons		
Gallery	**Newsletter**	
Additional	On / Off	
Author options		
Post options		

Figure 10-29. *Newsletter is disabled*

Note   If you would like to use a custom version of the Mono theme that allows you to edit the text for the newsletter sign-up feature, here is a modified version of the Mono theme: `https://github.com/bjazmoore/mono-modified`.

Next focus on fonts. The default fonts are OK, but I like the Raleway font. To change it, click the "Fonts" menu item in the Custom settings menu and locate the "Main font settings" section at the top of the right panel as shown in Figure 10-30.

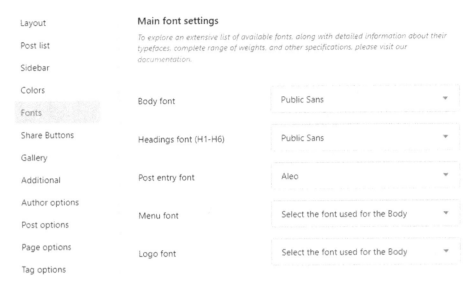

Figure 10-30. *Main font settings*

Change the Body font and the Headings font to Raleway as shown in Figure 10-31. Note that the font fields are drop-down fields. All available fonts are listed in the field organized by type as shown in Figure 10-31.

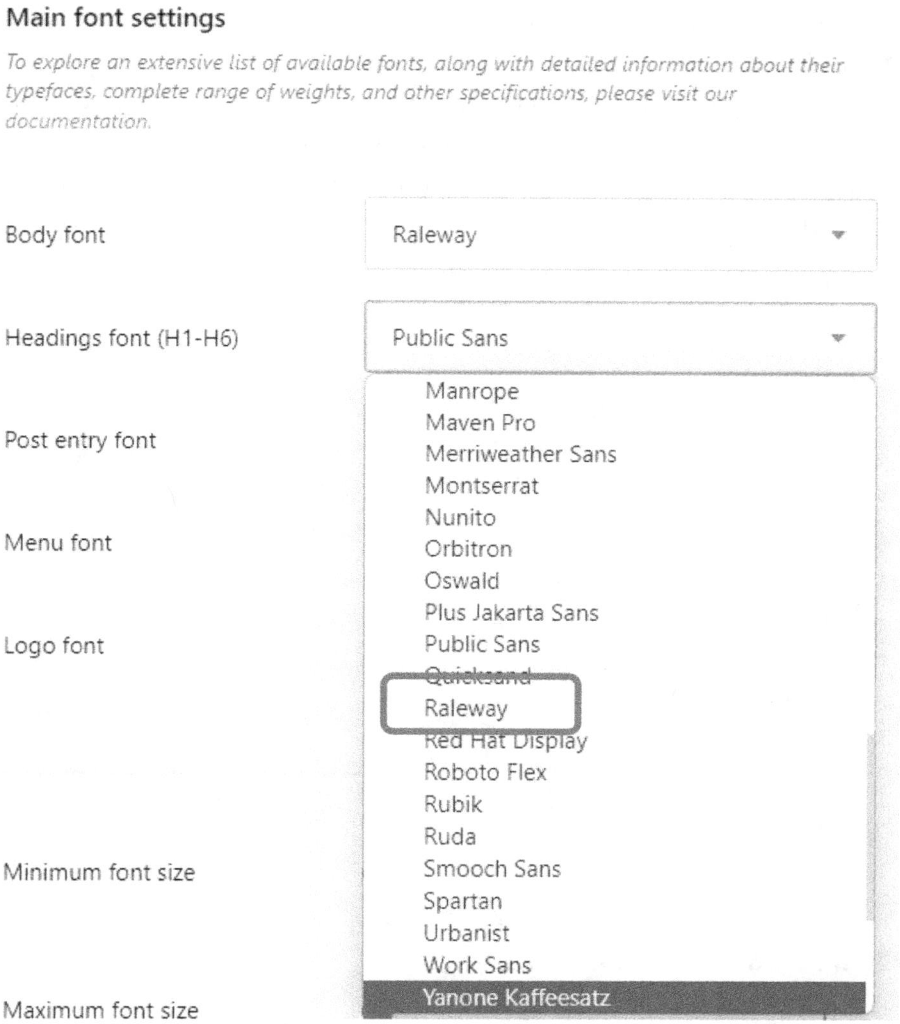

Main font settings

To explore an extensive list of available fonts, along with detailed information about their typefaces, complete range of weights, and other specifications, please visit our documentation.

Body font	Raleway ▾
Headings font (H1-H6)	Public Sans ▾
Post entry font	Manrope
	Maven Pro
	Merriweather Sans
	Montserrat
	Nunito
Menu font	Orbitron
	Oswald
	Plus Jakarta Sans
Logo font	Public Sans
	Quicksand
	Raleway
	Red Hat Display
	Roboto Flex
	Rubik
	Ruda
Minimum font size	Smooch Sans
	Spartan
	Urbanist
	Work Sans
	Yanone Kaffeesatz
Maximum font size	

Figure 10-31. *Main font settings and fonts listed in the font drop-down menu*

Select Raleway as highlighted in Figure 10-31. No other changes are required in the font settings section.

The Favicon was lost when the new theme was installed. To add it back in, click the "Additional" menu item in the Custom settings menu and locate the "Favicon" section at the bottom of the right panel as shown in Figure 10-32.

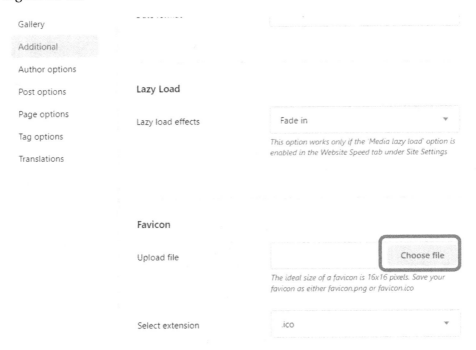

Figure 10-32. *The Favicon section*

Locate the favicon.png file used in Chapter 4. It is in the GitHub repository for this book in Chapters 4 and 10. You can access that at `https://github.com/Apress/Designing-Websites-with-Publii-and-GitHub-Pages`. Download the file to your computer if it is not already there from when we did this in Chapter 4.

Click the "Choose file" button in the Upload file field which is highlighted in Figure 10-32. Select the favicon.png file (remember the file must be called favicon.png) in the Windows open file dialog window and click the "Open" button. You should see a path to the file as shown in Figure 10-33.

Also change the extension in the Select extension drop-down field so that it says ".png", also shown in Figure 10-33.

Favicon

Upload file	media/website/favicon.png ×
	The ideal size of a favicon is 16x16 pixels. Save your favicon as either favicon.png or favicon.ico
Select extension	.png ▼

Figure 10-33. *Favicon settings*

Another area you might want to visit is the Share Buttons – also accessed from the Custom settings menu. The default buttons are for sharing on Facebook, X (formerly Twitter), and Pinterest.

Click the "Save Settings" or "Save & Preview" button on the bottom right side or the top of the top right side of the Theme Settings panel when you are done as shown in Figure 10-34. Your settings will not be saved if you neglect this step.

Figure 10-34. *Save Settings and Save & Preview buttons*

Featured Posts

I wanted to point out one other thing about this specific theme that is very useful. It supports featured posts. Featured posts allow the post author to highlight certain posts as being of specific importance – thereby featuring them to the readers of the blog. Here is how that works.

Click the "Posts" menu item in the main menu on the left side of the application as shown in Figure 10-35.

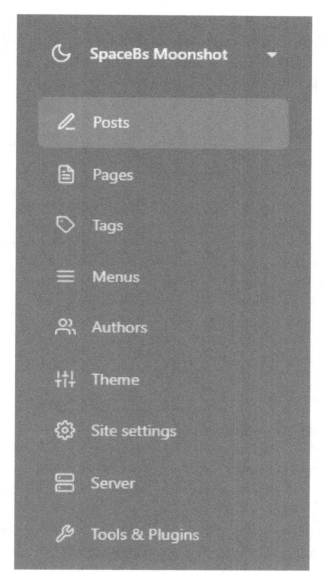

Figure 10-35. *Posts menu item in the Publii CMS main menu*

The right-side Posts panel displays the posts list as discussed in Chapter 5. Select one of the posts by clicking the check box to the left of the post. I selected the post titled "Inspired by a Dream" as shown in Figure 10-36.

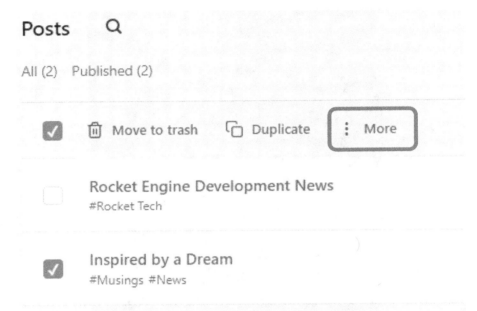

Figure 10-36. *Posts list on the Posts panel*

A quick action menu is displayed above the topmost post in the list. Click the "More" menu item denoted by the three stacked dots as highlighted in Figure 10-36.

A menu of additional actions will drop down. Click the menu item "Mark as featured" as highlighted in Figure 10-37.

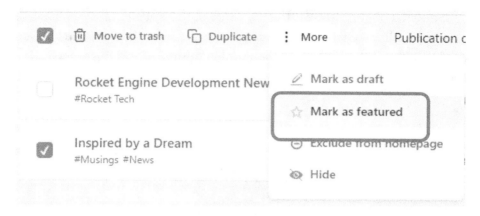

Figure 10-37. *Mark as featured*

Now look at how the Mono theme handles featured posts. Click the "Preview your changes" button at the bottom of the Publii CMS main menu as shown in Figure 10-38.

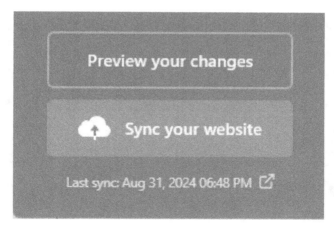

Figure 10-38. *Preview your changes*

Shown in Figure 10-39 is the right side of the website that was generated when I clicked the "Preview your changes" button. You can see that there is a new item in the sidebar highlighting one of the posts as a featured post.

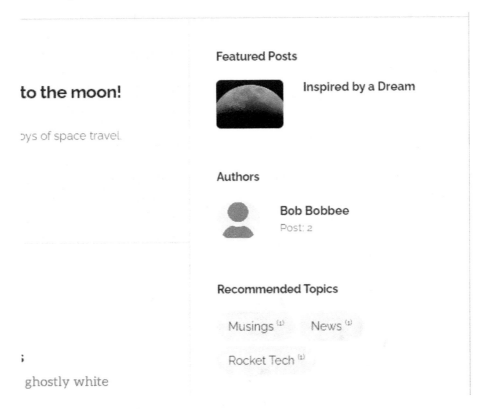

Figure 10-39. *Featured posts on the website rendered by Publii CMS*

Summary

As you saw in this chapter, themes add new functionality and a new look and feel to an existing Publii CMS website.

Publii CMS offers official themes which are desirable as they are always updated to take advantage of new features of Publii CMS – something that community themes often fail to keep pace with.

Publii CMS offers a good selection of free themes and additional premium themes that you can purchase from the good folks at Publii CMS.

Applying a theme to a website involves three steps:

1. Getting the theme from the Publii Marketplace

2. Installing the theme globally

3. Activating (called installing) the theme locally into a specific website

Themes have their own set of similar but potentially different Custom settings. Sometimes these settings can cause harm to your site. Always backup your site before activating/installing a theme locally.

In this chapter, we learned how featured posts are supported within a theme with that support built in. This is a good way to call attention to specific posts on a site that has many posts.

CHAPTER 11

Single-Page Sites

Publii CMS was originally designed to create and maintain blogs – websites with a homepage containing a hero followed by a list of blog entries. This is what the first project in this book focused on. Blogs have built-in pagination allowing Publii CMS to render sites with hundreds of blog posts. These posts are linked one to the next through the underlying structure of the site that Publii CMS creates. Additionally, a blog site supports tag and author pages permitting alternative methods of navigating posts and articles.

The blog is a natural application for news sites, hobbyist sites, and other journal-type websites. There is another form of website structure common on the Internet – the single-page website or landing page website. Many times, these are landing pages that act as a map to multiple other resources included on a website. Other times these are just one page that contains all the information the author needs to communicate to their readers.

Calling them a single-page website is misleading. This type of website is simply a collection of free-standing pages that must be manually linked to each other in the context of menu system or inline links. They do not leverage the built-in blogging structure that Publii CMS offers.

This is not a bad thing. There are many applications where a blog is not what you need. This is where this type of site becomes powerful. These might be landing pages that direct readers to multiple website resources, pages that communicate a single message supporting a cause, business, or organization. Think about a church or a medical office – they would use this type of page to provide information about who, what, and where they are.

In this chapter, I will be developing just such a website. You should follow along so that you can better understand these features in Publii CMS and learn some new tricks for getting the most out of the application. Open your instance of Publii CMS and let's get started.

More About Pages

In this section, I will explain how to set up a Publii CMS site as a Page-based site using a page as the site homepage.

The site we have been working on so far has been a basic blog. It consists of a simple structure with a homepage and a list of posts or articles that have been written. Sometimes this is not what you need. Perhaps you have a small company that just needs a page describing your services and contact information. Maybe you are a nonprofit and you just need to hang your shingle and let people know you exist. In these cases, perhaps blogging does not make sense.

Publii CMS can display a single page instead of a blog. That single page could be a place for you to communicate your message without the hassle of maintaining and constantly updating a blog. Publii CMS has supported this functionality in a limited form for some time; however, with the release of version 0.46.x, this functionality is baked into Publii in the form of Pages.

Those running a version prior to 0.46.x had to make do with tweaking a post to act like a page and then configuring that post to act as the site home page. With the addition of Page support, this functionality is much simpler to use. Additionally, the blog index page (what is normally the site home page) can be redirected so that Page-based sites can still support blogs natively.

Leveraging Earlier Work

Currently we have a nice blog that is working well. Instead of starting over, I plan to leverage this site to bootstrap the next site. This will save me from having to repeat some of the configuration work done in Chapters 3 and 4. It will also give me a ready-to-use set of blog posts when I add the blogging feature back into this single-page site.

Go to the "Sites management" interface that we worked with in Chapter 9. Remember that this can be accessed by clicking the current site title in the Publii CMS main menu as highlighted in Figure 11-1.

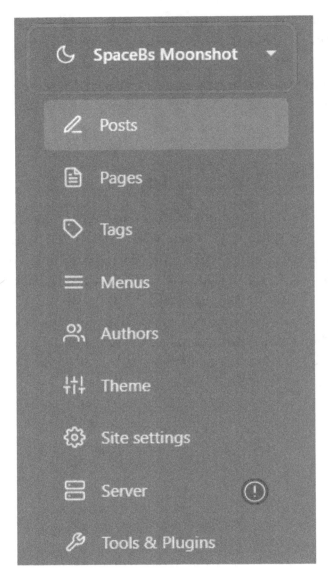

Figure 11-1. *Click the site title to access the "Sites management" interface*

Duplicate the site called "SpaceBs Moonshot" – or whatever your site is named – as shown in Figure 11-2.

SpaceBs Moonshot

Figure 11-2. *Duplicate a site*

Name the new site "Visiting Space" if you are following along with me, or the name of your choosing if you would like to be creative. Refer to Chapter 9 if you need additional guidance around these steps.

Adding a New Page

Click "Pages" in Publii CMS's main menu as highlighted in Figure 11-3.

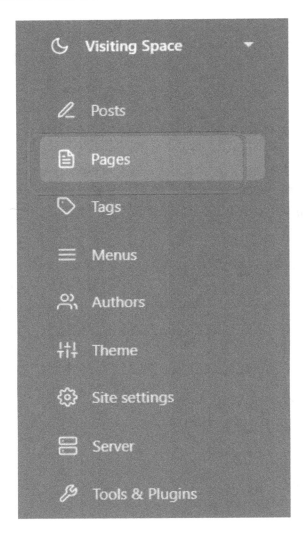

Figure 11-3. *Pages in the Publii CMS main menu*

There is currently a single page listed in the Pages list called "Terms and Conditions" which was created in Chapter 6. Click on the drop-down arrow on the right of the "Add new page" button and select the "Use WYSIWYG editor" as shown in Figure 11-4.

Figure 11-4. *Select the WYSIWYG editor*

Remember that we covered several features of the WYSIWYG editor in Chapter 5. As this page is developed, I will be detailing how to do new things, but I will not spend a lot of time on the techniques covered in Chapter 5. Refer to that chapter if you need help.

Equally I will be discussing what I have done to the page I developed including naming, layout, and text with the assumption that you will be following along identically. You are welcome to deviate from my design and do your own creative thing.

Before you begin adding content to the editor, look at the proposed finished page rendered in a web browser. Figure 11-5 shows the upper half of the page, and Figure 11-6 shows the lower half of the page.

Vacation in Space

Space-B is BOOKING trips to space and the moor now!

Book your trip now to avoid long waiting lines.

For tens of thousands of years humans have looked up to the moon and wondered about and dreamed about walking on its surface.

The moon is no longer out of reach. Even for person of average means.

Visit the moon by traveling with Space-B

We are going - you can too!

Check out the resources below to learn more about Space-B's space and moon travel packages. They are affordable and available right now. We launch in 2030!

Figure 11-5. *The top half of the finished web page*

Book a Trip

FAQs

Photo Gallery

Read our Blog

Contact Us

We are already putting people into low earth orbit and will have an operational space hotel for guests to visit in 2028.

Read testimonies of some who traveled into low earth orbit with us.

Lorem ipsum dolor sit amet, consectetur adipiscing elit. Vivamus convallis efficitur massa, a ornare diam maximus vitae. Nulla quis quam a leo vehicula ultricies. Aliquam venenatis odio lorem, quis pellentesque sapien lobortis vitae. Suspendisse dictum.

-- Jewl Roberts

Lorem ipsum dolor sit amet, consectetur adipiscing elit. Suspendisse elementum risus neque, lacinia mollis orci pretium ac. Morbi hendrerit ipsum in quam dapibus, id egestas sapien pellentesque. Quisque sollicitudin ut tortor vel semper. Nulla vitae neque luctus est lobortis lobortis.

-- John Doe

BOOK NOW

Figure 11-6. *The bottom half of the web page*

The first thing to do when working with either a post or a page is to give it a title. I have titled this one: "Vacation in Space".

Next add some text to the top of your page. You can format it after it has been added. Add the following two sentences:

Space-B is BOOKING trips to space and the moon now!

Book your trip now to avoid long waiting lines.

Make sure there is a blank line between the first and the second sentence. Format the first sentence by selecting it and then applying the "Heading H2" format to it. That tool is here on the toolbar as highlighted in Figure 11-7.

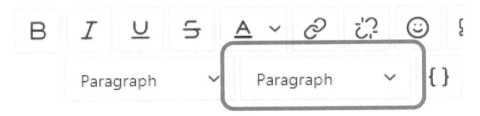

***Figure 11-7.** Text formatting tool in the toolbar*

Select the word "BOOKING" and click the link tool in the toolbar. Remember it looks like two links of chain. That will open the Insert/Edit link dialog window. I don't have anything to link to, so I will use placeholder links. Add a hashmark ("#") to the Custom link field as shown in Figure 11-8. Save the changes by clicking "OK".

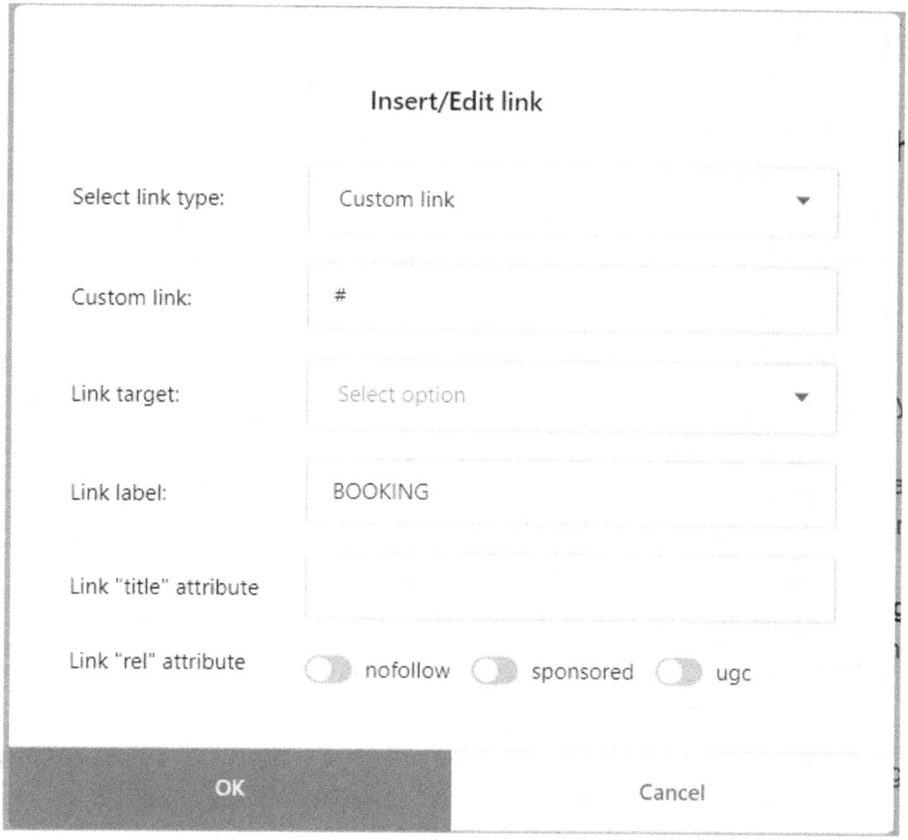

Figure 11-8. *Insert/Edit link dialog window*

Next, I want to place two elements side by side. Publii CMS handles content rendering in a way that makes it difficult to do this without resorting to using a table. Using tables for layout is so 1999! But it is what we must work with. The HTML and CSS that Publii CMS renders do a nice job of making tables responsive.

Learn More   Let's take a little side trip into responsive website design. This is not something you will need to know about to create nice looking sites with Publii CMS. Publii CMS's official themes take care of responsiveness automatically – but it is nice to understand the concept. Simply put, responsive web design is the application of special HTML and CSS directives and design principles that allow content to dynamically size and look good and readable on any device.

Target devices are typically desktop computer displays, tablets, and phones. Each comes in a variety of sizes. Responsiveness is all about the techniques used to get your site's rendering of information and web elements displayed so they look best on the device they are being viewed on. W3Schools offers a nice, guided tour of responsive website design for those interested in learning more: `https://www.w3schools.com/css/css_rwd_intro.asp`.

To place an image and text side by side, you will need to insert a table. I have not explained using tables yet. The WYSIWYG editor has good support for tables. The Block editor does not support tables currently.

Place the cursor in the editor where you want to insert a table. Click the table drop-down tool in the toolbar as highlighted in Figure 11-9.

Figure 11-9. *Table tool in the toolbar*

To add a table with a single row and two columns, click the table tool, click the "Table >" menu item. A grid is shown to the left of the menu. Highlight two cells wide and one row deep (the table grid will report the size as 2x1 on the bottom of the grid), and click in the rightmost, lowest cell in the area desired as shown in Figure 11-10.

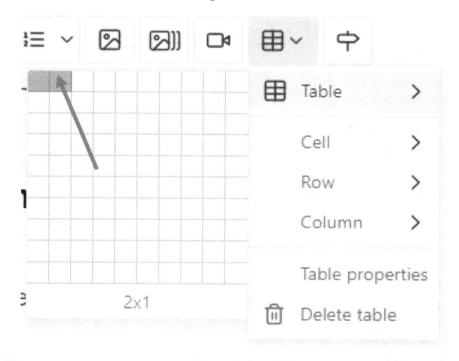

Figure 11-10. *Inserting a table – click in the cell indicated by the arrow*

In Figure 11-10, I have indicated the cell to click in, as shown by an arrow, to form a two-column single-row table. Figure 11-11 shows the table inserted into the editor. Note the context-related toolbar that the table makes available.

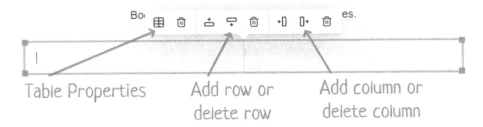

Figure 11-11. Inserted table with table context menu

In the right cell of the table, type or paste some text. Below is the text I used – if you are following along, then copy and insert that text.

For tens of thousands of years humans have looked up to the moon and wondered about and dreamed about walking on its surface.

The moon is no longer out of reach. Even for a person of average means.

Visit the moon by traveling with Space-B

We are going - you can too!

Select the sentence "The moon is no longer out of reach" and make it bold. Select the sentence "We are going – you can too!" and format it as "Heading H3". Select all the text and click the "Align center" toolbar button as highlighted in Figure 11-12.

Figure 11-12. The Align center toolbar button

Next, I will add an image to the left cell. The images I used in the site example in Figures 11-5 and 11-6 were created by DALL-E with the assistance of ChatGPT. Download these images from the book's GitHub repository: `https://github.com/Apress/Designing-Websites-with-Publii-and-GitHub-Pages`.

Place the cursor in the left cell of the table by clicking there. Click the Insert/Edit Image toolbar button (covered in Chapter 5, section titled "The WYSIWYG Editor") to insert an image. The image I am inserting is "Rocket-headed-to-the-moon-2.webp" as shown in Figure 11-13.

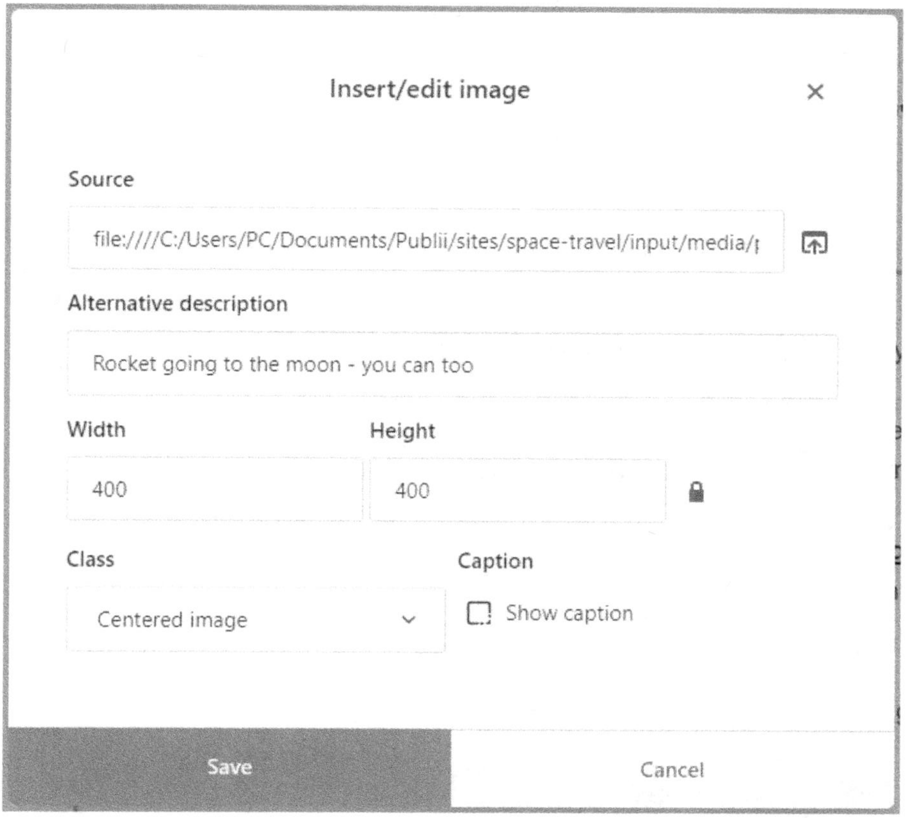

Figure 11-13. *Insert/edit image dialog window*

Notice in Figure 11-13 that I have given this image an Alternative text and set the size to 400x400. Under the Class drop-down field, I have selected "Centered image". The centered class will keep the image constrained to the cell it is assigned to. Save these settings to insert the image.

I do not want the table border or cell border to be visible. Click inside the table and then click on the "Table properties" icon in the menu as shown in Figure 11-11. Click "Advanced" on the left side of the Table properties dialog window. Select a Border style of "None" from the Border style drop-down field as shown in Figure 11-14.

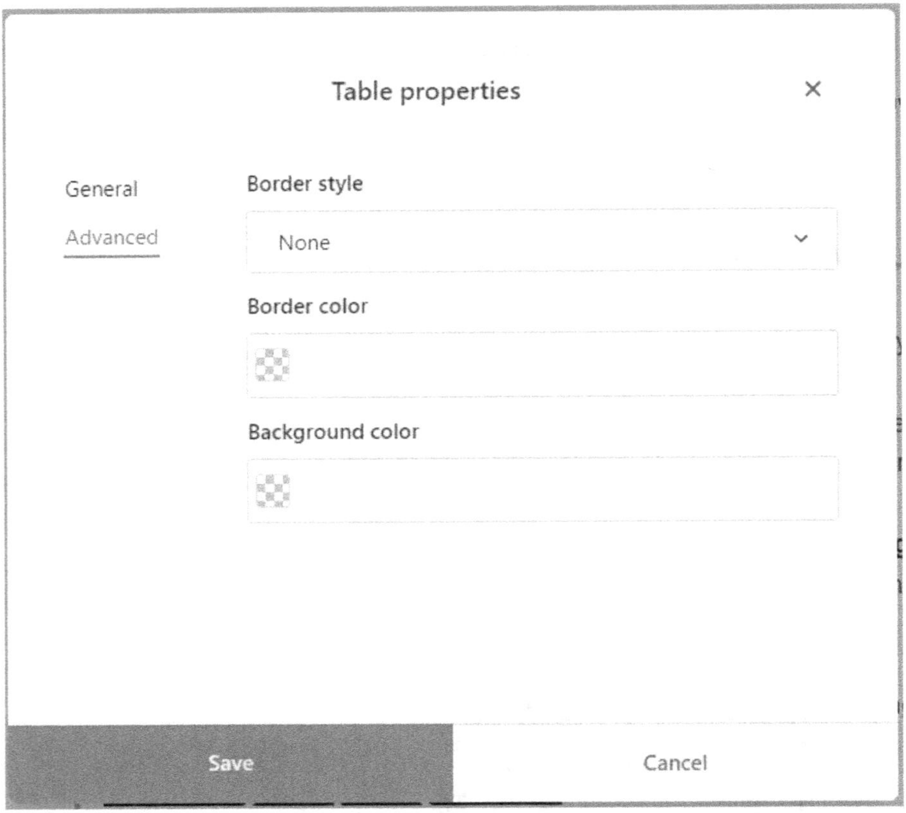

Figure 11-14. *Table properties dialog window*

Click "Save" to commit the settings.

We removed the table border in the previous step, but the cell borders are still visible. Preview the page and look if you would like. To remove these borders, select both cells by clicking in one and dragging through into the other. Now click the "Table tool" icon in the toolbar. Click "Cell" and then click "Cell properties" in the submenu that pops out from the side as highlighted in Figure 11-15.

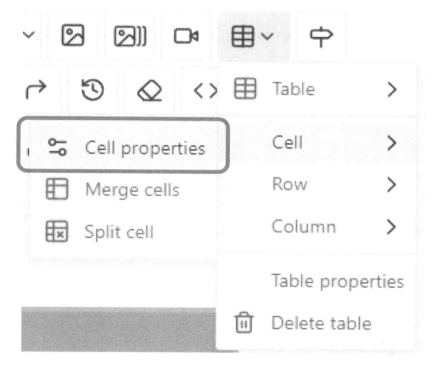

Figure 11-15. *Cell properties*

This opens the Cell properties dialog window which is like the Table properties dialog window. The initial section displayed is the "General" Cell properties. While on this view, set the Horizontal align drop-down field to "Center" and the Vertical align drop-down field to "Top" as highlighted in Figure 11-16.

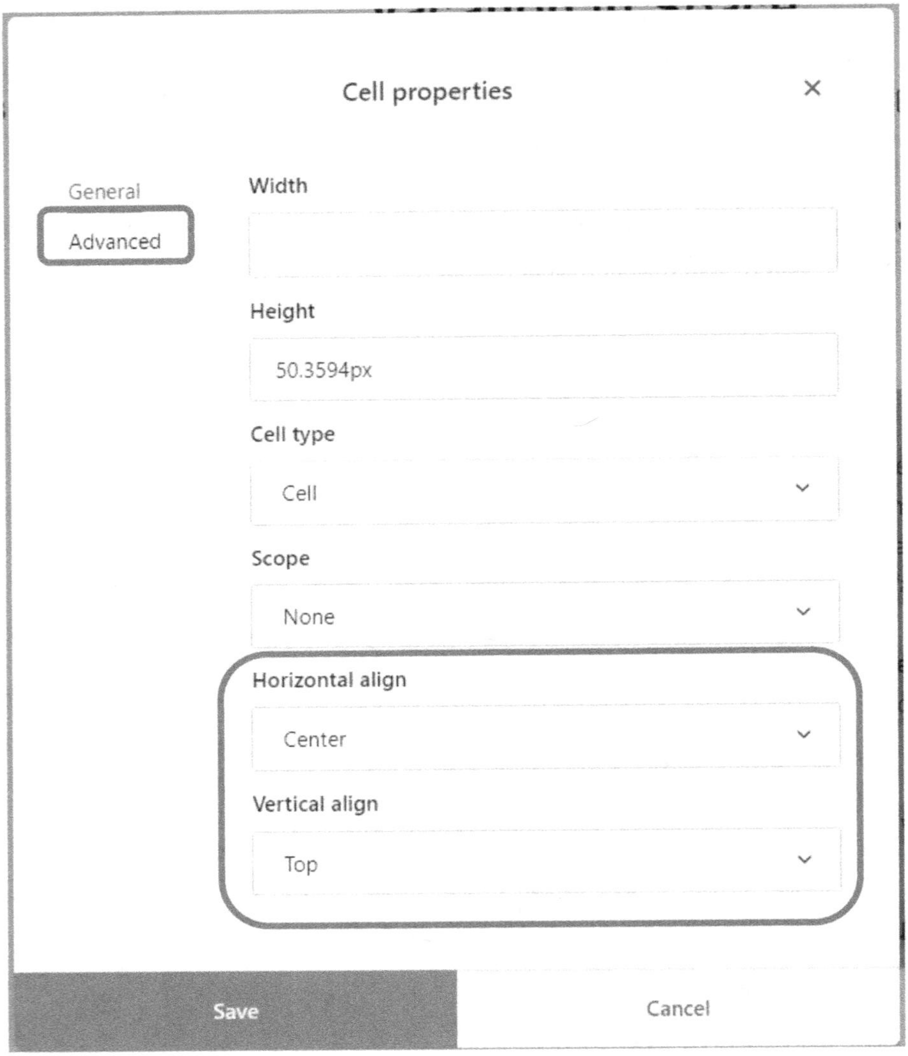

Figure 11-16. *Cell Alignment – Cell Properties "General" view*

Don't click save yet – instead click "Advanced" on the left side of
the Cell properties dialog window (also highlighted in Figure 11-16).
Select a Border style of "None" from the Border style drop-down field as
highlighted in Figure 11-17.

496

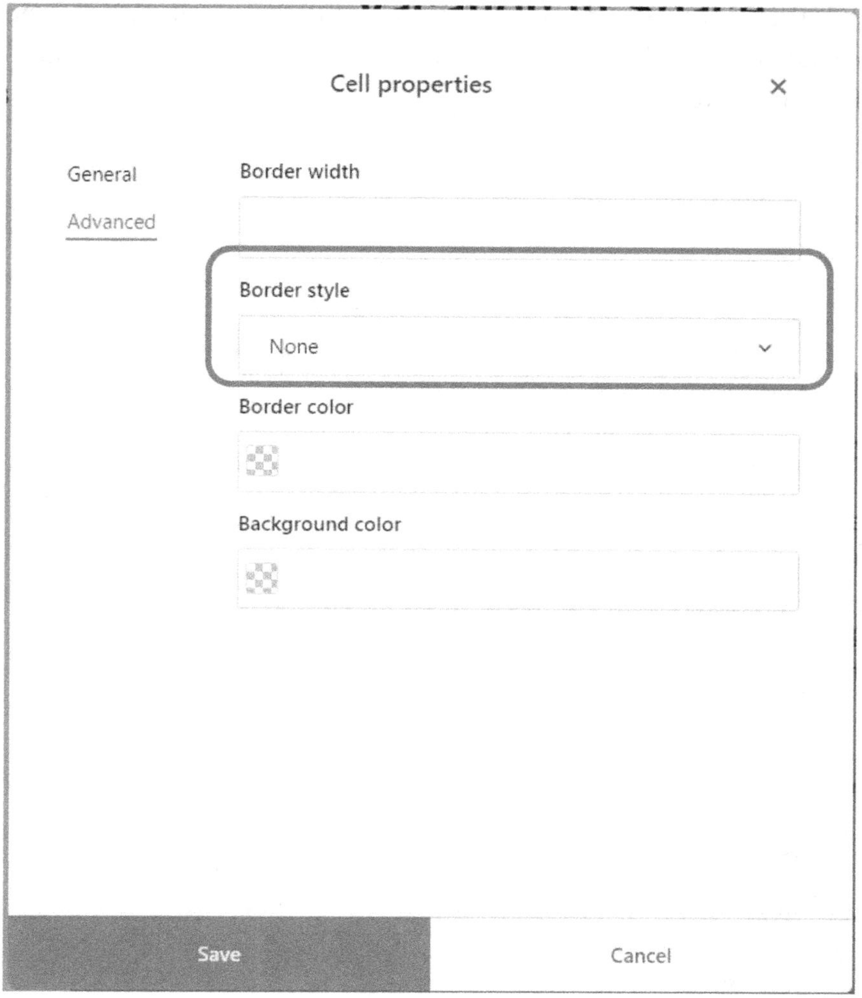

Figure 11-17. *Cell properties dialog window*

Click the "Save" button to commit the changes.

There is one more cosmetic change I want to make to the table. I want to reduce the width of the left cell to 45%. This will give the text in the right cell some breathing room visually. To do this, click in the left cell. Repeat the steps above to open the Cell properties dialog window. This time I will be changing only the properties of the left cell since it is the only cell selected.

497

In the General section of the Cell properties dialog window, change the width of the cell by typing 45% into the field below the label "Width" as shown in Figure 11-18.

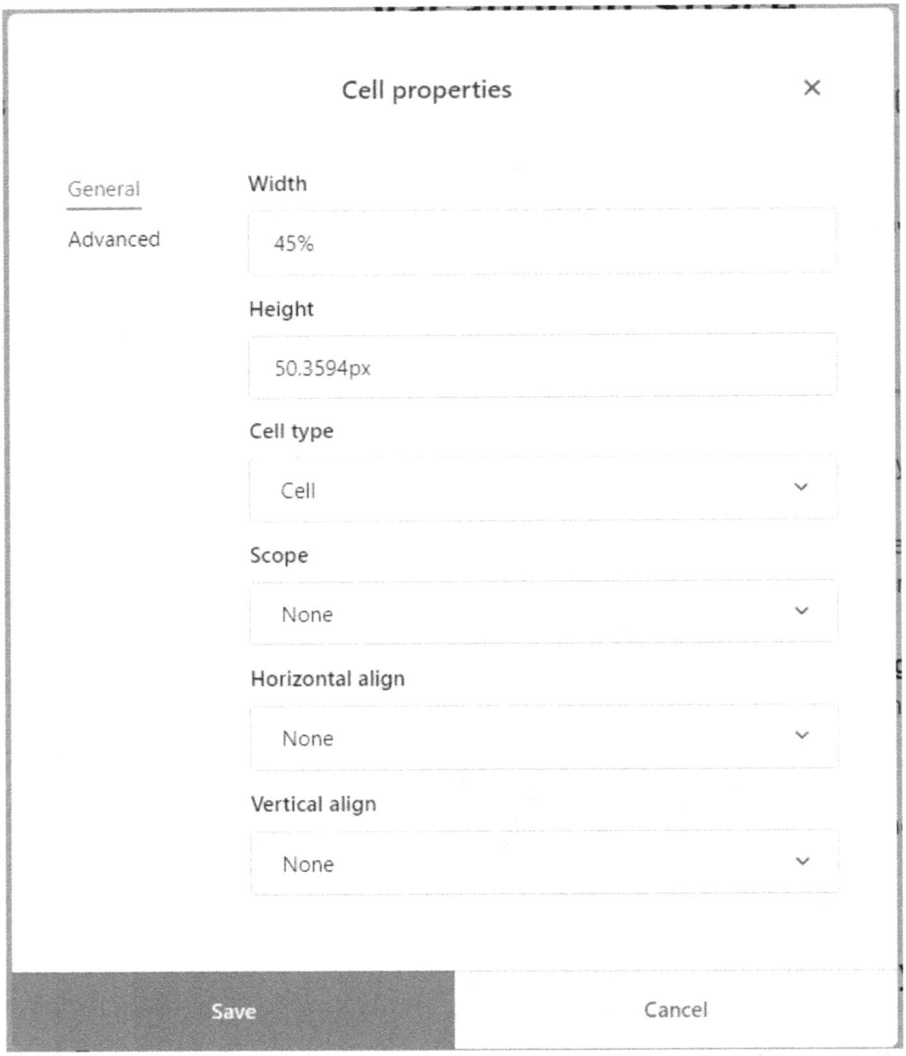

Cell properties   ×

General

Advanced

Width

45%

Height

50.3594px

Cell type

Cell   ⌄

Scope

None   ⌄

Horizontal align

None   ⌄

Vertical align

None   ⌄

Save   Cancel

Figure 11-18. *Setting Cell Width – "General" Cell properties*

Don't forget the percent symbol ("%") or you will be setting the width to 45 pixels – that's pretty small.

Click the Preview link in the upper left corner of the editor to see how the page is coming along.

Add some text to the editor to break up the next major page element. I have added the following sentences:

> *Check out the resources below to learn more about Space-B's space and moon travel packages. They are affordable and available right now. We launch in 2030!*

The next major element once again will be side by side image and text enclosed in a two-cell table. Put the image "Astronauts-boarding-capsule-2.webp" (found in the book's GitHub repository for Chapter 11 here: `https://github.com/Apress/Designing-Websites-with-Publii-and-GitHub-Pages`) into the right cell. Figure 11-19 shows the configuration for the image – much like that of the previous image.

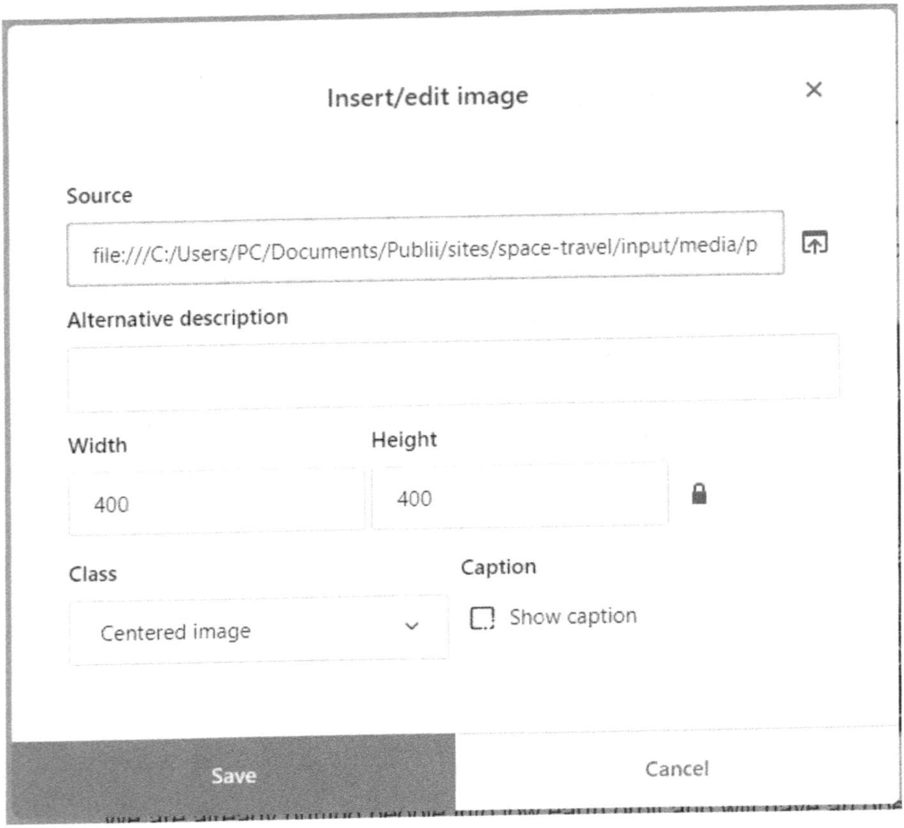

Insert/edit image   ×

Source

file:///C:/Users/PC/Documents/Publii/sites/space-travel/input/media/p

Alternative description

Width   Height

400   400   🔒

Class   Caption

Centered image   ⌄   ☐ Show caption

Save   Cancel

Figure 11-19. *Insert/edit image dialog window*

In the left-side cell, I added text for five links. These are

Book a Trip

FAQs

Photo Gallery

Read our Blog

Contact Us

Configure each of these as a link with a placeholder of "#" for the Custom link URL value as was done in Figure 11-8.

Configure the table borders and cell borders as we did for the previous table above. Set the cell properties for Horizontal and Vertical align as well. It should look like Figure 11-20 when complete.

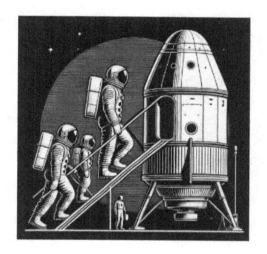

Book a Trip

FAQs

Photo Gallery

Read our Blog

Contact Us

Figure 11-20. *Completely formatted table*

Below this table, add some text introducing the testimonial portion of the page. This is the text I added:

We are already putting people into low earth orbit and will have an operational space hotel for guests to visit in 2028.

Read testimonies of some who traveled into low earth orbit with us.

If you are following along, then add this text it into the editor below the table you just created. Format the second sentence to be bold.

Add one more two-cell, single-row table like the last two we have added. Format the table so that it does not have table borders or cell borders as we did for the previous two tables above. Set the cell properties for Horizontal and Vertical align as well.

501

The testimonials that I am using were created by a Lorem Ipsum generator located here: `https://www.lipsum.com/`. Below is the text of the first testimonial. Generate your own, copy and paste it into the left cell of the table.

> *Lorem ipsum dolor sit amet, consectetur adipiscing elit. Vivamus convallis efficitur massa, a ornare diam maximus vitae. Nulla quis quam a leo vehicula ultricies. Aliquam venenatis odio lorem, quis pellentesque sapien lobortis vitae. Suspendisse dictum.*
>
> *-- Jewl Roberts*

The second testimonial reuses the same Lorem ipsum as above. Copy and paste it into the right cell of the table.

> *Lorem ipsum dolor sit amet, consectetur adipiscing elit. Suspendisse elementum risus neque, lacinia mollis orci pretium ac. Morbi hendrerit ipsum in quam dapibus, id egestas sapien pellentesque. Quisque sollicitudin ut tortor vel semper. Nulla vitae neque luctus est lobortis lobortis.*
>
> *-- John Doe*

I have formatted these as italic text to make them more distinctive. I wanted to use the blockquote but did not like how it looked on the finished page. The table is shown in Figure 11-21.

Lorem ipsum dolor sit amet, consectetur adipiscing elit. Vivamus convallis efficitur massa, a ornare diam maximus vitae. Nulla quis quam a leo vehicula ultricies. Aliquam venenatis odio lorem, quis pellentesque sapien lobortis vitae. Suspendisse dictum.	*Lorem ipsum dolor sit amet, consectetur adipiscing elit. Suspendisse elementum risus neque, lacinia mollis orci pretium ac. Morbi hendrerit ipsum in quam dapibus, id egestas sapien pellentesque. Quisque sollicitudin ut tortor vel semper. Nulla vitae neque luctus est lobortis lobortis.*
-- Jewl Roberts	
	-- John Doe

Figure 11-21. *Completed testimonials displayed in a table*

One last element is needed to complete the page. A final call to action – a simple but bold "BOOK NOW" link. Style this text as a "Heading H2" to make it large and bold. Select the text and click the Insert/Edit link button in the toolbar to add a hyperlink to the text. This is a Custom link like the others we have made, and it links to "#" as a placeholder for the link address as shown in Figure 11-22.

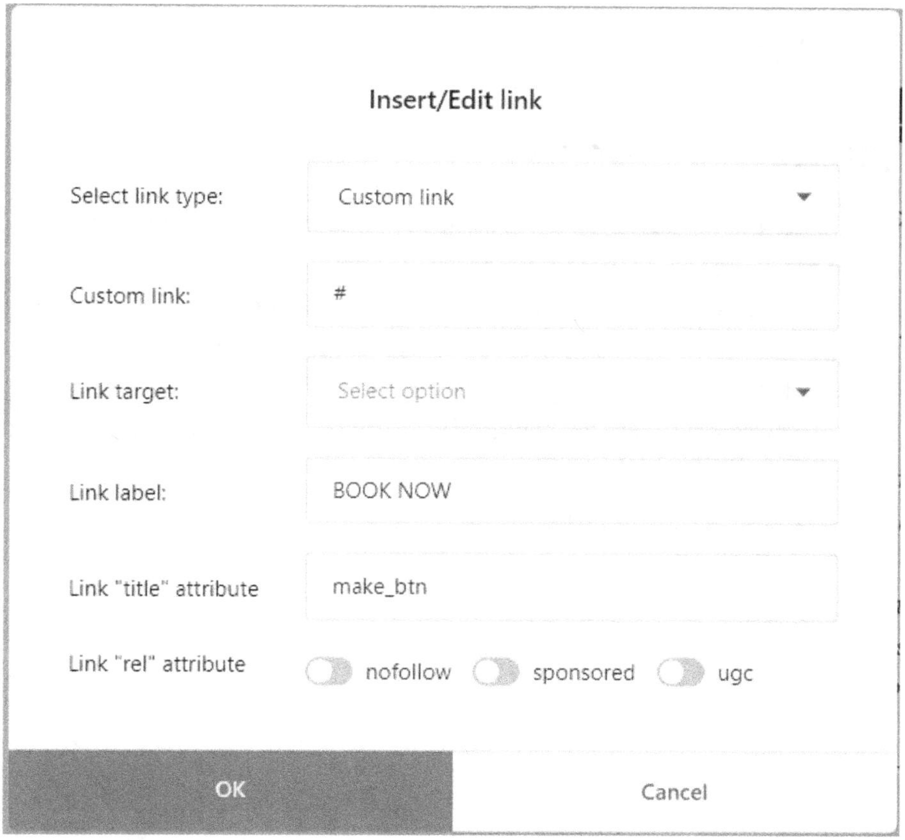

Insert/Edit link

Select link type:	Custom link ▼
Custom link:	#
Link target:	Select option ▼
Link label:	BOOK NOW
Link "title" attribute	make_btn
Link "rel" attribute	◯ nofollow ◯ sponsored ◯ ugc

OK   Cancel

Figure 11-22. *Custom link settings for the BOOK NOW link*

Notice also that I have added a Link "title" attribute. I will show you later how to leverage that to turn the link into a button using a little CSS generated by ChatGPT.

This completes the page. We will come back to it to attach some additional pages to the links that we initially populated with placeholder links.

Save your work then click the "Pages" link in the upper left corner of the editor to leave the editor window.

Selecting a Theme

At the time I copied this new site from the SpaceB Moonshot site, the theme for that site was Mono. We therefore have copied Mono as the theme for this site. This is a nice theme for a blog website but is not as well suited for a single-page site or landing page site like we have been working on. Click the "Site settings" menu item in the Publii CMS main menu to access the Basic site settings where the site theme is managed as shown in Figure 11-23.

Site settings

Basic settings

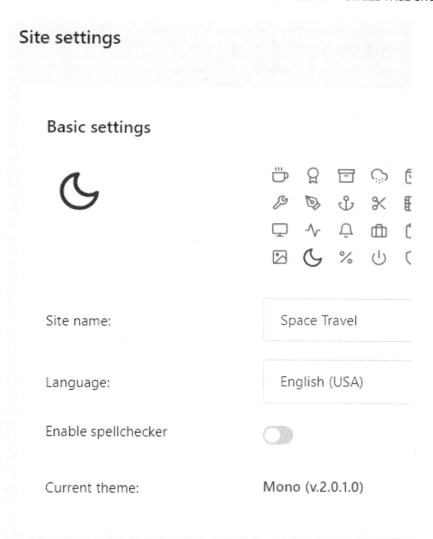

Site name: Space Travel

Language: English (USA)

Enable spellchecker

Current theme: Mono (v.2.0.1.0)

Figure 11-23. *Site settings - Basic settings showing the current theme*

As it turns out, the Simple 3.0.0.0 theme works quite well for a landing page-type website. To better support this site as a landing page, I will change the theme to Simple 3.0.0.0. This is also done in the Basic settings section of Site settings. To the right of the current theme is a drop-down field where we can select a theme to use, install themes locally, and delete them locally as we learned in Chapter 10. Click the drop-down and then select "Simple(v.3.0.0.0)" from the "Use" section as highlighted in Figure 11-24.

Figure 11-24. *Selecting a theme from the Theme drop-down field*

After selecting the theme, click the light blue "Save settings" button in the upper right corner of the Site settings panel.

You will be prompted to regenerate thumbnails because of the change. This is always a good idea. If you became lost changing themes, then refer to Chapter 10, section titled "Activating a Theme", where this topic is discussed in detail.

Sometimes moving between themes will cause a feature from one theme to be disabled, and later when returning to that theme, there may be unusual side effects. Going from Simple to Mono and back to Simple does this to the Hero image if one was specified.

You should remove the hero image from the Simple theme or replace it to correct just such an issue. To do that, click the "Theme" menu item in the Publii CMS main menu on the left side of the application. Scroll down to the "Custom settings" panel and click the "Layout" menu item in the custom settings menu. Now scroll the right side of the custom settings panel down to the "Hero section". Locate the image field. Click the red "remove image" link below the image field.

You can add an image back into this field after removing the lost image if you choose to. I left mine empty. Don't forget to save the changes.

If you got lost here, go back and read about the hero settings in Chapter 4, section titled "Layout: Hero Section".

Setting the Homepage

Previewing your site reveals that the homepage is the default posts list page. This is because we have not yet told Publii CMS to make the new page created above the homepage. This change is made in the Site settings area of the application where the theme was just changed.

This time you will need to scroll down to the "Advanced options" section and click the "SEO" menu of that section. Scroll down the right side of the Advanced options panel until you see the "Homepage" section as shown in Figure 11-25.

Figure 11-25. *The "Homepage" section of the SEO section of the Advanced options section of the Site settings*

Click the "Set page as homepage" toggle switch highlighted in Figure 11-25 so that it slides right and becomes colored blue. Once enabled, the "Page Title" field becomes a drop-down field labeled "Select page". Click the drop-down and select the page created above. In my project, it is called "Vacation in Space" as highlighted in Figure 11-26.

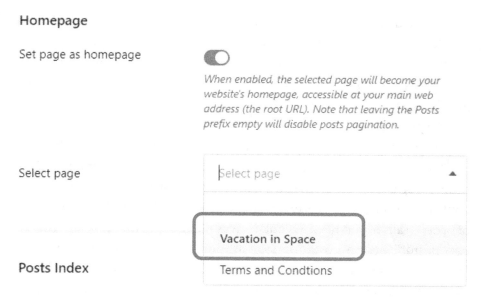

Figure 11-26. *Select the page to act as your homepage*

Click the darker blue button on the upper right corner of the Site settings panel labeled "Save & Preview" to save the changes and see a preview of your website.

Congratulations – you now have a landing page as your homepage. If you followed along with the examples provided, it should look like the one shown in Figures 11-5 and 11-6.

Adding a Blog

Originally the website for this project, it had a blog attached to it. Unfortunately, we no longer have access to the posts list page. This is because we have defined a new home page which replaced the posts page (which originally was the site's home page). We can access the tags list page because we added a menu item that was linked to it.

To add access to the blog feature back into this site, we will need to tell Publii CMS to generate the posts list page in a subfolder. This will allow the underlying blog structure of the website to be created when the site is previewed or published. Version 0.46.0 introduced a mechanism to do just this.

We just ditched the blog because we wanted to have this neat single-page website – why would I want to add a blog to a single-page website?

There are several use cases where a single-page website would benefit from a blog as well. The strength of the single-page website is that you control the entire look and feel of the homepage. No basic hero and lists of posts – rather, you have a blank canvas to paint the picture you desire to communicate with your message to your readers. Sometimes this is an evolving message. Cases where a business or organization has events, needs to share evolving information about their operation, or publishes tips, recipes, and how-to articles. These things are best managed in a newsletter or blog format.

Adding a blog to this imaginary space travel organization will allow it to share planned events and trips, stories from previous trips, and other articles that can add color to the overall mission of the company. It is all about reader engagement. Blogs help enhance that element of your interface to the public.

To add a blog, we need a place to redirect the posts list to. Three things must be done to redirect the posts list. The first replace the default homepage with a specific page created for that purpose. We did that in the previous section.

Second enable pretty URLs in the site settings - this also has been completed earlier. The final thing is to set a new value for the "Posts prefix" which will define the root folder where posts will appear in the site structure. We will need to go to the "Site settings" panel to do both of those things.

Pretty URLs

Click the "Site settings" menu item in the Publii CMS main menu on the left side of the application to access the Site settings panel. Scroll down below the "Basic settings" section to the "Advanced options" section and click the "URL" menu item in the Advanced options menu as shown in Figure 11-27.

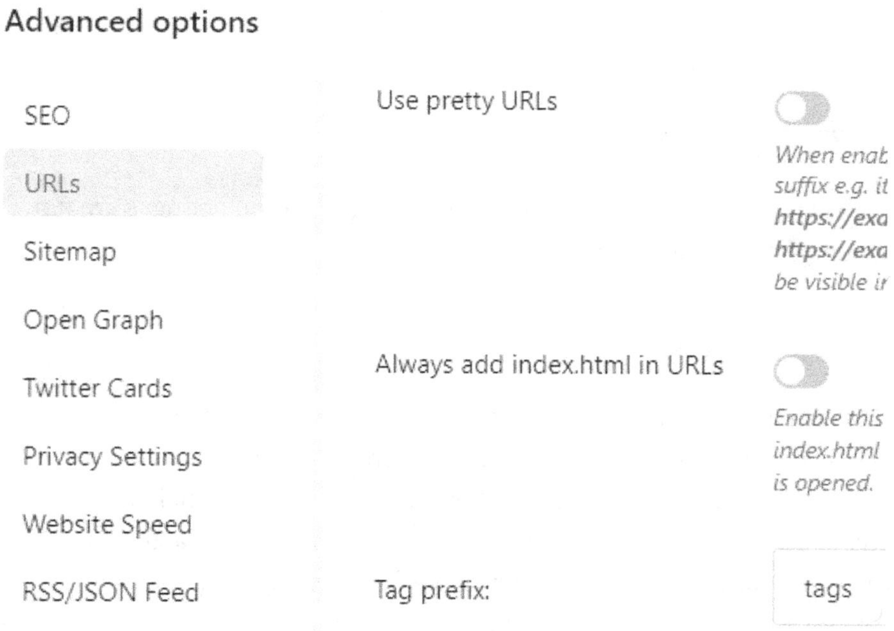

Advanced options

SEO	Use pretty URLs	⬭
URLs		*When enab*
		suffix e.g. it
Sitemap		*https://exa*
		https://exa
Open Graph		*be visible ir*
Twitter Cards	Always add index.html in URLs	⬭
		Enable this
Privacy Settings		*index.html*
		is opened.
Website Speed		
RSS/JSON Feed	Tag prefix:	tags

Figure 11-27. *Advanced options panel*

If you recall, we enabled pretty URLs in Chapter 3. If it has become disabled, so slide the toggle switch to the right to enable the option "Use pretty URLs". It will turn blue when enabled as shown in Figure 11-28.

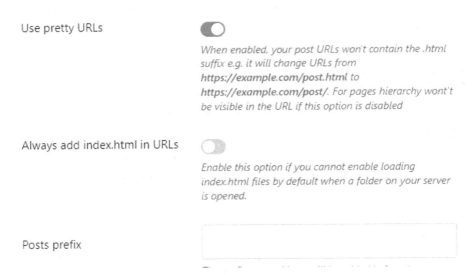

Figure 11-28. Use pretty URLs

If pretty URLs is still enabled in your project, then changes are not required at this step – move on to the next step.

Posts Prefix

Enabling pretty URLs has revealed a previously hidden field labeled "Posts prefix". The text explaining the operation of this field (located below the field) can be hard to interpret. Essentially this field allows you to give a new name and location to the posts list that acted as the blog homepage. The redirected posts list will be placed into a sub-folder with the given name you have defined in the "posts prefix" field.

Locate the "Posts prefix" field in the same section as the pretty URLs as shown in Figure 11-29. Give the Posts prefix the value of "blog".

Posts prefix	blog

Figure 11-29. *Posts prefix setting*

Scroll to the top of the Site settings panel and click the "Save settings" button.

Add Links to Blog

We have defined a folder for the blog list page, but we still cannot access it because we do not have any links pointing users to it. Remember that when working with single-page sites, we must provide all the links to all the various pages we want our readers to find. The new blog list is the same.

I want to link it two ways. I want a menu item that will open the blog list page, and I want to have a link from within the content of the new homepage. If you remember, we added a placeholder link for that when building the page.

First, the site menu. Click the "Menus" menu item in the Publii CMS main menu on the left side of the application. The Menu list will be displayed in the right panel. If you are following along, then you will have a single menu named "Main" like I do.

Click the menu named "Main" to display its menu items as shown in Figure 11-30.

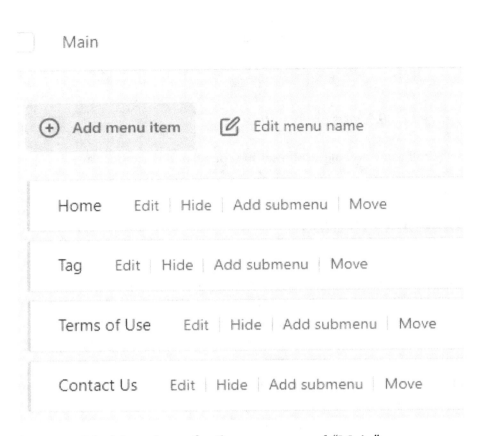

Figure 11-30. *Menu items for the menu named "Main"*

Instead of deleting, adding, and moving menu items around, I am going to just repurpose the menu item "Tag". I do not want that menu item in the future, but I do want a menu item that reads "Blog" in exactly that same place. Click on the action to the right of the "Tag" menu item labeled "Edit" as shown in Figure 11-31.

514

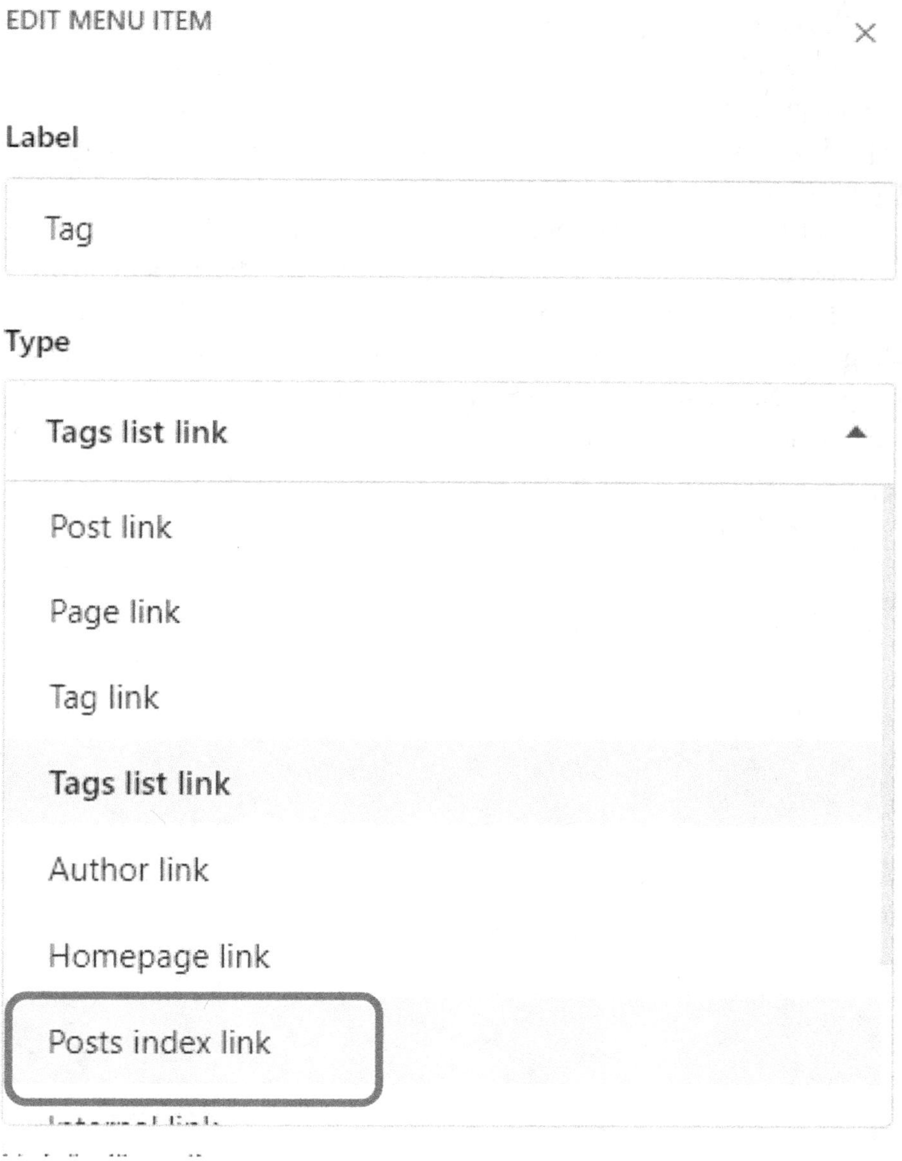

EDIT MENU ITEM   ✕

Label

Tag

Type

Tags list link	▲

Post link

Page link

Tag link

Tags list link

Author link

Homepage link

Posts index link

Figure 11-31. *Edit Menu Item dialog*

The Edit action opens a panel form that flies out from the right side titled "EDIT MENU ITEM". Change the name of this menu item by changing the value in the Label field from "Tag" to "Blog". In the Type drop-down field, select the "Posts index link" as highlighted in Figure 11-31.

Click the blue "Save Changes" button to save these changes.

Next click the "Pages" menu item in the Publii CMS main menu on the left side of the application. Locate the page you created earlier in the chapter to be the site's new homepage. I created a page called "Vacation in Space". Notice that Publii CMS has attached the notation that this is the current homepage at the end of the page name as shown in Figure 11-32.

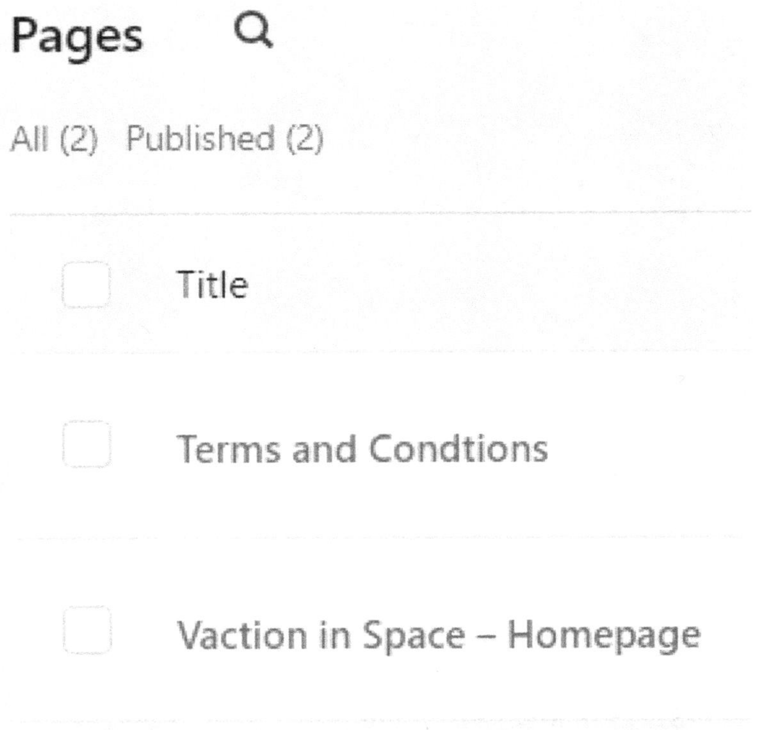

Pages   Q

All (2)   Published (2)

Title

Terms and Condtions

Vaction in Space – Homepage

Figure 11-32. *Pages list*

Click on the name of the page to open it up in the editor it was created in. Scroll down to the middle of the page where you added links to other pages we hoped to add in the future as shown in Figure 11-33.

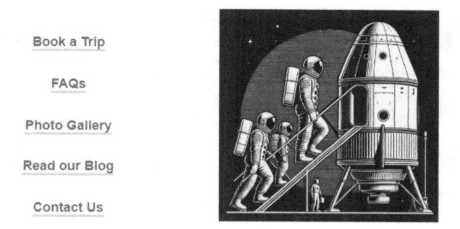

ᵉ̶ady putting people into low earth orbit and will have an operational space

Figure 11-33. *Links to be added in the future*

It is time to add the link to the blog. Click on the link text and then click the link icon in the context menu that is displayed as highlighted in Figure 11-34.

Figure 11-34. *Link icon in the context menu*

This opens the Inset/Edit link dialog window as shown in Figure 11-35. Click in the "Select link type" drop-down field and select "Posts index link" from the drop-down menu.

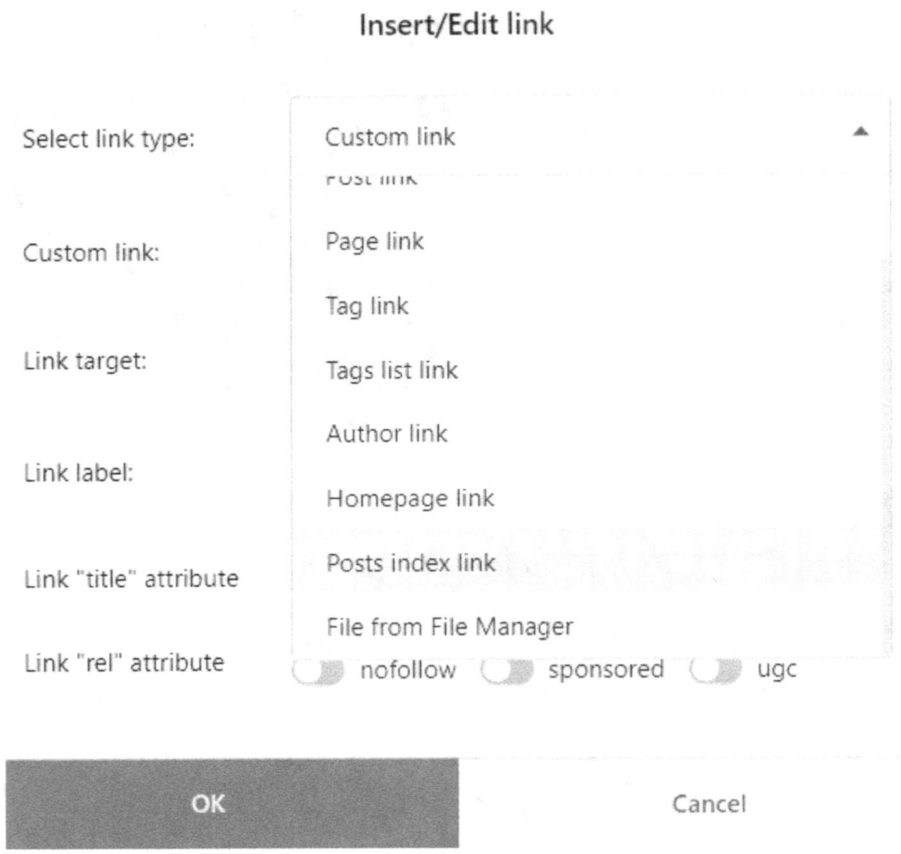

Insert/Edit link

Select link type:	Custom link ▲
	Post link
Custom link:	Page link
	Tag link
Link target:	Tags list link
	Author link
Link label:	Homepage link
Link "title" attribute	Posts index link
	File from File Manager
Link "rel" attribute	⬤ nofollow ⬤ sponsored ⬤ ugc

OK	Cancel

Figure 11-35. *Select "Posts index link" as the link type*

Click the blue "OK" button to commit the changes. Click the blue "Save" button in the upper right corner of the editor to save the changes to the page.

Click the "< Pages" link in the upper left corner of the editor to exit the editor and return to the Pages list panel.

Click the "Preview your changes" button at the bottom of the Publii CMS main menu on the left side of the application to see and test the blog links. As we move into the next section, keep the preview of the website open.

Create a Footer Menu

One of the last things to do to embellish the new homepage is to add a footer menu and improve the footer text to reflect who we are. To do this, you will be working in two different areas of Publii CMS.

Begin with the footer menu. It will be very similar to the main menu. The process is the same as creating the main menu called "Main". Click the "Menus" menu item in the Publii CMS main menu on the left side of the application. Currently there is one menu listed in the Menu list. Click the "Add new menu" button in the upper right corner of the Menu list panel. It will ask for a name for this new menu as shown in Figure 11-36. Name it "Footer".

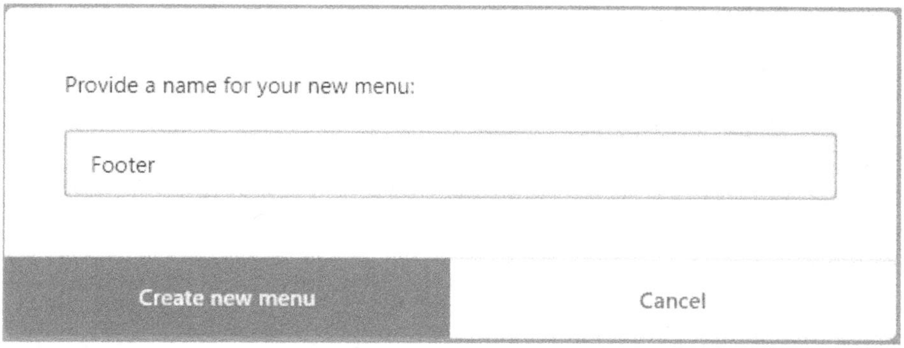

Provide a name for your new menu:

Footer

Create new menu   Cancel

Figure 11-36. Name the new menu

Click the blue "Create new menu" button on the dialog window. Open the new menu named "Footer" by clicking the menu name. Currently there are no menu items associated with this menu.

Click the "Add menu item" button and add the following menus:

Menu item 1

Label: Home

Type: Homepage link

Menu item 2

Label: Terms & Conditions

Type: Page link

Page: Terms and Conditions

Menu item 3

Label: Cookie Policy

Type: External link

External URL: #

Menu item 4

Label: Contact Us

Type: External link

External URL: #

When complete, the Footer menu should look like Figure 11-37.

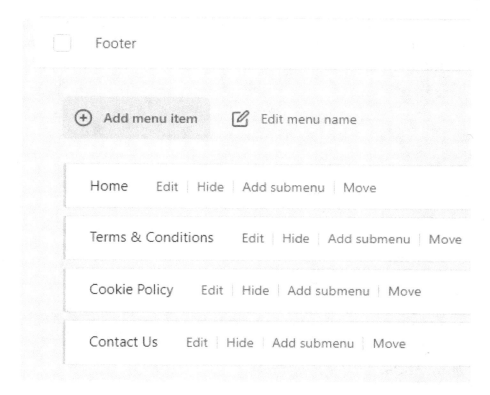

Figure 11-37. Footer menu with menu items assigned

Click the "Unassigned" link below the label "Assigned menu" for the
Footer menu to assign it as highlighted in Figure 11-38.

Name	Assigned menu
Main	Main menu
Footer	Unassigned

Figure 11-38. Assigning the Footer menu

Enable the Footer menu location by sliding the toggle for that selection to the right as shown in Figure 11-39. The toggle switch will turn blue when enabled.

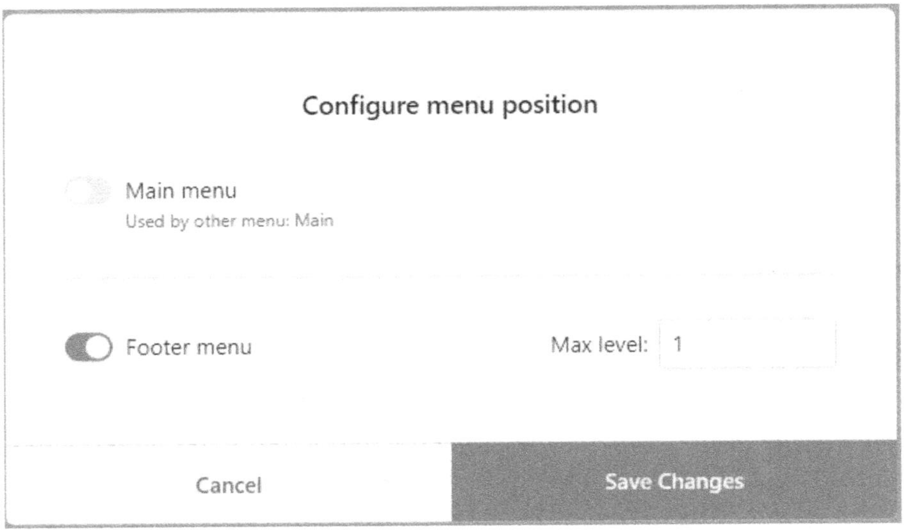

Configure menu position

Main menu
Used by other menu: Main

Footer menu   Max level: 1

Cancel   Save Changes

Figure 11-39. *Enable Footer menu*

Click the blue "Save Changes" button to save the selection. When the site is previewed, the new footer menu looks like the one shown in Figure 11-40.

Home   Terms & Conditions   Cookie Policy   Contact Us

Powered by Publii

Figure 11-40. *New footer menu*

While in the Menus panel, click the menu named "Main" to view the menu items assigned to it. Delete the menu item "Terms of Use" since this is in the footer now – as shown in Figure 11-41.

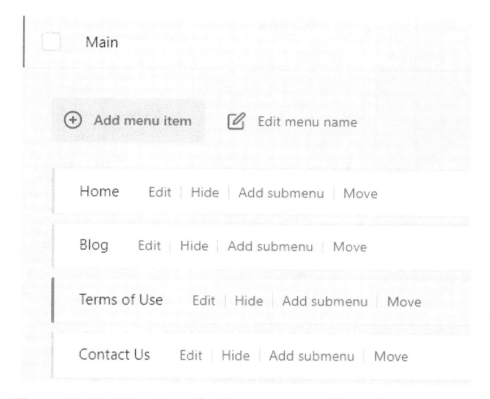

Figure 11-41. Menu items for the menu named "Main"

There is one more change to make to the Footer. I want to add some information about SpaceB (all made up, mind you) to the footer text. Access the footer text from the "Theme" menu item in the Publii CMS main menu on the left side of the application. Scroll down to the Custom settings for the theme and locate the "Footer" menu item in the Custom settings menu. Click on it.

Enter the following information into the "Copyright text" field:

SpaceB Technologies | 2345 Any St., Any Town USA | (456)-555-5555Site designed in house | Powered by Publii

Copyright 2024 - All rights retained

Looking at Figure 11-42, you can see how this text is formatted.

Figure 11-42. *The footer copyright text*

Paste the text into the field and format it as shown. Each of the line feeds is a soft line feed which is created by pressing the SHIFT key while pressing the ENTER key. A soft line feed will keep the text grouped closer together without extra white space between lines.

Save the changes and preview the site.

Summary

In this chapter, you learned how to assemble a page and use it as the home page for your website, creating a single-page site. Sometimes these types of sites are called landing pages.

A single-page site does not necessarily have to have just one page. What they do require is that you, as the site designer, manually link all site pages together with links so that the reader can navigate the site properly.

When creating the page, we covered some new topics such as using tables to force page layouts that are not native to the Publii CMS page format. Tables are only available in the WYSIWYG editor.

Continuing the theme of single-page sites, we discussed in depth how to configure SEO settings to use an existing page as the homepage for your site. This left the blog orphaned as there was no way to access the blog post list.

You learned how to redirect the posts list to another folder and make links to it so that your single-page website could support a blog.

The last thing we did in this chapter was create a footer menu and add some more information to the footer about our imaginary space company.

CHAPTER 12

Gallery and Contacts

In this chapter, I will be discussing adding a gallery page as well as integrating a third-party contact provider. Most contact mechanisms on any given Content Management System (CMS) like Publii CMS use HTML forms for collection of data, usually forwarding the data to a backend service for storage. This is how things work with larger tools like WordPress, but Publii CMS does not have a backend server. It is a static website that is simply a collection of HTML files some CSS and the occasional JavaScript file. This means that Publii CMS needs to use other methods of integrating contact forms or supporting commenting systems. In this chapter, we will examine several options and implement one of them.

Photo galleries are a much simpler technology to implement in a static website as they require no backend processing. Publii CMS ships with a well-rounded set of tools that will allow you to do a lot of different things within the limitations of a static website. The benefit of these built-in features is that you can implement nice design solutions on your site without ever touching a single line of HTML or CSS. One of the neat built-in features is the image gallery support. Support for galleries is provided by a lightweight third-party add-on called PhotoSwipe, which is fully integrated into Publii CMS. Image (photo) gallery support is embedded in the WYSIWYG and Block editors. It is extremely easy to use.

© Brad Moore 2025
B. Moore, *Designing Websites with Publii and GitHub Pages*,
https://doi.org/10.1007/979-8-8688-1195-1_12

Adding a Gallery

I will be adding a gallery page to this site to demonstrate the operation and use of the gallery. The images that I will be using are all space related and are from Unsplash.com and available under their free-to-use license. All 18 images used in the example are available in the "Gallery" folder in the "Chapter 11" folder in the book's GitHub repository here: `https://github.com/Apress/Designing-Websites-with-Publii-and-GitHub-Pages`. Links to each original individual file are available in the same folder. Download the images to your computer.

Begin by creating a new page. Remember that pages are managed from the "Pages" menu item in the Publii CMS main menu on the left of the application. Add a new page by selecting "Use WYSIWYG editor" from the "Add new page" button drop-down menu as shown in Figure 12-1.

Figure 12-1. Add new page drop-down menu

Give the page a title – I think "SpaceB Gallery" would work just great. I choose to add some text before inserting the gallery. The text I used is

Check out some of the space images that we are
pretending are all related to SpaceB's rocket and
space development and tourism efforts.

You can copy and paste, or type, that into the editor if you choose or go with your own. I centered the text for a better appearance.

With the cursor located on the page where you want to insert the gallery (an arrow points this out in Figure 12-2), click the "Insert gallery" button in the toolbar – which you can see highlighted in Figure 12-2.

Figure 12-2. Insert gallery button

The gallery button will add a block to the editor that has a button labeled "Add images" as shown in Figure 12-3. This looks like a drag and drop image picker field like those we have seen before, but it is not. Do not drag and drop images onto this object.

Figure 12-3. *Image Gallery Add Images field*

Click the "Add images" button to add images to the gallery. This will open an open file dialog window. In this window, you will be able to select one or more images. If you are following along with this project, then select all the images that were downloaded from the "Gallery" folder in the "Chapter 11" folder of this book's GitHub repository (`https://github.com/Apress/Designing-Websites-with-Publii-and-GitHub-Pages`). Once you have selected all the images, click the "open" button in the dialog window.

The images will be uploaded into the gallery as shown in Figure 12-4.

Figure 12-4. *Images uploading into the gallery*

Wait until the upload is complete.

Once all the images have uploaded into the Insert/Edit Gallery dialog window, they will be displayed with fields for image alternative text and image caption for every image as shown in Figure 12-5.

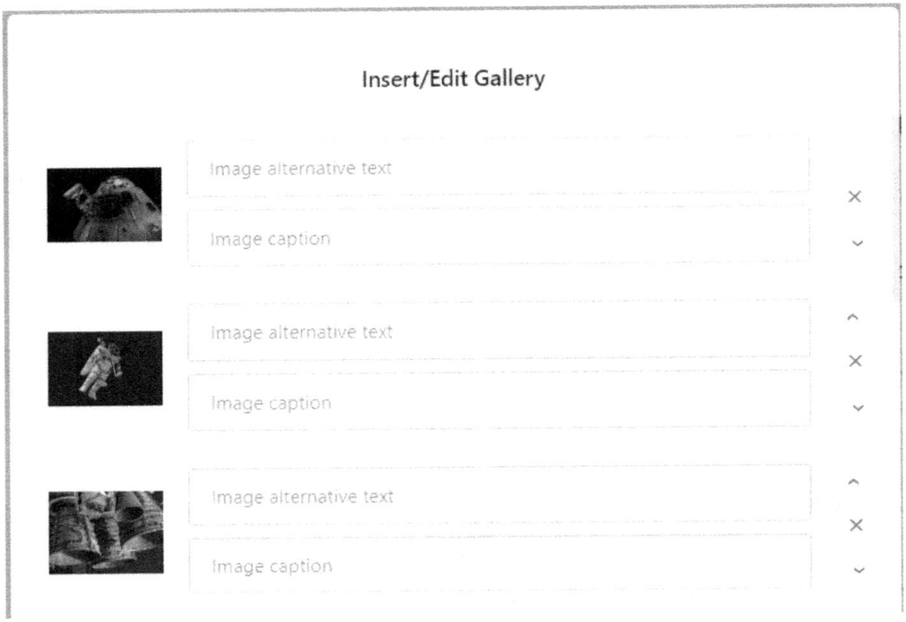

Figure 12-5. *Insert/Edit Gallery dialog window*

Notice also on the right side of these fields there are controls for managing image location as well as removing images. Clicking the caret symbols that point up and down will move the image in that direction in the list of images respective to the image next to it. Clicking the red "X" will delete the image.

I have discussed the importance of giving images an Alternative text whenever the option is available. It is good practice from a usability perspective for those with vision impairments as well as from an SEO perspective for improving page and site ranking.

Give each of the images an Alternative text value. This text will not appear in the gallery but will be attached to each image in the page source.

The Image caption is optional. You can use the caption to credit the original image artist, to describe the image, or both. In Figure 12-6, I have chosen to copy the Alternative text from the first image into the caption. In the second image, I have credited the photo's author.

I have left the fields blank for the third image so that you can tell which field is which when reading this book as you can see in Figure 12-6.

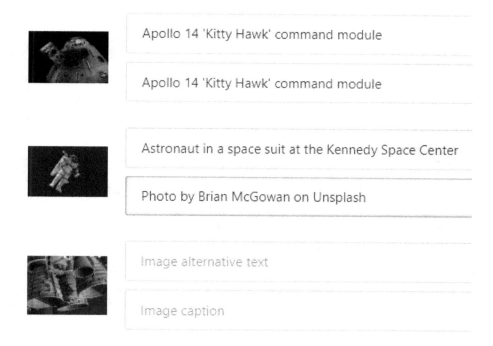

Figure 12-6. *Image alternative text and Image caption*

Notice that at the bottom of the Insert/Edit Gallery dialog window, there are options to configure the gallery layout. The default layout is three columns, which feels about right when viewed; however, it can be configured to values between 1 and 8. The align option tells Publii CMS how wide to render the gallery in comparison to the page content. If you select "None" (the default), the gallery will be the same width as the page content. Selecting "Full width" will cause it to stretch from one site to another with very little padding. The "Wide" option is a nice balance between the other two, and my favorite setting for the gallery.

Clicking the "Add images" button will open the computer's open file dialog window and permit adding more images to the gallery. You can see these settings and button in Figure 12-7.

Figure 12-7. *Gallery layout options and Add images button*

Click the blue "OK" button to complete the addition of the gallery to the editor. In Figure 12-8, you can see the gallery that was added to the page. It has been cropped to improve readability.

Apollo 14 'Kitty Hawk' command module   Photo by Brian McGowan on Unsplash   En

Figure 12-8. *A gallery once complete (cropped)*

Notice that the first three images have captions while the remaining images do not. Captions are rendered differently when the gallery is published. They will only appear when the mouse pointer is hovering over an image as shown in Figure 12-9.

Figure 12-9. Rendered gallery in the web browser (cropped)

To render this page as seen in Figure 12-9, I have clicked the "Preview" link in the upper left corner of the editor. The mouse pointer is hovering over the image of the space-suited astronaut – notice the caption that is displayed.

Clicking an image will cause it to be enlarged so that it fills the entire browser width. This is a feature of the PhotoSwipe library driving the gallery behind the scenes. At the top of the image are controls for viewing the image full screen, zooming in further, and sharing the image (as shown in Figure 12-10).

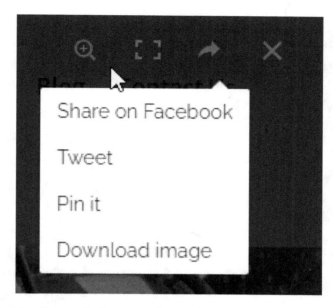

Figure 12-10. *Controls for an enlarged image from gallery*

An enlarged image also has navigation controls on the right and left side of the image permitting navigation between the previous and next images without needing to return to the galley view.

Options that a gallery supports such as those mentioned above must be supported by the theme. Gallery support in themes may differ. Under the "Custom settings" of a "Theme", you will find options for the gallery if the theme supports special gallery features.

The Simple theme allows for item spacing, Lightbox style (light or dark), and Lightbox overlay transparency. It also has an option for enabling advanced settings which permit enabling and disabling core PhotoSwipe functions shown above.

Now that we have created a Gallery page, we should add a link to it from elsewhere on the site so that our readers can enjoy the page. If you remember, we had just such a placeholder link on the "Vacation in Space" homepage.

After saving your work click the "< Pages" link in the upper left corner of the editor to return to the Pages list panel. Open the "Vacation in Space" page in the editor by clicking the page title.

Scroll down until you come to the in-page "menu" that looks like the one shown in Figure 12-11.

Book a Trip

FAQs

Photo Gallery

Read our Blog

Contact Us

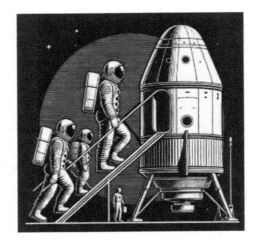

Figure 12-11. *In-page "menu"*

Click the link titled Photo Gallery to edit that link. Click the chain icon in the context menu that pops up to edit the link.

In the Insert/Edit link dialog window, change the link type to "Page link". In the "Page name" drop-down field, select the page named "SpaceB Gallery" as shown in Figure 12-12.

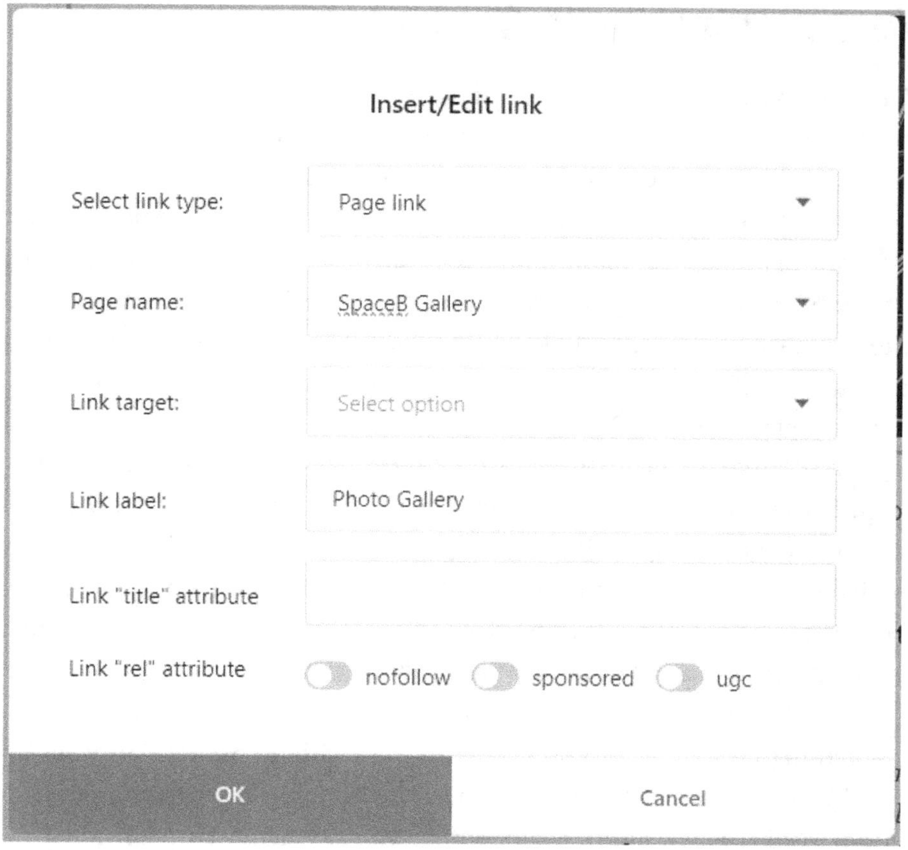

Figure 12-12. *Insert/Edit link dialog window*

Of course, the name of the gallery page may be different in your project if you are not following along exactly – make the necessary adjustments as needed.

Click the blue "OK" button to commit the changes.

Don't forget to save the page now that you have made changes. Return to the Pages list again. Click the "Preview your changes" button on the bottom of the Publii CMS main menu to see the new gallery in action.

Add a Third-Party Contact Page

One area we can use to greatly enhance the user experience with our website would be adding a contact page instead of opening the reader's email client when they click the contact link in the main menu.

Having a contact page instead of relying on the reader's email client as a means of contact serves several purposes in improving the functionality of your site. First, it keeps the reader on your website rather than giving them a reason to move on to something else. Second, it increases your appearance of professionalism. Finally, it provides a consistent mechanism for contact that readers are accustomed to using.

Traditional contact pages rely on the HTML form functionality which requires a backend server to process the form when submitted. HTML does not have the capability to manage, validate, and store form data natively. Most CMS products in use like WordPress, for instance, are hosted on servers that can execute code behind the scenes to process form submissions and store or otherwise handle the data.

Publii CMS does not have this capability built in as it is simply a collection of HTML, CSS, and JavaScript files with no backend processing. For this reason, Publii CMS does not support form processing natively. Publii CMS is slowly adding some integration services in the form of plugins that support third-party backend processing providers. Most of these are for the integration of commenting systems. Currently Publii CMS does not have a contact form plugin, but we still can add this functionality to your site.

To add a third-party contact page to your website, we must choose a provider that supports embedding a form using JavaScript. That form will be created, managed, and hosted on the third-party website.

Learn More   JavaScript is a programming language primarily used to create interactive and dynamic content on websites, such as responding to user inputs, animations, and updating content without reloading pages. It typically runs on the client web browser and not on a server. It was created in 1995 by Brendan Eich while he was working at Netscape Communications.

Finding a provider is just a matter of trial and error. There are many companies that offer this kind of service on the Internet. Generally, all of them charge for their services, although many offer limited free starter plans. For our needs, this type of plan will be great. Here are some providers and the free plans they offer at the time of this writing:

1. Jotform – Free plan

   a. https://jotform.com/

   b. 100 submissions per month

   c. 5 forms

2. Formspark – Free plan

   a. https://formspark.io/

   b. 250 lifetime submissions (buy more as you go)

   c. Unlimited forms

3. Getform – Free plan

   a. https://getform.io/

   b. 50 submissions per month

Note   The providers and their offerings will change over time.

Neither the author nor the publisher endorses any specific third-party provider. Use of a specific provider is merely for demonstration purposes.

I have selected Jotform to create my form for the new "Contact Us" page. You can follow along using the same provider and content or experiment on your own. The examples in the book will be for this specific provider.

When choosing a provider, it is important to select one that uses JavaScript for embedding their forms. Currently Publii CMS is not able to embed forms as native HTML in a page.

The form I will be creating will collect the readers' full name, email address, and their message. When following along, you first need to sign up for the service being demonstrated. Begin first by visiting the URL for Jotform: `https://www.jotform.com/`, as shown in Figure 12-13.

EASIEST ONLINE FORM BUILDER

Powerful forms get it done.

We believe the right form makes all the difference. Go from busywork to less work with powerful forms that use conditional logic, accept payments, generate reports, and automate workflows.

Figure 12-13. *The Jotform.com website*

Click the big orange button in the middle of the page that is labeled "Sign Up with an email". Use the email address you created in Chapter 2 to sign up for an account as shown in Figure 12-14.

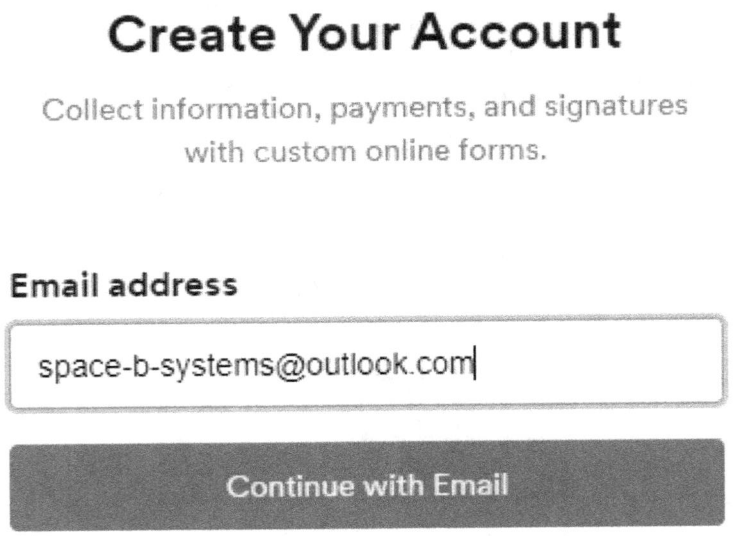

Create Your Account

Collect information, payments, and signatures
with custom online forms.

Email address

space-b-systems@outlook.com|

Continue with Email

Figure 12-14. *Sign up with your email account*

Click the blue "Continue with Email" button after providing your email address. The signup process continues with requesting your Name and a Password for this account as shown in Figure 12-15.

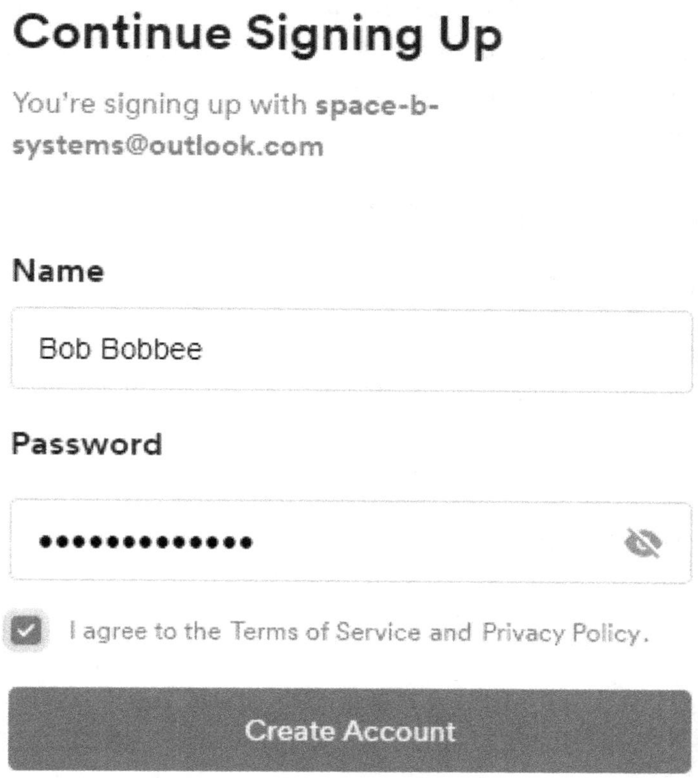

Continue Signing Up

You're signing up with **space-b-systems@outlook.com**

Name

Bob Bobbee

Password

•••••••••••••   👁

☑ I agree to the Terms of Service and Privacy Policy.

Create Account

Figure 12-15. *Signup continued*

Tip   Remember the tips about passwords that were discussed in Chapter 2. Use several short words in mixed case, creating a password that is at least 12 to 15 characters long. Be aware that some systems require the inclusion of a number or special character or both. **Never** use the same password on more than one system.

Read the Terms of Service and the Privacy Policy (if you are into that sort of thing) and checkmark the box that says you agree with both. Click the blue "Create Account" button.

Jotform will proceed to ask you a little bit about you and your organization in the next page loaded as shown in Figure 12-16. You can fill this out like I did or just skip this step by clicking the "Skip" link below the "Finish" button.

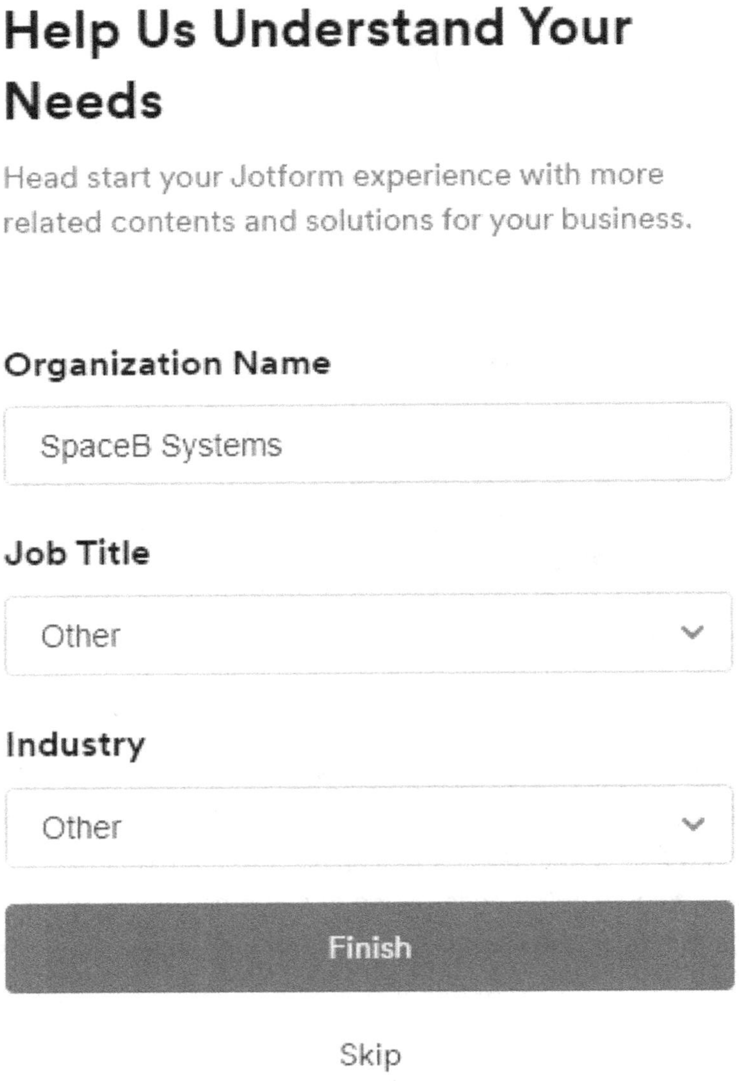

Help Us Understand Your Needs

Head start your Jotform experience with more related contents and solutions for your business.

Organization Name

SpaceB Systems

Job Title

Other ⌄

Industry

Other ⌄

Finish

Skip

Figure 12-16. *Final step in signing up*

Click the blue "Finish" button after providing some answers if you have not chosen to skip this part.

You should get an email after completing the account signup. It will be a request to verify your email address. Most sites require this when signing up for services. I discovered the email went into my "Junk" folder. Locate the email in your email client and confirm your account as requested. This will be necessary before using Jotform's services.

Part of Jotform's onboarding process is to walk you through the creation of your first form. It supercharges the process by letting you search for a form that best matches what you want to do. Jotform has hundreds of templates. You can also make a form from scratch by selecting that option as shown in Figure 12-17.

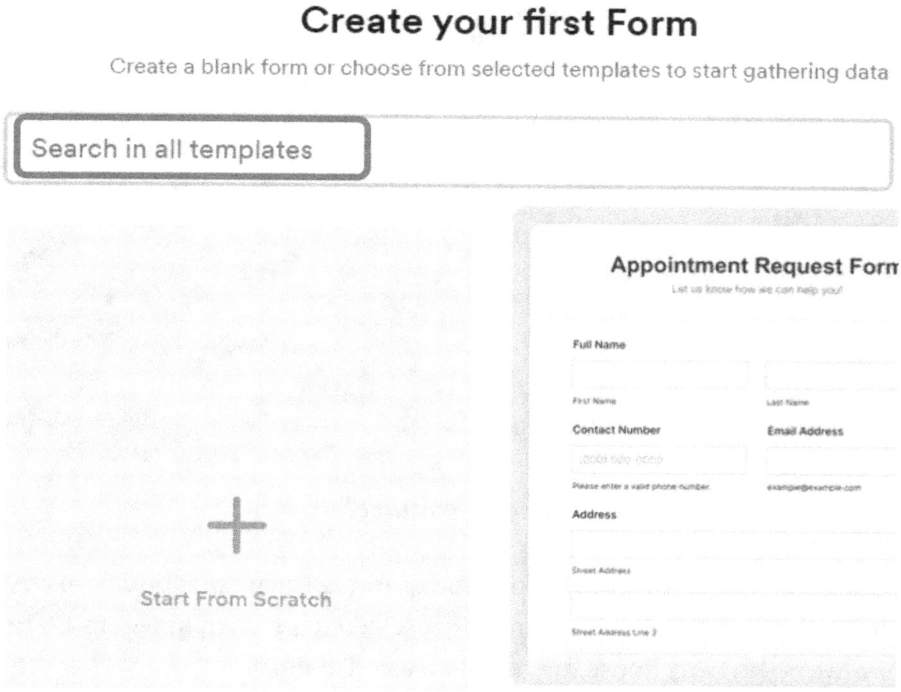

Figure 12-17. *Your first form*

I searched for a form from the huge library of existing form templates. I did this by typing "contact" into the Search field as highlighted in Figure 12-17. That search returned over 2000 results as shown in Figure 12-18. I specifically wanted Contact Forms which appeared as a category in one of the columns with 477 templates. I clicked that pink colored button/link as highlighted in Figure 12-18.

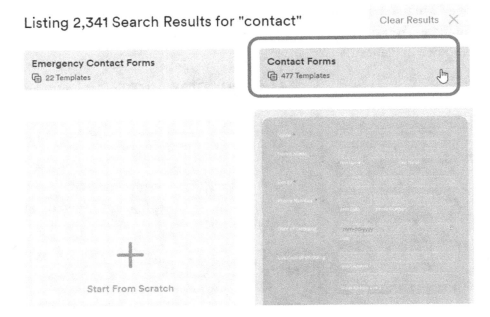

Figure 12-18. *Search results for "contact"*

I scrolled down a ways looking for a form template that both looked nice and met my needs. The template I selected is shown in Figure 12-19. As always you can choose the template you like most.

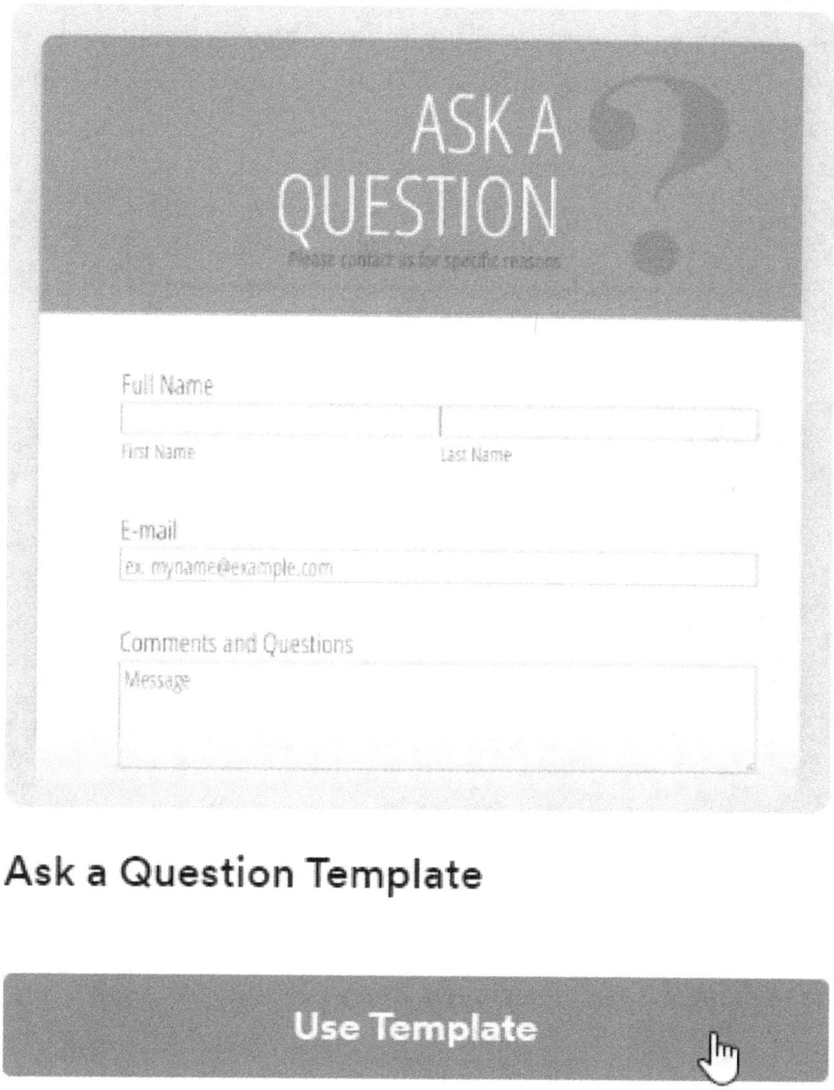

Ask a Question Template

Figure 12-19. *Using a template you like*

Click the green "Use Template" button below the template you have selected.

Jotform continues the configuration of the form in three steps: Build, Settings, and Publish as shown in Figure 12-20. Note that you can go between these steps in any order by clicking the step that you wish to make changes in.

Figure 12-20. Phases of setting up and publishing your form

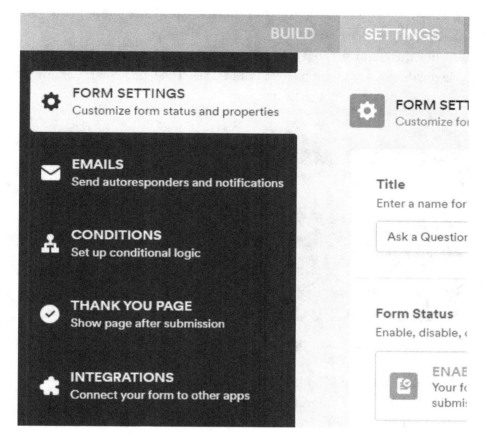

Figure 12-21. *Form Settings (cropped)*

If you want to add additional elements to your form – do it on the "Build" step.

Go to the "Settings" section as shown in Figure 12-21. The most important settings – for a form that collects information and then emails it to your email address – are found in the first four sub-sections: Form Settings, Emails, Conditions, and Thank You Page. The settings enabled by default meet our needs and do not need to be changed at this time. Feel free to look them over though.

There are additional settings not shown below "Integrations", but you will not need to use them.

Click the "Publish" step to publish your form. Here you will get the code needed to add it to a page in Publii CMS. The Quick Share section tab is active as shown in Figure 12-22.

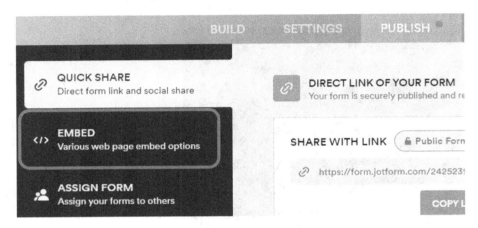

Figure 12-22. *Publish options*

Click the tab titled "Embed" tab as highlighted in Figure 12-22.

There are a lot of different ways to embed the form, but all we need is the simple JavaScript code that is displayed at the top of this section as shown in Figure 12-23.

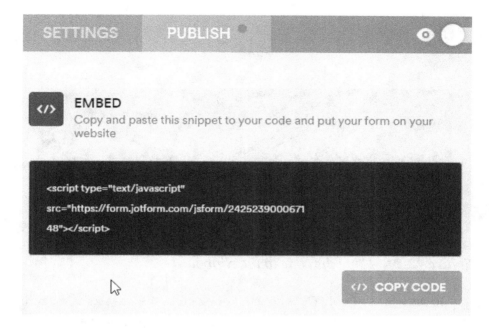

Figure 12-23. *Embed form section*

Click the green "Copy Code" button as highlighted in Figure 12-24. Notice the message "Copied to Clipboard!".

Figure 12-24. *Copy the code to the clipboard*

Go back to the Publii CMS now but don't close the browser tab where Jotform is now open. It is time to create a Contact Us page and embed this code into it. You should be accustomed to navigating the main parts of Publii CMS by now. You will need to go to the Pages section of the application. Click the "Pages" menu item in Publii CMS's main menu.

Create a new page using the WYSIWYG editor. Normally the last editor used is the default editor for the next time a page is added using the "Add new page" button. If you are not sure, then click the drop-down menu on the right side of the "Add new page" button and select "Use WYSIWYG editor".

Give the new page a title. I called my new page "Contact Us" as shown in Figure 12-25. Click the button on the toolbar labeled "<> HTML" as highlighted in Figure 12-25.

Contact Us

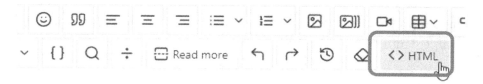

Figure 12-25. *The new Contact Us page with the HTML button highlighted*

Here is where I sort of break my promise – we will be seeing some code this time around, but you will not need to edit it. Don't worry – it will be fine.

The HTML button opens a code editor for the page. Pages created using the WYSIWYG editor can be edited and tweaked (if desired) in the code editor. In this case, we will use it just to paste in the JavaScript we copied from Jotform.

The cursor will be on the first line of the editor when it is opened. Press the key combination of the "Ctrl" key and "v" key to paste the code that is in the clipboard into the editor as shown in Figure 12-26.

Source code

```
1 <script type="text/javascript"
2   src="https://form.jotform.com/jsform/              ">
3 </script>
4
```

Figure 12-26. *JavaScript pasted into the HTML editor*

I broke the JavaScript into three lines so that it would better fit the format of a book. You should not be typing the code you see in the book into the HTML editor. The code given as an example here will not work for your project. Ensure that you are copying the code from Jotform and pasting it into the HTML editor.

Tip   If nothing is pasted into the editor, go back to the web browser and locate the tab where we were working with Jotform. Copy the code again as you did in Figure 12-24. Now try pasting it back into the Publii CMS HTML editor using the Ctrl-V key combination.

Once you have pasted the code into the editor, click the blue "Apply changes" button in the upper right corner of the HTML editor as shown in Figure 12-27.

Figure 12-27.   *The Apply changes button*

Save the page by clicking the blue "Save" button in the upper right corner of the editor. Click the "< Pages" link in the upper left corner of the editor to return to the Pages list.

Now that you have a "Contact Us" page, it is time to link it up to the homepage so that website visitors can access it. Open the "Vacation in Space" page in the editor. You should be looking at the Pages list panel so just click the page title of the homepage to open it. Scroll down the page to the in-page menu which we edited earlier in this chapter when linking the gallery. Click the "Contact Us" link as shown in Figure 12-28.

Book a Trip

FAQs

Photo Gallery

Read our Blog

Contact Us

Figure 12-28. *Edit the "Contact Us" link*

Click the chain icon in the context menu that pops up above the link. It will open the Insert/Edit link dialog window as shown in Figure 12-29.

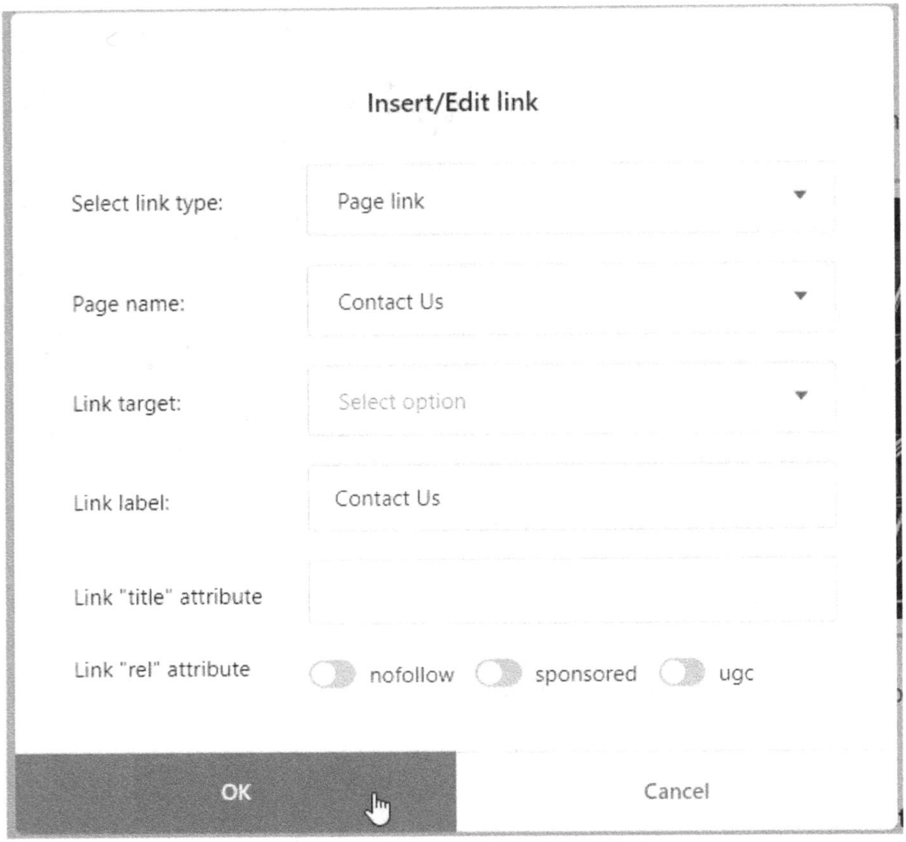

Figure 12-29. *Insert/Edit link dialog window*

Change the link type from a Custom link to a Page link in the link type drop-down field. In the Page name field, select the "Contact Us" page from the list of pages in the drop-down field.

Click the blue "OK" button to commit the changes. Remember to save the page by clicking the blue "Save" button in the upper right corner of the editor. Return to the Pages list by clicking the "< Pages" link in the upper left corner of the editor.

Test out the "Contact Us" form by clicking the "Preview your changes" button on the bottom of the Publii CMS main menu. Scroll down in the web page that loads into your web browser until you see the "Contact Us" link. Click it and fill out some information as shown in Figure 12-30.

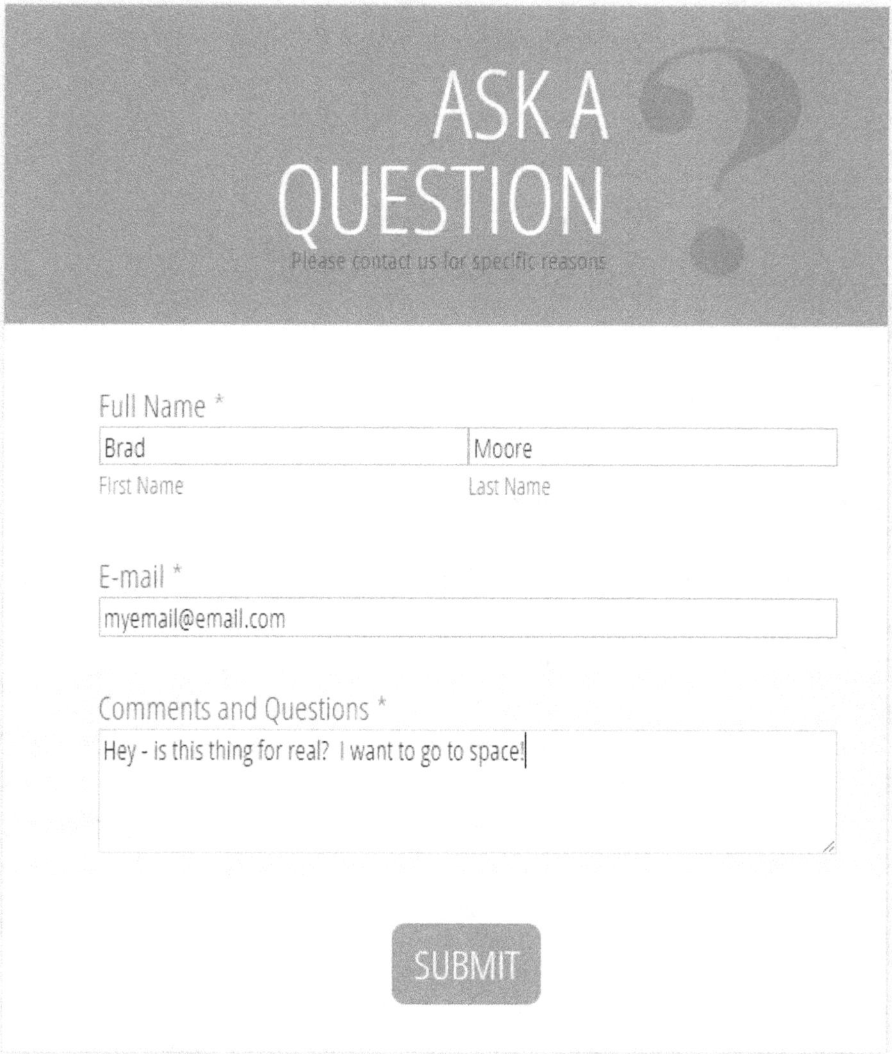

Figure 12-30. *Testing the Contact Us form*

Click the "Submit" button. After submitting the form, you get a very pleasant thank you notification as shown in Figure 12-31.

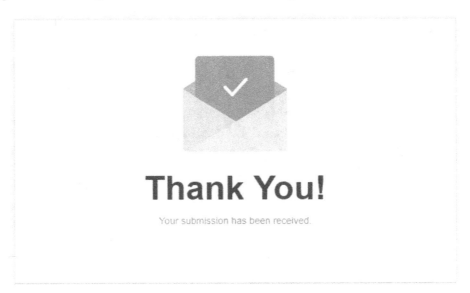

Figure 12-31. *Thank you for your submission*

Open your email client where the email address registered in Chapter 2 recieves emails. I use the Windows Outlook Mail client. Find the email from Jotform.com. I found these were going into the "Junk Email" folder. Move them to the Inbox to open them. In the Windows Outlook Mail client, you can drag and drop them into the Inbox, or you can right-click the email message and select "Inbox" from the "Move" option as shown in Figure 12-32. This may work differently if you use a different email client.

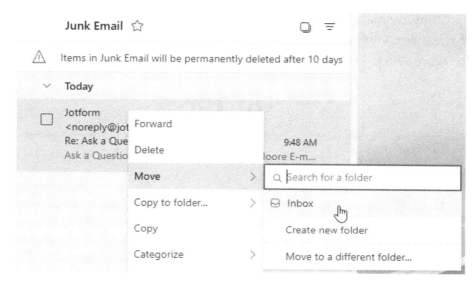

Figure 12-32. *Moving a message to the Inbox*

Moving the message to the Inbox will trigger a dialog window asking whether all emails from "noreply@jotforms.com" should be delivered to the Inbox as shown in Figure 12-33.

Figure 12-33. *Move to Inbox dialog window*

561

Confirm that all future emails from "noreply@jotforms.com" should go to the Inbox. Once the message is in the Inbox, open and read it as shown in Figure 12-34.

Figure 12-34. *The message sent via email from my website using Jotform*

It appears that things are working successfully. If you run into issues, go back and double-check all your settings. Jotform has several options for getting help if you are running into trouble getting it to work. Check out the help options under the "Support" option found on the top menu of the Jotform site as seen in Figure 12-35.

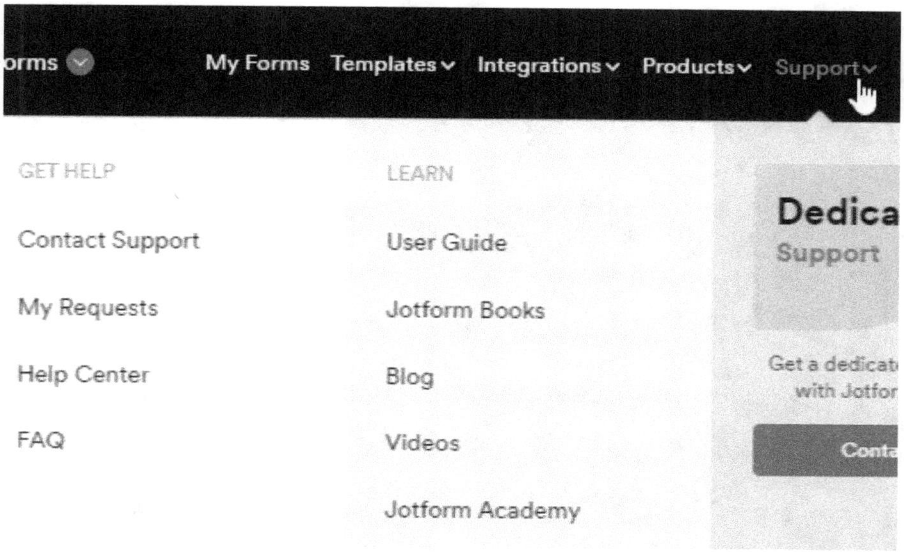

Figure 12-35. *Support options are available in Jotform*

There is still more to do getting the "Contact Us" form fully linked up on the website. If you remember, there are two "Contact Us" links in the menu systems that you built: one on the Main menu and one on the Footer menu. Open the Menu list by clicking the "Menus" menu item in the Publii CMS main menu.

Locate the menu that was named "Main" and click it to reveal the menu items assigned to that menu. Locate the "Contact Us" menu item and click the "Edit" action in the actions listed to the right of the menu item as shown in Figure 12-36.

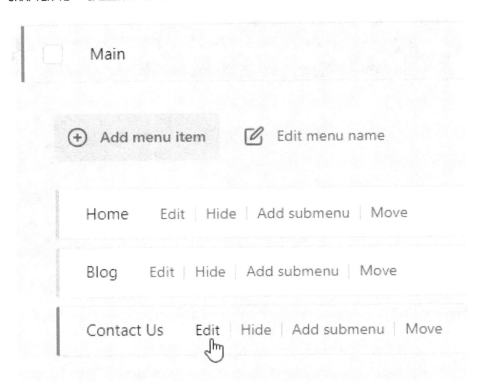

Figure 12-36. *Menu items belonging to the menu named "Main"*

A panel titled "Edit Menu Item" will fly out from the right side of the application. Change the Link Type in the drop-down field to "Page link". Select the page named "Contact Us" from the Page drop-down field as shown in Figure 12-37.

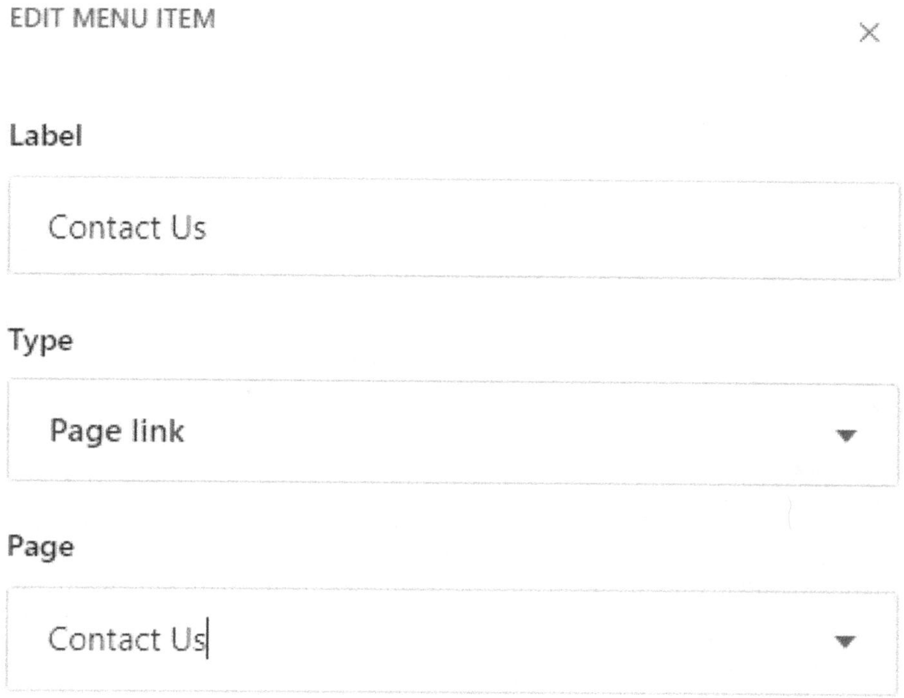

EDIT MENU ITEM   ✕

Label

> Contact Us

Type

> Page link   ▼

Page

> Contact Us| ▼

Figure 12-37. Edit Menu Item panel

Click the blue "Save Changes" button at the bottom of the "Edit Menu Item" panel. Expand the menu items assigned to the menu titled "Footer". Edit the menu item "Contact Us" as shown in Figure 12-38 in the same way you did the previous menu.

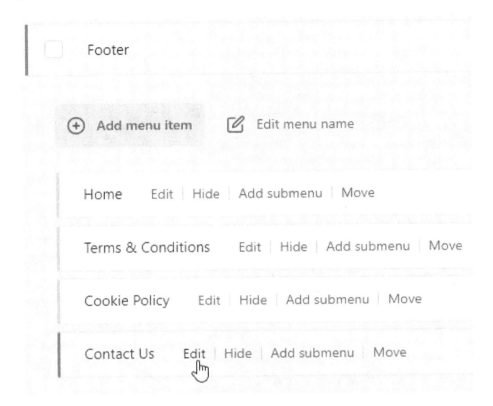

Figure 12-38. *Footer menu items*

Click the "Preview your changes" button on the bottom of the Publii CMS main menu to experience your completed website.

Configuring Server

I have called the website complete, but there is one major piece missing – something I lost when I cloned the original blog website. That is the server configuration.

Switch back to the site "SpaceBs Moonshot" – or whatever you called your first blog website. Remember we discussed switching between sites in the section "managing Sites" in Chapter 9 in case you need a refresher.

Click the "Server" menu item in the Publii CMS main menu. Make a note of the following items from that page:

- Website URL

- Username/Organization

- Repository

- Branch

Observe in Figure 12-39 that these items are highlighted to help you locate them.

Website URL   https:// ▼   space-bob.github.io/moonshot

This will be your GitHub repository path, which should use the
YOUR_USERNAME.github.io/YOUR_REPOSITORY_NAME.
If you are using a custom domain name, set this field to just th

⬤ Use relative URLs

Note: while using relative URLs, some features like Open Grap
JSON feeds etc. will be disabled.

API Server   api.github.com

Change this value only if you are using your own GitHub inst

Username / Organization   space-bob

Repository   moonshot

Branch   main

Figure 12-39. *SpaceBs Moonshot Server Settings*

Switch back to the "Visiting Space" website. Click the "Server" menu
item in the Publii CMS main menu. Click the "GitHub" server type as
shown in Figure 12-40.

Select server type:

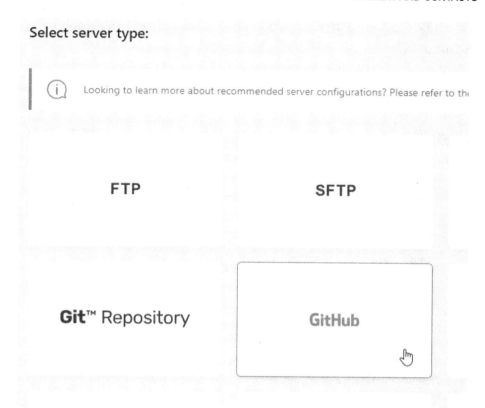

Figure 12-40. *Selecting the GitHub server type*

Transfer the information noted from Figure 12-39. One of the items we could not copy from the "SpaceBs Moonshot" server configuration was the Token. Publii CMS stores this as an encrypted item and obscures it when displayed in the Server connection panel.

If you saved the access token string in Notepad or some other text editor when it was generated in Chapter 8, then simply copy and paste it into this field. If you no longer have access to the token you generated in Chapter 8, then you will need to delete the token on GitHub and start over. Go to the section titled "Token" in Chapter 8 and follow those steps again to generate a new token. Save it somewhere like Notepad for future reference.

Once you have a token, paste it into the Token field as shown in
Figure 12-41.

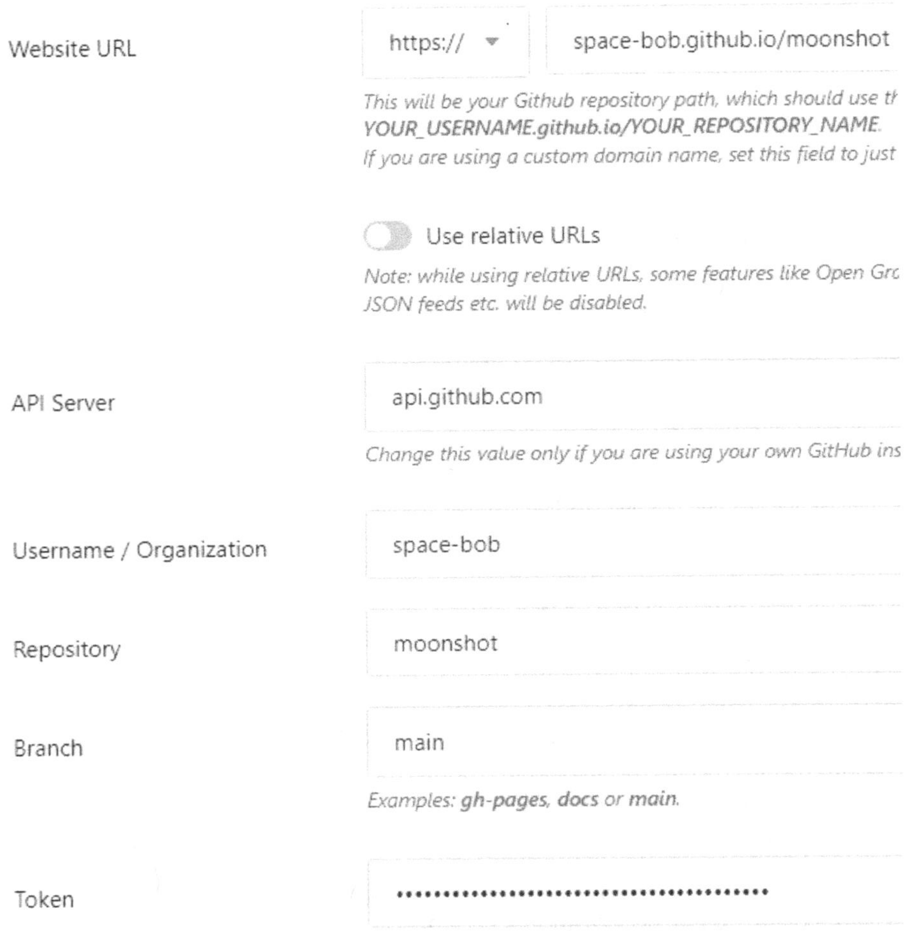

Website URL	https:// ▼	space-bob.github.io/moonshot

This will be your Github repository path, which should use th
YOUR_USERNAME.github.io/YOUR_REPOSITORY_NAME.
If you are using a custom domain name, set this field to just

⚪ Use relative URLs

Note: while using relative URLs, some features like Open Gra
JSON feeds etc. will be disabled.

API Server

api.github.com

Change this value only if you are using your own GitHub ins

Username / Organization

space-bob

Repository

moonshot

Branch

main

Examples: **gh-pages**, **docs** or **main**.

Token

•••••••••••••••••••••••••••••••••••••••

Figure 12-41. *The server configuration for the site "Visiting Space"*

Click the light blue "Test connection" button at the bottom right of the
Server configuration panel. Note that testing the connection will save the
connection settings. Hopefully you get a message of success as shown in
Figure 12-42.

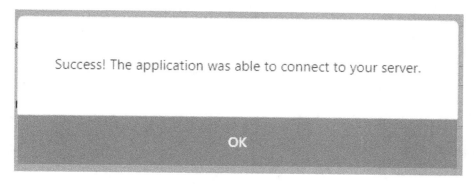

Figure 12-42. Successful connection

If you run into problems, see the "Troubleshooting" section in Chapter 8.

Presuming you were able to establish a connection to your GitHub repository, then you are ready to synchronize your website, which, as we discussed in Chapter 8, means that your site on GitHub will match your site on your local PC for this website.

Hover over the "Sync your website" button. Click it when it becomes yellow. In the "Website synchronization" window, click the "Sync your website" button as shown in Figure 12-43.

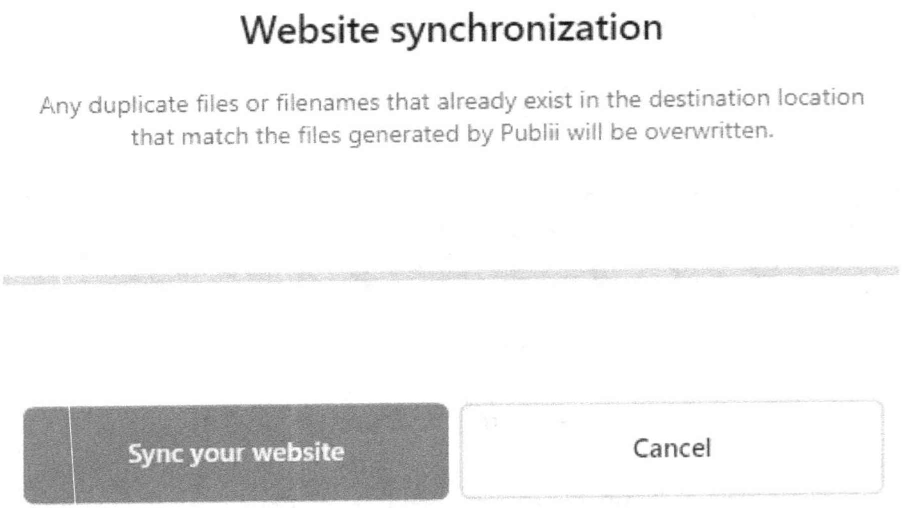

Website synchronization

Any duplicate files or filenames that already exist in the destination location that match the files generated by Publii will be overwritten.

| Sync your website | Cancel |

Figure 12-43. *Website synchronization*

Click the green "Visit your website" button to check out how your site looks live and available to the whole world.

If you get an error message instead of the green "Visit your website" button, then please check out the "Troubleshooting" section in Chapter 8.

Summary

A lot was accomplished in this chapter as you learned how to put the finishing touches on your website and create a more polished product.

Adding a gallery of images demonstrated a technique that could be used in many different use cases, from an organization that shows off its success stories through images to family events for a personal website to products offered by a small business.

You learned that galleries are supported in two of the three editors, specifically the Block editor and the WYSIWYG editor.

Galleries are supported by the integration of a JavaScript library called PhotoSwipe and specific gallery support that must be built into the theme you are using. Most themes provided by the makers of Publii CMS support the gallery.

Each theme that supports the gallery will have gallery settings that can be enabled or disabled as well as default values for some basic formatting.

In this chapter, you also learned how to embed a JavaScript code snippet into a WYSIWYG page using the HTML editor. This allowed you to integrate a third-party contact form onto your website.

The use of third-party-hosted forms allows you to take advantage of their backend form processing capabilities while continuing to work with a static web page like the type Publii CMS generates.

We specifically looked at Jotform as we explored how to create a form from an existing template and get the code needed to integrate it into our website.

CHAPTER 13

Internet Real Estate

I have a nice bridge in Brookland that exists only on the Internet that I would like to sell to you... No, not really. The idea of Internet real estate is simply obtaining your own domain name – a name which Internet users of the world can use to access your website. Where would the google.com's of the world be if they had to be known by their IP address, such as `http://142.250.191.174`[1], or as a subdomain of another parent named site, `http://google.search.cern.ch`[2]?

Domain names let you, as a website operator, obtain an appropriate easy-to-remember name that can be used to point to your website. The name is unique and belongs to you alone. This is what makes the Internet so intuitive. We are in the habit of just spouting off Internet domain names to our friends as well as using them ourselves without a second thought. Owning your own name is not hard or particularly expensive, but they are not free unfortunately.

---

[1] The string of numbers is called an IP address. This is the way computers know how to find things on the Web. Learn more about that in the section called "What Is DNS."

[2] The first website was created by Tim Berners-Lee and was hosted at `http://info.cern.ch`. Imagine if cern.ch was the only root domain and all URLs were this ugly.

© Brad Moore 2025
B. Moore, *Designing Websites with Publii and GitHub Pages*,
https://doi.org/10.1007/979-8-8688-1195-1_13

Until now, everything we have done, can be done without monetary investment. A domain name will require a yearly commitment of $15 or $20. The good news is that getting and having a domain name is completely optional as far as this project is concerned.

What we have created so far is fully functional and completely free and will remain that way. Your domain name is not quite as easy to use in its current form. For instance, the name of my site is `https://space-bob.github.io/moonshot/`. You can type that into a web browser and visit that site and it will work just fine.

This chapter covers the process of getting your own personal domain name and configuring the required systems to use that name. It is perhaps the most technical chapter in the book. It is also a completely optional chapter. If you don't plan to obtain a domain name, you can skip ahead to Part 3 and learn about advanced topics in Publii CMS. If you are skipping the domain name but want to understand the technology – then keep on reading. If you want your own domain name, then you are in the right place.

I am going to presume if you are still with me – that you are thinking the same as I am. Specifically, that you want a simpler domain name than something like `https://space-bob.github.io/moonshot/` (or whatever your domain on GitHub is called). How about spaceb.com? I like the feel of that one. If that name is available – meaning no one else is using it – then I can register it and make it my domain name. Let's find out.

Domain Names

In this section, I will be discussing more about domain names, how they are constructed, and how to get one. I will explain how to find an available domain name and the steps we need to take to register for it.

By default, your GitHub Pages URL is comprised of your GitHub username, GitHub's URL (github.io), and your repository name. In the case of our example in this tutorial, that is `https://space-bob.github.io/moonshot/`.

Not exactly pretty, is it? Let's break this down and discuss the parts of the URL so it can be better understood. In Figure 13-1, the URL for my website that I developed in this project is broken into various parts.

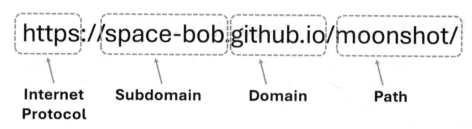

Figure 13-1. *Dissecting a URL*

Internet Protocol: This tells your web browser how to connect to the website.

Subdomain: This is like a specific section or area of the main website. If github.io is the main neighborhood, space-bob is a particular house or unit within that neighborhood.

Domain: This is the main address of the website. It's like the street name where you'll find the website. It consists of the "github" domain and the ".io" top-level domain (TLD).

Path: This part shows you a specific page or folder on the website. Maintaining the street and house analogy is like telling your browser which room within the house you want to visit.

We can simplify this URL by obtaining our own domain name and then configuring it to point directly to the resource we want to share with the world. Using the street and house analogy, we would configure this special address to point directly to the room without needing to worry the visitor about where the house is located.

I mentioned earlier that the domain spaceb.com would be desirable if available. This domain name would eliminate the need for the user to tell the browser specifically where the resource we want to find is located – the resource will be directly linked to the domain name.

But before we can do that, we need to secure a domain name of our own.

Registering a Domain Name

Domain names are registered with a specially appointed service provider called a registrar. In this section, we will cover how a domain name is constructed, how to find one that is available, and how to register it as your own.

Selecting a Name

Domain names are a form of property. They are unique, and only one person or entity can have a specific name. Who owns them and for how long is managed by the Internet Corporation for Assigned Names and Numbers or ICANN for short. ICANN works with third-party companies who host special records that tie domain names together with the servers that hold the content.

A domain name consists of two parts. Looking at the example in Figure 13-1, the domain name was "github.io". The "github" portion is the unique domain belonging to the ".io" top-level domain (TLD).

The TLD is the most granular division of the Internet naming system, serving as the final segment of a domain name and helping to categorize and identify the type or origin of a website. As a result, nothing prevents "github" from being assigned to other TLDs. In fact, it is assigned to several other TLDs including ".net" and ".org".

In the early years of the Internet, there were seven TLDs – at that time TLDs were controlled by a US nonprofit organization:

- **.com:** Originally intended for commercial organizations, but it has since become the most widely used TLD for all kinds of websites

- **.org:** Originally intended for noncommercial organizations, such as nonprofits

- **.net:** Originally intended for network-related entities, like Internet service providers and infrastructure organizations

- **.edu:** Reserved for educational institutions, mainly universities and colleges

- **.gov:** Reserved for US government entities

- **.mil:** Reserved for the US military

- **.int:** Reserved for international organizations established by treaties between governments

Today there are about 1700 TLDs, and the list is growing. The most desirable are ".com", ".net", and ".org".

As you consider a domain name, you will first need to decide what top-level domain you will be targeting. Most business as well as general websites operated for general appeal prefer the ".com" TLD. Most nonprofits and religious and other similar organizations prefer the ".org" TLD. Many opt for the ".net" TLD when an associated ".com" TLD is unavailable or if the site is technical in nature.

Domain names must be unique. Before you can register a domain name, you will need to find one that is not in use. The domain name industry is a bit predatory,[3] so the tools you use to locate an available domain name are important. If you are looking for an unused domain name, use the WHOIS tool located at this site: `https://lookup.icann.org/en`.

This is run by ICANN. Searching for a domain name here goes unnoticed by bad players in the domain registration business. Try it out by searching for the registration information for "google.com" as shown in Figure 13-2.

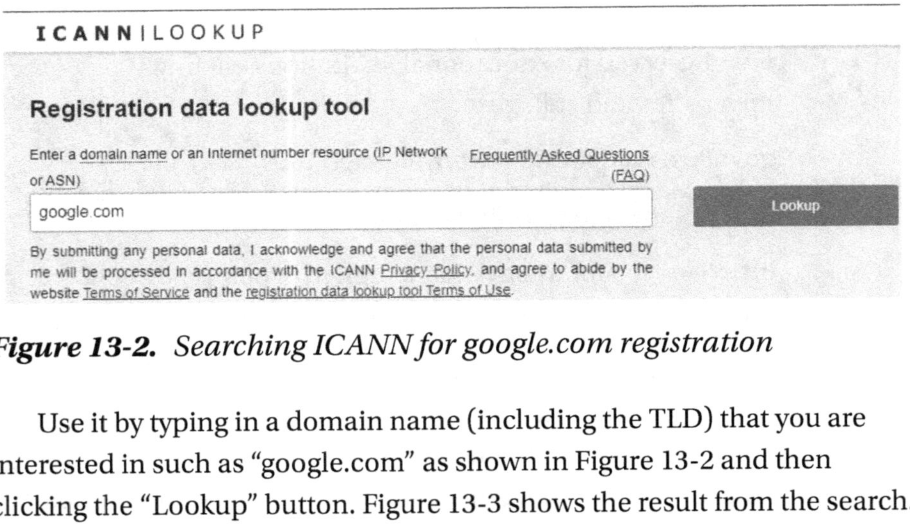

Figure 13-2.   *Searching ICANN for google.com registration*

Use it by typing in a domain name (including the TLD) that you are interested in such as "google.com" as shown in Figure 13-2 and then clicking the "Lookup" button. Figure 13-3 shows the result from the search.

---

[3] Registars like GoDaddy.com have options to search for available domain names. Some less reputable registars will buy up names that are searched hoping to sell them at a profit later. This is called cybersquatting.

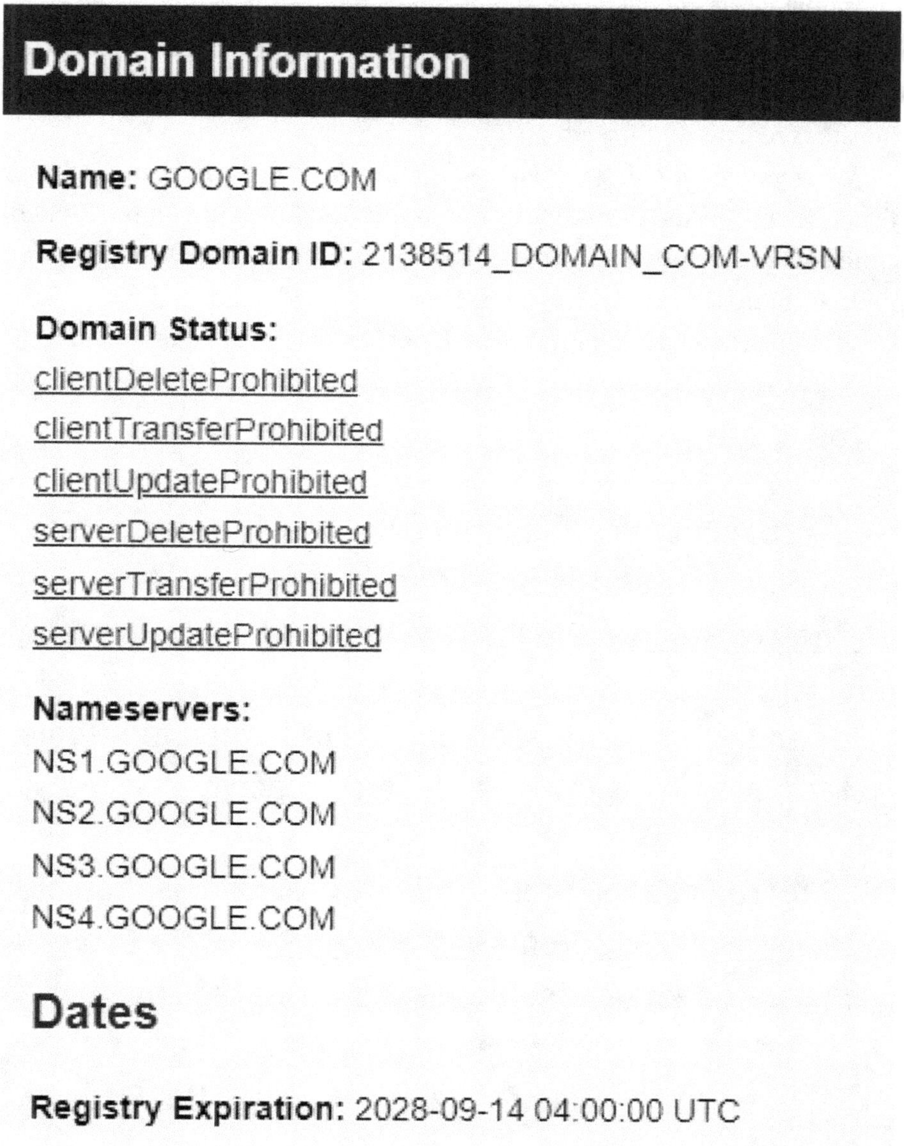

Domain Information

Name: GOOGLE.COM

Registry Domain ID: 2138514_DOMAIN_COM-VRSN

Domain Status:
clientDeleteProhibited
clientTransferProhibited
clientUpdateProhibited
serverDeleteProhibited
serverTransferProhibited
serverUpdateProhibited

Nameservers:
NS1.GOOGLE.COM
NS2.GOOGLE.COM
NS3.GOOGLE.COM
NS4.GOOGLE.COM

Dates

Registry Expiration: 2028-09-14 04:00:00 UTC

Figure 13-3. *Google.com registration information*

Searching for google.com reveals that someone already owns that name. Surprise! We can see some basic domain information – most of it without meaning to us. We really are not interested in this data. Notice that the site is registered through 2028.

What you are looking for when searching for a domain name is the response "requested domain was not found" as shown in Figure 13-4. I did some basic searching using the lookup tool and found that "SpaceB" was a popular name for various websites. I was surprised.

I finally tried a search for "space-b.net" as shown in Figure 13-4.

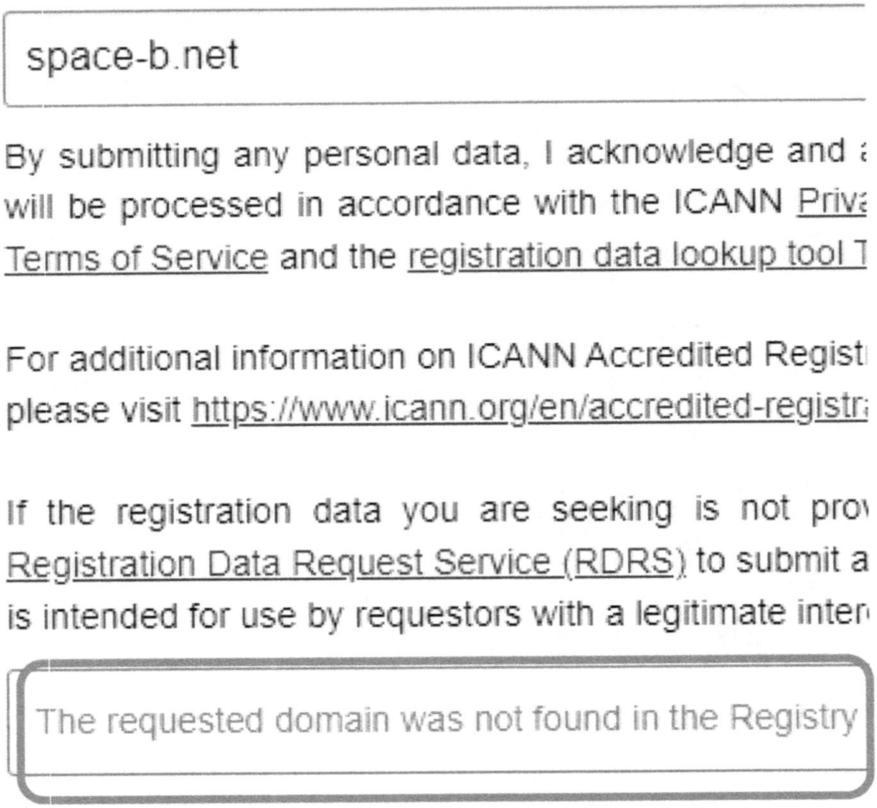

space-b.net

By submitting any personal data, I acknowledge and a will be processed in accordance with the ICANN Priva Terms of Service and the registration data lookup tool T

For additional information on ICANN Accredited Regist please visit https://www.icann.org/en/accredited-registr

If the registration data you are seeking is not prov Registration Data Request Service (RDRS) to submit a is intended for use by requestors with a legitimate inter

The requested domain was not found in the Registry

Figure 13-4. *Results searching for space-b.net (cropped)*

Here are the results I was hoping to find as highlighted in Figure 13-4. The domain "space-b.net" is available. I can proceed to register this name as my own. I will need to do that using a reputable domain registrar after which I will own a small piece of the Internet!

Registering a Domain Name

To register this domain name, we will want to find a reliable domain registrar. These are the third-party organizations that ICANN has entrusted the registration of domain names with.

Prior to 2024 I would have recommended using Google domains as a registrar. They offered favorable pricing and WHOIS privacy[4] and had a simple interface for managing your domain. Unfortunately, Google sold that part of their business to Squarespace.com.

There are literally dozens of companies that you can choose from to purchase a domain name – they offer a variety of prices and tools. I am going to suggest Squarespace as a reliable for several reasons. First, Google placed confidence in them to manage millions of domains that were part of a successful business. Second, they are transparent in their upfront pricing without hidden fees. Third, they offer the tools needed for anyone to successfully manage a domain including WHOIS privacy. Finally, they are well established and will be around for the long haul. Their prices are not the cheapest available, but they will tell you exactly what to expect to pay year after year. Yes, there are cheaper options, so if you want to save a buck – go ahead and shop around.

---

[4] WHOIS privacy is a level of obfuscation that hides your personal name, address, and other personal information that is typically stored in a domain record.

Note   While I am suggesting you use Squarespace.com as a domain registrar, I am not specifically endorsing or recommending their service. In addition, Apress does not officially endorse or recommend any specific service. Your mileage may vary – shop around.

Make sure, when you are shopping around, that the registrar is offering the following in the features in the price they are quoting (sometimes these are add-on costs):

- Full DNS control

- WHOIS privacy

- Domain transfer protection

Sometimes the registrar will offer a free SSL certificate[5] if you host with them. You will not need this, but it is an indication that the company is a good choice to work with.

Squarespace offers all the above with their registrations. I will be using them in the steps outlined throughout the rest of this chapter.

Point your web browser here to start the process (if you will be following along): `https://domains.squarespace.com/domain-search`.

Figure 13-5 shows the search page and the domain names that Squarespace suggests and confirms that "space-b.net" is available.

---

[5] SSL (Secure Sockets Layer) certificates are used to form a secure contract between your web server and a user's browser insuring that data passed between them is encrypted and secure and cannot be intercepted and tampered with by bad actors.

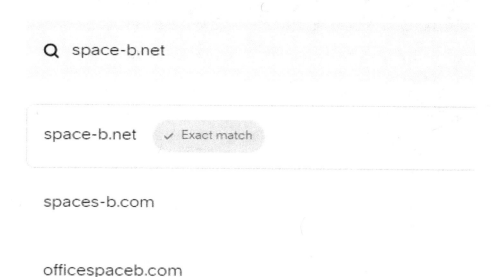

Figure 13-5. *Domains available that match the search query*

On the right side of the web page, we see the price for the site as shown in Figure 13-6.

Figure 13-6. *Purchase price for this domain for one year*

Currently this domain costs $4 for the first year. We can expect that it will renew at the full price of $20 in future years. Click the shopping cart as highlighted in Figure 13-6 to add this domain to your cart. At the bottom of the web page, you will see a summary of your purchase decision and a button to check out as seen in Figure 13-7.

Figure 13-7. *Purchase summary and Checkout button*

Click the "Checkout" button to begin the purchase process. I am not logged in currently, so I am given the option to create an account as shown in Figure 13-8. I recommend creating the account using the email address set up in Chapter 2.

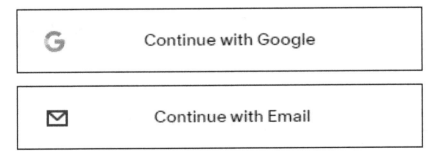

Figure 13-8. *Create Your Account*

You will be asked to provide the basic information needed for most account registrations – name, email address, and a password – as shown in Figure 13-9.

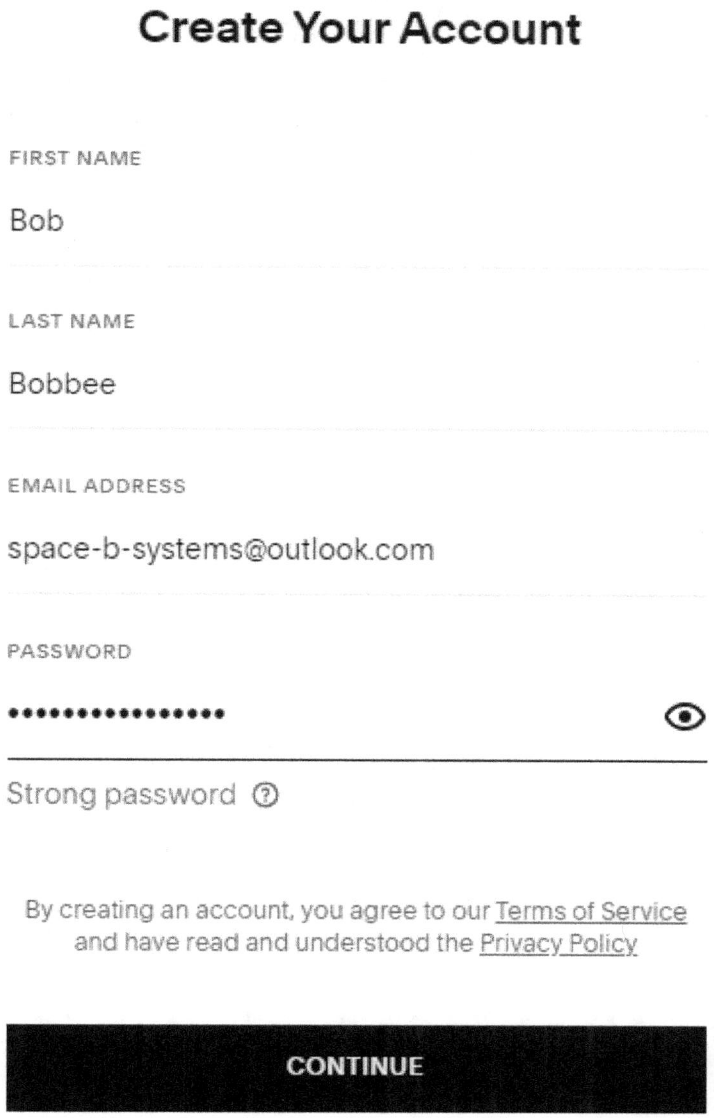

Create Your Account

FIRST NAME

Bob

LAST NAME

Bobbee

EMAIL ADDRESS

space-b-systems@outlook.com

PASSWORD

●●●●●●●●●●●●●●●●   ◉

Strong password ⓘ

By creating an account, you agree to our Terms of Service and have read and understood the Privacy Policy

CONTINUE

Figure 13-9. *Continuing to Create Your Account*

I have used the email account that I set up in Chapter 2. I have also provided a strong password. The Squarespace site will measure the strength of your password. Provide a strong password that conforms to the advice around creating passwords provided in Chapter 2. Specifically use four or five short words that are easy to remember and capitalize as desired. Provide numbers and/or special characters only if the site requires this. Your password should be about 15 characters in length. Most importantly do not use passwords used on other sites or services.

Click the "Continue" button to complete the account creation and continue with the purchase. You will be given a summary of the registration term on the left side of the next page as shown in Figure 13-10.

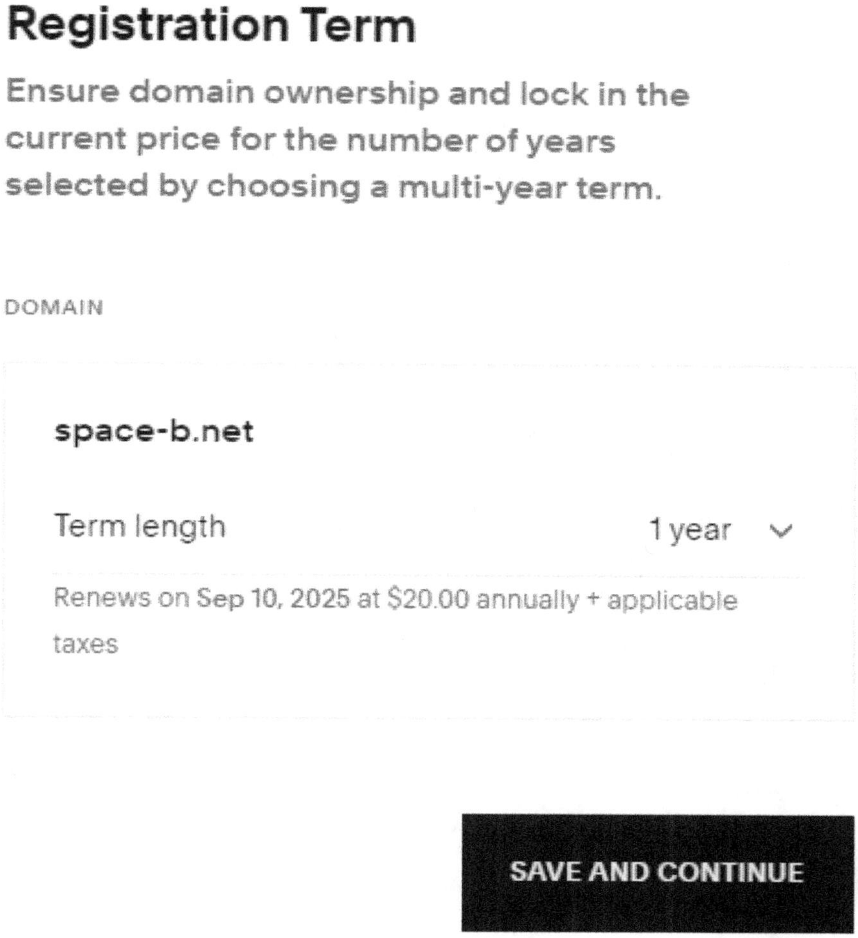

Registration Term

Ensure domain ownership and lock in the current price for the number of years selected by choosing a multi-year term.

DOMAIN

space-b.net

Term length   1 year ˅

Renews on Sep 10, 2025 at $20.00 annually + applicable taxes

SAVE AND CONTINUE

Figure 13-10. *Purchase summary*

Notice that the Term is one year and that additional years will automatically renew at the cost of $20 per year. You can opt to buy more than one year at a time, but only the first year will receive the discount.

The costs are shown on the right side of the same web page in the "Order Summary" as seen in Figure 13-11. Here you will see that I am getting a $16 discount for the first year.

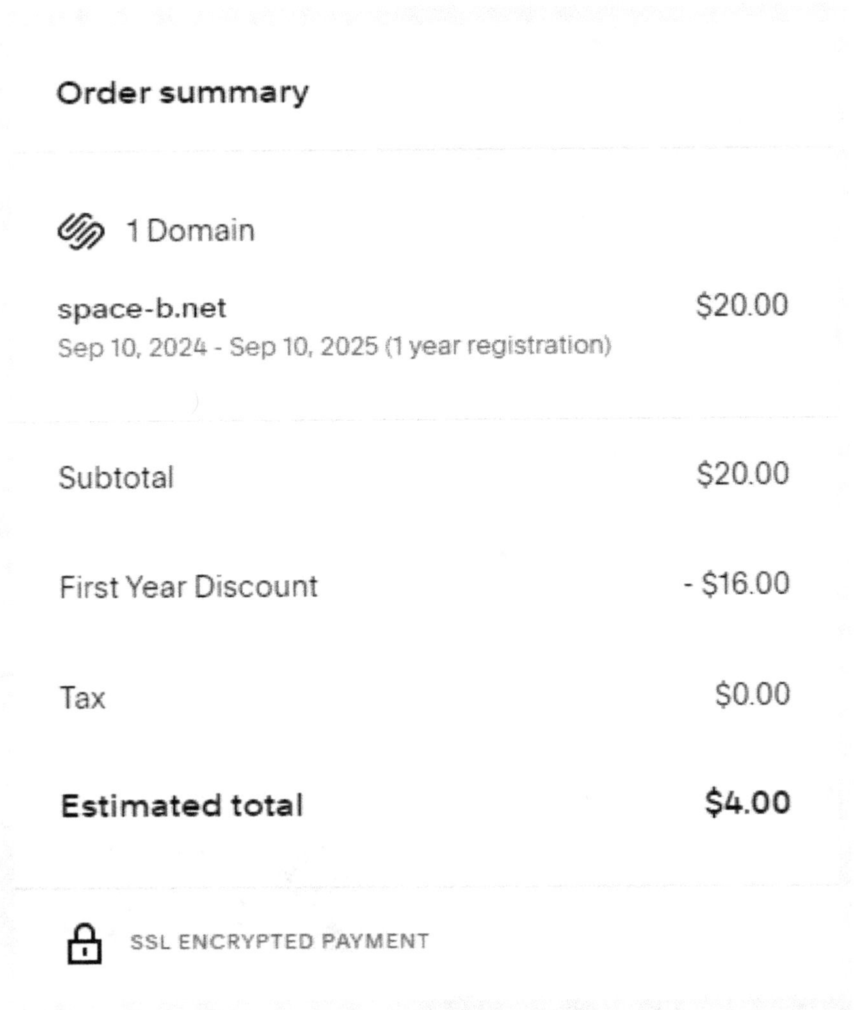

Order summary

1 Domain

space-b.net	$20.00
Sep 10, 2024 - Sep 10, 2025 (1 year registration)	

Subtotal	$20.00
First Year Discount	- $16.00
Tax	$0.00
Estimated total	**$4.00**

SSL ENCRYPTED PAYMENT

Figure 13-11. *Order summary*

Click the "Save and continue" button as shown in Figure 13-10. On the left side of the web page, the Registration section has been revealed as shown in Figure 13-12. The right side of the web page still shows the Order summary shown in Figure 13-11. ICANN requires that this information be accurate and maintained to remain in compliance with their terms of service.

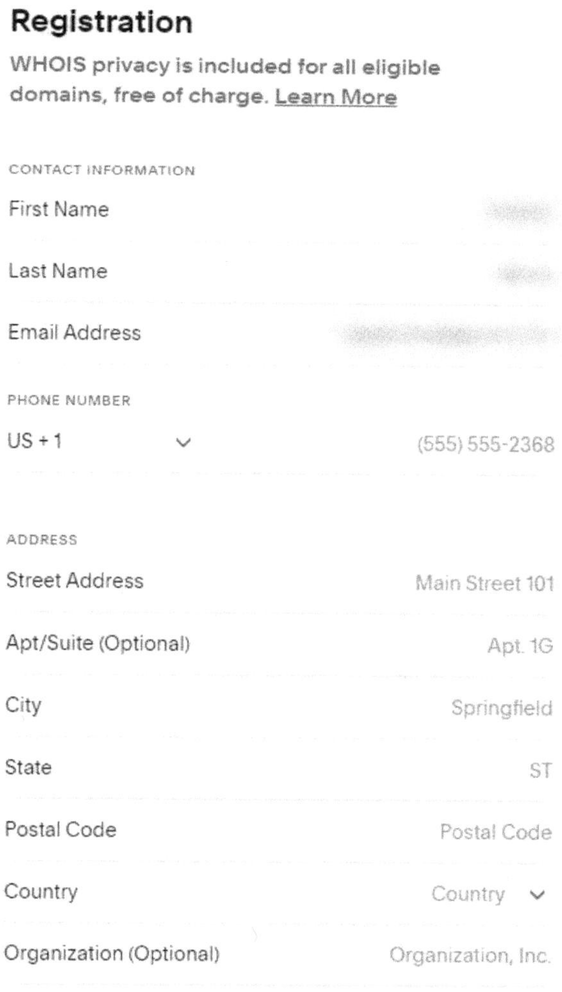

Registration

WHOIS privacy is included for all eligible domains, free of charge. Learn More

CONTACT INFORMATION

First Name

Last Name

Email Address

PHONE NUMBER

US + 1   (555) 555-2368

ADDRESS

Street Address   Main Street 101

Apt/Suite (Optional)   Apt. 1G

City   Springfield

State   ST

Postal Code   Postal Code

Country   Country

Organization (Optional)   Organization, Inc.

Figure 13-12. Registration

Complete the registration accurately. One of the benefits of registering with Squarespace is the free WHOIS privacy that is included in your registration. It will protect the information that is sent to ICANN from being publicly available.

Click the "Save and Continue" button (not shown in Figure 13-12) at the bottom of the Registration page once filled in.

The final step in the process is to supply payment information and pay for the domain as shown in Figure 13-13. Note that on the right side of the web page, the Order summary remains unchanged reminding you what you are purchasing.

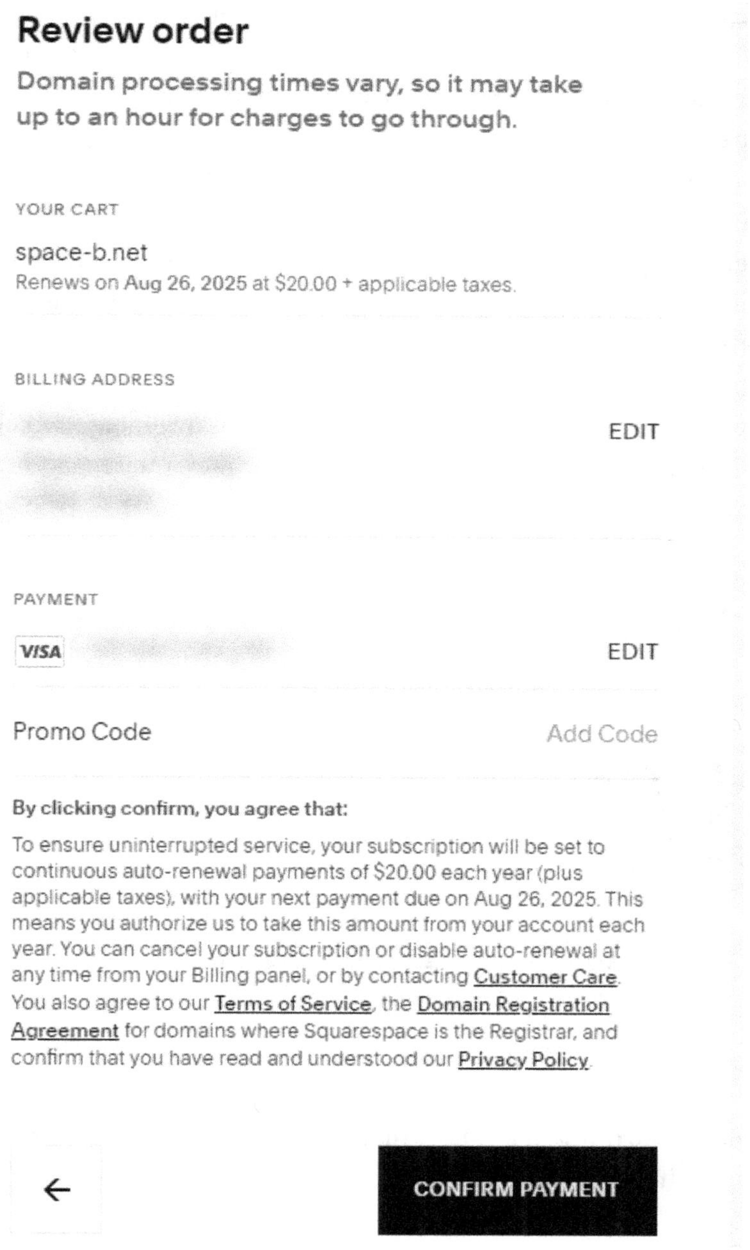

Review order

Domain processing times vary, so it may take up to an hour for charges to go through.

YOUR CART

space-b.net
Renews on Aug 26, 2025 at $20.00 + applicable taxes.

BILLING ADDRESS

EDIT

PAYMENT

VISA   EDIT

Promo Code   Add Code

By clicking confirm, you agree that:

To ensure uninterrupted service, your subscription will be set to continuous auto-renewal payments of $20.00 each year (plus applicable taxes), with your next payment due on Aug 26, 2025. This means you authorize us to take this amount from your account each year. You can cancel your subscription or disable auto-renewal at any time from your Billing panel, or by contacting Customer Care. You also agree to our Terms of Service, the Domain Registration Agreement for domains where Squarespace is the Registrar, and confirm that you have read and understood our Privacy Policy.

←   **CONFIRM PAYMENT**

Figure 13-13. *Review order and confirm payment*

Click the Confirm Payment button to purchase the domain name. It can take anywhere from a few minutes to several hours for the provider to provision the backend systems so that you can use the domain you have purchased.

Squarespace will send you an email when the provisioning is completed.

I personally registered the domain "space-b.net" under my personal Squarespace user account where I have a dozen or more domains registered and under management. This was done to simplify management by keeping it together with my other domains.

After getting notified that my new domain was available – which took about three minutes in my case – I logged back into Squarespace to view the configuration as shown in Figure 13-14.

Figure 13-14. *Domains assigned to my account*

Click on the domain in the domain list to view the details for that domain as shown in Figure 13-15.

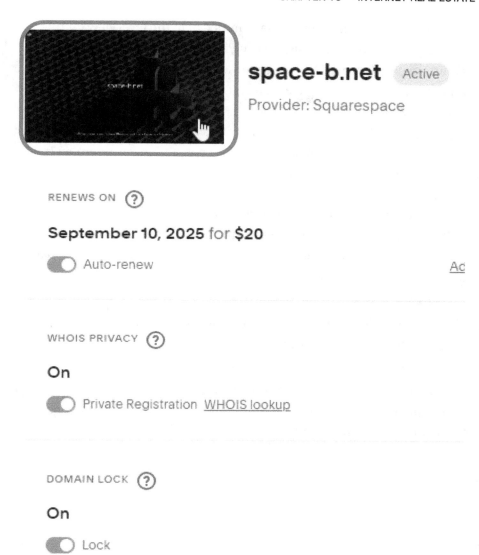

space-b.net Active

Provider: Squarespace

RENEWS ON (?)

September 10, 2025 for **$20**

Auto-renew   Ac

WHOIS PRIVACY (?)

On

Private Registration WHOIS lookup

DOMAIN LOCK (?)

On

Lock

Figure 13-15. *Domain details*

There are a couple things to take notice of in the Overview for this domain. First is that the default setting for new domains purchased from Squarespace is for them to auto-renew. Leave this enabled if this is a domain name you plan to use for a real website (and not a make-believe project like this one).

Also notice that WHOIS privacy is enabled by default. This will protect your personal information provided when registering your domain from being publicly available. Keep this enabled.

Finally, notice that the feature called "Domain Lock" is enabled. This prevents someone other than the owner (you) requesting a domain migration from this DNS provider to another. That is a sneaky way some bad actors would steal domains from others in the past. Keep this enabled as well.

Tip   Keep this page's browser tab open, as we will return to it to make a couple of changes soon.

Squarespace has parked your new domain and provides a basic web page explaining that a new site is coming soon. Click the page image highlighted in Figure 13-15 to visit that page as shown in Figure 13-16.

Figure 13-16. *Parked web page for your new domain*

Next you will need to link your new domain name to your existing
GitHub Pages web page.

Configuring DNS

In this section, I will explain how Domain Name System (DNS) works at a
high level. I will provide an overview of the DNS settings I will be changing
to get the new domain name that I just purchased to resolve to the website
hosted on GitHub Pages.

What Is DNS

Domain Name System (DNS) serves a simple purpose. It translates the human-readable name attached to a server or other computing device into a numeric address used to locate that device within a network or on the Internet. Computers work well with numbers.

In the early days of the development of networking, a numeric addressing method was developed called the Internet Protocol Address (or IP address). Computers still use this method today for locating other devices on the Internet.

The job of a DNS server is to look up a name for a resource on the Internet and return its IP address. This is explained in Figure 13-17.

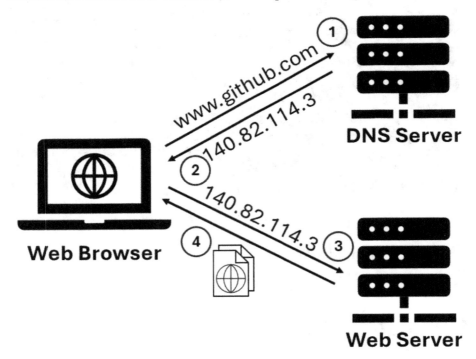

Figure 13-17. *DNS explained*

The process of getting a web page loaded into your web browser when typing and clicking on a URL depends heavily on the structure of DNS servers that support the Internet. Here is what happens when you type in a URL of a website and press the ENTER key.

1. The browser sends a request to one of the Domain Name System (DNS) servers it knows about. It asks for the IP address of the server that belongs to the URL "www.github.com".

2. The DNS server will cross reference the name to a table of IP addresses. After finding a match, it will send that address back to the web browser. In this case, 140.82.114.3.

3. The web browser will send out a message asking for the server at 140.82.114.3 to identify itself and return some specific website content.

4. The specifically requested website content is located on the server and returned to a web browser which will convert the information into a web page that the user can read and appreciate.

There are several settings that will need to be changed both on the GitHub site and the Squarespace domain hosting site to link your new domain to the GitHub Pages website you created earlier.

GitHub Settings

In this section, I will be guiding you through making the necessary changes to GitHub settings to link it to your new domain name. I will be using my project as an example.

To begin, go to GitHub.com in your web browser and log in. Navigate to the repository that you set up for this project. In my case, that was a repository called "moonshot". Repositories always open to the "Code" page. Click the "Settings" link on the right side of the links menu bar at the top of the page as highlighted in Figure 13-18.

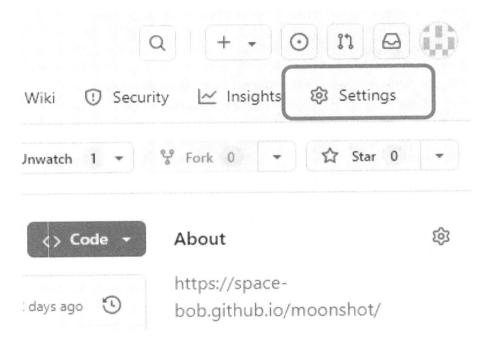

Figure 13-18. Settings link on the links menu bar on GitHub.com

Click the "Pages" menu item in the "Code and automation" menu on the "General" panel on the left of the page as highlighted in Figure 13-19.

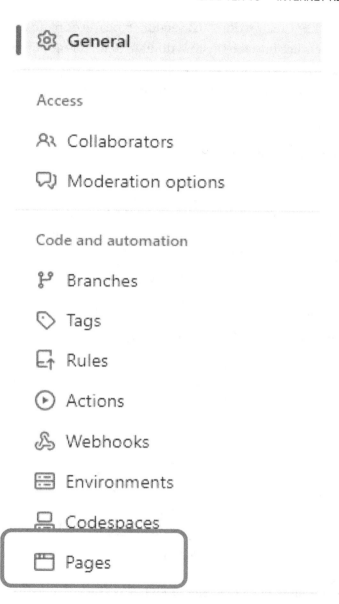

Figure 13-19. Pages menu item in the General panel

Under the "Custom domain" section, type the domain name that you purchased earlier into the Custom domain field. It is about two-thirds of the way down the GitHub Pages web page. As you can see in Figure 13-20, I have typed "space-b.net" into the Custom domain field.

Custom domain

Custom domains allow you to serve your site from a domain
more about configuring custom domains.

| space-b.net | Save | Remove |

Figure 13-20. *Add the domain name to the Custom domain field*

Click **Save** to commit the setting. You will get a message shown in Figure 13-21 that a DNS check is underway.

Custom domain

Custom domains allow you to serve your site from a domain other than space-bob.github.io. Learn more about configuring custom domains.

| space-b.net | Save | Remove |

● DNS Check in Progress

> (!) space-b.net DNS check is in progress.
> Please wait for the DNS check to complete.

Figure 13-21. *DNS check underway*

Unfortunately, the DNS check will fail as shown in Figure 13-22. Don't panic. This was expected. The DNS settings that link the domain name to the GitHub.com site have not been configured yet.

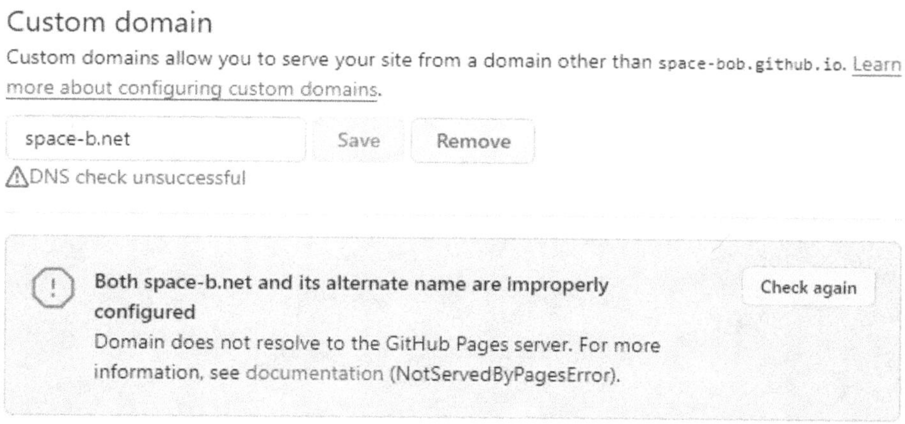

Custom domain

Custom domains allow you to serve your site from a domain other than space-bob.github.io. Learn more about configuring custom domains.

| space-b.net | Save | Remove |

⚠DNS check unsuccessful

> (!) **Both space-b.net and its alternate name are improperly configured**
> Domain does not resolve to the GitHub Pages server. For more information, see documentation (NotServedByPagesError).
>
> Check again

Figure 13-22. *DNS check failed*

Keep this tab open in your web browser. You will be coming back to this page to check the settings again.

Configuring Your DNS

Return to the web browser tab where you left the Squarespace page open as seen in Figure 13-15. If you no longer have that tab open or the connection timed out, then log back into Squarespace and open the domain overview from the domain list by clicking the domain name as shown in Figure 13-14.

Click the "DNS" menu item on the left side of the web page as shown in Figure 13-23.

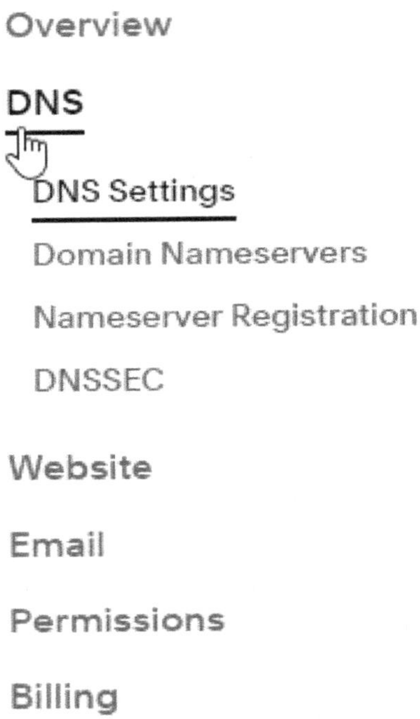

Overview

DNS

DNS Settings

Domain Nameservers

Nameserver Registration

DNSSEC

Website

Email

Permissions

Billing

Figure 13-23. *DNS menu item*

The DNS entries provisioned when your domain was created are default values pointing to Squarespace. These will need to be deleted. Click the red trash can on the upper right corner of the "Squarespace Defaults" box as shown in Figure 13-24.

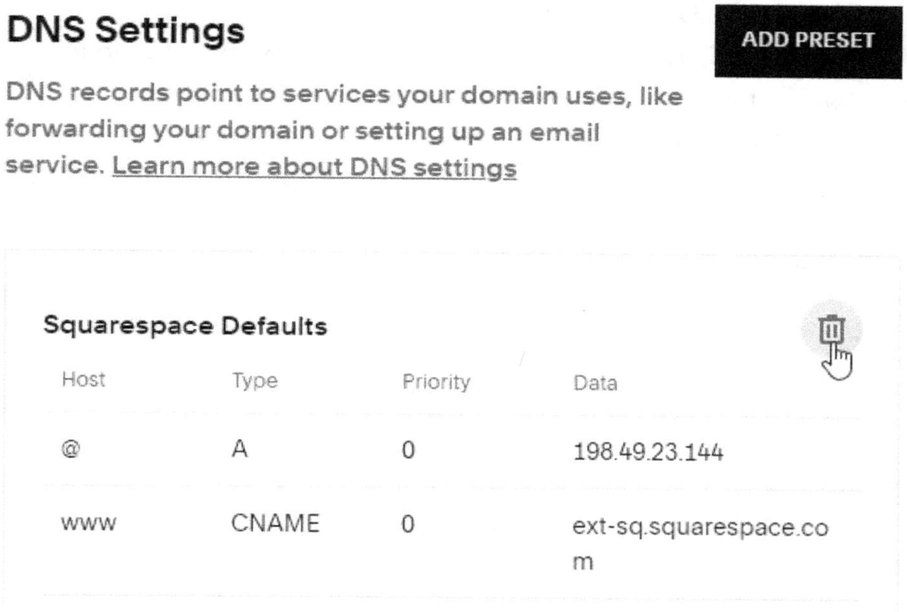

DNS Settings

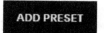

DNS records point to services your domain uses, like forwarding your domain or setting up an email service. Learn more about DNS settings

Squarespace Defaults

Host	Type	Priority	Data
@	A	0	198.49.23.144
www	CNAME	0	ext-sq.squarespace.com

Figure 13-24. *Delete the Squarespace Defaults*

Squarespace will warn you about the actions you are taking and advise you to forward your domain as shown in Figure 13-25.

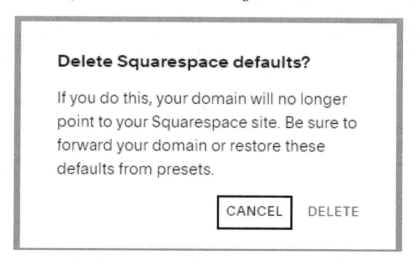

Delete Squarespace defaults?

If you do this, your domain will no longer point to your Squarespace site. Be sure to forward your domain or restore these defaults from presets.

CANCEL   DELETE

Figure 13-25. *Confirmation dialog window*

Click the red Delete button in the dialog window.

Now you will need to add some custom records so that this domain can correctly be resolved to GitHub.com. GitHub has some documentation[6] you can reference to configure the new custom DNS records. To add a new custom record, click the "Add Record" button as shown in Figure 13-26.

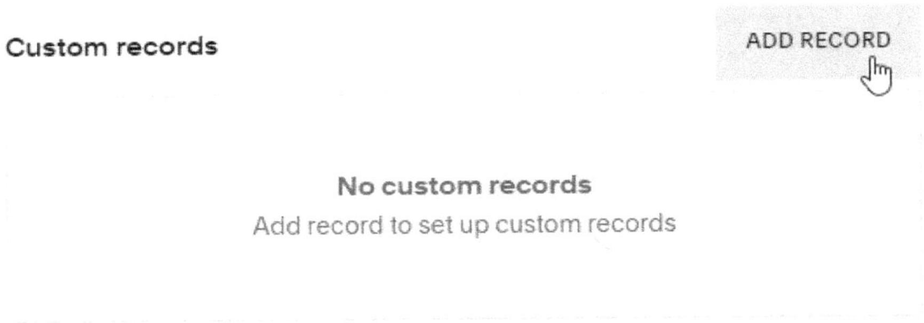

Custom records   ADD RECORD

No custom records
Add record to set up custom records

Figure 13-26. *Custom records*

There is a little bit of technical jargon here. Don't worry about it too much – just follow along. In the next few steps, you will create four "A" type records that are used to point your domain to GitHub.com. You will also create a "CNAME" record that helps the resolution process.

Begin with the first "A" type record. Due to the width of the web page, I will be showing you the left half first and then the right half of the same record. In Figure 13-27, the "Host" and the "Type" are defined.

---

[6] GitHub DNS Configuration Documentation: https://docs.github.com/en/pages/configuring-a-custom-domain-for-your-github-pages-site/managing-a-custom-domain-for-your-github-pages-site

Custom records

Host ⑦   Type ⑦

HOST   TYPE

@   A   ⌄

Figure 13-27. *Right side of the custom record fields*

Type the symbol "@" for the Host. This is a wildcard which is typically used in this field. The Type field is a drop-down list of many options. Right at the top is the "A" – select it.

On the left side of the same record, you will need to provide an IP address as shown in Figure 13-28.

Priority   Data ⑦

                      IP ADDRESS

—   185.199.108.153   CANCEL   SAVE

Figure 13-28. *Right side of the custom record fields*

Type "A" records do not require a priority, so this field is disabled. The data for an "A" type record is an IP address as specified by the field label. The GitHub documentation specified the address of 185.199.108.153.

After typing in the IP address, click the "Save" button on the right of the record as shown in Figure 13-28.

Figure 13-29 shows the newly added record. Click the "Add Record" button again to add the next "A" type record.

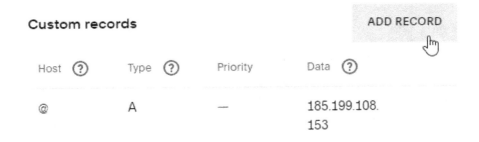

Figure 13-29. *Click Add Record to add another record*

Proceed to add an "A" type record with a Host of "@" for the following three IP addresses:

- 185.199.109.153

- 185.199.110.153

- 185.199.111.153

You need to add a "CNAME" record as well, so after the four "A" type records have been added, click the "Add Record" button one more time as shown in Figure 13-30.

Figure 13-30. *Adding a "CNAME" record*

Add the following to the record:

- Type "www" in the Host field.

- Select "CNAME" from the Type drop-down field list.

- Type the domain name you purchased earlier in the "Alias Data" field. In my case, it is "space-b.net".

When adding these values, be sure to type them without the quotation marks.

Click the SAVE button as shown in Figure 13-30 to commit the changes. The complete set of custom DNS records is shown in Figure 13-31.

Custom records   ADC

Host ?	Type ?	Priority	Data ?
@	A	—	185.199.108. 153
@	A	—	185.199.109. 153
@	A	—	185.199.110. 153
@	A	—	185.199.111. 153
www	CNAME	—	space-b.net

Figure 13-31. Custom DNS records

Be aware that it can take anywhere from a couple of minutes to 72 hours for your custom DNS records to propagate through the Internet. Some providers are much more responsive than others. I find Squarespace to be one of the most responsive.

Verifying the DNS Settings

The next thing that needs done is verifying the DNS settings back on the GitHub Pages site. Hopefully you left that open in one of your browser tabs as suggested earlier. If not, then go back up to the GitHub settings section and make your way to the GitHub Pages web page.

Last time we looked at that page, it had an error message telling us that the DNS check had been unsuccessful as shown in Figure 13-32.

Custom domain

Custom domains allow you to serve your site from a domain other than space-bob.github.io. Learn more about configuring custom domains.

| space-b.net | Save | Remove |

⚠DNS check unsuccessful

(!) Both space-b.net and its alternate name are improperly configured
Domain does not resolve to the GitHub Pages server. For more information, see documentation (NotServedByPagesError).

Check again

Figure 13-32. *Unsuccessful DNS check*

Click the "Check again" button as highlighted in Figure 13-32. GitHub will proceed to validate the DNS settings to ensure that the site is resolvable by name. If the check fails, then double-check the settings in the previous sections. If things look right, then you might need to wait. DNS information must be passed from server to server propagating through the Internet before resolution can work reliably. That should not take more than a couple hours but in certain situations can take up to 72 hours.

Go catch a movie or do some bingeing on Netflix. If it is a nice day, try taking a refreshing walk.

While you wait, consider a simple poem about waiting...

I have always been a patient soul,

I've learned to wait while others toil.

But now as years pass by, I feel

My work is held, and time does spoil.

I wait for tasks beyond my hand,

For others' labor to be done.

I watch and hope for progress made,

So that my path can yet be run.

I wait in stillness, biding time,

For when their task will reach its end.

And then, at last, I'll take my turn,

To move ahead, my work to tend.

Back to it folks! After having checked GitHub Pages again, I found that the DNS settings have successfully resolved as shown in Figure 13-33.

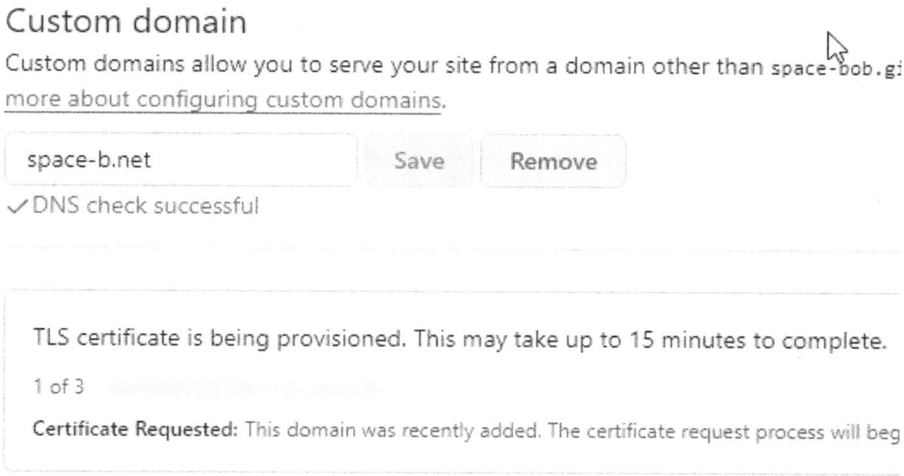

Custom domain

Custom domains allow you to serve your site from a domain other than space-bob.gi
more about configuring custom domains.

| space-b.net | Save | Remove |

✓ DNS check successful

TLS certificate is being provisioned. This may take up to 15 minutes to complete.

1 of 3

Certificate Requested: This domain was recently added. The certificate request process will beg

---

Figure 13-33. *DNS check successful*

GitHub will issue a special security file to your site called a TLS (Transport Layer Security) certificate. It is a digital ID for your website that proves its trustworthiness and helps keep data secure. When someone visits your site, the TLS certificate verifies that your site is legitimate and ensures that the data transmitted has been encrypted by a known party on each end. TLS (Transport Layer Security) is a more secure and updated version of SSL (Secure Sockets Layer).

The TLS certificate supports data encryption of the data exchanged between your website and the visitor, making it unreadable to anyone trying to intercept it. It provides the secure layer of the "Hypertext Transfer Protocol Secure" (HTTPS), ensuring that sensitive information like login credentials, personal details, and confidential information remain private and protected during transmission.

Having a TLS certificate boosts security, builds trust by displaying a padlock symbol in the browser, and can improve your website's ranking on search engines like Google.

It can take up to 15 minutes for the TLS certificate to be issued. Refresh the web browser page after about that long. If the message about provisioning the TLS certificate is gone, you can enable the "Enforce HTTPS" option as highlighted in Figure 13-34.

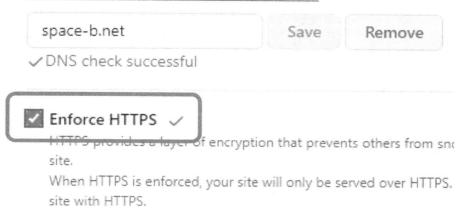

Figure 13-34. Enforce HTTPS

Testing the Domain Name

It is time to put all the work done to the test. You should be able to open a web browser tab and type in the domain name that you purchased earlier in this chapter and see your website displayed.

The domain name I purchased was "space-b.net". Typing that into the browser address bar for a new tab and pressing the ENTER key should have revealed my web page. Unfortunately, there was a fly in the ointment, and I was rewarded with a view of the parked domain page as shown in Figure 13-16.

This is the same problem we ran into in Chapter 8 after uploading our first website to the GitHub repository and then viewing that site with a browser. We got a locally cached page and not the live page hosted by GitHub.

As you will recall, we performed a procedure that has come to be known as clearing the browser cache. Do this by opening the browser settings menu (three vertical dots in the upper right corner of the browser) and selecting the "Delete browsing data..." menu option.

Select the options "Cookies and other site data" as well as "Cached images and files". Set the Time range to "Last 7 days" and click the Delete data button as shown in Figure 13-35.

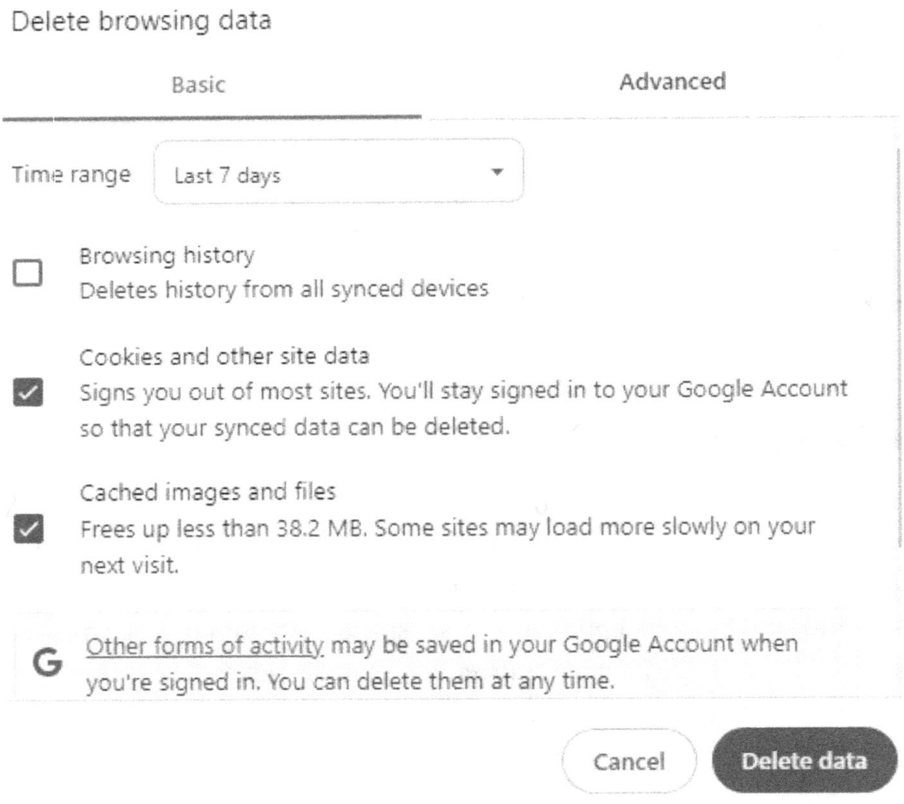

Delete browsing data

Basic	Advanced

Time range   Last 7 days   ▼

☐ Browsing history
Deletes history from all synced devices

☑ Cookies and other site data
Signs you out of most sites. You'll stay signed in to your Google Account so that your synced data can be deleted.

☑ Cached images and files
Frees up less than 38.2 MB. Some sites may load more slowly on your next visit.

G Other forms of activity may be saved in your Google Account when you're signed in. You can delete them at any time.

Cancel   **Delete data**

Figure 13-35. *Delete browsing data*

I find that I often need to close my web browser and open it back up before the cached data is truly eradicated.

Once the cached data is out of the way, open a new tab in your web browser again and type into the address bar your domain name. I did this for "space-b.net" and pressed the ENTER button.

Voilà – the site is up and working on the new domain as shown in Figure 13-36.

Vacation in Space

Space-B is BOOKING trips to space and the moon now!

Book your trip now to avoid long waiting lines.

For tens of thousands of years humans have looked up to the moon and wondered about and dreamed about walking on its surface.

The moon is no longer out of reach.
Even for person of average means.

Visit the moon by traveling with Space-B

We are going - you can too!

Figure 13-36. *space-b.net website*

Modifying Publii CMS Server Settings

There is just one other modification that needs to be made when changing the domain name for a Publii CMS website. In the "Server" settings, you will need to update the website URL.

Click the "Server" menu item in the Publii CMS main menu on the left side of the application. Locate the Website URL field as highlighted in Figure 13-37.

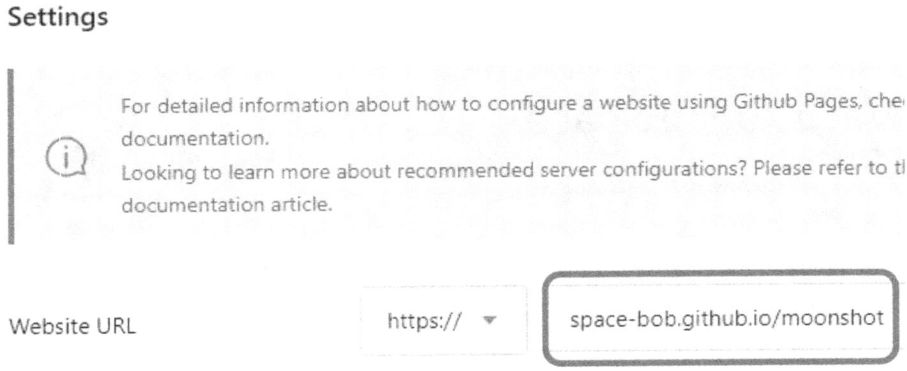

Settings

For detailed information about how to configure a website using Github Pages, che documentation.
Looking to learn more about recommended server configurations? Please refer to tl documentation article.

Website URL   https:// ▼   space-bob.github.io/moonshot

Figure 13-37. *Website URL in Server Settings*

Change the URL so that it is the same as your new domain name. In my case, I will replace the existing value with "space-b.net" as shown in Figure 13-38.

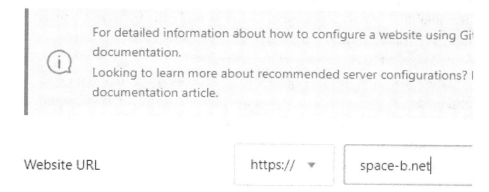

Figure 13-38. Website URL updated to new domain name

Click the blue "Save Settings" button in the upper right corner of the GitHub Pages settings panel to commit the changes.

Synchronize your website. Refer to the detailed process in Chapter 8 to sync the website to GitHub if needed.

Summary

This has been an optional chapter explaining and demonstrating the acquisition of a custom domain name and how to set it up as the primary domain name for your GitHub Pages site.

Domain names are like a virtual property that you own (or perhaps rent).

Your GitHub Pages website will have a domain name that is part of the GitHub.com domain structure. Having your own domain name is desirable as it can impart a level of professionalism to your site and as well as usually being easier to remember and share with others.

Domain names are obtained from a registrar who is certified by the Internet Corporation for Assigned Names and Numbers (ICANN). Search for available domain names using a website tool called a "WHOIS search". Many sites offer this functionality, but the safest to use is offered by ICANN located here: `https://lookup.icann.org/en`.

I demonstrated using a registrar called Squarespace to purchase and manage a custom domain. Squarespace offers a complete solution with all the needed features. They are desirable as they are transparent with their pricing structure.

In this chapter, we covered several technical elements of how things work on the Internet including how a URL is structured, how DNS works, and what a TLS security certificate is used for.

You were guided through setting up both GitHub and Squarespace to link the two systems together so that the DNS records from Squarespace pointed to GitHub and GitHub resolved your web page to the custom DNS.

We ran into the specter of cached web pages again in this chapter just like we did in Chapter 8 where I explained how to flush the browser cache to resolve this issue.

PART III

Advanced Customizations

In Part 3, I will be discussing some more advanced topics that will help you take your Publii CMS website to the next level. These things include using the plugin system to add a comment section to each of your blog posts using a third-party commenting service as well as managing cookie notices and other important Internet compliance requirements.

I will also introduce the concept of tweaking the look and feel of your site using Cascading Style Sheets or CSS. We will also use some HTML and CSS to add an interactive FAQ section to our site. This last section involves some coding. I will give you access to all the code on the book's GitHub page, so you will not need to type it into your system. The scope of this book unfortunately prohibits me from going into a great deal of explanation about how CSS and HTML work, but I will provide plenty of links to sites where you can learn more.

CHAPTER 14

Plugins and Cookies

This chapter is the first of two chapters covering advanced topics. What you have learned up to now has resulted in a fully functional website with a blog, contact page, and other features. What has been created so far is a presentable website that will function well for your small business, organization, or personal website. It is simple and highly maintainable in its current form.

You can take it further, and that is what the next two chapters are all about – adding functionality and dressing up the site a little bit more. Topics covered in these chapters fall into the advanced category of enhancements. They are optional but serve to put that polished shine on your site. I recommend reading and trying the examples.

We begin by discussing Publii CMS's plugin infrastructure. The developers of Publii CMS have created a system that permits expanding on the basic core by adding plugins to deliver additional features. I will be presenting a plugin to permit website visitors to leave comments on the posts they read.

The second half of this chapter will cover the enabling of the built-in cookie banner. Cookie banners are a highly recommended feature for any website which advise readers regarding the cookies that your site uses. Alerting visitors of cookies that are in use arose out of a 2002 European Union directive requiring member countries to have laws requiring website declaration of cookie practices.

I will be explaining how to add a cookie banner to your Publii CMS site in compliance with various laws and regulations around that requirement.

B. Moore, *Designing Websites with Publii and GitHub Pages*,
https://doi.org/10.1007/979-8-8688-1195-1_14

Plugins

In this section, I will be discussing Publii CMS plugins with specific focus on commenting plugins for a blog built with Publii CMS. I will discuss getting plugins from the Publii CMS Marketplace, installing plugins, and utilizing the plugin locally on a specific website. At the end of this section, I will make mention of other plugins that can add functionality to your Publii CMS–based system taking your site to the next level.

A plugin is an add-on module that is installed in your Publii CMS environment to provide additional functionality that is not present in the base version of the application. At the time of writing, Publii CMS offered 28 plugins. There are new plugins added regularly to the Publii CMS Marketplace. There are both free and premium plugins available in the Plugins Marketplace. Premium plugins offer unique features that the developers of Publii CMS have invested in bringing to the community. They are a great way to support the great folks who offer Publii CMS free.

Keeping with the overall theme of this book, I will be demonstrating the acquisition and implementation of a free plugin that uses a free backend service.

Getting a Comments Plugin

The Publii Marketplace offers six different comment system plugins. They vary significantly in price and capabilities:

Hyvor Talk

> Pros: Real-time comments; voting; reactions; automatic spam detection; analytics

> Cons: No free plan; busy interface

Commento

> Pros: Spam filtering; voting; solid privacy; simple
> interface; anonymous commenting
>
> Cons: No free plan

GraphComment

> Pros: Free plan; solid privacy; EU hosted data
>
> Cons: Busy interface; no Anonymous commenting

Cusdis

> Pros: Free plan; very sparse interface; only
> anonymous commenting; open source
>
> Cons: Slow; no spam filtering

Facebook Comments

> Pros: Free; huge user base
>
> Cons: Complex interface; notorious privacy policies;
> no anonymous comments

Disqus

> Pros: Free plan; voting; spam filtering; very popular
> with bloggers; questionable privacy practices
>
> Cons: Free plan is ad supported; rather busy
> interface; no anonymous commenting

I personally like GraphComment and Cusdis as they are extremely easy to integrate, can be used without cost, and look good on the website. In this chapter, I will be demonstrating the GraphComment plugin. Configuring and integrating the other comment providers (except for Facebook) is very much the same as the process I will be demonstrating in the sections below.

Note   Neither the author nor Apress endorses or specifically recommends any service other than for demonstration purposes. You are encouraged to shop around and select the service that best meets your needs. As always, your mileage may vary.

I will need to access the Publii CMS Plugin manager panel to locate and install plugins. To do this, open Publii CMS and locate the Application settings and options icon – which is three stacked dots – in the upper right corner of the application. Click the icon to open the context menu as highlighted in Figure 14-1.

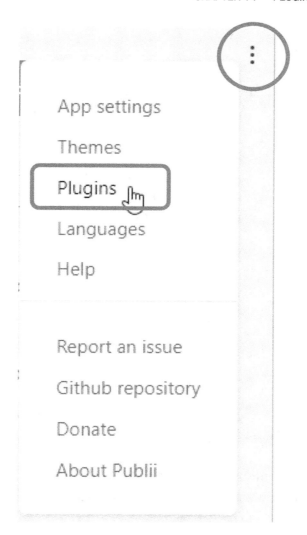

Figure 14-1. *Context menu for the application settings and options*

Click the "Plugins" menu item in the drop-down menu as highlighted in Figure 14-1. It has a tooltip that says, "Go to the plugins manager".

There are no plugins installed, so the only option available is the "Get more plugins" button as shown in Figure 14-2.

Plugins

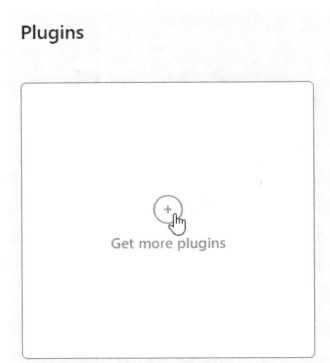

Figure 14-2. *Get more plugins*

Clicking this button will open your default web browser and load the web page for the Publii Marketplace for Plugins as shown in Figure 14-3.

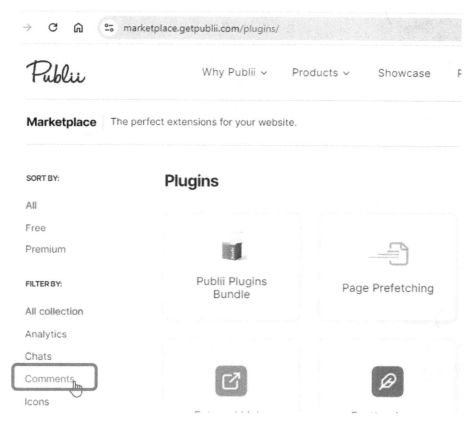

Figure 14-3. *Publii Marketplace - Plugins (cropped)*

Click "Comments" under the "Filter by" filters as highlighted in Figure 14-3 to limit the display of plugins to just those that support commenting systems. Click the "GraphComment" button as shown in Figure 14-4.

Plugins

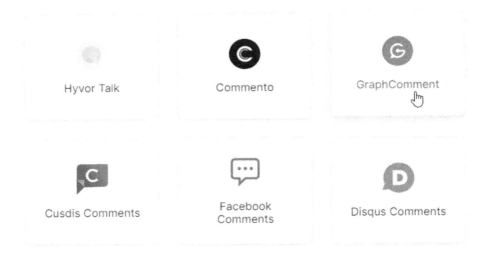

Figure 14-4. *Click the GraphComment button*

This navigates the web browser to the GraphComment plugin page as shown in Figure 14-5.

nting system into your Publii site with this plugin, you'll
ʲu stay on top of what your users have to say. Allow
ful tools that expand far beyond the standard

Figure 14-5. *The GraphComment page (cropped)*

Click the blue "Download" button to download this plugin. The
Chrome web browser will indicate the download is complete with a
message in the upper right corner of the browser as highlighted in
Figure 14-5 (indication of such in other browsers varies).

Installing the Plugin

The plugin is now downloaded to your local PC. Close or minimize the
web browser and return to the Publii CMS application. You should still
have the Plugin manager open. Focus on the upper right corner of the
application where you will see a button labeled "Install plugin" as shown
in Figure 14-6.

Figure 14-6. *Install plugin button*

Click the "Install plugin" button which will open an "Open file" dialog window as shown in Figure 14-7. Navigate to the Downloads folder and locate the zip file for the GraphComment plugin that was downloaded in the previous step as highlighted in Figure 14-7.

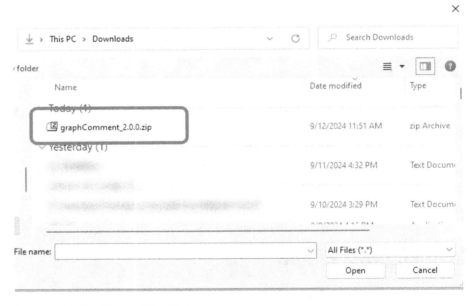

Figure 14-7. *Open file dialog*

Select the zip file and click the "Open" button to install the plugin. The plugin will be installed as shown in Figure 14-8.

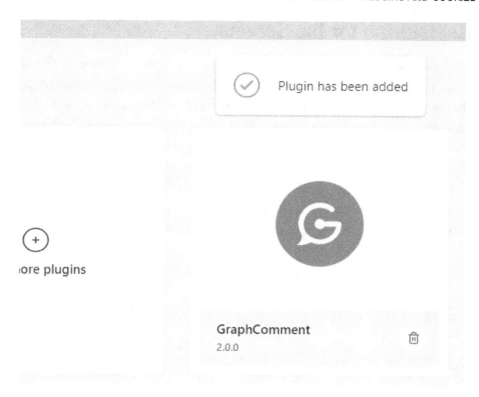

Figure 14-8. *GraphComment installed*

Close the Plugin manager by clicking the "Go back" link located in the upper right corner of the application next to the "Install plugin" button, as shown in Figure 14-9.

Figure 14-9. *Go back link*

631

Registering for the Service

GraphComment is a third-party service which is not affiliated with Publii CMS. Like the Contact Us functionality added to our website in Chapter 12, this provider operates a system that provides backend processing of forms and storage of data. Services are provided in various plan levels with the most basic being a free-to-use tier. See the plans available and select one of them for your project by visiting their website here: `https://www.graphcomment.com/en/products/graphcomment/pricing`. One of the goals of this project has been to implement a solution at no cost, so I will select the Free Basic plan as shown in Figure 14-10.

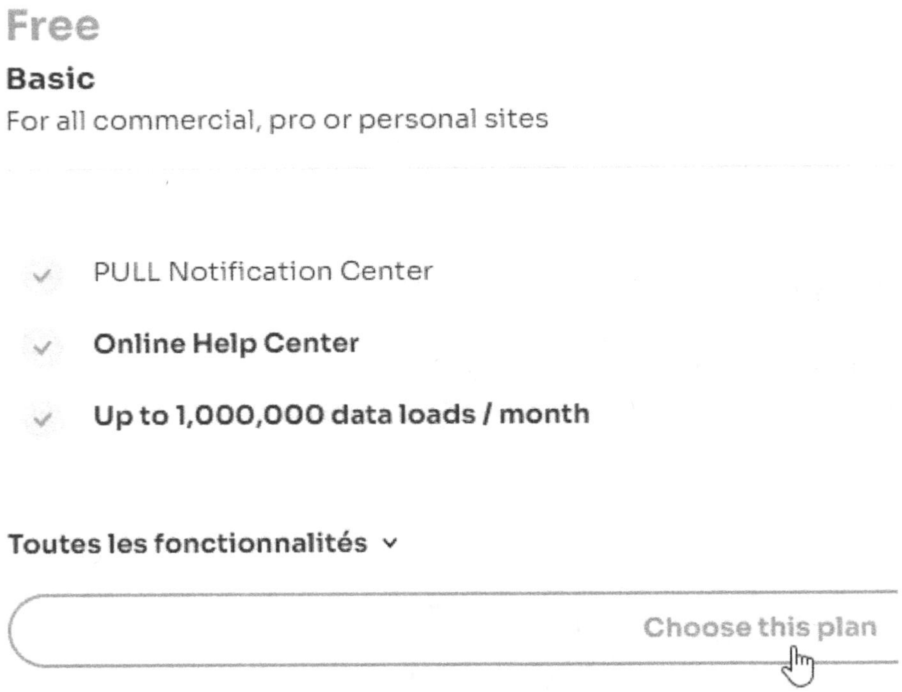

Free

Basic

For all commercial, pro or personal sites

- ✓ PULL Notification Center

- ✓ **Online Help Center**

- ✓ **Up to 1,000,000 data loads / month**

Toutes les fonctionnalités ⌄

Choose this plan

Figure 14-10. Select a plan from the GraphComment website (cropped)

Click the "Choose this plan" button as shown in Figure 14-10 to select the Free plan. GraphComment will ask you to log in with your account. We don't have an account yet, so click the "Register now!" link at the bottom of the dialog box as highlighted in Figure 14-11.

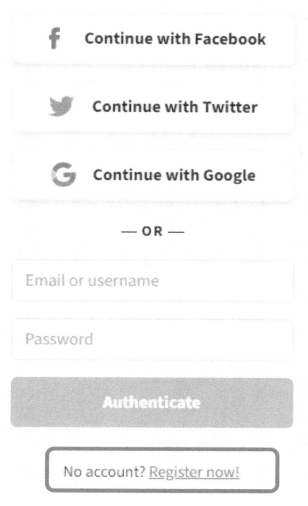

Figure 14-11. *Log in to GraphComment*

GraphComment provides several sign-on provider services with which to register and create a new account. I prefer using Google's sign-on provider when available. However, I will register with an email keeping all my various accounts for this project tied to that address for future simplicity.

Don't forget to write down the information as you create it. Click the link labeled "email" as highlighted in Figure 14-12.

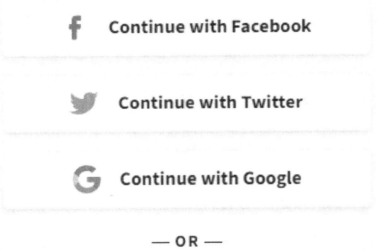

Figure 14-12. *Create an account*

Look at Figure 14-13 where I have provided a username, my email address, and a password. Remember the password guidelines we discussed earlier in this book. You can find those in Chapter 2.

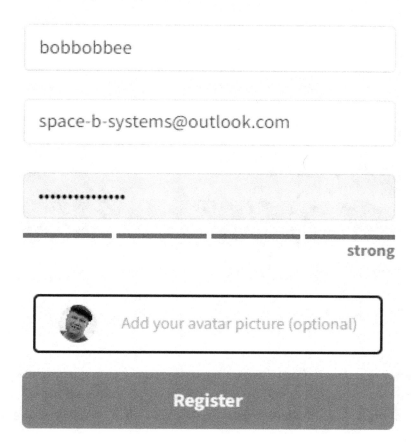

CREATE AN ACCOUNT

bobbobbee

space-b-systems@outlook.com

•••••••••••••••

strong

Add your avatar picture (optional)

Register

Figure 14-13. *Register an account with email*

I also added an avatar picture – because why not. This avatar will show up next to any comments or replies that you make in the comment system in Publii CMS.

Click the red "Register" button. In the next step, you will be asked to confirm your email address as shown in Figure 14-14.

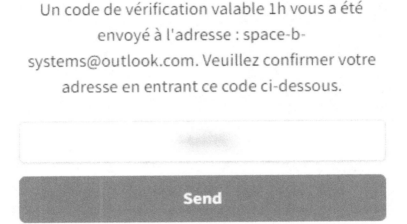

CONFIRM YOUR EMAIL

Un code de vérification valable 1h vous a été envoyé à l'adresse : space-b-systems@outlook.com. Veuillez confirmer votre adresse en entrant ce code ci-dessous.

Send

Figure 14-14. *Confirm your email*

The GraphComment provider is in France. Some of the localization of the website seems to have been missed when publishing the English version. I was surprised nonetheless to see a full paragraph of French.

I was pretty sure from the context of the page that the message was telling me that an email had been sent to space-b-systems@outlook.com and I should go get the code that was in that email and enter it in the field provided.

A quick visit to translate.google.com confirmed to me what the message did indeed say:

A verification code valid for 1 hour has been sent to you at: space-b-systems@outlook.com. Please confirm your address by entering this code below.

I found the email from GraphComment in my email client and read it. The code located in that email was typed into the form shown above in Figure 14-14. Finally, I was able to click the red "Send" button to complete the registration process.

I was greeted by a nice welcome message and some basic information about GraphComment. I knew that I would need to add the website that I wanted to integrate the commenting system into, so I looked for a button or link for that purpose. In the upper right side of the page, there is a button labeled "Add a new website" as shown in Figure 14-15.

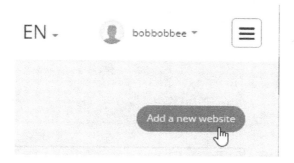

Figure 14-15. *Click the "Add a new website" button*

Clicking the "Add a new website" button opened a page where I could register my website as shown in Figure 14-16.

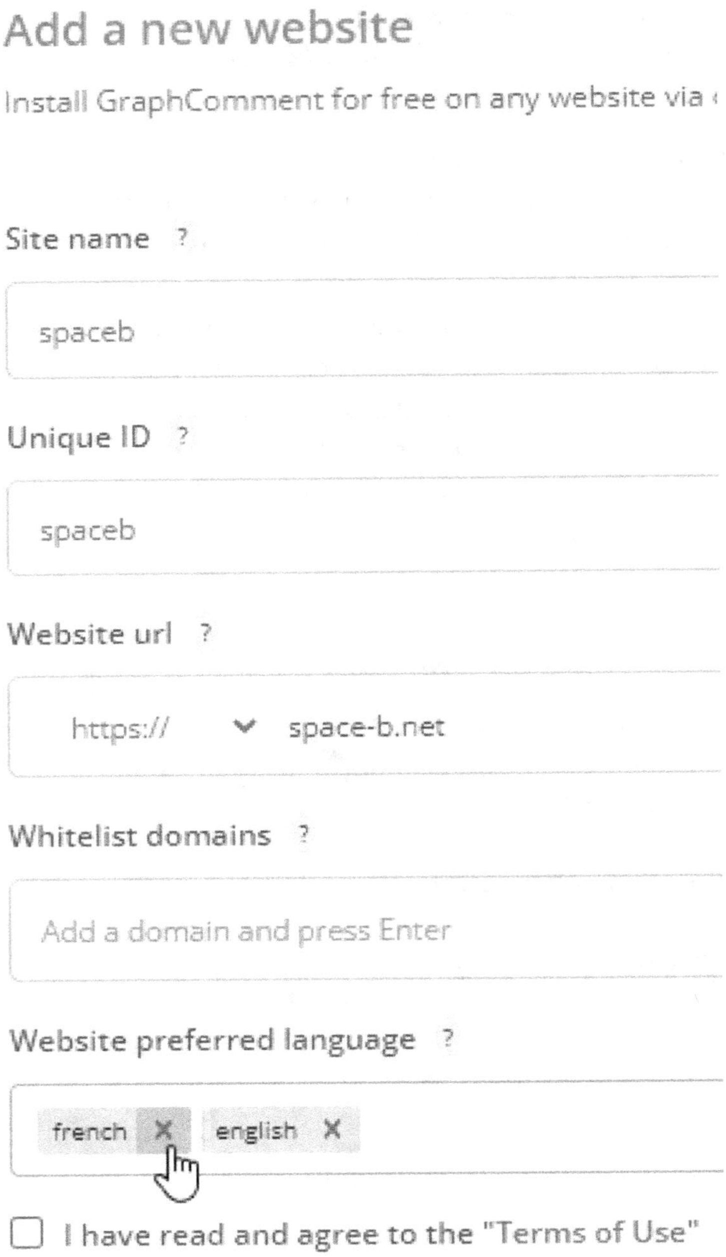

Add a new website

Install GraphComment for free on any website via ‹

Site name   ?

spaceb

Unique ID   ?

spaceb

Website url   ?

https://   ⌄   space-b.net

Whitelist domains   ?

Add a domain and press Enter

Website preferred language   ?

french   ✕   english   ✕

☐ I have read and agree to the "Terms of Use"

Figure 14-16. *Complete the website registration*

The important things needed in this form are the Site name, the Unique ID (which is automatically copied from the Site name), and the Website URL. I went with "spaceb" for the Site name and the Unique ID.

Notice that the Website preferred language is only "French" by default. I added "English" and then deleted "French" since my website is in English only.

Don't forget to agree to the "Terms of Use" as shown in Figure 14-17.

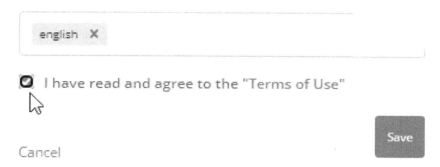

Figure 14-17. *Agree to the Terms of Use and click the red "Save" button*

Click the red "Save" button to complete the website registration process. The GraphComment Dashboard will be opened as soon as the registration is completed as shown in Figure 14-18.

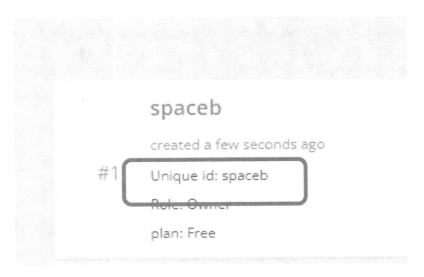

Figure 14-18. *GraphComment Dashboard*

You will need the Unique ID value to complete the plugin activation in the next section of this chapter. You can see that value for my account and website as highlighted in Figure 14-18.

Activating the Plugin

Return to the Publii CMS application. The plugin needs to be activated for the website project you are working on. Click the "Tools & Plugins" menu item in the Publii CMS main menu as shown in Figure 14-19.

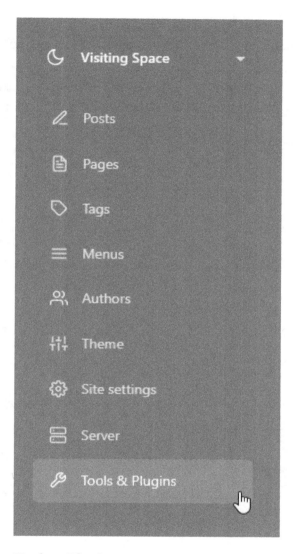

Figure 14-19. *Tools & Plugins*

Plugins are listed following the default system tools in the "Tools & Plugins" main interface. As you can see in Figure 14-20, the GraphComment plugin is displayed here since it is globally installed into Publii CMS. Initially the plugin is not active as can be evidenced by the gray colored toggle switch set to the left-hand position in the lower left hand of the GraphComment plugin button.

Click the toggle switch to enable it. It will slide into the right-hand position and will be colored blue as highlighted in Figure 14-20.

Figure 14-20. *Activate the plugin*

Configuring the Plugin

Open the plugin configuration interface by clicking the "GraphComment" plugin button as shown in Figure 14-20. We are particularly interested in the item labeled "GraphComment ID" in the Comments configuration section as shown in Figure 14-21.

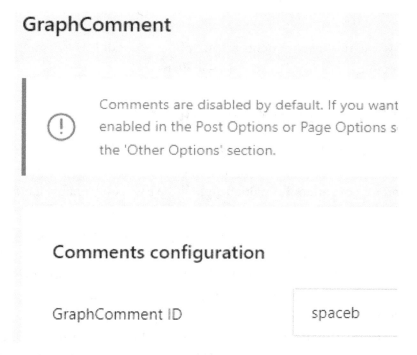

Figure 14-21. GraphComment configuration

Type the GraphComment ID from Figure 14-18 into this field. In my case, that value is "spaceb" in all lowercase. Click the light blue "Save Settings" button in the upper right of the application window to save the changes.

Note the message above the Comments configuration section preceded with an angry red exclamation mark. It reads:

> *Comments are disabled by default. If you want to allow comments on your entries, make sure the "Comments" option is enabled in the Post Options or Page Options sections of the Theme settings or, for individual entries, in edit mode via the 'Other Options' section.*

This means that comments are not on (or accessible) by default. We must enable them. That is what we will do next.

Enabling Comments in Publii CMS

Enabling comments can be done globally for an entire site in the Post and/or Page Options for the active theme. Commenting on a Page is rare, and it is therefore not generally enabled globally. We will only enable it globally for Posts.

Comments can be enabled or disabled individually on a Post and/or Page basis as needed. Do this from the editor where the item is being created. It will be listed as an option in the "Other Options" section of the Post or Page settings and options accessed by clicking the gear in the upper right corner of the editor.

For now, I want to enable comments globally for all posts. This is done in the settings for the active theme. Click the "Theme" menu item in the Publii CMS main menu shown in Figure 14-22.

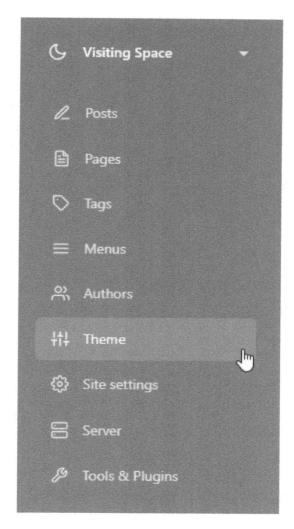

Figure 14-22. *Theme menu item*

Scroll down in the Theme Settings interface panel until you come to the "Custom settings". In the Custom settings menu on the left side of this section, click the "Post options" button as shown in Figure 14-23.

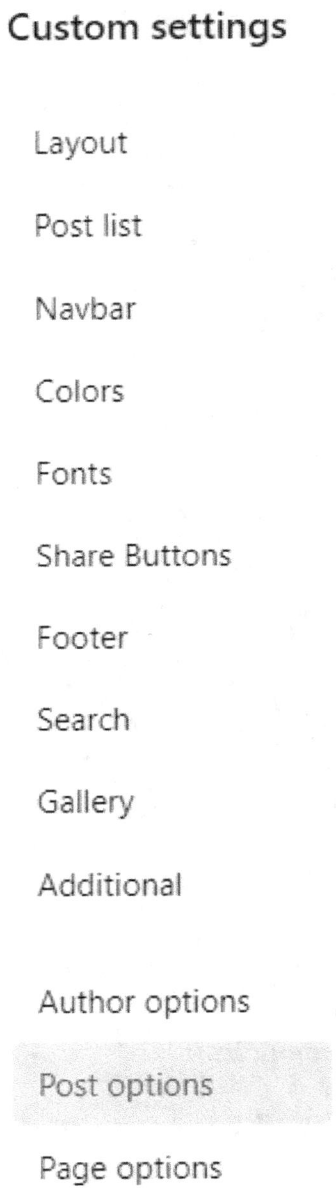

Custom settings

Layout

Post list

Navbar

Colors

Fonts

Share Buttons

Footer

Search

Gallery

Additional

Author options

Post options

Page options

Figure 14-23. Post options in the Custom settings menu

At the bottom of the list of Post options is an option labeled "Display comments". By default, this is set to Disabled. Click the drop-down field and select "Enabled" for this option as shown in Figure 14-24.

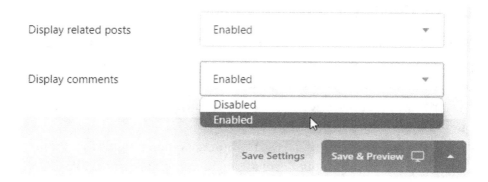

Figure 14-24. *Enable Display comments*

Save the settings by clicking the light blue "Save Settings" button on the bottom of the page shown just below the "Display comments" option in Figure 14-24.

Note   We are enabling the Display Comments globally in the theme; you can enable this on a post-by-post basis as well by changing the setting for the "Display comments" option in the Post options (under options panel accessed by clicking the gear in the upper right corner of the Post editor).

Test it out! Click the "Preview your changes" button at the bottom of the Publii CMS main menu. Open your blog and click on a blog post. Scroll to the bottom to view the comments section. It can take a few seconds for the resources and JavaScript component to load up before you can see the comments.

Here is another great idea: sync the local copy to your website on GitHub. Check it out online.

Other Great Plugins

Publii CMS has quite a few free plugins and several useful premium plugins. In keeping with the over-arching theme of this book, I will be discussing several of the highly useful free plugins. Some may require a third-party backend service provider. I will only be highlighting those who offer free access tier.

We have already discussed the Comment system plugins that Publii CMS offers. Another popular form of plugin many site owners like to use is an analytics toolset that can help gauge visitor engagement. Publii CMS offers four such plugins; two of them are supported by a provider with a free service tier. They are Umami Analytics and Google Analytics.

Google Analytics (GA) is notorious for their data sharing policies and massive amount of data collected as well as the vast number of tracking cookies they embed in visitors' browsers when visiting sites that use GA. I do not recommend using GA for this reason despite its free offering and high-quality analytics tools.

Plugins worth considering for your website:[1]

---

[1] Note that descriptions given for each plugin are taken verbatim from the Publii Marketplace.

Umami Analytics

Lucide Icons

Feather Icons

Umami Analytics

Umami is a user-friendly web analytics solution that aims to be more privacy-focused than Google Analytics while remaining free and open source; no subscriptions or other payments needed. With this plugin, you'll easily be able to integrate Umami into your site and start collecting data to improve your users' site experience.

Lucide Icons

The Lucide Icons plugin seamlessly integrates with Publii CMS, making it easy to add stylish and consistent icons to your website using simple shortcodes. It provides 1468 icons from the Lucide library, allowing you to enhance your site's visual appeal without sacrificing performance.

Feather Icons

The Feather Icons plugin is a fantastic addition to the Publii CMS, making it effortless to add stylish and modern icons to your website using shortcodes. This plugin allows you to enhance the visual appeal of your site with a beautiful, minimalist "Feather icons" design without sacrificing ease of implementation.

(continued)

Image Decoding

External Links

Image Decoding

The Image Decoding plugin has one job, but it can make for some helpful gains in your page load times. When enabled, it adds a decoding attribute to the elements of your site which can instruct the browser to start transferring image data while rendering the other page elements, instead of waiting until the base content in rendered. In practice, this can result in much better page performance, especially on posts that load a lot of images.

External Links

The External Links plugin enhances how external links are presented on websites powered by Publii CMS by offering a range of customizable features. This plugin allows you to add icons to external links, apply various rel attributes, and include additional CSS classes and titles. It provides comprehensive control and styling options for external links, ensuring they seamlessly blend with your site's design while maintaining a consistent look and feel.

(continued)

Meta Tabs

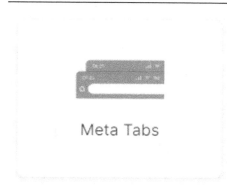

Meta Tabs

The simple Meta Tabs plugin has one job: to make your visitors' browser UI match the color style of your site. Enable the plugin, and with a couple of clicks, you can define the UI colors for both light and dark mode in supported browsers.

These are not the only plugins available in the Publii Marketplace. This also does not suggest that the paid plugins are somehow inferior to the free ones mentioned above. The theme of the book is a fantastic site hosted free, so I focused on free plugins. All of the paid plugins bring significant new features that can really enhance your site.

Cookie Banner Notice

In this section, I will be discussing how to utilize Publii CMS's built-in cookie banner options for your website. Some states in the United States, Canada, and most countries in the European Union as well as a handful of other nations have adopted privacy laws that require some form of notification to the end user regarding the tracking and operational cookies that your website uses.

Most websites use cookies for some form of functionality. The more dynamic the technology the site is built on, the greater the reliance on cookies. The good news is that websites generated by Publii CMS as static sites do not require any cookies when using official themes and having no plugins.

Plugins that you have installed may require cookies to enable their unique functionality. Non-official themes may also use cookies. It's important to know what types of cookies your site uses. This way, you can include the right consent requests where needed and make sure your site is GDPR compliant from the moment it goes live.

The Publii CMS built-in cookie banner offers two levels of functionality: a basic banner that simply informs visitors that cookies are used on the site and an advanced mode where visitors can give specific consent to different types of cookies. Configuring the former and deploying it is easy.

Deploying the advanced mode of operation for the cookie banner comes with some potential challenges. You must determine specifically what cookies are in use within your theme, Publii CMS, and each of your plugins and other linked resources (like the contact form we integrated via JavaScript in Chapter12).

Publii CMS and the official Publii CMS themes do not generate any cookies. However, many of the plugins that Publii CMS offers could require cookies to function correctly – these will need user consent. For example, analytics tools like Google Analytics use cookies to provide in-depth usage data for your site. You'll need to add these cookies to your cookie banner configuration if you are using the advanced functionality, so visitors can provide specific consent for their use.

Understanding how to specifically discover what cookies many of these plugins use is beyond the scope of this book; therefore, we will not be utilizing the advanced options for the cookie banner.

Note   As mentioned earlier, neither Publii CMS nor the Simple theme use cookies. This is also true of the GraphComment plugin which does not use cookies. Jotform, which was used as the solution for a contact form, sets two cookies: "guest" and "userReferer". Both cookies expire after 48 hours.

Having a Privacy Policy

It is considered best practice for a website to have a privacy policy as well as a set of terms and conditions in policy form. The privacy policy should outline what personal information is collected from users, how it is collected (e.g., through forms, cookies, or tracking technologies), and for what purposes it is used. It should specify whether this information is shared with third parties and under what circumstances.

The policy should detail how user data is protected, including any security measures in place. It's important to include information on users' rights regarding their data, such as the ability to access, correct, or delete their information. The policy should also address how the website complies with relevant data protection laws (e.g., GDPR, CCPA) and how it handles data from minors. Additionally, it should explain the use of cookies and similar technologies and provide contact information for privacy-related inquiries.

You should construct a comprehensive privacy policy and link it from somewhere within your system. The terms and conditions policy document that we created in Chapter 6 has some basic privacy policy language. You could leverage that to create a full-fledged policy.

There are dozens of policy generators on the Internet that you can leverage to create a policy. I have used the generator at Termly.io for projects in the past, and it is one option you could consider: `https://termly.io/products/privacy-policy-generator/`. Creating a privacy policy is also something that ChatGPT and Claude AI are particularly well suited for given enough background information about your website.

The source code folder for Chapter 14 located in the repository for this book on GitHub contains a file called "privacy.rtf", located here: `https://github.com/Apress/Designing-Websites-with-Publii-and-GitHub-Pages`. This is the privacy policy that has been created for the site: space-b.net.

You may use this policy as a starting place, adapting it to your needs. To use it, follow the procedure for creating a page in the WYSIWYG editor that was covered in Chapter 6.

These are the steps you should take:

1. Add a new page using the WYSIWYG editor.

2. Give your page a title. I used the title of the document "Privacy Policy."

3. Copy the content from the file "privacy.rtf" and paste it into the editor.

4. Change the things that do not apply to your site, such as site name and email address. Scan the document for other required modifications.

5. Save and close the editor.

Caution   All policies are potential legal instruments and should be reviewed by a qualified professional. The sample policy provided is intended only as a starting point for developing your own and is not a substitute for a legally binding document.

Enabling the Banner Notice

In this section, I will explain how to enable the basic cookie banner notice for your website using my own project site as an example. You should have created a new page in Publii CMS that contains your specific privacy policy for your website. If you have not completed this step, do it now.

Begin the setup process by clicking the "Site settings" menu item in the Publii CMS main menu as shown in Figure 14-25.

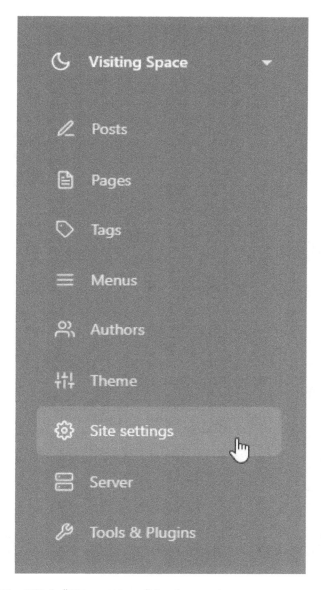

Figure 14-25. *Click "Site settings" in the main menu*

Scroll down to the Advanced options section of the Site settings. Click the "Privacy Settings" menu item in the Advanced options menu as shown in Figure 14-26.

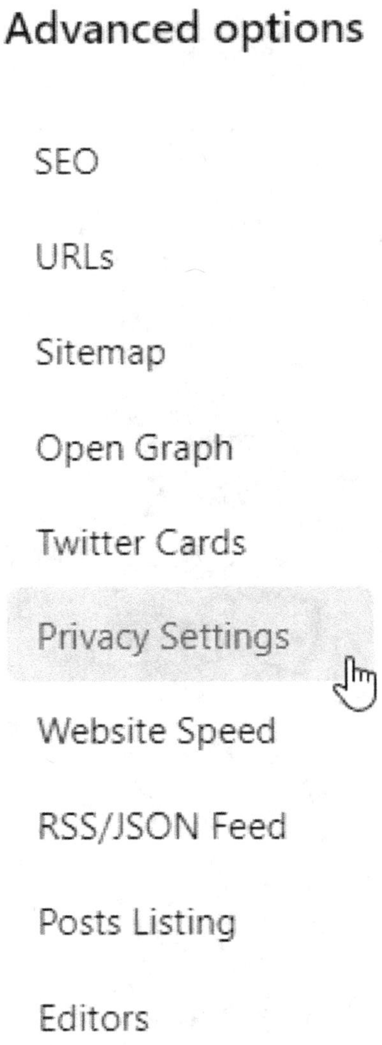

Advanced options

SEO

URLs

Sitemap

Open Graph

Twitter Cards

Privacy Settings

Website Speed

RSS/JSON Feed

Posts Listing

Editors

Figure 14-26. Click "Privacy Settings" in the Advanced options menu

In the section titled "Cookie Banner", enable the banner by sliding the toggle switch to the right as highlighted in Figure 14-27. The toggle switch will turn blue when enabled.

Cookie Banner

Enable banner

Enabling this option will display a cookie banner on your website. Please read the GDPR Cookie Banner Configuration article for more information on how to configure the banner correctly.

Figure 14-27.   Enable the cookie banner

The default banner message is more appropriate for the advanced banner setup. Since I will be disabling the advanced banner options, I chose to rewrite the cookie message as shown in Figure 14-28.

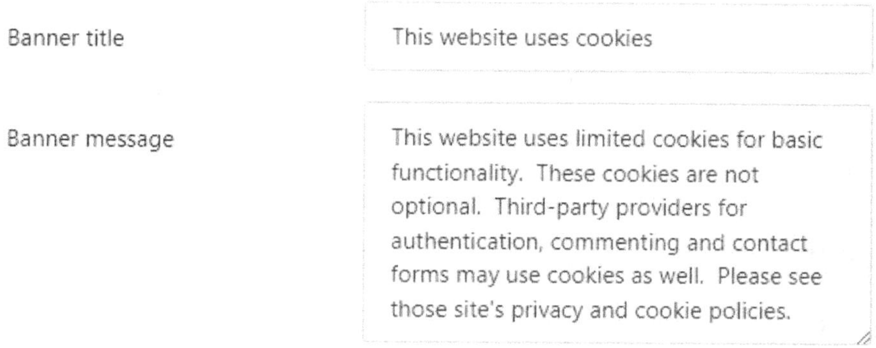

Banner title

This website uses cookies

Banner message

This website uses limited cookies for basic functionality. These cookies are not optional. Third-party providers for authentication, commenting and contact forms may use cookies as well. Please see those site's privacy and cookie policies.

Figure 14-28.   Cookie banner message

The new banner message reads as follows:

This website uses limited cookies for basic functionality. These cookies are not optional. Third-party providers for authentication, commenting and contact forms may use cookies as well. Please see those site's privacy and cookie policies.

The option "Show privacy policy link" is enabled by default. This is the best practice. Select the Privacy policy link source as "Internal page" from that field drop-down.

In the Select page drop-down field, select the page which contains your privacy policy. In my case, it is called "Privacy Policy". These options are shown in Figure 14-29.

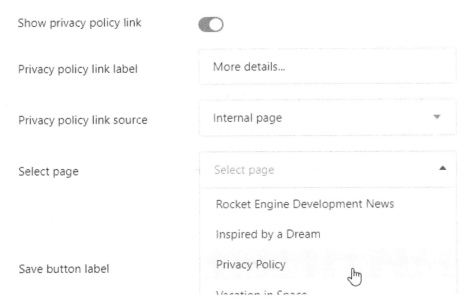

Figure 14-29. *Select the page "Privacy Policy"*

The default "Save button label" is "Accept All". I like to change it to a simple "OK" as that is more fitting with the basic banner operation. You can see this in Figure 14-30.

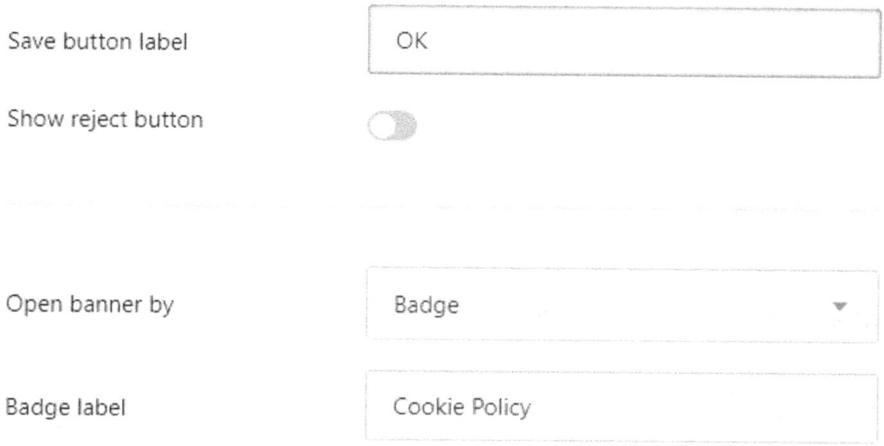

Save button label	OK
Show reject button	⬤
Open banner by	Badge ▾
Badge label	Cookie Policy

Figure 14-30. *Save button label*

Notice in Figure 14-30 that we retained the default values for the "Open banner by" and "Badge label". I will explain this shortly.

Scroll down a bit more to the section labeled "Advanced". This is where the Advanced cookie banner options are configured. I decided earlier that trying to understand all the potential cookies that could be used by Publii CMS extensions and plugins was beyond the scope of this book (remember Publii CMS and official Publii CMS themes do not use cookies). For this reason, disable the "Enable advanced cookies configuration" by sliding the toggle switch to the left from its enabled position as highlighted in Figure 14-31.

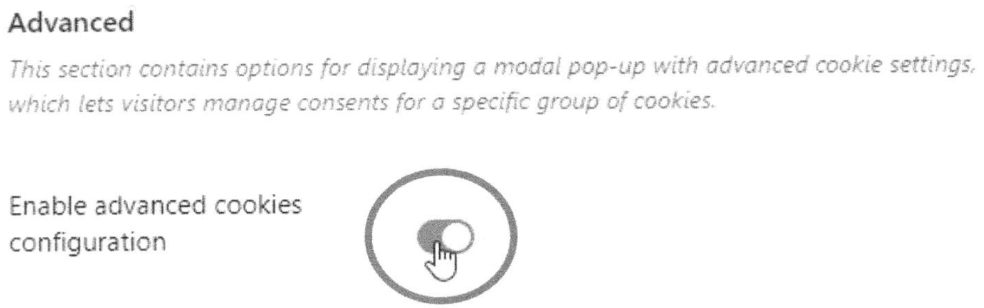

Advanced

This section contains options for displaying a modal pop-up with advanced cookie settings, which lets visitors manage consents for a specific group of cookies.

Enable advanced cookies
configuration

Figure 14-31. *Enable/disable advanced cookies*

The toggle switch will turn a gray color when disabled.

Observe in Figure 14-32 that the cookie banner sets its own cookie when the user accepts the terms and closes the button. That cookie is written to the user's browser and remains active for 90 days. This value can be changed.

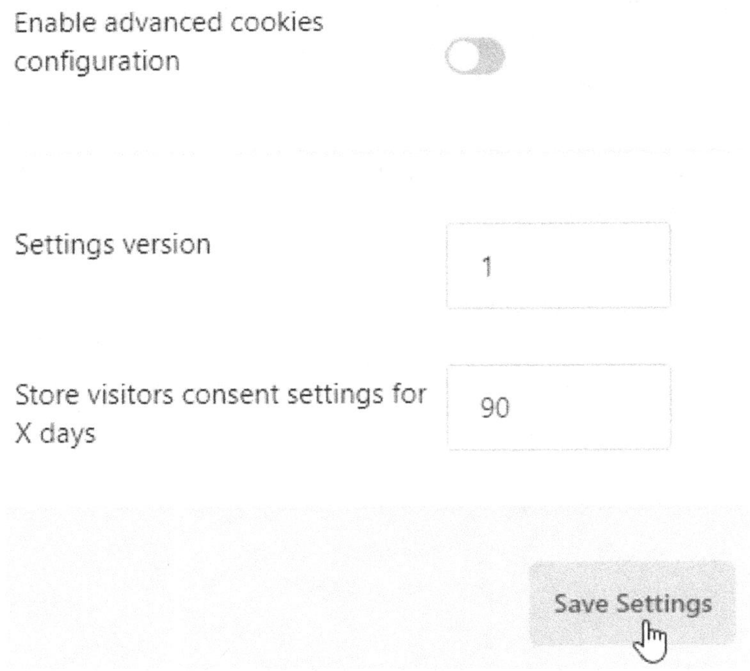

Enable advanced cookies
configuration

Settings version

> 1

Store visitors consent settings for
X days

> 90

> Save Settings

Figure 14-32. *Save the settings*

Click the light blue "Save Settings" button at the bottom of the Site Settings panel as shown in Figure 14-32.

Before verifying the operation of the cookie banner, you should close any tabs containing previews of your website and clear the browser cache for your web browser. The procedure was discussed in Chapter 8.

Preview your website by clicking the "Preview your changes" button on the bottom of the Publii CMS main menu. Notice the cookie banner displayed at the bottom of the web page as shown in Figure 14-33.

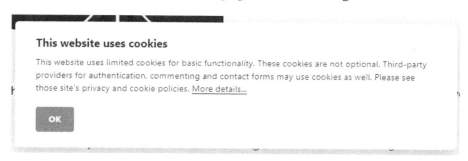

This website uses cookies

This website uses limited cookies for basic functionality. These cookies are not optional. Third-party providers for authentication, commenting and contact forms may use cookies as well. Please see those site's privacy and cookie policies. More details...

OK

Figure 14-33. *Cookie banner as seen in the browser*

Click the "OK" button to acknowledge the message and close the window. Notice the little cookie icon in the lower left corner of the web page as shown in Figure 14-34. This is the cookie badge. Clicking it will open the cookie banner again. This is the setting that we skipped over in Figure 14-30.

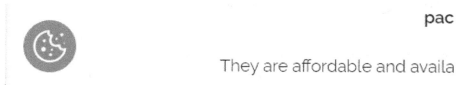

pac

They are affordable and availa

Figure 14-34. *The cookie badge*

The purpose of the cookie badge is to allow visitors to open and view their cookie choices when using the advanced cookie banner configuration. When using the basic cookie banner configuration, this may not be a desirable option. You can cause the badge to not be placed by changing the setting for "Open banner by" to "Custom link" from the options in that drop-down field as shown in Figure 14-35.

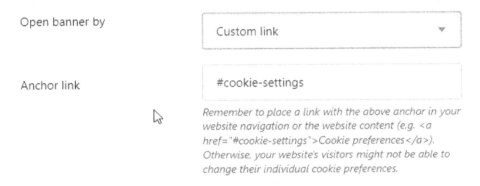

Figure 14-35. *Open banner by option*

There is an explanation of how to use the special anchor link below the Anchor link field. If you do not place an anchor link into the homepage, that is the same as disabling the link to reopen the cookie banner. This effectively removes the cookie badge shown in Figure 14-34.

Modifying the Footer Menu

In Chapter 11, I built and deployed a footer menu for the website. At that time, I intended to have a specific cookie policy. As it turns out, I have opted for a more comprehensive privacy policy. I need to now go back and edit the footer menu, changing the name of the menu item and linking it to the privacy policy. Join along with me making the change to your project site presuming you made the same error.

Click the "Menus" menu item in the Publii CMS main menu. Click the menu named "Footer" to expose the menu items assigned to that menu as shown in Figure 14-36.

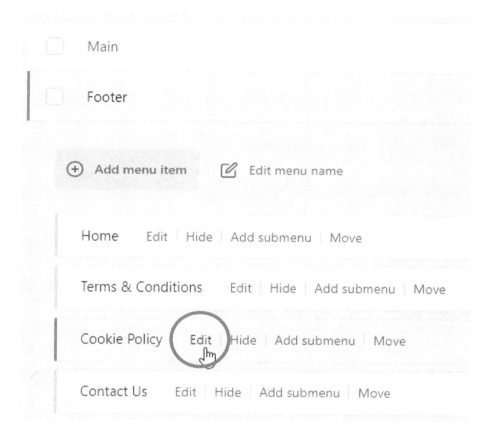

Figure 14-36. *Edit the Footer menu items*

Locate the menu item named "Cookie Policy" and click the Edit action on the right of the menu item name as highlighted in Figure 14-36.

The "Edit Menu Item" panel will fly out from the right side of the application as shown in Figure 14-37. Change the name of the menu item to "Privacy Policy". Change the link type in the "Type" drop-down field to "Page link". Finally, select the page "Privacy Policy" from the "Page" drop-down field list. All these changes are shown in Figure 14-37.

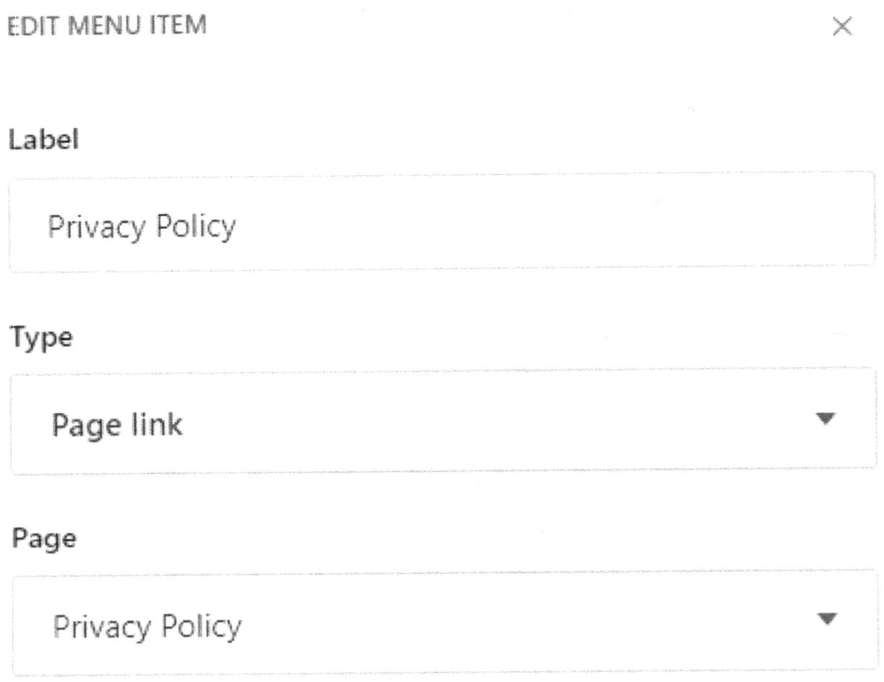

EDIT MENU ITEM   ✕

Label

> Privacy Policy

Type

> Page link   ▼

Page

> Privacy Policy   ▼

Figure 14-37. *Changes to the menu item*

Click the blue "Save Changes" button at the bottom of the "Edit Menu Item" panel to save the changes. Preview your changes to validate it looks and works as expected.

Synchronize your website with the publicly accessible version on GitHub.

Summary

In this chapter, you learned about the Publii CMS plugin infrastructure including getting plugins from the Marketplace, installing plugin files, and activating plugins.

We specifically explored plugins that add the capability to capture and display visitor comments on blog posts. There are a handful of choices in this category of plugin, each with its own pros and cons.

We selected the GraphComment system as it offered the best privacy, cost, and features of the lot. A good runner-up would have been Cusdis, which is an open source solution with a sparse feature set.

You learned how to register a downloaded plugin in Publii CMS, making it available to all sites globally. You also learned how to activate a plugin locally, allowing the local site to use the new feature set.

In the case of GraphComment, we needed to register for the service and obtain a unique ID to link the local plugin with the hosted service provider. Many plugins that integrate backend processing use this technique to link the service provider with the service.

We also learned that comments are not enabled in Publii CMS by default. We need to enable comments in the Theme settings.

You only installed one plugin as you worked through the chapter, but you did learn about several other useful plugins to try on your own.

I spent the second half of this chapter discussing privacy policies and the cookie banner that is integrated into Publii CMS.

We discussed cookies, what they are, and how they are used. We also discussed the difficulty determining every cookie that a site may use because of third-party integrations.

Every site should have a privacy policy as we discussed. The privacy policy should explain what information is collected from users, how it is collected, and how it will be used. It should state whether information is shared with third parties and when.

A good policy should explain how user data is protected and include information on users' rights regarding their data. It should also address how the website complies with relevant data protection laws (e.g., GDPR, CCPA). Finally, it should explain the use of cookies and similar technologies and provide contact information for privacy-related inquiries.

I provided a prewritten privacy policy that you can use as a starting point in developing your own privacy policy. It is in the Chapter 14 folder in the repository for this book on GitHub: `https://github.com/Apress/Designing-Websites-with-Publii-and-GitHub-Pages`.

In this chapter, you also configured the Publii CMS cookie banner notice which is part of the Site settings in the Privacy Settings section. We chose to implement the Basic cookie banner as determining all cookies in use on a site was beyond the scope of this book.

The final thing we did in the chapter was revisit the footer menu created in Chapter 11, modifying it to read "Privacy Policy" instead of "Cookie Policy" and linking the policy to the menu item.

CSS Tricks

This chapter covers a couple simple tricks that we can leverage to enhance our Publii CMS website. These tricks rely on knowing a little bit about the underlying structure of the website generated by Publii CMS as well as some basic Cascading Style Sheets styling language.

It is quite possible to follow along using the code in the book or in the repository and achieve the results I will be demonstrating without understanding how it works. I would recommend getting to know CSS just a little bit, as it can pay off in other web projects. Here are some great resources:

- CSS Tutorial at w3schools.com: `https://www.w3schools.com/css/css_intro.asp`

- Learn CSS in 20 minutes (video): `https://www.youtube.com/watch?v=1PnVor36_40&t=15s`

- Learn CSS – online course (free): `https://web.dev/learn/css`

- Learn CSS with Codecademy (free online course): `https://www.codecademy.com/learn/learn-css`

FAQ Section

A feature seen on many websites is an accordion-styled Frequently Asked Questions (FAQ) section or page. In this section, I will be showing you how to add an FAQ to a new page and link that page to the homepage. An FAQ could just as easily be integrated into an existing page.

© Brad Moore 2025
B. Moore, *Designing Websites with Publii and GitHub Pages*,
https://doi.org/10.1007/979-8-8688-1195-1_15

FAQs are designed to answer questions that visitors might have about your website, products, services, or information presented. Many times, they are built from real questions and answers given to site visitors. Other times they are simply the best attempt at constructing questions visitors might have and providing answers. FAQs always follow the same pattern – first a question and then an answer.

In the early days of the Web, these were just a page of questions and answers formatted in a way to distinguish one from another. Later as the Web matured and new technologies like jQuery (a JavaScript library) became available, the interactive accordion style became popular. With the advent of HTML version 5, JavaScript is no longer required to achieve this functionality.

Warning – things get a bit technical through the remainder of this section – you can skip ahead to the "Getting the Code" section without detrimental effect.

HTML5 introduced quite a few new features when it was released in late 2018 including the <details> tag. Technically this is a disclosure widget from which the user can retrieve additional information. This tag is often used to create an interactive element where users can click to reveal or hide extra content. It is ideal for formatting FAQ lists.

The typical usage of this HTML tag is shown here.

Listing 15-1. Example of the details tag

```
<details>
 <summary>More Information</summary>
 <p>This is the additional content that is revealed when the
 user clicks on "More Information".</p>
</details>
```

The <details> tag tells the browser to expect some interactive content. The <summary> tag is often used with the <details> tag to provide a heading or summary of the hidden content. Without it, the default label is "Details".

The content between the Details tag pair is automatically hidden by the browser as shown at the bottom of Figure 15-1. The full content is only made visible when the user clicks on the down arrow in the browser as shown in Figure 15-2 from codepen.com.

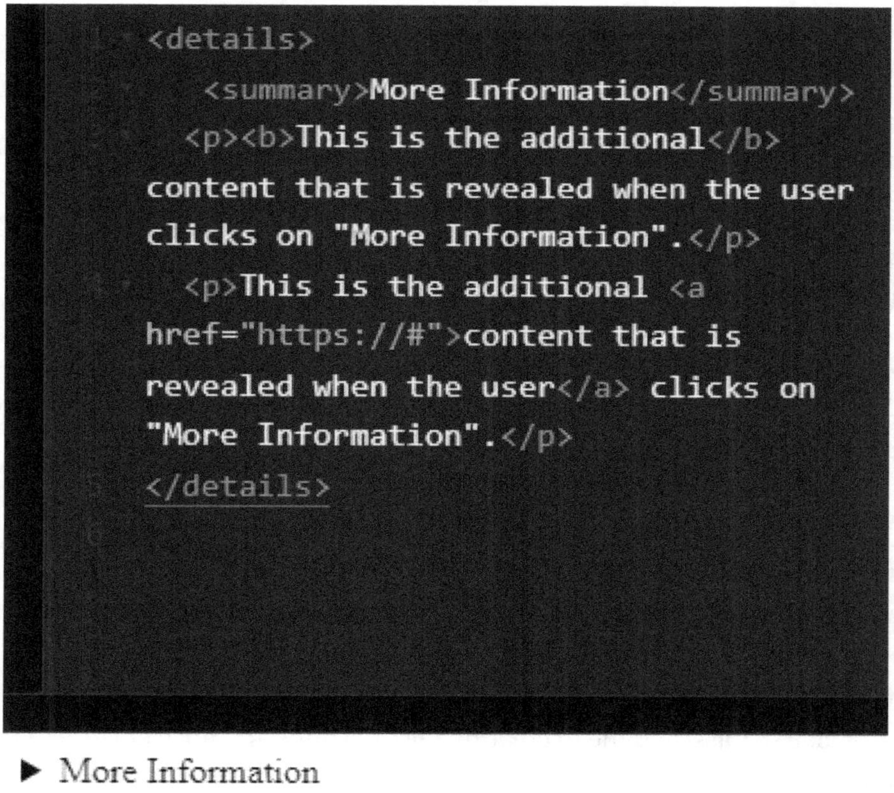

```
<details>
    <summary>More Information</summary>
    <p><b>This is the additional</b>
content that is revealed when the user
clicks on "More Information".</p>
    <p>This is the additional <a
href="https://#">content that is
revealed when the user</a> clicks on
"More Information".</p>
</details>
```

▶ More Information

Figure 15-1. *Example from https://codepen.io/Bradley-Moore/pen/qBzwzVZ*

The same example is shown in Figure 15-2 with the arrow clicked to reveal the content between the Details tags.

▼ More Information

This is the additional content that is revealed when the user clicks on "More Information".

This is the additional content that is revealed when the user clicks on "More Information".

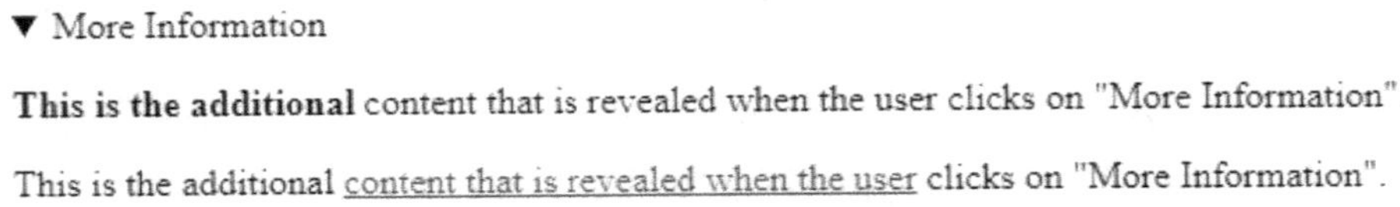

Figure 15-2. Example from `https://codepen.io/Bradley-Moore/pen/qBzwzVZ`

This is the functionality that I will leverage along with some very pleasant CSS styling to produce an appealing FAQ for my website. This is a reproducible component that can be used over and over in various projects. Just change the content between the Details tags and between the Summary tags.

Getting the Code

This project can be completed without understanding how or why the code works. Just copy and paste being careful not to introduce any changes into the code. I will be walking you through the whole process.

The first thing that you should do is get the source code for the project. The complete code is available in the Chapter 15 folder in the book repository on GitHub (`https://github.com/Apress/Designing-Websites-with-Publii-and-GitHub-Pages`). You can also experiment with it in CodePen here: `https://codepen.io/Bradley-Moore/pen/KKjYLwa`.

ChatGPT assisted me in creating the questions and answers for FAQ which I will be integrating into the website. It generated the six sets of questions and fictitious answers, which were then wrapped into the required "detail" tags.

Creating an FAQ Page

In this section, we will complete the first of two steps to make a functional and styled FAQ page.

Since we have the code already at our disposal, the process of creating the FAQ page will be greatly simplified. You will be using the WYSIWYG editor as we have done in the past. Review the procedure for creating a page in the WYSIWYG editor that was covered in Chapter 6 if you need a refresher on using it.

These are the steps you should take:

1. Add a new page using the WYSIWYG editor.

2. Give your page a title. I titled my page "FAQ."

3. After clicking in the page body, click the Source code tool in the toolbar which is labeled "<> HTML".

4. Open the file "faq.html.txt" in a text editor like Notepad. See Listing 15-2 for reference.

5. Copy the entire contents of the file "faq.html.txt" and paste it into the editor. (Remember you can copy with the key combination Ctrl-C and paste with Ctrl-V.)

6. Click the "Apply changes" button in the upper right of the code editor.

7. Save and close the WYSIWYG editor.

The FAQ page should look a lot like Figure 15-3 after step 6 above.

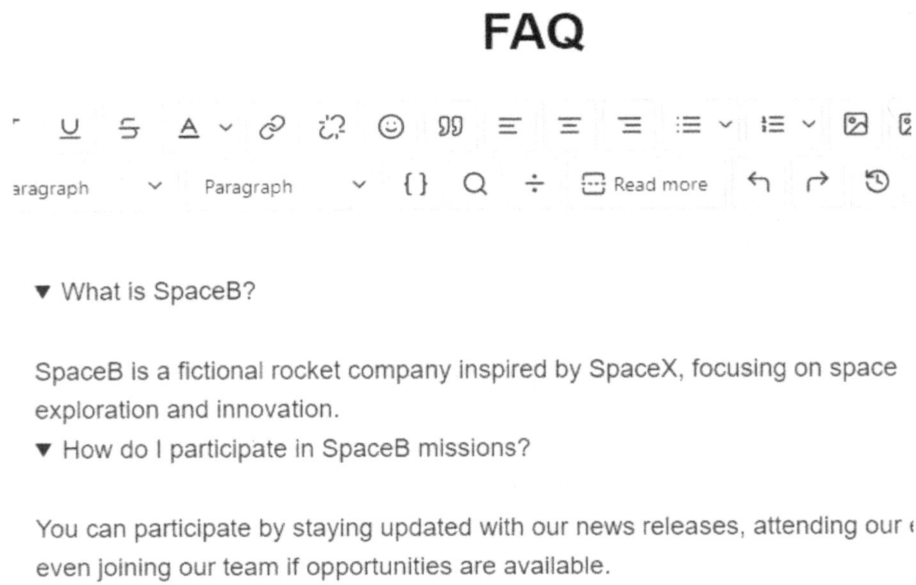

FAQ

U ⩗ A ⌄ ⌀ ⁇ ☺ 🙶 ≡ ≡ ≡ ☰ ⌄ ☰ ⌄ 🖼 🔖

aragraph   ⌄   Paragraph   ⌄   { }   Q   ÷   ⬚ Read more   ↶ ↷ 🕙

▼ What is SpaceB?

SpaceB is a fictional rocket company inspired by SpaceX, focusing on space exploration and innovation.

▼ How do I participate in SpaceB missions?

You can participate by staying updated with our news releases, attending our (even joining our team if opportunities are available.

Figure 15-3. *FAQ page after step 6 (cropped)*

The actual HTML code that should be entered into the HTML editor (either by pasting and typing) is found in Listing 15-2.

Listing 15-2. The complete HTML for the FAQ section

```
<div class="faq-list"><details>
    <summary>What is SpaceB?</summary>
    <p>SpaceB is a fictional rocket company inspired by
    SpaceX, ↵
Focusing on space exploration and innovation.</p>
</details>
<details>
    <summary>How do I participate in SpaceB missions?</summary>
    <p>You can participate by staying updated with our news ↵
releases, attending our events, or even joining our team if ↵
```

```
opportunities are available.</p>
</details>
<details>
    <summary>Where is SpaceB located?</summary>
    <p>SpaceB is based in Kentucky and operates globally.</p>
</details>
<details>
    <summary>What rockets does SpaceB develop?</summary>
    <p>SpaceB develops a range of rockets named after different
    types of ↵
turtles, such as the Terrapin and the Snapper, designed for
both cargo ↵
and crewed missions to the Moon and beyond.</p>
</details>
<details>
    <summary>What is the mission of SpaceB?</summary>
    <p>SpaceB aims to revolutionize space travel by making
    it more ↵
accessible and sustainable, with a focus on lunar
exploration, ↵
satellite deployment, and future missions to Mars.</p>
</details>
<details>
    <summary>Does SpaceB collaborate with other
    organizations?</summary>
    <p>Yes, SpaceB collaborates with various space agencies,
    research ↵
institutions, and private companies to advance space
technology and ↵
promote international cooperation in space exploration.</p>
</details>
</div>
```

Adding Custom CSS to Publii CMS

In this section, I will be demonstrating how to add custom CSS to Publii CMS. In the repository for Chapter 15, there is a source code file that contains all the CSS we will need to style the FAQ.

Explaining how CSS works is outside the scope of this book. Check out the references from earlier in the chapter where you can learn more about CSS.

To begin the process of adding the custom CSS to Publii CMS, click the "Tools & Plugins" menu item in the Publii CMS main menu as shown in Figure 15-4.

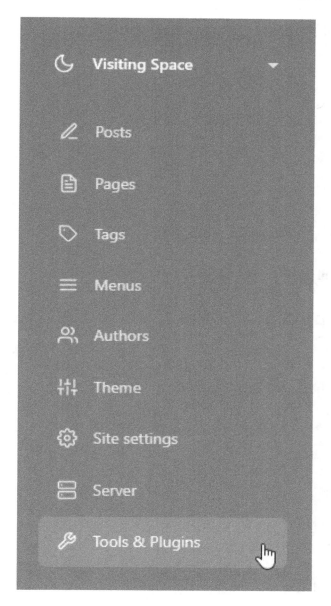

Figure 15-4. *Tools & Plugins menu item in the main menu*

Click the "Custom CSS" tool button in the Tools & Plugins panel on the right side of the application as shown in Figure 15-5.

Tools & Plugins

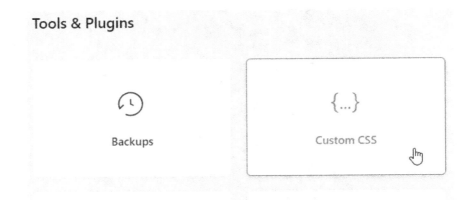

Figure 15-5. *Custom CSS button*

This will open a code editor as shown in Figure 15-6.

Custom CSS

```
1  /*
2   * Put your custom CSS code here
3   */
```

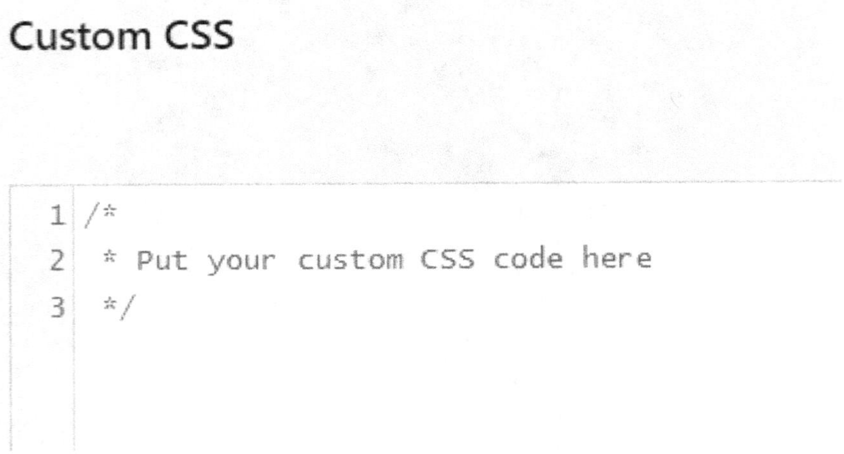

Figure 15-6. *Custom CSS code editor*

Delete all the code that is in the code editor as shown in Figure 15-6.

Open the file "faq.css.txt", which you downloaded from GitHub, in a text editor such as Notepad. Select all the text in the file and copy it. Returning to Publii CMS, paste the entire block of code into the code editor. (Remember you can copy and paste with the key combination Ctrl-C and paste with Ctrl-V.)

The code editor will look something like what you see in Figure 15-7 after pasting the code block into it.

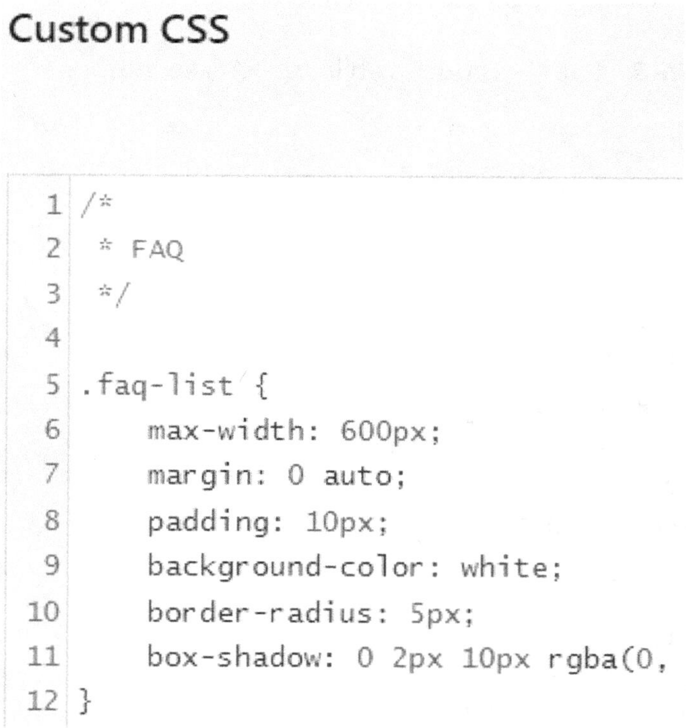

Custom CSS

```
 1  /*
 2   * FAQ
 3   */
 4
 5  .faq-list {
 6      max-width: 600px;
 7      margin: 0 auto;
 8      padding: 10px;
 9      background-color: white;
10      border-radius: 5px;
11      box-shadow: 0 2px 10px rgba(0,
12  }
```

Figure 15-7. Custom CSS code editor (cropped)

Click the light blue "Save Changes" button in the upper right corner of the code editor window as shown in Figure 15-8.

677

Figure 15-8. *Save Changes button*

The actual CSS styling that should be entered into the CSS editor (either by pasting or typing) is found in Listing 15-3.

Listing 15-3. The CSS code to style the FAQ section

```
/*
 * FAQ
 */

.faq-list {
    max-width: 600px;
    margin: 0 auto;
    padding: 10px;
    background-color: white;
    border-radius: 5px;
    box-shadow: 0 2px 10px rgba(0, 0, 0, 0.1);
}

details {
    margin-bottom: 10px;
    border: 1px solid #ddd;
    border-radius: 4px;
}

summary {
    cursor: pointer;
    padding: 10px;
    font-weight: bold;
```

```
    background-color: #f7f7f7;
    border-bottom: 1px solid #ddd;
}

details > p {
    margin: 0;
    padding: 10px !important;
    background-color: #fff;
    line-height: normal;
}

details[open] summary {
    background-color: #e7e7e7;
}
```

Linking the FAQ to the Homepage

The FAQ page is still an orphan page since it is not currently linked to any other page on the website. Early in the development of the single-page website, I had added a placeholder link just for an FAQ page. Now it is time to link these up.

Begin by clicking the "Pages" menu item in the Publii CMS main menu. In the Pages list, locate the page that is your homepage. Mine is called "Vacation in Space". Click that page title to open it in the editor.

Scroll down the page until you find the FAQ placeholder link. Click it and observe the context menu that appears which allows you to edit the link, break the link, or see the link as shown in Figure 15-9.

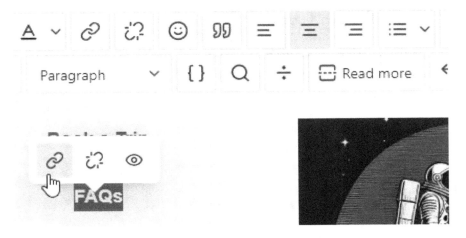

Figure 15-9. *Link context menu*

Click the icon of a link of chain to edit the link. In the Select link type drop-down field, select the "Page link" type. In the Page name drop-down field, select the page titled "FAQ" as shown in Figure 15-10.

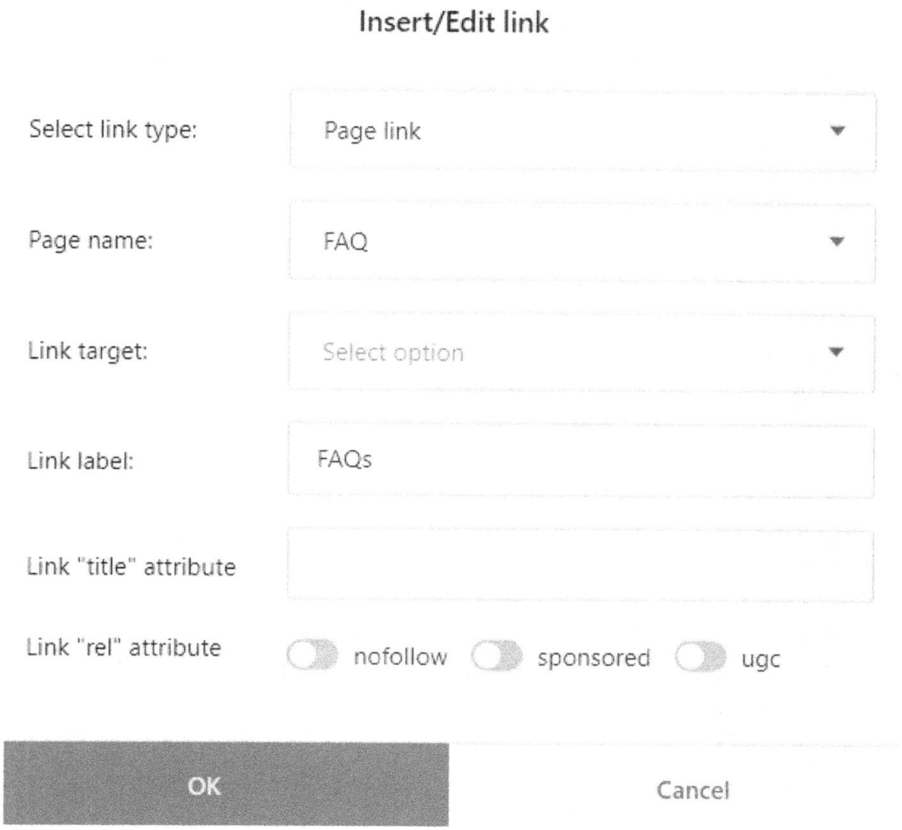

Insert/Edit link

Select link type:	Page link ▼
Page name:	FAQ ▼
Link target:	Select option ▼
Link label:	FAQs
Link "title" attribute	
Link "rel" attribute	◯ nofollow ◯ sponsored ◯ ugc

OK	Cancel

Figure 15-10. *Insert/Edit link*

Click the blue "OK" button to save the changes. Click the blue "Save and close" button in the upper right corner of the editor to save the changes.

Check out how the new FAQ page works. Click the "Preview your changes" button on the bottom of the Publii CMS main menu. In Figure 15-11, you can see the FAQs rendered in the web browser.

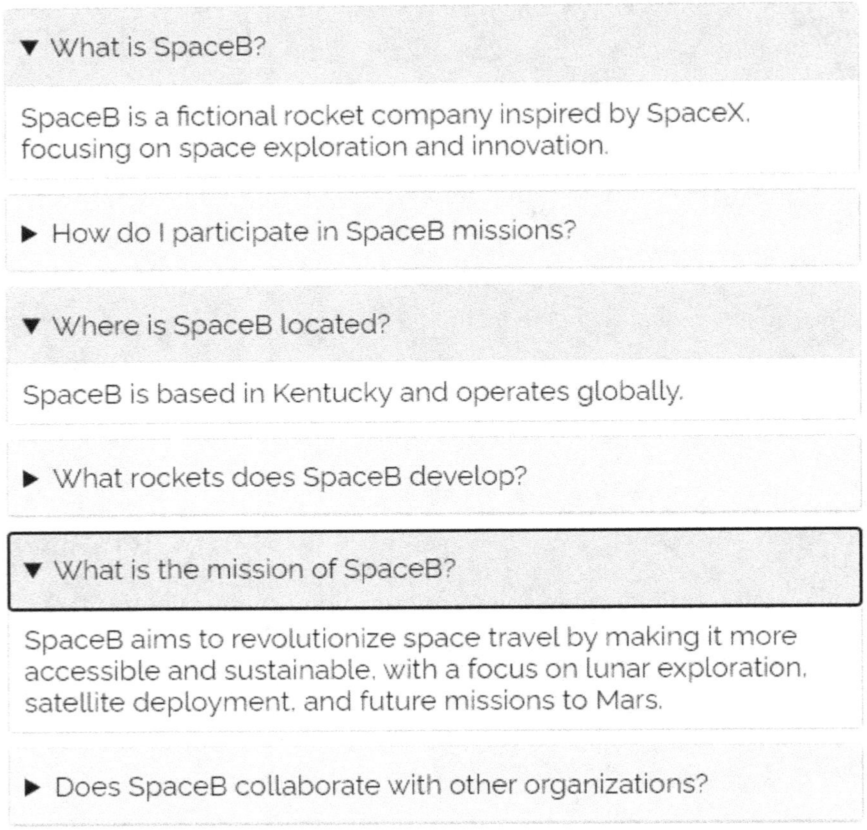

▼ What is SpaceB?

SpaceB is a fictional rocket company inspired by SpaceX, focusing on space exploration and innovation.

► How do I participate in SpaceB missions?

▼ Where is SpaceB located?

SpaceB is based in Kentucky and operates globally.

► What rockets does SpaceB develop?

▼ What is the mission of SpaceB?

SpaceB aims to revolutionize space travel by making it more accessible and sustainable, with a focus on lunar exploration, satellite deployment, and future missions to Mars.

► Does SpaceB collaborate with other organizations?

Figure 15-11. *FAQs as seen in the web browser*

Styling Links As Buttons

This section will explore how to style a standard link as a button in the WYSIWYG editor, allowing you to add a Call-to-Action feature to pages and posts. I will be discussing how to add styling to the custom CSS tool in Publii CMS and how to select the link to style.

One common element found on many websites is the Call-to-Action button. It is usually featured somewhere in the top part of the homepage where it is immediately visible and can attract the attention of the reader. These buttons often link to other resources on the website where the reader can learn more about your products, services, or ideas.

Many of the Publii CMS themes have default main pages that feature a Call-to-Action button, but if you replace the default homepage with a custom Page as we have done in our projects, this feature is lost.

What we need is a way to add a button to a Page, but none of the editors support that feature. We can, however, mimic a button with a link and some well-crafted CSS. As before I will be providing the code you require in a downloadable file in the Chapter 15 folder of the book repository on GitHub located here: `https://github.com/Apress/ Designing-Websites-with-Publii-and-GitHub-Pages`. I will comment a little on CSS; however, teaching you how to use CSS in practice is beyond the scope of this book.

Getting the Code and CSS

Styling a link to be a button is one of those rite-of-passage things that web developers go through. Today there are many CSS Button generators that will create the code needed to style a link as a button, no CSS knowledge needed – well, very little needed. The other great way to get some ready-made CSS for a link is to ask ChatGPT.

I tried this by visiting chatgpt.com and giving it the following query:

Style an anchor tag (link) as a pill shaped button with royal blue normal color and dark blue hovered using a 40px font.

Here is the code that was generated.

Listing 15-4. General CSS code to style a link as a button

```
[HTML]
<a href="#" class="pill-button">Click Me</a>
[CSS]
.pill-button {
    display: inline-block;
    background-color: RoyalBlue;
    color: white;
    padding: 10px 20px;
    font-size: 40px;
    text-decoration: none;
    border-radius: 50px;
    transition: background-color 0.3s ease;
}

.pill-button:hover {
    background-color: DarkBlue;
}
```

See this code in action in the CodePen located here: https:// codepen.io/Bradley-Moore/pen/XWLwNbz.

Note that the HTML is only relevant for the CodePen example. In Publii CMS, you will be modifying a link added into the WYSIWYG or Block editor using the link tool accessed from the context menu as highlighted in Figure 15-12. Click the existing link to access the context menu.

Figure 15-12. *The link tool from the context menu*

The code provided by ChatGPT works well, but it needs some changes to work with Publii CMS. The first thing that needs to be changed is the selector[1] used to target the element to style on the page. The selector in Listing 15-4 is a class called "pill-button". In the editor, we are not able to specify a class for inline links, so we will need to select the HTML using a different HTML attribute.

What we can set for a link in the editor which would allow us to select the link for styling is the title attribute – as we will see in the next section. In the code in Listing 15-5, I have specified the selector as an anchor (the "a" tag) combined with the title attribute:

```
a[title="Book Now"]
```

Other changes to the CSS provided by ChatGPT were necessary to override some of the Publii CMS native styling to achieve the look that I envisioned. I used the "!important" declaration after a couple style properties to increase their priority – essentially overriding the native Publii CMS styles that had a higher precedence. Overriding styles like this is considered a suboptimal practice – typically when modifying a page CSS, the developer should go back to the original CSS file and make the required changes there. It was necessary in this situation since I do not have full control of the page styling – Publii CMS does.

I also added a change in right/left padding when hovering over the button. This makes the button appear to grow wider. Specifying a transition effect for the padding ("transition: padding 0.3s") helps the effect to look smooth and pleasing.

It was also necessary to change the font sizing from "pixel" to "rem" measurement so that the font size can grow and shrink depending on the device it is viewed on. The final change, adding a nice touch to the styling, was specifying "pointer" as having the cursor attribute which is in line with how cursors work when encountering buttons.

---

[1] CSS selectors are the element, class name, or ID name used to target the specific HTML to be styled (https://www.w3schools.com/css/css_selectors.asp).

The final code is available in a file named "button.css.txt" in the Chapter 15 folder of the book repository on GitHub located here: `https://github.com/Apress/Designing-Websites-with-Publii-and-GitHub-Pages`. Download it so you can use it in the next section.

The final code to style a button with the title "Book Now" is shown below. The properties and attributes that were added or changed from what was suggested by ChatGPT are highlighted in gray in the code.

Listing 15-5. Finall CSS for styling a link as a button

```
/*
 * Button styling for buttons with title "make_btn"
 */

a[title="Book Now"] {
    cursor: pointer;
    background-color: RoyalBlue;
    color: white !important;
    padding: 10px 25px;
    font-size: 2.25rem;
    text-decoration: none !important;
    border-radius: 50px;
    transition: background-color 0.3s
    transition: padding 0.3s
}

a[title="Book Now"]:hover {
    padding: 10px 50px;
    background-color: DarkBlue;
}
```

Adding Custom CSS to Publii CMS

To begin the process of adding the custom CSS to Publii CMS, click the "Tools & Plugins" menu item in the Publii CMS main menu as shown in Figure 15-4 in an earlier section.

Next click the "Custom CSS" tool button in the Tools & Plugins panel on the right side of the application shown in Figure 15-5.

This will open the code editor that we saw in Figure 15-6. This time the code editor has code in it that we added to style the FAQs. Scroll to the bottom of that code block and place the cursor on line 39 as highlighted in Figure 15-13.

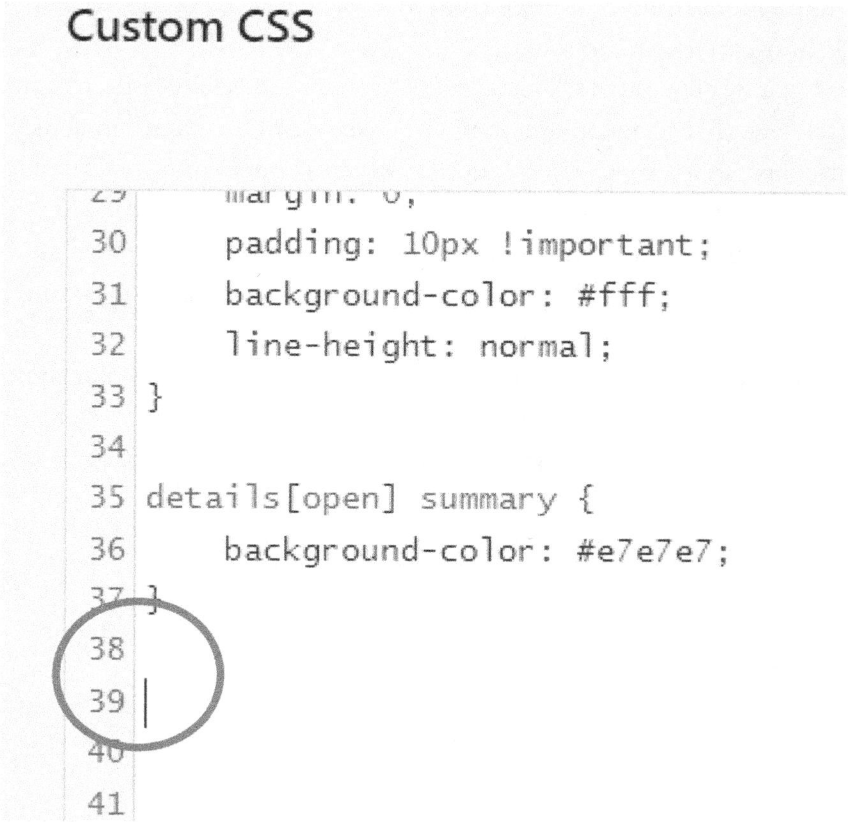

Custom CSS

```
29      margin: 0;
30      padding: 10px !important;
31      background-color: #fff;
32      line-height: normal;
33 }
34
35 details[open] summary {
36      background-color: #e7e7e7;
37 }
38
39 |
40
41
```

Figure 15-13. *Custom CSS editor*

Open the file that you downloaded from the Chapter 15 folder in the book repository in a text editor such as Notepad. Copy the styling code in that file and paste it into the editor beginning on line 39. Alternatively, you can type the code from Listing 15-5 into the editor being careful not to make any mistakes.

Click the light blue "Save Changes" button in the upper right corner of the Custom CSS panel.

Modifying the Homepage Page

With the CSS saved and ready for use, all we need to do is set the title attribute on the anchor link we want to act as a button. In this section, I will show you how to do that.

Begin by clicking the "Pages" menu item in the Publii CMS main menu. In the Pages list panel on the right, click the title of the page, which is your homepage. In my case, it is called "Vacation in Space", and it is denoted as the homepage in the list.

Clicking the title of the page will open it in the editor it was created in. If you followed along with me in the earlier chapters, then that should be the WYSIWYG editor.

Scroll all the way down the page to the bottom where the placeholder link "Book Now" is located. Select that link and then change the section style to "Paragraph" if it is not already styled that way – as shown in Figure 15-14.

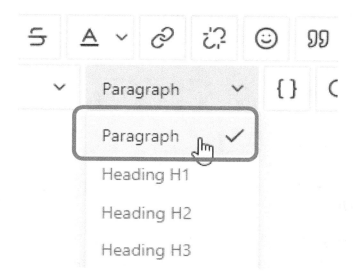

Figure 15-14. *Change the style of the link to paragraph style*

The link will immediately be right justified. Click the toolbar button labeled "Align center" to center it once more. While the link is selected, click the icon in the context menu that looks like two links of chain – the link menu item – as shown in Figure 15-15.

Figure 15-15. *The link tool from the context menu*

This opens the Insert/Edit link dialog window. Locate the 'Link "title" attribute' field as highlighted in Figure 15-16.

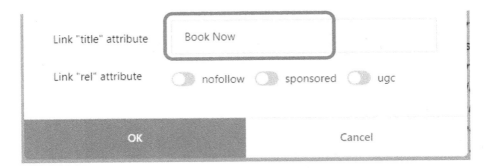

Figure 15-16. *The 'Link "title" attribute' field in the Insert/Edit link dialog window*

Type "Book Now" into the field as shown in Figure 15-16 being mindful to use the same case. Click the blue "OK" button to save the changes. Click the "Preview" link in the upper left corner of the editor to preview the changes. The link should be styled like a button as shown in Figure 15-18. Hover over the button and observe the hover effect. Compare that with how the link looked before styling in Figure 15-17.

Book Now

Figure 15-17. *Link before styling*

Figure 15-18. *Link after styling*

Return to Publii CMS and scroll up to the page to the top. This area – which extends down to the bottom of the first image on the page – is what is known as "above the fold" in web design terms. The phrase comes from the era of newspapers where the most important news went on the first page above where the page was folded.

In the world of web design, we must consider visitors with short attention spans; therefore, this portion of your website is the only part that you can reliably expect will be viewed by someone visiting your site. It is in this area where you will want to hook your visitor. Say what you need to say to keep the visitor reading the rest of the site.

This is the area where a Call-to-Action statement and/or button would appear. I am going to change up my main page to add a Call-to-Action button here. Delete the text as highlighted in Figure 15-19 to make room for a Call-to-Action button.

For tens of thousands of years humans have looked up to the moon and wondered about and dreamed about walking on its surface.

The moon is no longer out of reach. Even for person of average means.

Visit the moon by traveling with Space-B

We are going - you can too!

Figure 15-19. *Text to delete from homepage*

Scroll to the bottom of the page and click the "Book Now" link which we just completed styling. When clicking the link, you will notice that the entire link will be selected automatically – copy it by pressing the key combination Ctrl-C.

Scroll back up to the area where you deleted the text "Visit the moon by traveling with Space-B" and place the cursor in the empty area left behind. Paste the copied link where the cursor is by pressing the key combination Ctrl-V. You might need to add some blank lines between elements to break them up if they run together. When done correctly, it should look like Figure 15-20.

For tens of thousands of years humans have looked up to the moon and wondered about and dreamed about walking on its surface.

The moon is no longer out of reach.
Even for person of average means.

Book Now

We are going - you can too!

Figure 15-20. *Homepage with the "Book Now" Call-to-Action link*

Save and close the homepage. Click the "Preview your changes" button to see how your site looks – especially "above the fold." Admittedly the next image is a bit too small to appreciate, but my project site looks like Figure 15-21 in the web browser. I have cropped the page heading and menus off to assist in visibility.

Space-B is BOOKING trips to space and the moon now!

Book your trip now to avoid long waiting lines.

For tens of thousands of years humans have looked up to the moon and wondered about and dreamed about walking on its surface.

The moon is no longer out of reach.
Even for person of average means.

We are going - you can too!

Check out the resources below to learn more about Space-B's space and moon travel packages.

Figure 15-21.   space-b.net homepage in the web browser

The Final Word

This project has been a lot of fun. Thinking about going into space and following in the footsteps of some great astronauts has been exciting. As I was finishing this last chapter, a commercial space company launched a private mission that saw the very first spacewalk performed by private citizens.[2] The same mission was record setting for having flown humans further into space on a trip not going to the moon, 870 miles from the earth surface – a record set in 1966.[3]

We have also come a long way since the beginning of this book, although not nearly as far as those mentioned above. We now have a fully functional website with a landing page, a photo gallery, and a blog. Our site meets the minimum requirements of most laws regarding cookie notice and privacy policies. The site sports a nice Contact us page, and the integration of a commenting system on the blog is a smart feature.

You can visit the completed website and see it for yourself at space-b. net where it will be hosted for many years to come. Links on that page will take you to the book GitHub repository which you can also visit by typing the following into your web browser address bar: `https://github.com/Apress/Designing-Websites-with-Publii-and-GitHub-Pages`.

If you chose not to get your own personal domain name and stick with the default domain name given to you by GitHub, then you can claim to have built and hosted a website for free – that is a remarkable feat!

If you chose to go through this book following along with the example and learning the techniques with the idea that you would build the website you have always desired next, then this is your siren call. Hopefully you have taken some notes and put some bookmarks in the book where you wanted to remember things and you are ready to build that site.

So build that site.

As a parting gift – I have placed into the Chapter 15 folder of the book repository on GitHub (located here: `https://github.com/Apress/Designing-Websites-with-Publii-and-GitHub-Pages`) one additional file called extra.css.txt. This is some CSS that you can add to the end of the custom

---

[2] Space X Polaris Dawn mission (`https://polarisprogram.com/dawn/`).

[3] Astronaut Pete Conrad in NASA's Gemini 11 climbed to a record orbital altitude of 850 miles on Sept. 14, 1966 (`https://time.com/7020171/polaris-dawn-sets-new-space-altitude-record`).

CSS which we have already added to the project. This extra styling reduces the massive amounts of white space that the Simple theme seems to have embedded into it by overriding a few attributes with more sensible values.

This works because at compile time (when a site is previewed or synchronized) the custom CSS is saved into a CSS file and added to the head of the web page generated after all the other CSS. This allows the changes made to existing attributes to overwrite those from other CSS files.

The code may look complex. It is not necessary to understand it to use it. Just paste it into the custom CSS editor at the bottom of the code already present as we did in the section titled "Adding Custom CSS to Publii CMS" in this chapter. Here is the code should the repository not be available.

Listing 15-6. CSS code to add some additional white space to the page layout

```
.hero {
margin-top:-38px;
}

.hero__content {
    padding-bottom: calc(var(--baseline) * 1 + 1.5vw);
}

blockquote, figure, hr, pre, table {
    margin-top: calc(var(--baseline) * 2 + .5vw);
    margin-bottom: calc(var(--baseline) * 2 + .5vw);
}

dl, ol, p, ul {
    margin-top: calc(var(--baseline) * 1.25 + .25vw);
}
.btn {
    margin-top: calc(var(--baseline) * 2.5 + .25vw);
}
```

```
blockquote {
    font-variation-settings: unset;
}
```

Good luck on the journey.

Summary

In this chapter, we broke with our mantra of no code and dove headfirst into some CSS.

CSS is a styling language that defines what a website will look like by adding specific typography, spacing, color, and other visible styles to the basic HTML on a web page.

In this chapter, you learned what an FAQ was and how they are constructed using HTML and the <details> tag.

I did not explain the CSS used to style the details tag as presented in the book, as a primer on CSS was outside of the scope of this book, but I did provide some good resources to learn more about CSS.

The CSS used to style the FAQ section was provided as a completed block of code which could be downloaded and pasted into Publii CMS.

We discussed how Publii CMS manages custom CSS and pasted the code provided into the CSS editor.

We used techniques we learned in earlier chapters to link the new FAQ page to the homepage so that visitors can access it.

In the second half of this chapter, I presented a method of styling a link in a page or post created in the WYSIWYG editor or the Block editor to look like a button. We focused on the link to book a trip titled "Book Now".

We discussed how to derive some nice CSS for a given need using ChatGPT, and I suggested some additional styling that would take the button to the next level.

We discussed the importance of a Call-to-Action button (or buttons) and the criticality of the information presented in the top portion of a website – the part that is above the fold.

We copied the new button we styled from a humble link and added it to the upper portion of our page creating a Call-to-Action response area.

Index

© Brad Moore 2025
B. Moore, *Designing Websites with Publii and GitHub Pages*,
https://doi.org/10.1007/979-8-8688-1195-1

Enforce HTTPS, 612
Engaging, 75
ENTER key, 259, 525, 599
EV Code Signing certificate, 55
External links, 650
External menu item, 135–138

F

G

P